THE
ANNALS

of the American Academy of
Political and Social Science

VOLUME 681 | JANUARY 2019

Polarizing Polities:
A Global Threat to Democracy

SPECIAL EDITORS:

Jennifer McCoy
Georgia State University

Murat Somer
Koç University, Istanbul

Los Angeles | London | New Delhi
Singapore | Washington DC | Melbourne

The American Academy of Political and Social Science

202 S. 36th Street, Annenberg School for Communication, University of Pennsylvania,
Philadelphia, PA 19104-3806; (215) 746-6500; (215) 573-2667 (fax); www.aapss.org

Origin and Purpose. The Academy was organized December 14, 1889, to promote the progress of political and social science, especially through publications and meetings. The Academy does not take sides in controverted questions, but seeks to gather and present reliable information to assist the public in forming an intelligent and accurate judgment.

Meetings. The Academy occasionally holds a meeting in the spring extending over two days.

Publications. THE ANNALS of The American Academy of Political and Social Science is the bimonthly publication of the Academy. Each issue contains articles on some prominent social or political problem, written at the invitation of the editors. These volumes constitute important reference works on the topics with which they deal, and they are extensively cited by authorities throughout the United States and abroad.

Subscriptions. THE ANNALS of The American Academy of Political and Social Science (ISSN 0002-7162) (J295) is published bimonthly—in January, March, May, July, September, and November—by SAGE Publishing, 2455 Teller Road, Thousand Oaks, CA 91320. Periodicals postage paid at Thousand Oaks, California, and at additional mailing offices. POSTMASTER: Send address changes to The Annals of The American Academy of Political and Social Science, c/o SAGE Publishing, 2455 Teller Road, Thousand Oaks, CA 91320. Institutions may subscribe to THE ANNALS at the annual rate: $1191 (clothbound, $1345). Individuals may subscribe to the ANNALS at the annual rate: $130 (clothbound, $191). Single issues of THE ANNALS may be obtained by individuals for $40 each (clothbound, $56). Single issues of THE ANNALS have proven to be excellent supplementary texts for classroom use. Direct inquiries regarding adoptions to THE ANNALS c/o SAGE Publishing (address below).

All correspondence concerning membership in the Academy, dues renewals, inquiries about membership status, and/or purchase of single issues of THE ANNALS should be sent to THE ANNALS c/o SAGE Publishing, 2455 Teller Road, Thousand Oaks, CA 91320. Telephone: (800) 818-SAGE (7243) and (805) 499-0721; Fax/Order line: (805) 375-1700; e-mail: journals@sagepub.com. *Please note that orders under $30 must be prepaid.* For all customers outside the Americas, please visit http://www.sagepub.co.uk/customerCare.nav for information.

Printed on acid-free paper

THE ANNALS

© 2019 by The American Academy of Political and Social Science

Editorial Office: 202 S. 36th Street, Philadelphia, PA 19104-3806
For information about individual and institutional subscriptions address:
SAGE Publishing
2455 Teller Road
Thousand Oaks, CA 91320

For SAGE Publishing: Peter Geraghty (Production) and Mimi Nguyen (Marketing)

From India and South Asia,
write to:
SAGE PUBLICATIONS INDIA Pvt Ltd
B-42 Panchsheel Enclave, P.O. Box 4109
New Delhi 110 017
INDIA

From Europe, the Middle East,
and Africa, write to:
SAGE PUBLICATIONS LTD
1 Oliver's Yard, 55 City Road
London EC1Y 1SP
UNITED KINGDOM

International Standard Serial Number ISSN 0002-7162
ISBN 978-1-5443-6988-4 (Vol. 681, 2019) paper
ISBN 978-1-5443-6989-1 (Vol. 681, 2019) cloth
Manufactured in the United States of America. First printing, January 2019

THE
ANNALS
of the American Academy of
Political and Social Science

VOLUME 681 | JANUARY 2019

IN THIS ISSUE:

Polarizing Polities: A Global Threat to Democracy

Special Editors: JENNIFER McCOY and MURAT SOMER

Introduction

IV. The Illusory Promise of Democratic Reform: Success and Failure

Conclusions

Corrigendum

FORTHCOMING

The Evolution of Attitudes toward Work
Special Editors: GERBERT KRAAYKAMP, ZEYNEP CEMALCILAR,
and JALE TOSUN

The Future of Educational Assessment
Special Editors: MICHAEL FEUER, JAMES PELLEGRINO,
and AMY BERMAN

Introduction

Transformations through Polarizations and Global Threats to Democracy

By
MURAT SOMER
and
JENNIFER McCOY

This volume collects and analyzes eleven country case studies of polarized polities that are, or had been, electoral democracies, identifying the common and differing causal mechanisms that lead to different outcomes for democracy when a society experiences polarization. In this introduction, we discuss our goals for the volume, the comparative logic we apply to the cases, our overall methodological approach, and the concepts that ground the analyses. The goal of this volume is to explore pernicious polarization, i.e., when and how a society divides into mutually distrustful "us vs. them" blocs, which endangers democracy. Accordingly, we discuss the effects of such polarization on democracies, and start building a foundation for remedies. In this introductory article, we highlight and explain the inherently political and relational aspects of polarization in general and pernicious polarization in particular, present the concept of formative rifts, and discuss how opposition strategies should be part of an explanation of severe polarization.

Keywords: polarization; democracy; democratic erosion; populism; opposition strategies

Our main interests in this volume of *The ANNALS* are to explore when and how societies become *perniciously polarized* and how such polarization affects democracy. Building on previous work (McCoy and Somer 2018), this collection also starts to build a foundation for remedies. We depart from a conventional definition of political polarization that simply measures the distance between political parties and voters on policy issues or ideological stances. Instead, we explore political polarization that divides

Murat Somer is a professor of political science and international relations at Koç University, Istanbul. He specializes in comparative politics and democratization. His research on polarization, religious and secular politics, ethnic conflict and authoritarianism has appeared in books, book volumes, and journals such as Comparative Political Studies, American Behavioral Scientist, *and* Democratization.

Correspondence: musomer@ku.edu.tr

DOI: 10.1177/0002716218818058

electorates into mutually antagonistic "us" vs. "them" camps and collapses normal cross-cutting interests and identities into two mutually exclusive identities. It has a high potential to extend into social relations, whereby political identity becomes a social identity, and it takes on characteristics of political tribalism in which members of each camp feel loyalty and sympathy toward their own political group and distrust and antipathy toward the other. In the extreme, each camp comes to view the other as an existential threat to the nation or their way of life. This type of polarization severely undermines the capacity of democracies to survive and address critical policy problems, though we also explore when and how it can bring about democratic reforms.

Potential consequences for democracy include gridlock and paralysis, careening and instability, democratic erosion, and democratic collapse. In the most hopeful cases, political oppositions and electorates may be able to contain polarizing dynamics and polarizing figures and agree on democratic reforms, whereby the transformative potential of polarization can be tapped for democratization rather than democratic erosion.

Polarization, Democracy, and the Focus of this Volume

Anxieties are growing over the future of democracy in the world, and many democracies have already undergone serious erosion or, worse, breakdown (Diamond 2015; Bermeo 2016; Foa and Mounk 2016; Levitsky and Ziblatt 2018). Polarization and democratic erosion—the gradual deterioration of the quality of democracy from within, such as the weakening of institutional checks and balances, electoral processes, and/or civil liberties—are clearly interrelated. But the causality may work in several different directions (Somer and McCoy 2018), and the causal mechanisms linking polarization and different outcomes for democracy need to be uncovered (McCoy, Rahman, and Somer 2018).

One of the most troubling effects of pernicious polarization on democracy may be that, as polities become perniciously polarized, to the disbelief of both sides, the opposing blocs of electorates fundamentally disagree on whether ongoing substantive and procedural transformations of their country advance or undermine democracy. Take the United States, still the world's most sizable economic and military power, under the presidency of Donald J. Trump. Arguably, the dominant sentiment prevailing in recent years among the social, political, and

Jennifer McCoy is a distinguished university professor of political science at Georgia State University. As a specialist in comparative politics and democratization and Latin American politics, she coordinates the international research group on political polarization and democratic consequences. She is the author or editor of six books, the most recent being International Mediation in Venezuela *(with Francisco Diez; United States Institute of Peace 2011).*

NOTE: Jennifer McCoy acknowledges the financial support from the National Science Foundation, the International Studies Association, Georgia State University, and Central European University for research assistance and two international workshops during which earlier drafts of these and other articles in this volume were presented.

economic elites, including the "learned classes" and the academy inside and out-side the United States, has ranged from despair to growing concerns over the quality, sustainability, and future of American democracy. These democratic anxi-eties were present before Trump became president, but they have been elevated to a new and alarming level first by his election and thereafter by his policies, discourse, and governing style.

However, to the chagrin of Trump-skeptics, this viewpoint does not represent the whole of American society, not even necessarily the majority. In fact, Abramowitz and McCoy in this volume report findings indicating that Trump approvers view the quality of U.S. democracy under the Trump administration as *improving*. This viewpoint is not easy for Trump disapprovers to understand. It is a sign of growing polarization when people find the other bloc's views not only objectionable but also unintelligible and threatening. Such mutual incomprehen-sion is evident today in the United States; for example, a person from the Trump-disapproving side may express how uncomfortable they feel when they hear others say things like Trump is "the best president in a long while."[1] Such anec-dotes are commonplace not only in the United States but also in widely different polarized countries around the globe.

In Poland, the Philippines, Thailand, Turkey, or Venezuela, many people find it incredible that others vote for the party or president—frequently a relative newcomer to the political system or an existing one that adopted a new and heterodox style—that they find deeply unacceptable. Often, they attribute the others' political choices to apathy, ignorance, benighted self-interest, or, worse, treason. Meanwhile, the supporters of the actors in question feel upset, typically labeling their critics as arrogant, self-righteous, corrupt, and pro-status-quo.

Why is this happening in so many otherwise dissimilar countries? How does polarization turn pernicious, and how does this affect democracy as we know it? This volume addresses these questions in a large comparative analysis of eleven countries that come from many different regions of the world. The con-tributions to a previous special issue addressed these questions based on theo-retical, conceptual, and individual-level and large-N empirical studies (McCoy and Somer 2018). In this volume, we pursue these issues by presenting eleven country case studies of polarization that are, or had been, an electoral democ-racy. Hence, we bring together and comparatively examine—as we also do in the concluding article—a relatively large number of theoretically informed and in-depth studies of specific polities. By doing so, we aim to have a closer look at the conditions and causal pathways that help to determine when and how polarization becomes pernicious and harms democracy. While we do not directly take up the question of policy implications in this issue, the conclusion to this volume discusses the insights gained from our analysis vis-à-vis reme-dies. Finally, Nancy Bermeo's contribution offers reflections about the implica-tions of this analysis for the United States.

Polarization, difference, and a certain dose of agonistic competition are part of the democratic game and can even have democratizing consequences at times. They can do so for example by clarifying the choices facing citizens and helping political party systems to institutionalize (Campbell 2016; Carlin, Singer, and Zechmeister 2015; LeBas 2011, 2018; Stavrakakis 2018). However, our main concern is the pernicious consequences of polarization for democracy. For reasons we explore, polarization is a risky political tool even when intended as an instrument of democratization. Some potential by-products of polarization, such as political party institutionalization, that are normally thought to be assets for democratization, can become a liability depending on the nature of polarization (Enyedi 2016). Thus, in addition to developing policies to better manage and contain severe polarization, an additional benefit of studying and theorizing the dynamics of pernicious polarization may be to better specify to what extent and under which conditions polarization could serve democratization.

In polarized contexts, people can differ and become divided based on opinions, perceptions, and convictions of a seemingly subjective nature. Thus, they may also disagree on whether democracy is progressing or backsliding in their country. Nevertheless, this does not change that the effects of polarization and of such split opinions on democracy are often demonstrably concrete and should be beyond dispute. Identifying and documenting these lasting impacts is one of the goals of this volume.

Democratic regimes have various dimensions, such as majority rule, minority rights, freedom, and equality, which can sometimes contradict each other and can be supported by different people for different reasons. A variety of different forms of democracy exist, and novel and "non-Western" forms could emerge in the future (Youngs 2015). However, different democracies also share some fundamental pillars and minimum standards that political scientists have long been conceptualizing and trying to measure based on qualitative and quantitative indicators (Dahl 1989; Munck and Verkuilen 2002; Merkel 2004; Tilly 2007; Munck 2016). Through the operation of various causal mechanisms that we explore and discuss, severe forms of polarization tend to undermine these foundations and practices. These include, for example, free and fair elections, a reasonably independent judiciary, and some form of checks and balances in government. They also entail less quantifiable and less understood, but by no means less crucial, informal norms that sustain democracies, such as "mutual tolerance and institutional forbearance" (Levitsky and Ziblatt 2018). The case studies in this volume analyze and record how severe polarization negatively affects such foundations, norms, and practices of democracy.

The divisions we witness in polarized polities pertain not only to policy, interests, and ideology, which would be an expected and tolerable condition for democracy, but often reflect sharp differences over the formal procedural as well as informal democratic norms. Perhaps most perniciously, they frequently represent disagreements over the interpretation of the founding principles and identities of the respective states and societies. Or worse yet, disagreements over basic material facts that should be beyond questioning whenever supported by material evidence, say, whether a corrupt transaction has taken place or global warming is occurring.

The Empirical Scope and Methodological Approach of this Volume

We bring together and comparatively evaluate "positive cases of" polarized polities, which come from various regions of the world. Thus, technically, we do not investigate any "negative cases" of nonpolarized polities, that is, countries that could have become gravely polarized but have not (Eckstein 1975; Gerring 2004; George and Bennett 2005; Beach and Pedersen 2016).[2] By excluding nonpolarized cases, we forsake our ability to offer causal claims with some confidence regarding why polarization has been occurring in these and other cases, but we discuss the probable causes that emerge from our cases in our concluding article.

In return, however, focusing on polarized cases enables us to identify the common, as well as differing, causal mechanisms that lead from polarization to different outcomes for democracy, after a society begins to experience polarization. Even though we did not necessarily select our cases based on suffering democratic erosion, all our polarized cases have experienced some degree of deterioration in measures of liberal democracy, and outcomes that range from political gridlock and careening to democratic breakdown and autocratic takeover.

Accordingly, our first goal is to establish the common characteristics and causal mechanisms that prevail in polarized polities in general. Many of our cases can be classified as "most different cases" (George and Bennett 2005; Beach and Pedersen 2016). That is, they are different in many respects, such as geography, culture, democratic history, and level of economic development, but have in common the occurrence of polarization. This diversity in aspects other than polarization enables us to identify the common causal paths that lead to severe polarization in our cases despite their other differences. Second, we identify the common characteristics and logics of polarization across our cases.

Third, we aim to uncover and distinguish the *varying* causal patterns and mechanisms that lead to different experiences of polarization and different outcomes for democracy. More specifically, our objective is to understand when and how polarization becomes "pernicious" (McCoy, Rahman, and Somer 2018), thus taking on a life of its own, and which factors help to explain the consequences for the extent and quality of democracy as a result. We pursue these goals and summarize our comparative findings and the theoretical insights and hypotheses we reach in the concluding article to this volume.

There is a vast and interdisciplinary body of research on polarization and a growing one on polarization, democracy, and development, which draw on either single countries and regions or large-N and experimental research. To our knowledge, this is the first volume that is aimed at addressing the question of polarization and democracy based on a large number of theoretically informed and comparatively evaluated case studies coming from many different regions of the world.

Defining Polarization: A Political and Relational Definition

One reason research on polarization and democracy is inconclusive may be the conceptual definition of polarization. Most extant definitions of polarization focus on ideological distance (see, for example, Sartori 1976; Poole and Rosenthal 1997; Dalton 2008; Fiorina and Abrams 2008). However, even though distancing often goes together with polarization, it may be neither necessary nor sufficient for the type of severe polarization we analyze in this volume.

In response, following McCoy, Rahman, and Somer (2018) and Somer and McCoy (2018), we offer a *political* and *relational* definition of polarization.[3] Such a definition is crucial to understand and explain pernicious polarization and its consequences for democracy. Hence, polarization is a process whereby the normal multiplicity of differences in a society increasingly align along a single dimension, cross-cutting differences become reinforcing, and people increasingly perceive and describe politics and society in terms of "us" versus "them." Accordingly, we treat the related phenomenon of populism, which attempts to simplify politics by aligning cross-cutting differences along the "elites" vs "people" distinction, as a specific and widely used subtype of polarizing politics.

It is not growing difference itself that produces severe polarization. It is how this difference is interpreted and used by some actors and groups to create an antagonistic "us" vs "them" perception of other groups. Furthermore, it is how these other groups react to this differentiation and how they respond to and situate themselves vis-a-vis the first group(s). Hence, the inherently relational nature of polarization.

What we mean with the political nature of polarization may require some more discussion and elaboration. We note that polarization is frequently triggered by various conscious and deliberate policies and by the discourse of political entrepreneurs. These entrepreneurs often activate and reframe societal divisions, and, polarization is used as an effective—yet, as we argue, elusive and dangerous—tool to consolidate supporters and weaken opponents.

Hence, polarization is inherently linked to questions of power and domination, and, in many of the cases of polarized democracies we explore, with struggles of transforming governments and governing elites. This political aim of polarization clearly applies to salient polarizing actors such as political parties, movements, and charismatic leaders, who frequently drive polarized polities. But it is also true for smaller and informal groups and actors, such as peer groups, neighborhood communities, and NGOs, which are part and parcel of the processes of polarization. Thus, arguably, polarization has a political nature at both the macro and micro level.

At a macro level, more often than not polarization is a political strategy that actors employ to achieve wide-scale political ends. We have previously observed a pattern in which "contemporary polarizations often start when a previously disunited or marginalized segment of society becomes politically united and mobilized to achieve social, economic, cultural-ideological, or institutional goals" (McCoy, Rahman, and Somer 2018, 18). An ensuing backlash from previously dominant groups triggers political conflicts and polarizing dynamics that often reach a "pernicious" level and quality, involving a variety of social, psychological, and political dynamics. These take on a life of their own, regardless of the specific political intentions that prevailed at the beginning. Alternatively, similar polarizing dynamics can be unleashed in contexts of elite struggles, when one set of disgruntled political elites uses polarizing mass mobilization strategies to challenge dominant elites, as exhibited in some of the cases in this volume.

At a micro level, too, polarization can thrive on many dynamics of a political nature. Polarization feeds on people's fear of being excluded from social and political power structures and concerns with power, security, and hierarchy in groups. These qualities ensure that, when polarization advances in a society, many people feel the pressure to conform with one bloc or the other as their political preferences increasingly shape their social relations.

During this process, we can expect that facts and moral truths increasingly lose their weight, as more and more people begin to conform with the messages and "truths" of their own bloc. To use the famous polemic between two ancient philosophers here, people follow the behavior identified by Glaucon, who argued that people cared about appearances more than they cared about the truth, rather than Socrates, who advised strict adherence to honesty (Haidt 2012). Following Glaucon's claims, in situations of conflict that involve two sides and moral implications, people often instinctively and instantaneously feel sympathy toward the claim that fits with their interests. Rather than asking which moral response is justified by the facts on the ground, they focus on how they can justify the response that was predetermined by their social and political interests.

None of this is absolute, of course, and individuals often overcome these predispositions whereby individual factors, such as personality and education, and group level factors, such as culture and institutions, presumably play critical roles. What concerns us here is that severe polarization is a major factor that increases the social and political cost of acting on moral principles.

As polarization advances, it will be increasingly more difficult and less likely for people to act in a morally principled fashion. As the middle and neutral ground collapses in a context of partisan polarization, it becomes increasingly difficult to confront one's group interests by defending the truth and acting in ways dictated by one's values. Standing up to the group risks being called a traitor or sell-out and can result in social and political isolation.

This helps to explain why polarized societies often witness public controversies over factually provable questions, say, whether President Obama was born in the United States or whether a religious figure's face appeared on the moon in Bangladesh (Abramowitz and McCoy, this volume; Rahman, this volume). Pernicious polarization often develops hand-in-hand with the ascendance of post-truth politics, whereby more and more social and political actors such as journalists, academics, and politicians either become engaged in partisan truth-making or else incur growing social, political, and economic costs.

Thus, we consider the expansion of polarization from formal politics to the realm of social relations, and vice versa, a major sign that pernicious polarization is becoming self-propagating. When this happens, people will find it increasingly costly to defend a nonpartisan and "virtuous" position.

Formative Rifts

Polarizing actors do not create polarization from tabula rasa. They typically build on already-existing social-political cleavages. We refer to long-standing and deep-cutting divisions that either emerged or could not be resolved during the formation of nation-states, or, sometimes during fundamental re-formations of states such as during transitions from communism to capitalism, or authoritarian to democratic regimes, as *formative rifts*. Some examples would be the legacy of unequal citizenship rights that were conferred upon African Americans, Native Americans, and women during the foundation of the United States, the claim that political legitimacy is to be conferred only on those with national liberation war experience in Zimbabwe, and whether language and ethnicity or religion should be the basis of national identity in Bangladesh. Similarly, the ambivalent relationship the Greek national identity has to Europe, which goes back to the formation of the modern Greek state in the beginning of the nineteenth century, and the wedge generated by the civil war that took place along the Left/Right axis following the second World War in Greece can be seen as formative rifts, even though they are not made the basis of current political polarization in Greece.

We do not limit formative rifts to any particular type of social, economic, or political cleavage because different crises accompany the formation and re-formation of different states. At the same time, we do not include all cleavages that may become salient in a polity during any one specific period in our definition of formative rift. Rather, we denote those divisions that have been a constant undercurrent of politics since the state-formation or reformation and have a particular divisive quality because they cannot be eliminated without fundamentally reconfiguring these states, and because people often find themselves on one side of these rifts or the other by birth.

As a result, formative rifts can have a powerful impact on political attachments when activated. Polarizing political actors typically try to activate them to mobilize their constituencies and thereby build a cohesive and emotionally appealing group identity. Formative rifts typically but not exclusively arise during independence movements, revolutions, and civil wars, and pertain to regional conflicts and race, ethnicity and nationality questions, state borders, national identities, foundational myths and "truths," fundamental rights of citizenship, and the religion-state relationship. Whenever a polarization is made on the basis of a formative rift, we hypothesize, polarization will have a high potential to become socially and psychologically divisive and enduring, with pernicious consequences for democracy.

Nevertheless, while these formative rifts often play a major role in the occurrence and endurance of polarization, they cannot by themselves explain it. The presence and contribution of formative rifts to polarization differs from case to case and across time. In other words, it is variable and in need of explanation. As we see in the cases that we explore in this volume, while formative rifts or even underlying social cleavages in their respective societies remain constant, polarization took off in certain periods and not others as a result of social, economic, and political developments and purposeful political mobilizations.

The main challenges and skills of polarizing political entrepreneurs who start a durable process of polarization based on a formative rift lie, we maintain, in managing to activate, mobilize, and bundle the formative rifts together with other cleavages so that they can become the basis of a winning coalition. Thus, many political actors may try to capitalize on the formative rifts in their societies, but not all of them succeed in making them the basis of a successful political mobilization. Some formative rifts, such as those pertaining to a country's foundational myths and basis of citizenship, may be especially prone to pernicious polarization. We take up this issue again in the Conclusion article in this volume. The more such rifts are pronounced by polarizing actors, the more we expect the ensuing polarization to become pernicious.

Opposition Strategies Integral to Pernicious Polarization

In accordance with the relational definition of polarization, we argue that opposition strategies—what opposition actors do and do not do in response to a polarizing incumbent—are crucial to explain pernicious polarization and its consequences and to develop potential remedies. Thus, a great deal of the sources and remedies of pernicious polarization may lie in the choices, actions, and capabilities of the opposition.

Opposition political strategies include the basic decisions whether to reciprocate polarizing discourse and tactics or try to depolarize politics based on inclusive and unifying platforms; whether to compromise and share power with the incumbent or unite against the incumbent; and whether to use electoral mobilization, popular protest, institutional accountability mechanisms, such as judicial rulings or impeachment proceedings, or extra-constitutional and non-democratic efforts to constrain or remove the incumbent. An additional common phenomenon, though not an intentional strategy, is fragmentation of the opposition in which internal divisions severely hamper its ability to challenge the polarizing incumbent.

Our case studies illustrate these various strategies, sometimes within the same polarizing episode. For example, the military coup attempted against the polarizing incumbent Hugo Chávez in Venezuela failed to remove him and instead generated more support and sympathy for him. On the other hand, a unified opposition following an electoral strategy in Venezuela successfully achieved a stunning victory in the 2015 legislative elections, winning two-thirds of the seats for their first majority in 15 years.

Finally, the balance of power between the poles and the strategic and ideological aims of the polarizing political actors are critical factors in explaining outcomes for the democratic system. A rough balance of power between two poles may entail similar capacities to mobilize people at the polls or in the streets, resulting in alternating elections or clashing street protests, or it may entail an advantage in numbers at the polls or in the streets on one side, and an advantage in institutional control on the other. In the concluding article we examine the hypothesis that the relative balance of power between the poles, and in particular the existence of cross-class parties capable of mobilizing popular electoral support, shapes the strategies of political actors and the dynamics of polarization: where the party system has developed competing mass-based parties, political actors are more likely to engage in electoral competitions, as in Bangladesh; where the opposition is electorally weak, they are more likely to turn to constitutional or extra-constitutional mechanisms to constrain the executive, as in Thailand, the latter with potentially counter-productive outcomes.

Transformative aims of polarizing actors

The strategic aims of polarizing actors also matter. We find in our cases three basic patterns giving rise to the political use of polarization: the more stationary and pro-status quo pattern of intra-elite power struggles and party competition, illustrated by the Philippines case, and the inclusionary versus exclusionary versions of transformative politics in which mass-based popular demands for fundamental change are channeled and exploited by a political entrepreneur able to capitalize on this demand. We hypothesize that the inclusionary polarizing-cum-transformative aim, which begins by arguing that polarizing confrontation is required to achieve democratizing reforms, as in Turkey and Venezuela, is the most likely to end up with pernicious polarization becoming self-propagating and producing authoritarian outcomes under the new elites.

We argue that polarization is potentially transformative in its capacity to disrupt the status quo, thereby helping to address injustice, or an imbalance in the popular vs. oligarchic versions of democracy (Slater 2013; Stavrakakis 2018), or to open up a strong state as discussed by Somer in this volume. Democratic reform to enhance inclusion can be the goal when challengers organize to represent previously under-represented groups. But such challenges often provoke an elite backlash and counter-mobilization to stymie these transformative attempts, rather than a recognition of their reformist and inclusionary potential in building a constructively agonistic and pluralist, as opposed to antagonistic, democracy (Stavrakakis 2018). This elite backlash, in turn, can motivate the challengers to double down and strive to protect themselves by changing the rules and creating hegemonic power.

Thus, whether polarization serves a constructive or destructive purpose for democracy depends on the behavior of both governments and opposition, new political actors, and traditionally dominant groups. Whether these actors and groups pursue polarization or de-polarization, *how* they pursue these goals, for example, whether they focus on electoral mobilization or street protests, has consequences for democracy, as we discuss in the conclusion article.

Outcomes for Democracy

Our starting point for analyzing the effects of pernicious polarization on democracy begins with a quadruple typology of outcomes that polarization can produce vis-a-vis democracy: gridlock and careening; democratic erosion or collapse under new elites and dominant groups; democratic erosion or collapse with reassertion of old elites and dominant groups; or democratic reform (McCoy, Rahman, and Somer 2018; Somer and McCoy 2018). Nine of our eleven case study polities currently fit, to greater and lesser degrees, with one of these outcomes.

Bangladesh, Greece, the Philippines, and the United States suffer gridlock and "careening";[4] Hungary, Poland, Turkey, and Venezuela are undergoing democratic erosion or collapse under "new" elites and dominant groups; and Thailand moved from careening democracy to democratic collapse with the return of "old" elites and dominant groups. Further, some subperiods of some of our polities partially fit with the fourth outcome of democratic reforms, as in South Africa under Mandela, Greece in the early 2000s, and Turkey in 2002–2006.

However, Zimbabwe and post-Mandela South Africa have more ambiguous statuses vis-a-vis the quadruple classification, where the outcomes could perhaps be described as "precarious prospects of democratic reform." Accordingly, the relative democratic successes of post-apartheid South Africa are beyond question. However, the dominant party regime of the ANC also threatens to resemble the outcome of "democratic erosion under new elites and dominant groups." Likewise, the elite compromises in the form of power-sharing in Zimbabwe are actually elite co-optations short of genuine democratization. In both cases, very recent reform attempts within the dominant parties in 2017–18 present some hope for democratization, as discussed by the analyses of Southall, and LeBas and Munemo in this volume.

What is more, some of our cases vary cross-temporally and exhibit different outcomes in different periods. Turkey had careening combined with democratic reforms prior to 2007, which have been replaced by democratic erosion under new elites and dominant groups since then. Venezuela moved from potentially democratizing participatory reforms in the early polarization period to outright democratic collapse in the last few years. Other cases undergoing re-polarization or deepening polarization, such as South Africa, Greece, and the United States, have as yet dynamic and unclear outcomes, with the potential to move in various different directions in classification.

In the Conclusion article, we discuss seven risk factors that seem to be crucial for shaping outcomes for democracy: power asymmetry between the polarized blocs; reciprocal Manichean discourse; societal polarization; transformative ideology of the polarizing actor; institutionalized and mass-based party system; polarization formed around formative rifts; and majoritarian institutions. Within these seven, we argue, the various combinations or absence of two factors—polarization mobilized around formative rifts and mass-based political party institutionalization—are the most critical in helping to determine how enduring and democracy-eroding different types of polarizations will be. We thus highlight that agency—how political and institutional actors choose to act, and not just institutions or structures—is crucial to understanding polarization and its impact. We also acknowledge that additional factors not explored in this volume, such as international dynamics, may play a role in the outcome.

The Organization of the Case Studies

We present the cases in this volume based on our assessment of their current status in the quadruple typology of the outcomes for democracy. In the concluding article, we conduct a systematic comparison and aim to reach insights regarding the causal factors and a more refined typology of outcomes.

In the first two sections of this volume, we have Thailand, Turkey, Venezuela, Hungary, and Poland, whose ruling elites and governments have been very different in terms of their ideological makeup and institutional forms. Nevertheless, these five polities have been suffering severe polarization and democratic erosion combined with drastic shifts of governing elites, as analyzed in the contributions from Kongkirati, Somer, Garcia-Guadilla and Mallen, Vegetti, and Tworzecki, respectively. Relative newcomers to politics, Thaksin in Thailand, Erdoğan and the AKP in Turkey, and Chávez and the PSUV in Venezuela, achieved power by uniting and mobilizing the disenchanted and relatively disadvantaged segments of society based on polarizing politics and the promise of securing wide-scale changes in the political and economic status-quo. In turn, Viktor Orbán and Fidesz in Hungary and the Kaczyński brothers and the PiS in Poland were not newcomers to politics but have been employing similar strategies after reinventing themselves and their parties based on polarizing politics. In all five cases, with the possible exception of Hungary, the tactics and policies of the incumbents threatened and led to powerful backlashes from the state institutions, established elites, and their societal constituencies, who counter-mobilized via mass protests and other public and political campaigns, coup attempts, and judicial activism.

None of these polities has yet been able to democratically manage the ensuing and interactive dynamics of societal and political polarization, whereby deepening legal–political crises, mobilizations, and counter-mobilizations have led to democratic backsliding. However, polarization and the behavior of political actors produced the outcome of authoritarianism under the old elites who returned to power in Thailand, while new dominant elites consolidated their power in the other cases. Moreover, Turkey and Venezuela incrementally transformed to electoral authoritarian regimes, and now outright authoritarianism in Venezuela, whereas Poland and Hungary can be considered illiberal democracies with severe problems of executive degradation.

The third section features four polities where there has not been a decisive shift of the dominant governing elites, even though three of them saw the rise of populist newcomers in their political systems. Instead, in the Philippines, the United States, Greece, and Bangladesh, democracy is troubled and undermined by growing polarization and the resulting tensions, gridlocks, and "democratic careening" between different elite mobilizations and political realignments, and between state institutions and new elites. As the studies of Arugay and Slater, Abramowitz and McCoy, Stavrakakis and Andreadis, and Rahman, respectively, imply, the current polarizations have the potential to produce different outcomes for democracy, depending on the actors' choices and factors that we discuss in the conclusion to this volume.

Finally, two countries—South Africa and Zimbabwe—represent cases of national liberation elites emerging in state reformulations with unresolved questions over foundational myths, such as the symbols and heroes of national struggles. As discussed by the contributions of Southall, and LeBas and Munemo, respectively, to differing degrees both countries are conflict-ridden polities undermined by corruption, violence, and periodic episodes of polarizing crises and, in the case of Zimbabwe, outright government oppression. However, they each have the potential for further democratization through internal reform of the dominant liberation party, or for consolidation of hegemonic party control and electoral authoritarianism. South Africa more so, but with severe vulnerabilities; whereas in Zimbabwe, the outlook is bleaker.

Polarization is an expanding and disconcerting problem for many democratic polities across the world and has drawn the growing attention of scholars and policy-makers alike. This is not the first time that polarization is threatening democracies; when it has done so historically, as an alarming and thoughtful recent op-ed put it, it transformed politics as well as social and intellectual relations by pulling erstwhile friends and friendly competitors toward mutually antagonistic poles "like a flock of moths to an inescapable flame" (Applebaum 2018). This volume is an attempt to better understand and theorize pernicious polarization by presenting and comparing eleven otherwise dissimilar case studies of polarization. As our cases suggest, too, a multiplicity of different sentiments, rhetorics, and ideologies—such as populism, nativism, nationalism, religious conservatism, anticapitalism, and leftism—underlie current examples of polarization and democratic erosion. While the ideological manifestations, salient social cleavages, and cultural and institutional contexts vary in different examples, the driving causal mechanisms of polarization are quite similar—otherwise cross-cutting differences meld into one overarching division, political adversaries become enemies posing an existential threat, and polarization takes on a life of its own. Being preoccupied with particular ideologies and movements, many ordinary citizens and policy-makers may mistakenly think that the choices they make will not bear consequences similar to periods of democratic decay and authoritarianism in the past. Thus, achieving a better understanding of the causal processes underpinning severe polarization can help to explain and remedy not only pernicious polarization itself, but also related challenges to democracy such as unfettered populism and nationalism.

Notes

1. A (white male) cab driver in Cincinnati; incident reported by an academic colleague of author.
2. However, some of our case studies compare both negative and positive cases by examining and comparing less and more polarized subperiods within the same case, such as Zimbabwe, Turkey, and Greece.

3. For a review of different definitions, see McCoy, Rahman, and Somer (2018). Our definition is inspired by our past research, what we learned from the cases examined in this volume, and others with which we are familiar. However, individual contributions in our volume provide their own modifications or interpretations of this definition.

4. Careening captures "the sense of endemic unsettledness and rapid ricocheting that characterizes democracies that are struggling but not collapsing" (Slater 2013, 730).

References

Applebaum, Anne. October 2018. Polarization in Poland: A warning from Europe. *The Atlantic*. Available from https://www.theatlantic.com/magazine/archive/2018/10/poland-polarization/568324/.

Beach, Derek, and Rasmus Brun Pedersen, eds. 2016. *Causal case study methods: Foundations and guidelines for comparing, matching, and tracing*. Ann Arbor, MI: University of Michigan Press.

Bermeo, Nancy. 2016. On democratic backsliding. *Journal of Democracy* 27 (1): 5–19.

Campbell, James E. 2016. *Polarized: Making sense of a divided America*. Princeton, NJ: Princeton University Press.

Carlin, Ryan, Matthew Singer, and Elizabeth Zechmeister. 2015. *The Latin American voter: Pursuing representation and accountability in challenging contexts*. Ann Arbor, MI: University of Michigan Press.

Dahl, Robert A. 1989. *Democracy and its critics*. New Haven, CT: Yale University Press.

Dalton, Russell J. 2008. The quantity and the quality of party systems: Party system polarization, its measurement, and its consequences. *Comparative Political Studies* 41 (7): 899–920.

Diamond, Larry. 2015. Facing up to the democratic recession. *Journal of Democracy* 26 (1): 141–55.

Eckstein, Harry. 1975. Case studies and theory in political science. In *Handbook of political science. Political science: Scope and theory*, vol. 7, eds. Fred I. Greenstein and Nelson W. Polsby, 94–137. Reading, MA: Addison-Wesley.

Enyedi, Zsolt. 2016. Populist polarization and party system institutionalization: The role of party politics in de-democratization. *Problems of Post-Communism* 63 (4): 210–20.

Fiorina, Morris, and Samuel Abrams. 2008. Political polarization in the American public. *Annual Review of Political Science* 11:563–88.

Foa, Roberto Stefan, and Yascha Mounk. 2016. The democratic disconnect. *Journal of Democracy* 27 (3): 5–17.

George, Alexander, and Andrew Bennett. 2005. *Case studies and theory development in the social sciences*. Cambridge, MA: MIT Press.

Gerring, John. 2004. What is a case study and what is it good for? *American Political Science Review* 98 (2): 341–54.

Haidt, Jonathan. 2012. *The righteous mind: Why good people are divided by politics and religion*. New York, NY: Vintage Books.

LeBas, Adrienne. 2011. *From protest to parties: Party-building and democratization in Africa*. Oxford: Oxford University Press.

LeBas, Adrienne. 2018. Can polarization be positive? Conflict and institutional development in Africa. *American Behavioral Scientist* 62 (1): 59–74.

Levitsky, Steven, and Daniel Ziblatt. 2018. *How democracies die*. New York, NY: Crown.

McCoy, Jennifer, and Murat Somer, eds. 2018. Special Issue on polarization and democracy: A Janus-faced relationship with pernicious consequences. *American Behavioral Scientist* 62 (1).

McCoy, Jennifer, Tahmina Rahman, and Murat Somer. 2018. Polarization and the global crisis of democracy: Common patterns, dynamics, and pernicious consequences for democratic polities. *American Behavioral Scientist* 62 (1): 16–42.

Merkel, Wolfgang. 2004. Embedded and defective democracies. *Democratization* 11 (5): 33–58.

Munck, Gerardo. 2016. What is democracy? A reconceptualization of the quality of democracy. *Democratization* 23 (1): 1–26.

Munck, Gerardo, and Jay Verkuilen. 2002. Conceptualizing and measuring democracy: Evaluating alternative indices. *Comparative Political Studies* 35 (1): 5–34.

Poole, Keith T., and Howard Rosenthal. 1997. *Congress: A political-economic history of roll-call voting*. New York, NY: Cambridge University Press.

Sartori, Giovanni. 1976. *Parties and party systems: A framework for analysis*. New York, NY: Cambridge University Press.

Slater, Dan. 2013. Democratic careening. *World Politics* 65 (4): 729–63.

Somer, Murat, and Jennifer McCoy. 2018. Déjà vu? Polarization and endangered democracies in the 21st century. *American Behavioral Scientist* 62 (1): 3–15.

Stavrakakis, Yannis. 2018. Paradoxes of polarization: Democracy's inherent division and the (anti-) populist challenge. *American Behavioral Scientist* 62 (1): 43–58.

Tilly, Charles. 2007. *Democracy*. New York, NY: Cambridge University Press.

Youngs, Richard. 2015. *The puzzle of non-Western democracy*. Washington, DC: Carnegie Endowment for International Peace.

I. Democratic Collapse and Return of Old Elites

From Illiberal Democracy to Military Authoritar- ianism: Intra-Elite Struggle and Mass-Based Conflict in Deeply Polarized Thailand

By
PRAJAK KONGKIRATI

Thailand fits the pattern of pernicious polarized politics identified in this volume, where a previously excluded group successfully gains political power through the ballot box, governs unilaterally to pursue radical reforms, and produces a backlash from the traditional power elites. In Thailand, elite conflict has been a major part of the story, but this article argues that political polarization there cannot be merely understood as "elite-driven": conflict among the elites and the masses, and the interaction between them, produced polarized and unstable politics. Violent struggle is caused by class structure and regional, urban-rural disparities; elite struggle activates the existing social cleavages; and ideological framing deepens the polarization. While the Yellow Shirts and traditional elites want to restore and uphold the "Thai-style democracy" with royal nationalism, the Red Shirts espouse the "populist democracy" of strong elected government with popular nationalism and egalitarian social order.

Keywords: polarization; Thaksin Shinawatra; populism; Thai-style democracy; military authoritarianism

Since the mid-2000s, international media have regularly portrayed Thailand as a country engulfed by tumultuous street violence and a deep divide between two opposing political mass movements, called the Yellow Shirts and Red Shirts, whose differences of ideology and interests were signified symbolically by color codes. According to McCoy and Rahman's (2016) dynamic model of polarization, Thailand perfectly fit the causal pattern of pernicious polarized politics, in which "a previously

Prajak Kongkirati is an assistant professor, head of the Government Department, and director of the Direk Jayanama Research Center, Faculty of Political Science, at Thammasat University in Thailand. He is on the editorial board of Thammasat Review of Economic and Social Policy, *and the* Asian Democracy Review. *His current research project is the study of military authoritarianism in Thailand in comparative perspective.*

Correspondence: prajakk@yahoo.com

DOI: 10.1177/0002716218806912

excluded or marginalized sector of the population successfully gained political power through the ballot box, governed unilaterally to achieve the deep reforms they espouse, and produces a backlash from the previous power elites. The resulting conflict may end in a) gridlock and/or instability, with alternating governments failing to achieve governability; b) removal of the new group from power; or c) increasing authoritarian behavior by the incumbent to stay in power." (p. 2).

Dynamics of Polarization in Thailand: Divided Polity and Zero-Sum Politics

Political polarization in Thailand is a recent phenomenon. It emerged in 2005 with protests against the government of former prime minister Thaksin Shinawatra that gradually became the mass movement known as the Yellow Shirts. Polarization deepened when the triple alliance of royal-military-bureaucratic elites, supported by Yellow Shirt protesters comprised mainly of urban middle- and upper-classes, as well as big business groups, decided to overthrow the popularly elected Thaksin government by staging a military coup in 2006. The coup led to the formation of a pro-Thaksin mass movement (generally known as the Red Shirts), which mobilized to confront the traditional elites and the Yellow Shirts. The Red Shirt movement gained support from rural people, urban poor, Thaksin's party constituency, and progressive activists, as well as local and national politicians connected to Thaksin. The confrontation and clashes between the two opposing movements, and between state security units and the demonstrators, led to a large number of deaths and injuries, a paralyzed government, political instability, military intervention, and democratic breakdown. Over time, political polarization also spilled over into the societal sphere (including among families, friends, and communities). As polarization deepened, people were forced to choose sides, and political contestation became a deadly game.

In this article, I argue that the political polarization in Thailand should not be understood merely as an elite-driven conflict. Seeing Thailand's ongoing polarization as an elite power struggle between Thaksin and rival royal-military elites is not completely wrong, but it does not fully appreciate the dynamics of the polarized conflict. Fierce struggles between opposing sides of the elite are driven not only by control of state power and economic interests, but also by different notions about nationhood and political legitimacy. Furthermore, socioeconomic factors are not sufficient to account for the deep polarization that has evolved over time. The ideological component needs to be taken into account, as it produces the ingroup/outgroup division, and coalesces people from various socioeconomic backgrounds into two rival political camps.

To understand polarized conflicts in Thailand, it is thus important to understand two layers of conflict—the elite and the masses. The interaction of these two layers—shaped by individual, institutional, structural, and ideological factors—has led to the pernicious polarization witnessed in Thailand since the mid-2000s.

Dynamics of Polarization: The Rise of a "Populist" Party, the Awakening Masses, and the Backlash

The backdrop to the country's long and ongoing political crisis is the significant socioeconomic changes that have occurred in rural areas or rural/agrarian transformation since the 1980s (Walker 2012). But without the rise of Thaksin and his party, transformation would not have transpired in a way that led to deep polarization. It is therefore necessary to look at the rise of Thaksin in 2001, when his party won a landslide electoral victory and he became the prime minister.

To understand Thaksin's rise, one needs to go back to the dramatic political and economic changes that took place in the late 1990s. These changes significantly altered the rules of the game and the power balance among political forces. The rise of a new political player like Thaksin and his Thai Rak Thai Party (TRT) was a product of the financial crisis and the newly created constitution in 1997. These produced strong incentives, as well as opportunities, for national-level capitalists like Thaksin and his peers to form a political party and capture state power.

The 1997 constitution, which was supported by a reform coalition that consisted of liberal elites, technocrats, and civil society organizations, aimed to fix the enduring problems of Thai parliamentary democracy seen since the 1980s: a fragmented party system, weak coalition governments, and unstable democracy. To reform Thai politics, the constitution created several new organizations, mechanisms, and rules. For the first time in Thailand's history, voting became compulsory for all eligible voters, and party switching, a popular practice among Thai politicians, was restricted. The most far-reaching reform was a major overhaul of the electoral system. As part of an attempt to facilitate coherent political parties and party-oriented politics, it replaced the block-vote system with a mixed-member system.[1] Out of 500 House seats, 400 were elected from single-seat districts on a plurality basis (or first past the post); another 100 were elected from a single nationwide district on a proportional basis. All political parties had to submit a list of candidates for voters to consider, and those on the party list were ranked by top party leaders based on popularity, connection, and caliber. The aim of a party-list system was to give technocrats, businessmen, and professionals an opportunity to enter politics without electioneering. It also aimed to strengthen party building and party organization (Hicken 2006).

Thaksin and his TRT were the most skillful players in adapting themselves to the new rules and making use of the new system. The TRT introduced party-based and relatively more policy-oriented politics, a new style of electoral campaigning, and the ambitious goal of creating a single-party government. The political changes brought about by Thaksin and the TRT placed other elites in a completely new sociopolitical environment (Kongkirati 2013).

Thaksin Shinawatra (1950–), a telecommunication business tycoon turned politician, founded the TRT in 1998. He was born in Chiang Mai to a prominent business family, some of whom had successful political careers. He was a police officer until 1987, after which he became a full-time businessman, making a considerable fortune after obtaining government concessions for mobile phone and satellite networks. By the mid-1990s, he was a star in the business world and an advocate for economic and political reforms. He launched his political career in the mid-1990s (Phongpaichit and Baker 2009).

After the 1997 economic crisis and the promulgation of the new constitution, Thaksin launched the TRT, aiming to be the first prime minister elected in the postreform era. The 1997 crisis created strong incentives for prominent capitalists to directly capture state power. "Business was shocked by the severity of the economic slump, and by the refusal of the Democrat Party government (1997–2001) to assume any responsibility for defending domestic capital against its impact," Chaiwat and Phongpaichit (2008, 255) explain. Also, "the increased globalization of business raised the potential returns from holding the office of prime minister" (Chaiwat and Phongpaichit 2008, 256). Thaksin led a group of leading capitalists, who had not been severely damaged by the crisis, in pursuing a high-risk, high-return strategy of building their own political party, rather than building clientelistic relations with leading bureaucrats or sponsoring other people's parties like other capitalists had in the past. Thaksin's strategy was also different from that of other political oligarchs in the pre-1997 period. Rather than trying to win a plurality of votes and sharing power with other leaders in a multiparty coalition, he sought to win an absolute majority of votes and form a single-party government. In other words, he and his party strove for monopolistic control instead of the conventional mode of sharing power. The new electoral and party system, as explained above, was designed to promote strong executive power and large political parties. This, in turn, facilitated Thaksin and the TRT's political ambitions.

Beginning in 2001, the TRT was highly successful in every election, scoring landslide victories. To be precise, they won election contests six consecutive times (2001, 2005, 2006, 2007, 2011, and 2014) following the party's formation. The three most crucial factors that contributed to Thaksin's political domination were Thaksin's personality, populist policies, and shrewd campaign methods (Kongkirati 2013; Phatharathananunth 2008). For general voters, Thaksin offered strong and decisive leadership, which they had never found among bureaucratic leaders and old-style politicians. His responsiveness to the grievances of the urban and rural lower class and lower middle class, who together constituted the majority of the electorate, gave him a loyal political base and guaranteed his electoral success. TRT's policy package included universal health care, a village fund, debt moratorium for poor farmers, scholarships for village kids, cheap housing, and so on. This set of policies was highly popular with and admired by the poor, though pundits and critics called it "populist" (*prachaniyom* in Thai). During election campaigns, TRT ran a complementary two-pronged campaign strategy—a party-list centered campaign for the party-list seats and a candidate-centered campaign for constituency seats. The party was also savvy in using political marketing and the mass media to bolster its image (Kongkirati 2014; Chattharakul 2010).

Thaksin and his political party became an invincible force in electoral battle. In the 2005 election, TRT won a supermajority, securing 377 out of 500 seats.

The Democrat Party, the major opposition party and one of the oldest political parties in Thailand, came in second with only 96 seats. The TRT thus became the first political party in Thai history to establish a single-party government, and Thaksin became the first elected prime minister to duly serve the full four-year term and win elections twice.[2] He had achieved monopolistic control over the Cabinet and Parliament, and his domineering power and popularity made him a real threat to the old network of elites. While the landslide 2005 election victory and single-party government brought political aggrandizement to Thaksin, it generated fear and perturbation among his opponents. Beginning in 2001, Thaksin and his party employed various tactics to undermine his critics and rival political parties' power bases. But Thaksin had not been able to subvert extraparliamentary forces, in particular the royalist networks and the military—an alliance constituting the most formidable sources of traditional power in the Thai polity. A royal-military-bureaucratic alliance represents the old elites who dominated Thai politics from the 1950s until the late 1990s. Cold War politics, with the support of the American allies, propelled their power to its peak. The conservative elites underpinned their legitimate authority through the hegemonic discourse of Thai-style democracy guided by a benevolent monarch and patriotic military. Before Thaksin's rise, their political domination was secure, as political parties were weak and lacked mass support, and elected governments were feeble and unstable. The immense popularity and electoral success of the TRT made Thaksin the center of a new elite network of major capitalists and politicians. Thaksin's power network challenged the hegemony of the royal-military-bureaucratic alliance (McCargo 2005). The royal-military-bureaucratic political network did not embrace the basic democratic rules of the game, as such rules went against their traditional authority. They wanted to retain their power, privilege, and supremacy, and return the country to an old model of "semi-democracy," in which the bureaucracy and military dominated politics under the auspices of the monarchy. This conservative force was not willing to compete in electoral politics but still controlled critical parts of the state apparatus, notably the army, the courts and some parts of the bureaucracy (Baker 2016; Eugenie 2016). Consequently, it could destabilize elected governments. Nevertheless, given Thaksin's firm control of the government, his royal-military-bureaucratic opponents understood that the only way to unseat him was by nonelectoral, extraparliamentary means.

Soon after the 2005 election, those opposing Thaksin consisted of business rivals and personal foes, NGO activists, journalists, academics and professionals, human rights defenders, bureaucrats, and the urban middle class, all of whom joined forces against his government. By early 2006, Thaksin's legitimacy had been eroded by his controversial business dealings, and the antigovernment movement led by media mogul Sondhi Limthongkul and Major General Chamlong Srimuang gained crucial momentum.[3] In an attempt to revitalize his legitimacy, the embattled prime minister dissolved parliament and called for a snap election in April 2006. All main opposition parties decided to boycott the election, leaving the TRT running unopposed. Political party leaders claimed that Thaksin no longer had legitimacy and the snap election was an attempt to divert public attention from his business scandal. The sudden dissolution of parliament, they argued, also left opposition parties no time to prepare for an election campaign.[4] After the release of the election results showing that the TRT had won 460 of the 500 seats, anti-Thaksin leaders declared that they did not accept the results and "would go on rallying until Thaksin resigns and Thailand gets a royally appointed prime minister."[5] The political situation had reached an impasse.

On September 19, 2006, a group of army leaders staged a coup, the first in 15 years. The royal-military alliance could not defeat Thaksin and his political machine in an election, so Thai elites changed the game, staging a coup to eliminate Thaksin and his populist party. The 2006 coup further polarized the country, exacerbated political divisions, and radicalized political participation. The leaders changed frequently, and all prime ministers, whether from the Thaksin or anti-Thaksin camp, were faced with virulent protests. Violent street clashes and military crackdowns dominated political life. Deep polarization and hostility between the pro- and anti-Thaksin forces led Thai society to a continued cycle of violence and democratic breakdown for over a decade. Thaksin was forced to live in exile, but his allied parties have remained highly popular among marginalized voters, especially in the North and Northeast as well as among urban poor and the working class. Even though his allies kept winning elections without Thaksin, they could not govern the country, as they were continuously faced with fierce protests from the upper middle class and conservative elites, and they were undermined by the politicized independent organizations and Constitutional Court. From 2006 to 2014, Thaksin's allied parties were dissolved twice, and three of their prime ministers were disqualified by the Constitutional Court and independent organizations (Kongkirati 2016a).

In early 2014, urban middle-class protesters and staunch supporters of the Democrat Party from the south mobilized under the banner the People's Democratic Reform Committee (PDRC), protesting against the elected government of Yingluck Shinawatra, who is Thaksin's sister. The PDRC employed violence to disrupt and paralyze the government. The protesters repeatedly called for military intervention to unseat the Yingluck government. The violent protests by the PDRC ultimately paved the way for political intervention by the military. On May 22, 2014, General Prayuth Chan-ocha, the army chief, staged a coup to topple the government and brought the country back under the control of royal-military elites. General Prayuth was appointed by the coup-installed assembly to act as the country's new prime minister. Under his leadership, he recreated the old model of bureaucratic dominance and "Thai-style democracy," where the bureaucracy and military dominate politics under the auspices of the monarchy (see Chambers and Waitoolkiat 2016; Hewison and Kitirianglarp 2010). The military-controlled government aims to weaken political parties and civil society organizations, and to "tame" the majoritarian democracy that traditional elites had previously failed to harness. Under repressive military rule, civil liberties are restricted and political activity is prohibited. Thai society remains polarized, as the coup failed to transform ideological conflicts; it merely suppressed them (Kongkirati and Kanchoochat 2018).

The Linkage between Intra-Elite Power Struggle and Mass-Based Conflict

Since the conflict started, scholars of Thai politics have debated how to understand it. The debate is divided into two camps—those who view the polarized conflict as a typical elite power struggle of a type frequently witnessed in Thailand since the 1932 revolution, and those who see it as a "revolt of the downtrodden."[6] Those who propose that the crisis is centered on elite contestation argue that civil organizations and protesters in the streets are merely tools or pawns used by elites on both sides to win political battles. McCargo (2010), for example, describes it as "conflict between different elements of the Thai elite, who have mobilized rival patronage-based networks of supporters" (p. 9). The "elite struggle'" framework has several shortcomings, as I explain below.

By reducing supporters of both sides to pawns of the elite, this argument fails to explain the autonomous roles played by ordinary people. For one clear example, the Yingluck Shinawatra government's decision to pass a bill giving blanket amnesty to all conflicting parties was opposed strongly by a number of Red Shirt supporters. The "elite struggle" theory also fails to explain the longevity and intensity of social division among Thai people, which goes beyond the elite's agenda and control. Scholarship on social movements suggests that successful mass mobilization involves political opportunity, resource mobilization, organizational building, and resonated framing (McAdam, Tarrow, and Tilly 2001). Thaksin and his elite rivals were the prime movers of polarized conflict, but they did not dictate the direction and dynamics of conflict. If the polarization in Thailand were elite contestation first and foremost, it would not have lasted more than a decade—either one side would have won the political fight or both sides would have struck a political deal. Thaksin's policies and actions helped to activate the key social cleavages (regional, urban-rural, and class) that already existed in Thai society long before he came to power. Policies such as the village fund, debt moratorium, and universal health care empowered the rural lower and lower middle classes but made the urban middle and upper classes feel threatened and insecure. The royal-military network's decision to eliminate Thaksin through unconstitutional means worsened the situation and aggravated the conflict by upsetting the lower middle class that supported Thaksin. In turn, the radicalization of Thaksin and his supporters in defense of electoral democracy deepened the fear and insecurity of the establishment–middle-class nexus, which then struck back with more aggressive measures.

Different scholars have attributed polarization in Thailand to different factors and aspects of cleavages. However, it is rather misleading to argue exclusively for one factor or one aspect of the conflict. We need an integrative framework that combines several factors in a systematic way and has room for the dynamics and evolution of the conflict, rather than a static model of polarization (McCoy, Rahman, and Somer 2018). Several structural, institutional, and individual-level factors are involved, and each of them impacts the polarized conflict to varying degrees in different ways. To understand the crisis and ongoing polarized conflicts in Thailand, we need to understand both layers of conflict—the elite and the masses. The interaction of these two layers, aided by individual, institutional, structural, and ideological factors, has produced the pernicious polarization witnessed in Thailand since 2005.

Elite struggle and individual level factor

As discussed above, Thaksin strived for a monopoly of power in electoral politics. His campaign centered primarily on nationalist policies to rescue the business sector and populist policies to help the poor in both rural and urban areas. This strategy proved to be highly popular given the hardships faced by both these groups in the post-1997 economic crisis. In the process, this policy campaign helped to bring forth a political transformation from factional politics to party-dominated, policy-oriented politics led by a populist leader. Thaksin's party and its populist policies mobilized state resources to address the social grievances and political aspirations of the rural electorate, who had become a vital social force beginning in the late 1990s. In terms of electoral politics, the rural electorate is highly significant, as it accounts for two-thirds of the votes.

Thaksin, however, is not a left-wing populist in the style of Chaves and Morales in Latin America, nor a European-type right-wing populist (Mudde and Kaltwasser 2011; Roberts 2006). One scholar labeled his approach "populism for capitalism" (Kasian 2006). This populism evolved over time. In the beginning, Thaksin and his party did not position themselves as a populist party; it was his critics who labeled his policies "populist." (Yoshifumi 2009). Originally, Thaksin's policies were aimed primarily to win votes from the majority.[7] He also aimed to pacify the masses and prevent a mass uprising that might have resulted from shared discontent among the lower classes after the economic crisis. Only when Thaksin was attacked by the establishment did he begin using populist rhetoric and practices to mobilize the masses, personify his leadership, and strongly challenge the established elites. The Red Shirt movement emerged only after the 2006 coup, when Thaksin was ousted by his opponents. Without an organized mass movement, Thaksin realized that his government was vulnerable in the face of an attack by the old elites. Polarization in Thailand was thus being fueled by an action-reaction dynamic.

Why did traditional elites feel threatened by Thaksin? The answers lie in both material and psychological aspects. Thaksin's immense popularity and his dominant party challenged the power, interest, and prestige of the network monarchy, including the monarchy's "claim to be the sole focus of political loyalty" (Phongpaichit and Baker 2009, 89) and its role as the supreme political authority, guide, and final arbiter of Thai polity. Moreover, with a succession crisis, and the crown prince being unpopular and uncharismatic but close to Thaksin, the network monarchy feared that Thaksin would become a kingmaker during a succession and could assert strong influence over the palace in the next reign (Winichakul 2016).

We cannot downplay the psychological effects of the succession crisis, which seemed to cloud the judgement of those in the palace circle. Network monarchy is fundamentally a personalized network centered on the monarch and deriving its power from the king's charisma. When the network's head figure changed, the power of the whole network was reduced. Not only power and prestige are at stake. In terms of economic interest, the royal family's Crown Property Bureau (CPB) is one of the largest business conglomerates in Thailand, with assets worth some US$41 billion in 2005 (Hewison 2012, 149–50; Ouyyanont 2008). CPB is an opaque organization: exempt from taxes, protected by the palace, and lacking transparency and public accountability. Beginning in the 1950s, the power of the royal-military alliance had increased and never been subdued or reformed, giving them the capacity to intervene in and destabilize politics when they deemed the situation threatening to their interests.

Nevertheless, Thaksin's authoritarian, illiberal tendencies (Satha-Anand 2006; cf. Zakaria 2007) worsened the situation by pushing a number of media figures, nongovernment organizations (NGO) activists, and academics, who would have been expected to support democracy, to instead ally with the royal-military elite. With Thaksin's strong rule and divisive rhetoric and practices, these civil society actors were intimidated and suppressed. They were also concerned by the erosion of democratic institutions under Thaksin, and his government's human rights violations and suppression of civil liberties and freedom. They disapproved of Thaksin's attempts to undermine checks and balances. While the poor admired Thaksin because he spoke for them, his critics thought he had become increasingly autocratic. They felt that, under Thaksin, their political space shrunk and their influence disappeared. Eventually, they chose to support the anti-Thaksin elite in bringing Thaksin down. Unfortunately, in 2006 and 2014 the royal-military elite replaced Thaksin's illiberal democracy with military authoritarianism, deepening the crisis of Thailand's democracy. In comparative perspective, the dynamic of Thailand's polarization was similar to the situation in Venezuela and Turkey under the leadership of Hugo Chavez and Recep Tayyip Erdoğan, respectively, in which the elected populist leader turned more authoritarian and illiberal, provoking angry protests from the middle class and old elites. In Thailand, however, where the establishment is powerful, the end result of the tussle was the ousting of the elected populist leader and democratic breakdown.[8]

Institutional factors: Changing the rules of the game

It should be noted here that the constitution's rules and its institutional mechanisms played a part in creating a crisis in two ways. First, with its intent to strengthen the position of prime minister and stabilize the government, the 1997 constitution gave enormous power to the prime minister over Members of Parliament (MPs) and his own party members, and made it relatively difficult for the Lower House to hold the prime minister accountable. Second, the mixed member proportional (MMP) electoral system, with its disproportional nature, gave Thaksin's party a lot of "extra" seats, so they overwhelmingly dominated the parliament. For example, in the 2011 election, TRT gained 44 percent in constituency votes and 48 percent in party list votes, but obtained 53 percent of the seats in parliament.

The opposition party's inability to reform itself, come up with a viable alternative policy platform, and play under democratic rules was another important factor in the crisis. With its narrow support base, the Democrat Party has failed to win elections since 1995. It mainly positioned itself as the party of the urban middle class in Bangkok and relatively affluent voters in the South (both of which are minorities in national politics), while failing to win support from rural voters in the North and Northeast due to its elitist outlook and urban-biased policies. It is important to understand the regional composition of MP seats in Thailand, which explains Thaksin's success and the failure of the opposition: MP seats in the South and Bangkok combined total is 86, while the North and Northeast have 193. As long as the Democrat Party fails to win support in the relatively poor North and Northeast regions, it will not be able to win elections. Since Thaksin came to power, the Democrat Party has lost to Thaksin-backed parties in every election. During the crisis in 2005–2006, the party boycotted the election and decided to side with the Yellow Shirts and network monarchy in toppling Thaksin through extraparliamentary tactics. In 2014, it boycotted the election again and this time directly led the mass protests that eventually paved the way for the coup in May of that year (Kongkirati 2016a).

The quasi-judiciary and independent institutions created by the 1997 constitution to function as checks and balances also failed to do their job because of a lack of capacity and integrity, unclear jurisdictions and scope of power, and interference from Thaksin and the old elites. When Thaksin was dominant, these institutions ruled in his favor. But later, when the establishment decided to eliminate Thaksin, they switched sides. The constitutional court disbanded the Thaksin-allied parties twice and banned hundreds of their party members, disqualified two prime ministers from Thaksin's camp, blocked constitutional amendment attempts, and nullified the elections in 2006 and 2014, leading to political deadlock and military coups in both years. The highly partisan nature of these accountability mechanisms, and especially the politicization of the judiciary (Dressel 2010), polarized the country even further, as it undermined the rule of law and detracted from peaceful means to settle conflicts under a democratic polity.

Structural and ideological factors: Inequality, political disenfranchisement, and contested ideologies

Beyond the elite level, polarization in Thailand has deep structural roots. Social and economic inequality and political disenfranchisement constitute significant structural factors and grievances. These problems of inequality and exclusion are related to underlying social cleavages based on class, ideology, the rural-urban divide, and regional identity. We cannot single out one cleavage as the only explanatory factor in polarized conflicts. In Thailand's context, these cleavages were reinforcing and interrelated in establishing conditions for the emergence of both the anti- and pro-Thaksin movements.

As mentioned earlier, polarization in Thailand involved not only the elite but also a large number of ordinary people. At its peak, both the Yellow Shirt and Red Shirt movements mobilized 200,000–300,000 of their supporters to join protests on the street (Nostitz 2014). Several more millions support them through movement-owned media channels (radio stations, magazines, and satellite TV stations). The Thaksin-backed party and the Democrat Party had 15 million and 11 million voters on their side, respectively, in the 2011 election.

Socioeconomic and ideological factors can account for the division between the Yellow and the Red camps. Socioeconomic factors explain the social origin of each movement, and ideological factors help to explain the commitment and enthusiasm of movement participants. Polarization between the pro-Thaksin and anti-Thaksin coalitions is broadly based on regional, urban-rural, and class division. Considering the voting pattern in the elections from 2001 to 2014, we see a clear repeated pattern in which Thaksin gained an overwhelming number of votes in the North and Northeast regions plus some provinces in the Central region and the surrounding provinces of Bangkok, while the Democrats dominated in the South and among Bangkok's urban districts. The political division exhibited in this stable pattern of voting is a result and indication of Thailand's social inequality. Several pieces of research demonstrate that structural inequality is the underlying cause of political and social polarization in Thailand. Compared with neighboring countries in Southeast Asia, Thailand's income distribution is more unequal (UNDP 2010). The Gini coefficient, a measure of income inequality, has gradually worsened, and, with the exception of a brief period in the early 2000s, has shown no sign of improvement (0.341 in 2017). By 2012, the income differential between the top 20 percent and the bottom 20 percent of the population was approximately 13 times, compared with four times in Japan and Scandinavia and six to eight times in North America and Europe. The only countries that have a worse record of income distribution than Thailand are in Latin America (Phongpaichit and Baker 2012, 218–19). In this sense, the crisis manifested in Thailand corresponds to the argument that inequality tends to undermine the stability of a democratic regime "because elites have more to lose from redistributive policies that tend to result from majority rule" (Acemoglu and Robinson 2006, 35–8).

Support for Thaksin has been strong in the North and Northeast, where incomes are relatively low and poverty is pronounced. Even though absolute poverty has fallen over time, the income disparity has widened. More than 80 percent of the population with the lowest income is concentrated in rural areas in the North and Northeast (and the Deep South). In 2007, average incomes in the North and Northeast were about one-third of those in the capital. Data also show that the provinces that voted for the Democrat Party have average per capita gross provincial product of 221,130 baht per year, contrasted with 92,667 baht for provinces that voted for the Thaksin-backed party (UNDP Report 2009 quoted in Hewison 2012, 156). In addition, a national survey found that people who joined the Red Shirt movement had lower incomes, less education, and lower levels of job/life security (as the majority of them work in agriculture and the informal economic sector) than those who supported the Yellow Shirts (Sathitniramai et al. 2013).

It is not a coincidence that the majority of Red Shirt supporters come from the North and Northeast and suburbs of Bangkok, where migrant workers from the

Northeast are concentrated. Core members of the Red Shirt movement are drawn from rural farmers from these poor regions. Though many of them also obtain a chunk of their family income from nonfarm jobs, they still maintain their peasant, rural identity (Walker 2012; Keyes 2014). In Thailand, regional cleavages, the urban-rural divide, and class division are mutually reinforcing. But the polarizing conflict between the anti- and pro-Thaksin forces makes the multiplicity of interests and identities in Thai society "align along a single dimension, splitting into two opposing camps with [an] impermeable boundary and perceived zero-sum interests and mutually exclusive identities. Adversaries become enemies to be eliminated" (McCoy and Rahman 2016, 26). In Thailand, a constructed, color-coded identity has become a fixed political identity that defines the people's political positions and interests.

It is true that wealth disparities, and the underdevelopment of the North and Northeast, have existed in Thailand for decades, so the question is why polarization has developed now. The underlying condition of inequality was activated by several intervening factors in the late 1990s. The critical juncture was 1997, when the country witnessed three developments: the most severe financial crisis in its modern history; the new constitution, which changed the rules of the game; and the decentralization program, which affected state structure. The financial crisis made poor people more distressed and changed the power balance among the elite. The new constitution provided an advantage to a large party that could come up with a policy-based campaign and vast resources. And decentralization empowered local voters and made them aware of the power of the ballot. Frequent local elections strengthened electoral democracy at the grassroots level and decreased the power of the old bureaucratic machine.

Prior to 1997, almost no political parties offered concrete policies to voters, as the parties were built around a small network of business or bureaucratic cadets who lacked a clear ideological platform. Weak coalitions meant that elected governments failed to last long enough to implement policies and respond to voters. The Thaksin party's populist package and strong government changed Thai politics, making democracy "eatable" (the Red Shirt term) in the views of a marginalized electorate. Under Thaksin, these voters felt empowered, and they aspired to better opportunities in life—education for children, cheap health care for the elderly, micro-credits for investment, and so on. When Thaksin was ousted unconstitutionally, they felt that not only had "their leader" been brought down illegitimately, but also that progress in their lives had been put on hold by the establishment and urban elites. Unfulfilled political and social desires and yearning for political recognition played very important roles in the political mobilization of the Red Shirts (cf. Sopranzetti 2012; Ferrara 2015). The Red Shirt movement is neither an anticapitalist movement nor revolutionary. Its members demand basic equal political rights under electoral democracy, responsive government, and wider opportunities for social mobility. The Red Shirts perceived Thaksin's policies as an attempt to attenuate through redistribution the negative effects that the capital-wielding urban elites have on the social mobility of the disempowered rural and urban working class.

On the other side of the political division, the urban middle class opposed Thaksin because they found his "populist" rhetoric and practices repugnant and irresponsible. Given Thaksin's populist platform, which emphasized the rural and informal sectors, the urban middle class also felt that they were the ones who would bear the cost (through the income tax) of populist programs that benefited the lower class much more than them. They feared that their living standards and status would cease to improve or even deteriorate. The anxiety of the middle class was "about the threat to its social status and economic position presented by more inclusive political systems that confer upon provincial voters the power to choose the country's government" (Ferrara 2015, 273).[9]

Usually in Thailand, urban middle-class citizens are influential in shaping public opinion and social agendas through public space. But when it comes to electoral politics, they become a minority who are outnumbered by their rural countrymen, a situation that makes them feel powerless. When Thaksin cemented electoral support from rural voters in a way no politician had successfully done before, the middle class eventually turned against not only Thaksin but electoral democracy itself. In 2014, middle-class protesters led by the PDRC disrupted the voting process and publicly stated that the basic principle of "one man, one vote" is not suitable for Thailand, where the majority of voters are still poor, uneducated, and ignorant. This notion on the part of the urban middle class was based on their longstanding cultural bias toward rural people. The cultural bias was not new; what was new was the way the urban elites appropriated this cultural prejudice to legitimize their political campaign to deprive rural people of the right to vote. The PDRC was the first social movement in Thailand that mobilized mass support against the electoral process and institutions (Kongkirati 2016a).

It should be noted, however, that Thaksin's rise did not change the attitudes of the middle class immediately. In 2001 and 2005, TRT won the majority of seats in Bangkok by a wide margin. So the middle class's opposition to Thaksin grew gradually over time along with Thaksin's aggrandizement and the traditional elite's maneuvers to eliminate him. Therefore, both objective reality and the framing of the conflict came into play in shaping attitudes and behaviors that led to polarization. Royalist elites and anti-Thaksin media were "effective in arousing the insecurities and fears of urban middle-class voters, warning that Thaksin's populism would come at the expense of their economic well-being and social status" (Ferrara 2015, 257).

The changing media landscape helped to stoke political tension. The anti-Thaksin camp used social media and satellite TV (owned by a Yellow Shirt leader, Sondhi Limthongkul) to spread rumors, slander, false and distorted information, and accusations against Thaksin and his supporters. Later, the Red Shirts copied the same tactics, using their own TV stations and radio channels to propagate information and narratives to counter the Yellow Shirt media. The media has become a space of fierce political battle, flooded with hate speech and malign messages rather than public deliberation. Demonization and dehumanization are pervasive. The Yellow Shirts called the Red Shirts "buffalo," "lizard," and "scum of the earth," while the Red Shirts called the Democrat Party the "cockroach party." One observer points to "the increasing segmentation of information markets" in Thai society, which provided "little scope for negotiating principled political differences." (Unger 2012, 321). Thai people perceived political contestation with fervent emotions of love and hate, as if they were watching sports or reality TV (see McCargo 2009). People on opposing political sides have different political realities, consuming different news and living in two different worlds. Since 2014, cyber policing, cyber witch-hunts, and mass propaganda by state-controlled media and electronic media under the military regime have further exacerbated social conflict (see Laungaramsri 2016).

To conclude, class structure along with regional and urban-rural disparities provided the conditions for mass mobilization and the resulting polarization in Thailand. But elite struggle is what activated the existing social cleavages, and ideological framing exacerbated and deepened the polarization to the extent that it spiraled out of the elites' control. Political conflicts in Thailand have been gradually framed and perceived by both sides as "warfare"—black/white; us/them; uncompromising fighting between the "good" and the "bad"; "moral, clean, enlightened" and "immoral, corrupt, stupid" people; "patriots" and "traitors"; and "aristocrats" and "commoners." Political entrepreneurs on both sides have produced divisive discourse and rival images and symbols. The Yellow Shirts and traditional elites want to restore and uphold "Thai-style democracy" (i.e., despotic paternalism or elitist democracy), with royalist nationalism and a hierarchical social order drawing on traditional cultural values. By contrast, the Red Shirts espouse "populist democracy" with a strong elected government, popular nationalism, and an egalitarian social order drawing on the basic principle of political equality.

Consequences: Street Violence, Political Instability, and Democratic Breakdown

Deep polarization has made Thai politics a deadly game that is dysfunctional and unstable. Since the crisis started in 2005, there has been no consensus among power elites or civil society groups around basic "rules of the game," which made the country highly volatile. Dysfunctional politics has also disrupted growth and bred more deadly conflict. Since 2005, Thailand has had seven prime ministers (five elected, two installed by military coup), four general elections (and two nullified elections), two military coups, and four violent crackdowns on public protests. Two popularly elected prime ministers have been ousted by outright military coups, and the other two by court rulings. The April–May 2010 military crackdown on the pro-Thaksin movement under the Democrat Party was the most violent political suppression in modern Thai history, with an official death toll exceeding those of previous political crises (Kongkirati 2013).

With the latest coup in 2014, Thailand is back to being ruled by strong military authoritarianism, the most repressive since 1976. The coup was an attempt by the royal-military elites to eliminate Thaksin's influence in Thai politics and restore the power of the unelected minority elite. Political and social division have not been resolved but have been suppressed with brute force. The country has remained torn apart by various forms of civil strife and deep division, and it is still far from being able to reach a new political order deemed legitimate and acceptable by all conflicting entities. The new constitution promulgated in 2017 is likely to further exacerbate the conflict and deepen confrontation between opposing movements, as it clearly establishes a political system that maintains the dominance of the royal-military power bloc and unelected institutions at the expense of politicians and civil society groups (Kongkirati 2016b).

Notes

1. The block vote system is the use of plurality voting in multimember districts. Voters have as many votes as there are seats to be filled in their district, and are free to vote for individual candidates regardless of party affiliation. The block vote system normally produces a weak and fragmented political party system. For a mixed-member system, there are two electoral systems using different formulas running alongside each other. Voters cast their votes for candidates in a district and from a party list.

2. Usually, elected prime ministers in Thailand are short-lived. Before Thaksin, no one had ever finished their term in office. They were either forced to resign or to dissolve parliament, or ousted by military coup.

3. In January 2006 Thaksin's family sold its shares in Shin Corporation, a big telecommunication company, to Temasek Holdings of Singapore for US$1.88 billion. His family gained an enormous profit from this deal and paid no tax, which is legal under Thai law. The "tax evasion" issue, however, sparked a series of angry demonstrations in Bangkok.

4. Also, opposition parties' belief that they were going to lose to the TRT again. See "Opposition to boycott election," *Bangkok Post*, 26 February 2006.

5. http://nationmultimedia.com/breakingnews/read.php?newsid=30000759.

6. For studies that present the conflict as "elite" power struggle, see Crispin (2012), Lintner (2009), and McCargo (2010).

7. In Thailand, *populist* is a highly politically loaded term and conveys negative meaning. Thaksin's opponents intentionally used the term as a political weapon to attack Thaksin. So we need to be aware of the politics of meaning.

8. See Somer (2016) for the case of Turkey, and Garcia-Guadilla and Mallen (2016) for polarized politics in Venezuela.

9. It was striking that in the 2014 election, the Red Shirt's political campaign was "Respect my vote," while the anti-Yingluck's was "Respect my tax."

References

Acemoglu, Daron, and James Robinson. 2006. *Economic origins of dictatorship and democracy.* Cambridge: Cambridge University Press.

Baker, Chris. 2016. The 2014 Thai coup and some roots of authoritarianism. *Journal of Contemporary Asia* 46 (3): 388–404.

Chattharakul, Anyarat. 2010. Thai electoral campaigning: Vote-canvassing networks and hybrid voting. *Journal of Current Southeast Asian Affairs* 29 (4): 67–95.

Chaiwat, Thanee, and Pasuk Phongpaichit. 2008. Rents and rent-seeking in the Thaksin Era. In *Thai capital after the 1997 crisis*, eds. Pasuk Phongpaichit and Chris Baker, 249–66. Chiang Mai: Silkworm Books.

Chambers, Paul, and Napisa Waitoolkiat. 2016. The resilience of monarchised military in Thailand. *Journal Of Contemporary Asia* 46 (3): 425–44.

Crispin, Shawn. 2012. Thailand's classless conflicts. In *Bangkok, May 2010: Perspectives on a Divided Thailand*, eds. Michael Montesano, Pavin Chachavalponqpun, and Aekapol Chongvilaivan, 108–19 Singapore: Institute of Southeast Asian Studies.

Dressel, Björn. 2010. Judicialization of politics or politicization of the judiciary? Considerations from recent events in Thailand. *The Pacific Review* 23 (5): 671–91.

Eugénie Mérieau. 2016. Thailand's deep state, royal power and the constitutional court (1997–2015) *Journal of Contemporary Asia* 46 (3): 445–66.

Ferrara, Federico. 2015. *The political development of modern Thailand*. Cambridge: Cambridge University Press.

Garcia-Guadilla, Maria, and Ana Mallen. 2016. Polarized politics: The Experience of Venezuela under 21st-century socialism. Memo prepared for Polarized Politics Workshop, Georgia State University, March 14–15, 2016. Atlanta, GA.

Hewison, Kevin. 2012. Class, inequality, and politics. In *Bangkok, May 2010: Perspectives on a divided Thailand*, eds. Michael Montesano, Pavin Chachavalponqpun, and Aekapol Chongvilaivan, 143–60. Singapore: Institute of Southeast Asian Studies.

Hewison, Kevin, and Kengkij Kitirianglarp. 2010. "Thai-style democracy": The royalist struggle for Thailand's politics. In *Saying the unsayable. Monarchy and democracy in Thailand*. eds. Søren Ivarsson and Lotte Isager, 179–202. Copenhagen: Nordic Institute of Asian Studies Press.

Hicken, Allen. 2006. Party fabrication: Constitutional reform and the rise of Thai Rak Thai. *Journal of East Asian Studies* 6: 381–407.

Keyes, Charles. 2014. *Finding their voice. Northeastern villagers and the Thai state*. Chiang Mai: Silkworm Books.

Kongkirati, Prajak. 2013. Bosses, bullets, and ballots: Electoral violence and democracy in Thailand 1975–2011. PhD diss., Australian National University, Canberra.

Kongkirati, Prajak. 2014. The rise and fall of electoral violence in Thailand: Changing rules, structures and power landscapes, 1997–2011. *Contemporary Southeast Asia* 36 (3): 386–416.

Kongkirati, Prajak. 2016a. Thailand's failed 2014 election: The anti-election movement, violence and democratic breakdown. *Journal of Contemporary Asia* 46 (3): 467–85.

Kongkirati, Prajak. 2016b. Thailand's political future remains uncertain. ISEAS Perspective, Available from https://www.iseas.edu.sg/images/pdf/ISEAS_Perspective_2016_42.pdf (accessed 5 January 2017).

Kongkirati, Prajak, and Veerayooth Kanchoochat. 2018. The Prayuth regime: Embedded military and hierarchical capitalism in Thailand. *TRaNS: Trans-Regional and -National Studies of Southeast Asia* 6 (2): 279–305.

Laungaramsri, Pinkaew. 2016. Mass surveillance and the militarization of cyberspace in post- coup Thailand. *ASEAS – Austrian Journal of South-East Asian Studies* 9 (2): 195–214.

Lintner, Bertil. July/August 2009. "The battle for Thailand: Can democracy survive?" *Foreign Affairs*.

McAdam, Doug, Sidney Tarrow, and Charles Tilly. 2001. *Dynamics of contention*. Cambridge: Cambridge University Press.

McCargo, Duncan. 2005. Network monarchy and legitimacy crises in Thailand. *The Pacific Review* 18 (4): 499–519.

McCargo, Duncan. 2009. Thai politics as reality TV. *The Journal of Asian Studies* 68 (1): 7– 19.

McCargo, Duncan. 2010. Thailand's twin fires. *Survival* 52:5–12.

McCoy, Jennifer, and Tahmina Rahman. 2016. Polarized democracies in comparative perspective: Toward a conceptual framework. Paper presented at the International Political Science Association conference, 23 July–28 July 2016. Poznan: Poland.

McCoy, Jennifer, Tahmina Rahman, and Murat Somer. 2018. Polarization and the global crisis of democracy: Common patterns, dynamics and pernicious consequences for democratic polities. *American Behavioral Scientist* 62 (1): 16–42.

Mudde, Cas, and Cristóbal Rovira Kaltwasser. 2011. Voices of the peoples: Populism in Europe and Latin America compared. Working Paper no.378. The Helen Kellogg Institute for International Studies.

Nostitz, Nick. 2014. The red shirts from anti-coup protestors to social mass movement. In *"Good coup" gone bad: Thailand's political developments since Thaksin's downfall*, ed. Pavin Chachavalpongpun, 170–98. Singapore: Institute of Southeast Asian Studies.

Ouyyanont, Porphant. 2008. The Crown Property Bureau in Thailand and the crisis of 1997. *Journal of Contemporary Asia* 38 (1): 166–89.

Phatharathananunth, Somchai. 2008. The Thai Rak Thai Party and elections in Northeastern Thailand. *Journal of Contemporary Asia* 38 (1): 106–23.

Phongpaichit, Pasuk, and Chris Baker. 2009. Thaksin's populism. In *Populism in Asia*, eds. Kosuke Mizuno and Pasuk Phongpaichit, 66–93. Singapore: NUS Press.

Phongpaichit, Pasuk, and Chris Baker. 2012. Thailand in trouble: Revolt of the downtrodden or conflict among elites? In *Bangkok, May 2010: Perspectives on a Divided Thailand*, eds. Michael Montesano, Pavin Chachavalpongpun, and Aekapol Chongvilaivan, 214–29. Singapore: Institute of Southeast Asian Studies.

Roberts, Kenneth. 2006. Populism, political conflict, and grass-roots organization in Latin America. *Comparative Politics* 36 (2): 127–48.

Satha-Anand, Chaiwat. 2006. Fostering "authoritarian democracy" with violence: The effect of violent solutions in Southern Thailand. In *Empire and neoliberalism in Asia*, ed. Vedi R. Hadiz, 169–87. London: Routledge.

Sathitniramai, Apichart, Yukti Mukdawijitra, and Niti Pawakapan. 2013. *Phum mi that lae kanmueang khong kan phatthana chonnabot thai ruam samai* [*Landscape and politics of contemporary rural development*] Chiang Mai: Public Policy Studies Institute.

Somer, Murat. 2016. Religious versus secular and power sharing versus hegemonizing politics and polarization in Turkey. Memo prepared for Polarized Politics Workshop, Georgia State University, March 14–15, 2016. Atlanta, GA.

Sopranzetti, Claudio. 2012. Burning red desires: Isan migrants and the politics of desire in contemporary Thailand. *South East Asia Research* 20 (3): 361–79

Tejapira, Kasian. 2006. Toppling Thaksin. *New Left Review* 39:5–37.

UNDP (United Nations Development Programme). 2010. *Human security, today and tomorrow: Thailand human development report*. Bangkok: UNDP.

Unger, Danny. 2012. Flying blind. In *Bangkok, May 2010: Perspectives on a divided Thailand*, Eds. Michael Montesano, Pavin Chachavalponqpun, and Aekapol Chongvilaivan. 313–22. Singapore: Institute of Southeast Asian Studies.

Walker, Andrew. 2012. *Thailand's political peasants: Power in the modern rural economy*. Madison, WI: University of Wisconsin Press.

Winichakul, Thongchai. 2016. Thailand's hyper-royalism: Its past success and present predicament. Trends in Southeast Asia, no.7. Singapore: ISEAS-Yusof Ishak Institute.

Yoshifumi, Tamada. 2009. Democracy and populism in Thailand. In *Populism in Asia*, eds. Kosuke Mizuno and Pasuk Phongpaichit, 94–111. Singapore: NUS Press.

Zakaria, Fareed. 2007. *The future of freedom: Illiberal democracy at home and abroad*. New York, NY: W. W. Norton & Company.

II. Democratic Erosion under New Elites

Turkey: The Slippery Slope from Reformist to Revolutionary Polarization and Democratic Breakdown

By
MURAT SOMER

Under the Justice and Development Party AKP and Recep Tayyip Erdoğan, Turkey has become one of the most polarized countries in the world, and has undergone a significant democratic breakdown. This article explains how polarization and democratic breakdown happened, arguing that it was based on the built-in, perverse dynamics of an "authoritarian spiral of polarizing-cum-transformative politics." Furthermore, I identify ten causal mechanisms that have produced pernicious polarization and democratic erosion. Turkey's transformation since 2002 is an example of the broader phenomenon of democratic erosion under new elites and dominant groups. The causes and consequences of pernicious polarization are analyzed in terms of four subperiods: 2002–2006, 2007, 2008–2013, and 2014–present. In the end, what began as a potentially reformist politics of polarization-cum-transformation morphed into an autocratic-revolutionary one. During this process, polarization and AKP policies; the politicization of formative rifts that had been a divisive undercurrent since nation-state formation; structural transformations; and the opposition's organizational, programmatic, and personal shortcomings fed and reinforced each other.

Keywords: polarization; Turkey; democratic backsliding; Justice and Development Party AKP; presidentialism

Numerous studies—for example, on political party polarization, voter preferences, and social distrust—characterize Turkey as one of the most socially and politically polarized countries in the world (Erdogan 2016; Aydın-Düzgit and Balta 2018; Aytaç, Çarkoğlu, and Yıldırım 2017; KONDA 2017; Yılmaz 2017;

Murat Somer is a professor of political science and international relations at Koç University Istanbul. He specializes in comparative politics and democratization, and his research on polarization, religious and secular politics, and ethnic conflict has appeared in books, book volumes, and journals, such as Comparative Political Studies, American Behavioral Scientist, *and* Democratization.

Correspondence: musomer@ku.edu.tr

DOI: 10.1177/0002716218818056

Erdogan and Uyan Semerci 2018; McCoy, Rahman, and Somer 2018). Accordingly, the greater part of the political discourse and, in critical elections and referendums in recent years, the lion's share of voter behavior appears to have been frozen into two mutually disagreeable and obstinate blocs.

For instance, in the 2014 and 2018 presidential elections, where voters and election campaigns were divided almost evenly between those adamantly supporting and fiercely opposing President Recep Tayyip Erdoğan, he won with 51.79 and 52.59 percent of those voting, respectively.[1] Similarly, constitutional changes replacing Turkey's formal parliamentary system with an executive presidential system passed in a 2017 referendum with 51.41 percent of the voters approving the changes. The remaining portion of the body politic was highly mobilized against the changes, arguing that the new system would formally end democracy and establish strong-man autocracy. The high participation rates in these votes— 74.13 percent in 2014, 85.43 percent in 2017, and 86.24 percent in 2018—also suggested an increasingly polarized and politically mobilized electorate.[2]

The country is now widely viewed as having undergone a democratic breakdown and degenerating into an autocracy (Özbudun 2014; Diamond 2015; Esen and Gumuscu 2016; Somer 2016; Freedom 2018; Levitsky and Ziblatt 2018). This is striking because Turkey had long been hailed in the world as having built a rare, long-standing, developing, and exemplary case of secular democracy in a Muslim-majority society, while its many serious shortcomings were also noted (Rustow 1970; Özbudun 1996; Hale and Özbudun 2010; Turan 2015). What is more, many scholars had praised Turkey for being on the path of consolidating liberal democracy, and they had commended the Justice and Development Party (AKP) and its leader, Erdoğan, for building a "Muslim (or conservative) democracy" in the twenty-first century (Özbudun 2006; Kuru and Stepan 2012; Yavuz 2009). Hence, a seasoned observer had argued in 2008 (though also citing the warning signs):

> Turks have at long last begun winning the civic revolution they have been waging for decades. Turkey's democratic institutions have proven strong enough to contain and guide this revolution, allowing it to proceed peacefully and within the bounds of law. This is a transcendent vindication of the system shaped by revolutionaries of the 1920s, and of the Turkish Republic they created. (Kinzer 2008, xiii–xiv)

What happened, and what can we learn from the Turkish case regarding the relationship between polarization and political regime change? My goal in this article is to answer the question by examining how and why polarization emerged and became pernicious in Turkey, and how and why this contributed to democratic erosion, through several periods during the past two decades. How does polarization help to explain the utter collapse of democratic institutions in recent years, which Kinzer had applauded in 2008 for their ability—despite their inadequacies—to maintain an ongoing peaceful and lawful "civic revolution"? In turn, how did democratic backsliding reinforce polarization? What options have been available for depolarizing the country and for protecting and reforming democracy?

I also discuss a related question of bottom-up versus top-down polarization. To better understand both the Turkish case and the phenomenon of polarization at large, it is crucial to explain to what extent, and in what sense, one can attribute Turkey's polarization to its "formative rifts" (Somer and McCoy, this volume), in particular a "center-periphery" or "religious-secular" division, which emerged during late-Ottoman and early-republican processes of modernization. After all, Samuel Huntington once ominously described Turkey as a "torn country" (Huntington 1996). He referred to well-known and long-existing social-cultural cleavages (Mardin 1973; Berkes 1998; Kalaycıoğlu 2012), but, by treating them as if they were culturally and historically given and fixed, he also implied that they were decisive.

In fact, the level of politicization and impact on polarization of these cleavages are variable over time. The critical question to explain is how such divisions in some periods become, or, more accurately, how they are made the basis of a "pernicious" type of polarization, i.e., a polity's division into mutually distrustful "us vs. them" blocs (McCoy, Rahman, and Somer 2018; Somer and McCoy, this volume). For example, even though the fault lines Huntington and others described remained the same, polarization varied across time, as extant measurements of political party polarization also indicate. During the 1980s and 1990s, the Turkish party system had been called "a borderline case between moderate and polarized pluralism" (Ozbudun 1981, 234; Kalaycıoğlu 1994). By contrast, in 2015, Turkish politics was the most polarized among the thirty-eight countries included in the Comparative Study of Electoral Systems (CSES) data, based on Dalton (2008)'s index of party system polarization (Erdogan and Semerci 2018, 37–38).

In response to the above questions, I argue that Turkey's transformation under the AKP and Erdoğan since 2002 fits with, and helps to further develop, theory regarding a certain causal pattern: "polarization (leading to) democratic erosion or collapse under new elites and dominant groups" (McCoy, Rahman, and Somer 2018; Somer and McCoy 2018).

Further, I maintain that a great deal of democratic backsliding in Turkey can be explained by the built-in perverse dynamics of what I call the "authoritarian spiral of polarizing-cum-transformative politics." The very same polarizing tactics the AKP employed to mobilize a winning majority, undermine the opposition, and overcome societal and institutional resistance to its transformative policies— and to redistribute power, status, and resources to its own bloc—triggered changes that transformed the AKP itself and the mainstream political field at large. Together with the responses of the opposition and state institutions, this logic of polarization locked both the party and its rivals in a web of intended, unintended, and mutually reinforcing policies and discourses, which were anti-democratic or had democracy-destroying consequences.

In the end, what initially looked like reformist polarization with democratizing potential was transformed into revolutionary polarization, which had destructive, uncertain, and uncontrollable implications for Turkey's democratic regime. This suggests an important indicator of an authoritarian spiral turning pernicious: when polarization begins to irreversibly transform the polarizing political actor itself.

Transformation through Polarization in Turkey

Echoing the causal pattern of polarization leading to democratic backsliding under new groups (McCoy, Rahman, and Somer 2018; Somer and McCoy 2018), the AKP represented "new" (i.e., from the outskirts of the mainstream) political actors who had previously been marginalized, mainly because of their background as political Islamists. Turkey's secular laws and pro-secular institutions and elites—the country's "center"—had treated them with suspicion and some disdain. Though they had been allowed to participate in the political system, they had periodically been reprimanded with legal and political sanctions (Somer 2007 and 2014; Hale and Özbudun 2010).

How have these political outsiders (relatively speaking) come to dominate Turkey's politics, society, and, increasingly, economy? They did so by coalescing and mobilizing a winning coalition from a diverse, cross-class and cross-ideological base of elite and constituency support (Çarkoğlu and Kalaycıoğlu 2009; Ocakli 2015). A financial meltdown in 2001, among other factors, provided opportunities, and the party managed to use different degrees of polarizing politics in different periods, as I elaborate below. Hence, it mobilized diverse groups based on a simplified and polarizing framing of Turkish society and by promising wide-ranging changes in political and economic structures.

Over time, and with growing polarization, this coalition formed into a partisan bloc that was increasingly personified in Erdoğan. It thus amassed sufficient weight to challenge the well-established institutions of the Turkish "strong state" (Heper 1992; Migdal 2001; Somer 2016).

When the AKP came to power, Turkey's legacy of a strong state—which had successfully overseen modernization and transition to a multiparty, partial democracy but had also prevented the establishment of full democracy during the twentieth century—had long been in need of reform (Heper 2002; Kinzer 2008; Somer 2016). Strong states can impede democratization (Slater 2012). In Turkey, democratic reforms were necessary, for example, to ensure a transparent and accountable state and to redesign the state-religion relationship based on societal consensus.

Previous elected governments had failed to push through reforms because, among other reasons, they had been too fragile in terms of their support base and vis-à-vis their political rivals, an activist and rowdy media, and the guardian state institutions such as the military and the judiciary. By comparison, the AKP gathered sufficient power and stability to make wide-ranging changes, as I elaborate below, partly thanks to its polarizing-cum-transformative politics.

Many of the earlier changes secured economic growth, made potentially democratizing reforms, and subdued the meddlesome military. The latter was achieved through a mix of legitimate democratic and "new authoritarian," underhanded, or at times outright criminal, methods (Cizre and Walker 2010; Somer 2016; Yavuz and Balcı 2018). The party could often get away with this because its (over time, perniciously) polarized and captive constituencies in civil society and politics were willing to overlook and sometimes actively support these policies.

During this process, both the AKP and its antagonists often justified their positions in terms of democracy. Similar to other cases in this volume, pro-Erdoğan Turks saw democratization and promise in the same developments in which anti-Erdoğan Turks saw authoritarianism and decay.

At the end of the day, the cost of all this for Turkish democracy and society has been high. In addition to severe polarization, in 2018 Freedom House downgraded Turkish democracy from "partially free" to "unfree" for the first time since the 1980–83 military regime (Erdogan and Semerci 2018, 37–38; Freedom 2018). Accordingly, the three elections and one referendum the AKP has won since November 2015 have not been free and fair, because, among other reasons, plummeting media freedoms and building of a party-state unleveled the playing field against the opposition (Esen and Gümüşçü 2017; Freedom 2018). All in all, democracy broke down under new elites and dominant groups (Özbudun 2014; Esen and Gümüşçü 2015; Taş 2015; Somer 2016; Öktem and Akkoyunlu, eds 2017; McCoy, Rahman, and Somer 2018).

Analyzing how this happened helps to uncover the causal mechanisms through which polarization becomes pernicious and undermines democracy. I identify ten mechanisms, which I will summarize in the last section, by tracing how four causally important periods unfolded:

- 2002–2006: Trimodal, moderate, and "micro-textual" polarization, and reforms led by the AKP. Significant interparty cooperation.
- 2007: Micro-textual polarization culminates in a political confrontation. Beginning of "macro-textual" polarization.
- 2008–2013: Growing macro-textual polarization, decreasing trimodal and reversible polarization. Incremental democratic erosion. Opposition polarization emphasizes secularism. AKP side highlights the "new Turkey and reforms" theme as an upper text, but Islamism exists as a subtext. Trimodal polarization ends with the 2013 political confrontation.
- 2014–present: Full-fledged bimodal and pernicious (self-propagating) polarization spiraling out of control and democratic backsliding. Polarization is increasingly personalized and ossified into pro- and anti-Erdoğan camps. Islamism-secularism frame continues as a subtext.

But polarization under AKP governments was not created from a tabula rasa. The party capitalized on what might be called Turkey's "protean formative rifts," which took on different names and forms when represented by different actors in different periods.

Turkey's Two Formative Rifts

Periodic polarization and polarizing politics have been part of Turkish politics since late Ottoman times, based on two types of formative rifts. The first rift concerned "outsiders" in Turkey's historical processes of modernization and

"Turkish" nation-building, i.e., the cultural, religious, and linguistic groups that the ruling elites saw (or who saw themselves) as too different to be part of their sociocultural and political-economic projects. Hence, minority groups such as non-Muslims, Kurds, and Alevis were either denied citizenship or treated as citizens with suspicious loyalties unless they culturally assimilated into state-defined "Turkishness" in public life. Hence, the state and ruling elites used polarizing politics to mobilize the Turkish-speaking Sunni Muslim majority population and to justify policies against these other groups (Göçek 2011; Öktem 2011).[3] This type of formative rift might have produced a historical legacy, mode, and repertoire of polarizing politics that current governments can tap into.

However, my main concern—because of its more direct link with the current polarization—is a second type of rift that researchers have described with terms such as "center-periphery," "state-society," and "secular-religious" (Mardin 1973, 2006; Bozdoğan and Kasaba 1997; Berkes 1998; Findley 2010). This rift is a division within the Turkish-speaking Muslim majority, i.e., the "insiders" and main "target population," so to say, of the state-led processes of modernization and nation-building.

Until the AKP period, one side of this rift consisted of Turkey's transformative, developmental, and authoritative central state and the institutions and social-political groups that were its primary defenders and beneficiaries. On the other side were societal segments that felt overlooked and objectified by the state and by the people whom they perceived as enjoying a closer and more favored relation with the state. For lack of better terms, let us call these two sides "republican-centrist" and "provincial-revisionist," respectively.

Even though the "haves" of society were by definition overrepresented in the first and the "have-nots" were overrepresented in the second—education and formal employment being the key determinants of upward social mobility and socialization into state-favored lifestyles and identities—both categories have cut across class boundaries. Initially, urban-dwellers and the agents of state-led modernization such as civil servants and teachers were the mainstays of the first category (Mardin 1973). But both groups became more diverse and dynamic through socioeconomic modernization, rural-urban migration, and more market-based growth, after the 1980s (Bozdoğan and Kasaba 1997). This rift also cuts across ethnic-linguistic divisions, except perhaps for unassimilated ethnic Kurds (Demiralp 2012).

At first sight, the rift seems to overlap with a Left-Right division, because right-wing political actors have predominantly represented provincial-revisionist groups. Yet, periodically, leftist politics (including pro-Kurdish parties) has also represented it with some success, for example during the 1970s and early 1990s. Finally, the cultural-ideological nature of the "center" has changed depending on which political groupings control the state (Somer 2014a; Bilgin 2018).

This legacy produced two competing "foundational" narratives of Turkish modernization. The centrist right-wing and left-wing versions of these narratives have not been mutually exclusive. Both upheld the main myths and truth-claims of Turkish nation-building during the 1920s and 1930s, the difference being that right-wing actors aimed to curb its excesses through more religion- and market-friendly policies (Somer 2014a). However, these narratives also had versions, held by Islamist and secularist elites, that more or less excluded each other (Somer 2010).

Furthermore, before the AKP, power was to some degree balanced between the political representatives of the two sides. In party politics, right-wing political parties dominated the system. The Republican People's Party, CHP—originally founded by Atatürk—and other "left-wing" parties could rule only in coalition governments with right-wing parties. But the secular-republican ideology was dominant in the military, the judiciary, and various other state institutions, as well as the mainstream media, civil society, and big business. These horizontal and vertical forces balanced the power of right-wing elected governments.

These discursive ideological (partially overlapping narratives) and institutional (power balance) factors help to explain why pre-AKP polarization did not become pernicious despite the presence of formative rifts. For example, the Left-Right ideological polarization of the 1970s did not produce two ossified blocs as we see today; on the contrary, volatility and fragmentation were recurring features of the post-1960s party system (Sayarı, Musil, and Demirkol 2018).

The AKP was rooted in political Islamism, whose foundational narratives were in many respects mutually exclusive with the republican-centrist narratives, and they represented "new actors" with a "passive-revolutionary" and "state-conquering" agenda (Tuğal 2009; Somer 2010 and 2017). Yet, initially, the AKP formed a center-right coalition based on a more inclusive upper-text or "macro-text." This macro-text bundled center-right narratives with themes such as globalism, economic development, Muslim Turkish nationalism, neo-Ottomanism, anti-elitism, and EU membership (Öniş 2007; Çarkoğlu 2008; White 2014), while Islamist narratives continued as a subtext or "micro-text" (Somer 2007).

Causes, Dynamics, and Periods of Polarization under the AKP

Polarization is a multidimensional and relational process, and we need indicators that measure it as such (Lauka, McCoy, and Firat 2018). The causal narrative below focuses on qualitative signs and processes. Simultaneously, it is worthwhile to note that extant measurements of party-ideological polarization also indicate that Turkey became increasingly polarized during these periods.[4]

2002–2006: Moderate and micro-textual polarization and reforms

The AKP came to power in 2002 when major segments of the Turkish electorate had grown weary of the existing political elites and were ready to support large-scale changes, following a decade of political-economic instability. The first AKP period in government generated only moderate and what I call "micro-textual" polarization, because polarization in this period could be described as trimodal or bisected. In the middle of those who approved and disapproved of the party, mainly because of its Islamist credentials, stood many elite and societal groups. These groups lent their conditional backing to the new elites because they saw them as agents for change, EU membership, and ending military tutelage. Thus, these groups and many external observers were willing to overlook subtle but deeply polarizing micro-text discourse and behavior from the AKP (Tepe 2005; Somer 2007, 2010; Kinzer 2008).

Unlike the inclusive, reformist, compromising, and thus nonpolarizing upper-text, this polarizing subtext was "passive-revolutionary" (Tuğal 2009). It was revealed by behaviors and expressions at the local level and oblique statements at the national level (Somer 2007), and it reflected an orientation toward gradual state-capturing and redefining society based on Islamist foundational narratives (Somer 2010, 2017). These factors raised ontological insecurity among pro-secular groups (Somer 2007; Öktem and Akkoyunlu 2017).

Reinforcing these undercurrents were "state-conquering" government policies—e.g., gradual staffing of state agencies with partisans, including members of the Gülen Islamist movement (*Gülen Hareketi* [GH]), and subtle signs of Islamization in social life (Somer 2007; Toprak et al. 2008; Öktem and Akkoyunlu, eds 2017; Yavuz and Balcı 2018). On the macro-level, the government's discourse and policies were shaped by reformism, democratization, and EU membership (Özbudun 2007; Hale and Özbudun 2010). Many legal-political reforms were passed through inter-party cooperation. Reflecting the trimodal polarization, although pro-Islamic and pro-secular elite views in the press diverged on issues such as secularism, religion's role in society and state, and social pluralism including gender rights, they converged on issues such as political democracy—neither group being "exemplary democrats of a principled and inclusive kind"—and each group exhibited significant internal diversity (Somer 2010b; Somer 2011, 514).

2007: Political confrontation and the beginning of "macro-textual" polarization

At this critical juncture, pernicious polarization and authoritarianism could have been prevented in the decade ahead if Turkey's "old" political elites could have united and reformed the discourses, programs, and campaign strategies of the opposition parties, thus democratically checking and balancing the AKP's growing power (Somer 2007; Kumbaracıbaşı 2009). But they performed these tasks rather poorly. Instead, they resorted to mass polarizing politics and legal measures, which often had questionable constitutional legitimacy, to remove or discipline the AKP in a context of economic growth and AKP popularity.

Furthermore, secularists drew on the Islamism vs. secularism cleavage at a time when this division was growing in importance among significant pro-secular segments of society but might have been subsiding among a majority consisting of religious conservatives and moderate secularists. Reflecting the latter trend, in a 2006 survey, about half the respondents—presumably mostly AKP supporters—thought the party "believes in democracy (53.7 percent) … defends fundamental rights and freedoms more than other parties (50.8 percent) [but protects] an Islamic way of life more than other parties (53.3 percent)." Moreover, the proportion of those believing that religious people were repressed had fallen from 42.4 percent in 1999 to 17.0 percent in 2006. But other major segments of society thought that the party intended to "impose an Islamic way of life (50.3 percent) . . . seeks EU membership to legitimise [sic] an Islamic political system (45.2 percent) . . . did not soften the Islamist-secularist conflict (44.4 percent) . . . seeks to infiltrate the bureaucracy with Islamist cadres (43.8 percent) and . . . intends to reverse the advances concerning women's rights (36.7 percent)" (Çarkoğlu and Toprak 2006; Hale and Özbudun 2010, 38–39). There was also a split among pro-secular elites, among whom secularist sensitivities were either increasing or decreasing (Somer 2010b, 568–71).

Then the parliament's impending election of a new president prompted a political confrontation (Hale and Özbudun 2010, 39). The outgoing president was a secularist and former head of the Constitutional Court (CC) who had obstructed various AKP policies and appointments. Hence, secularists saw him "as a symbol and 'the last citadel' of the secular republic [and] reacted strongly to the election of a formerly Islamist politician" (Hale and Özbudun 2010, 40).

In essence, the constitution encouraged "forbearance," inter-party consensus, and a nonpartisan president by requiring a two-thirds majority of the parliament's full membership in the first two rounds of the election. Technically, however, it allowed the AKP to elect its own candidate—initially expected to be Erdoğan—because the vote of a simple majority was sufficient in the third and fourth rounds, with no quorum requirement specified for any round.

When the AKP nominated its number two figure, Abdullah Gül, secularist elites mobilized pro-secular members of the middle class in massive antigovernment "republican rallies" (Somer 2007). Further, the opposition CHP went to the CC claiming that a two-thirds quorum must be required during the first round so that the majority party would feel compelled to compromise. Meanwhile, the military issued an online ultimatum accusing the government of undermining secularism and threatening an intervention, amid pro-secular media criticism of the government.

Soon after, the Court upheld the CHP's case (Hale and Özbudun 2010, 39–40). With these moves, and the AKP's responses, micro-textual polarization became macro-textual. The AKP mobilized its base against this "affront to democracy" and called a referendum on various constitutional amendments that, among other changes, would explicitly abolish any quorum requirement for the impending presidential election and bring direct popular elections of future presidents. The CC agreed that the proposed changes were constitutional. The AKP carried the vote with 68.95 percent, elected Gül president, and won early parliamentary elections held "under the shadow of the constitutional crisis" with 46.58 percent support (Hale and Özbudun 2010, 40–41).

2008–2013: "Macro-textual" and increasingly bimodal polarization and incremental democratic erosion

This period began with a fierce war of nerves, words, and legal-political maneuvers at the elite level and ended with massive bottom-up uprisings against the government, known as the Gezi Protests, in 2013. Yet, arguably, the authoritarian spiral of polarizing-cum-transformative politics was still reversible, if the opposition parties could reform themselves to increase their electoral weight, link with the growing grass-roots opposition, and employ polarizing politics based on a constructive rather than an obstructive platform.

Early on, two judicial interventions, one from the secularist establishment and the other from the growing Islamist elements within the state, further polarized Turkish society. First was the chief public prosecutor's case to close the AKP in March 2008. The CC found that the party was guilty of being a "focal point of antisecular activity" but not seriously enough for closure. Instead, the Court issued a financial penalty and a "serious warning," while simultaneously citing concerns for democracy in the event of banning an elected governing party. The AKP declared this a "victory for democracy" (Tait 2008). However, it became apparent that it was celebrating a triumph for vertical accountability in democracy alone. From then on, and by increasingly framing the necessity of judicial reform as a struggle against "oligarchic rule," the party implemented policies that incrementally weakened judicial independence and undermined horizontal accountability.

Second, in July 2008, the growing AKP-GH camp within the judiciary opened a series of lawsuits against secularist military officers, intellectuals, and civil society actors, on what later turned out to be mainly trumped-up charges (Cizre and Walker 2010; Jenkins 2011).[5] Coming on the heels of smaller campaigns in 2004 and 2005 against military and secularist actors, including a university rector, and lasting until 2010, these legal maneuvers effectively subdued the secularist armed forces and parts of the pro-secular establishment. Reflecting the continuing trimodal polarization, pro-secular elites in political parties, media, and civil society became split between cynical democrats who viewed these cases—and in general cooperation with the AKP—as necessary to end military praetorianism and alarmists who saw them as anti-secular conspiracies.

The opposition parties could not form a positive and unequivocally prodemocratic agenda uniting the cynics and alarmists. The main opposition party, CHP, strongly condemned the antisecularist trials while sending ambiguous signals about, if not passively approving, the anti-AKP case. The party's leader supported the legal basis of the AKP-closure case but expressed concerns about the consequences for democracy if the AKP were banned.

Further, opposition parties took an uncompromising and arguably polarizing stand vis-à-vis various legal-constitutional changes that the AKP attempted or passed in this period, arguing that these changes were stepping stones for regime change. Opposition parties had legitimate reasons for concern, among them questions regarding the constitutionality of many amendments. In the case of a 2013 inter-party commission for partially rewriting the constitution, they also maintained that an apparent consensus collapsed in the eleventh hour because AKP insisted on introducing a presidential system, which the opposition believed would be authoritarian.

But the opposition parties appear to have had two main shortcomings. First, they focused on alarmist-obstructive rather than proactive and constructive politics of polarization, thereby neglecting to develop alternative programs of reforms. Second, they did not make any path-breaking changes in their organizations, programs, and electoral strategies, for example, by advancing new methods of civic engagement and political communication, even though the elections were mainly free and fair in this period. Preoccupied with the question of how to stop the AKP's transformations and inversion of the system's formal and informal rules, the opposition was trapped in a pro-status-quo position.

By comparison, the AKP managed to maintain an image as the main party that promised change and prosperity, and effectively communicating with its constituencies. The party and Erdoğan employed numerous discursive, coercive, financial, and legal (and at times extra-legal or illegal) methods of polarizing-cum-transformative politics that mobilized their base and weakened their opponents. A comprehensive account is beyond the scope of this article, but one consequential confrontation between the AKP and the media will serve as a representative example.

Early in 2008, Turkey's then–most influential media corporation, the Doğan Media Group (DMG), began covering news of corruption linked to the AKP, based on convictions in Germany (Daloğlu 2009; Higgings 2009). While the DMG was mainly pro-secular, it also harbored many outlets that were examples of the moderate or "cynical democratic" position.[6]

In response, the then–Prime Minister Erdoğan launched a fierce campaign against the DMG, displaying archetypal tools of polarizing-cum-transformative politics. He accused the DMG of spreading false news and blackmailing his government for financial favors, and asked people to boycott it. At the height of his campaign, Erdoğan described the dispute in terms of a broader political conflict taking place in the country, using a textbook example of a "polarizing speech act," which he later wielded against other critics such as Turkey's biggest and pro-secular business association, Tüsiad. "Those who do not take sides [in this battle]" he threatened, "will be sidelined." Only months later, the DMG was charged a record penalty of 500 million dollars for alleged tax evasion (Daloğlu 2009; Higgings 2009).

Acting as a polarizing political entrepreneur and displaying a "rival image" of the contenders in this conflict (Somer 2001; McCoy, Rahman, and Somer 2018), Erdoğan was urging people to interpret political events, and to position themselves politically, in terms of a major rivalry in society. While he invited people to support his own side in the struggle, which according to him would be the winning side, he also strongly discouraged anybody from seeking a middle ground, warning that they would also be targeted and eventually find themselves to be weak and politically irrelevant. As such, his rhetoric had a chilling and Machiavellian undercurrent of politics understood as pure power, where "the power and capacity to determine a friend and an enemy overlaps with the legitimate authority to establish a new legal order" à la Carl Schmitt (Kutay 2018, 1).

Against this background, many moderates and would-be bridge-makers became divided. Some argued that these forceful, confrontational tactics were necessary to reshuffle rigid institutions and dethrone established political-economic elites. Others opined that the government's means—whatever its ends might be—were dangerous and destructive.

The AKP framed the vote on a second crucial constitutional referendum, which it introduced in 2010, as a battle between those defending their privileges in the "old Turkey" and those supporting a "new Turkey," similarly polarizing society in a trimodal fashion. The proposed amendments looked like an omnibus bill. They included generally undisputed changes expanding some rights and liberties, such as collective bargaining for civil servants (Kalaycıoğlu 2012). The disputable changes seemed to democratize the election of the high judiciary, but simultaneously cracked open the door to speeding up the progovernment transformation of the judiciary and the military (Kalaycıoğlu 2012, 6; Arato 2010; Cizre and Walker 2010; Jenkins 2011). All of this split the opposition between those supporting the changes as "incomplete but good" and those warning of the end of secular democracy and judicial independence (Kalaycıoğlu 2012).

The AKP government won the referendum with a 58 percent majority, tipping the balance of power in the state from pro-secular to proreligious AKP and GH actors. This outcome was solidified by an electoral victory in 2011.

The period came to a close in 2013 with two polarizing episodes that ended trimodal polarization. The first involved the antigovernment Gezi protests, which were triggered by police violence against young environmentalists in Istanbul. They soon spread throughout the country, gathering millions of supporters. Even though pro-secular sensitivities were a main unifying theme, the participants were a cross-generational and cross-ideological lot brought together by opposition to AKP authoritarianism and the demand for real democracy (Özbudun 2014; Yörük and Yüksel 2014). This grass-roots mobilization offered a golden opportunity for the opposition parties to unify their fragmented constituencies based on an anti-AKP, prochange and prodemocratic politics of polarization. But the major opposition parties—except, perhaps, for the pro-Kurdish minority party—missed this opportunity, arguably because of their ideological divisions and rigidity and their organizational shortcomings as mainly "cartel parties" (Sayarı, Musil and Demirkol 2018).[7] As the AKP tightened its grip on civil society and the media, Gezi was unable to develop into a lasting social movement with a concrete agenda. Hence, it enhanced polarization and solidified the pro-AKP bloc without necessarily strengthening the anti-AKP bloc.

In the second episode, Islamist infighting between the AKP and GH produced a full-blown conflict. Antigovernment forces in the judiciary and police, led by GH-linked elements, brought massive corruption charges against the government (Gümüşçü 2016). The allegations were spread on the Internet through sound and video recordings of party members, including Erdoğan and his family. In addition to increasing Erdoğan's authoritarianism and accelerating his purge of AKP moderates, this conflict forced more people to choose between two evils: government corruption, on one hand, and antigovernment and illegal formations within the state, on the other. The opposition again failed to open a third, prodemocratic path, encumbered as it was not only by its own deficiencies but also by its disadvantages on an increasingly unlevel playing field.

2014–present: Pernicious polarization and democratic breakdown

While referring the reader to other contributions for the numerous and momentous socio-political developments in this period (see Başkan 2015; Taş 2015; Esen and Gumuscu 2016; Gumuscu 2016; Somer 2016; Esen and Gümüşçü 2017; Öktem and Akkoyunlu 2017; Yavuz and Balcı 2018), suffice it to say here that this period has witnessed incremental backsliding (Bermeo 2016) and collapse of democracy and the emergence of an electoral-authoritarian regime. The AKP's initial rise as a dominant party gradually gave way to Erdoğan's personalized rule, with an executive presidential system and a largely instrumental AKP.

Major developments have included: Erdoğan's election to the presidency in 2014 and his declaration of a "de facto presidential system," defying the constitutional order based on parliamentarism and a neutral (nonpartisan) presidency; the repeated legislative elections of 2015, where the AKP first lost the majority and then seized it back in unfair and only partially free snap elections; Erdoğan's de facto efforts to revamp and dominate governmental institutions; the resignation of the elected AKP prime minister under pressure from Erdoğan in the spring of 2016; a failed coup attempt, allegedly led by the GH, in the summer of 2016, after which the government declared a state of emergency and started an anti-GH and anti-opposition witch hunt; a 2017 constitutional referendum establishing a de jure executive presidential system; and snap legislative and presidential unfair and unfree elections in 2018, won by the AKP and Erdoğan despite a highly mobilized opposition.

All these transformations took place in a context of polarizing-cum-transformative politics where the ensuing social-political polarization became increasingly self-propagating, personalized, and based on negative partisanship and fear.

For example, in the 2017 referendum, voters' preferences vis-à-vis presidentialism were highly partisan (Aytaç, Çarkoğlu, and Yıldırım 2017). With few people understanding the difference between the presidential and parliamentary systems, most voters took their cues from their party preferences, but people with more knowledge of presidentialism were more likely to vote "No." Religiosity and Kurdish ethnic-linguistic background were significantly and positively correlated with a "Yes" vote, while "No" votes increased along with one's level of education. These three factors were discussed earlier in relation to Turkey's formative rift. However, partisanship was not the sole determinant of the vote; satisfaction with the economy was another significant factor in increasing "Yes" votes (Aytaç, Çarkoğlu, and Yıldırım 2017, 9).

What is more, support for presidentialism began to rise primarily "as a result of rising ontological security concerns" after the June election, when a spree of terror attacks broke out and petrified the public (Aytaç, Çarkoğlu, and Yıldırım 2017, 17). Simultaneously, the polarizing-cum-transformative arguments increasingly adopted the form of "either a presidential system or instability and terror." The "positive" polarizing frame of "either the old elites or new elites and a more democratic Turkey" that had prevailed earlier in the AKP was long gone. It was replaced by a negative frame of "either the new elites or insecurity."

In this context of full-fledged, pernicious bipolarization, the AKP increasingly saw itself as a hegemonic actor situated in a revolutionary moment and having a mandate to unilaterally rebuild both the state and civil society. Accordingly, AKP-engineered structural changes in the media and economy began more and more to sustain and feed polarization. For example, a decade after the confrontation with Erdoğan discussed above, the DMG—with its owner facing charges—was bought by a progovernment mogul, using a state bank loan with highly favorable conditions. This completed a process begun in 2008, as a result of which most of the media came under the control of progovernment outlets and cronies and the Turkish media became "unfree" (Economist 2018; Freedom 2018; Yeşil 2016). At these outlets, common ground disappeared not only through social, psychological, or intellectual mechanisms but also because journalists and commentators who refused to toe the party's or leader's line were sacked or simply no longer given a platform.

As Erdoğan had proclaimed a decade earlier, those who did not want to take sides were indeed left behind. Moreover, the bar of "taking sides" rose as polarizing-cum-transformative politics shifted power to new actors. In the process, many of the earlier agents or apologists of polarization—such as the GH, AKP politicians who refused to become Erdoğan loyalists, liberal writers, and at first independent and then semi-independent journalists and public intellectuals—were marginalized.

As of 2018, Turkey is both politically and socially polarized based on negative partisanship, i.e., how distant voters feel emotionally from the parties they oppose (Erdogan and Uyan Semerci 2018, 38–42), and "perceived threat, but not empathy" shapes "social distance toward Kurds, AKP supporters and AKP opponents" (Bilali, Iqbal, and Çelik 2018, 74). Polarization has transformed the media, public discourse, and social relations. To give just one example, in a 2016 survey, 74 percent of respondents opposed the idea of their children playing "with the children of someone voting for another party" (Erdogan 2016, 2; KONDA 2017).

Conclusions and Ten Causal Mechanisms

Certainly, multiple factors, including ideology and the international environment, contributed to the AKP's and Turkey's authoritarian transformation (see Öniş 2012; Grigoriadis 2014; Somer 2017). Notwithstanding those influences, I have argued that polarizing-cum-transformative politics and the dynamics of the resulting pernicious polarization were a crucial part of Turkey's recent, unfortunate, political history.

The Turkish case helps to uncover the causal mechanisms of pernicious polarization, not only because it tallies with the aforementioned causal pattern but also because it can be analyzed as a theory-disconfirming "crucial case" (Somer 2014b, 3, 7–9). Democratization failed under the AKP despite many auspicious conditions identified in extant theories of democratization (and related theories such as those involving religious actors and democratization). For example,

Turkey defies modernization theory, which would not predict that a country with "rising GDP per capita, a burgeoning civil society, and a rising middle class in the past decades … [would] slide into competitive authoritarianism" (Sarfati 2017, 395). It is hard to explain the outcome without taking into account the causal mechanisms of pernicious polarization.

My analysis suggests ten causal mechanisms that were at work when polarizing-cum-transformative politics spiraled out of control, became "normalized," and replaced what we understand as democratic competition.

First, polarizing politics and discourse empowered opportunistic and revanchist actors within the AKP while weakening more coolheaded actors with a stronger commitment to democracy, pluralism, the rule of law, and compromise. Hence, political actors who could support de-polarization and genuine democratization lost leverage within the AKP bloc.

Second, polarization supported post-truth politics, undermining any existing common ground for democracy. The AKP's rhetoric vilified the opposition, "old elites," and the existing political system, often by exaggerating and distorting the truth, if not by fabricating outright lies. These discursive developments crowded out views within the pro-AKP partisan discourse that were relatively more grounded in truth, while justifying more and more authoritarian policies. The polarizing discourse seems to have reached a critical mass (Somer 2001) and gained a self-propagating momentum, perhaps even spiraling out of the control of party leaders—at least of moderate leaders who would have resisted the pernicious kind of polarization.

Hence, third, all these factors increasingly nurtured a captive and partisan constituency. This constituency became increasingly willing to support, overlook, and, at times, demand not only the reformation but also the capturing and revolutionary dismantling of existing democratic institutions and divisions of powers. Captive audiences became increasingly ready to condone growing corruption, violations of the rule of law, and opportunistic grabbing of power and wealth by the party and its clients.[8]

This third mechanism triggered the fourth one, which can be called the "dwindling channels of bridge-making." Relatively nonpartisan agencies and institutions that harbored actors with mixed or noncommitted orientations and thus had the potential to contribute to bridge-building and de-polarization—such as those in the media, business, and civil society—were wiped out. Their ownership and control shifted to progovernment partisan actors as pro-opposition institutions were radicalized. Hence, polarizing-cum-transformative politics became more effective and forceful alongside the creation of crony capitalism, a partisan welfare state, and progovernment civil society and media, which became the financiers, justification, and mouthpieces of such politics (Yoruk 2012; Aytaç 2014; Kaya 2014; Gürakar 2016; Yeşil 2016).

Fifth, as the AKP increasingly captured the state, the vilification of state institutions became a self-defeating strategy. To continue the politics of polarization and maintain their support base, pro-AKP actors had to shift the blame onto other internal and external targets, which included many potential agents of de-polarization.

Sixth, all these policies—and the reactions of the state institutions—meant that progovernment actors increasingly began to perceive the institutions of horizontal accountability, such as an independent judiciary, as a barrier to their goals. This suggests an extension of the argument by Slater (2013) and Slater and Arugay (2018), who see divided societal preferences— favoring either horizontal (elite-institutional) or vertical (i.e., popular) accountability—as a cause of polarization. Rather than, or in addition to, being a source of polarization, aversion to horizontal accountability can develop as a product of polarization. Indeed, while all right-wing Turkish political actors had prioritized popular support over institutional accountability, the more the AKP relied on polarizing-cum-transformative politics, the more it grew hostile toward any autonomous institution enforcing horizontal accountability (Özbudun 2014).

Seventh, polarization encouraged the personalization of politics and the demand for an executive presidential system within the AKP. By definition, polarization simplifies politics to a choice between "either-or" options (McCoy, Rahman, and Somer 2018). With growing polarization, these choices increasingly resemble path-dependent and identity-based attachments, as in fanhood and tribalism, rather than interest- or value-based choices, as in ideological loyalty and preference for a political program.

By its very nature, I would argue, presidentialism—and executive presidentialism—is likely to emerge as the institutional form that represents and organizes a severely polarized polity, because it has a similar logic. Presidentialism and the personalization of politics, too, simplify politics in the form of either-or choices between the personas of a few strong leaders. Hence, it seems to be no coincidence that, as political choices in Turkey became increasingly simplified to a choice of supporting one bloc or the other, they increasingly took the form of either trusting or distrusting President Erdoğan. In this way, the AKP as a party and other contenders for power within the party were overshadowed by Erdoğan's personalized power (Lancaster 2014). Hence, there may be a causal relation between the synchronous rises of polarization and presidentialism—or rather "one strong man rules" (Stepan 2009; Svolik 2014; Diamond 2015).

Eighth, these developments equally affected the opposition, which found itself between a rock and a hard place. It has oscillated between two strategies since the political confrontation in 2007. Trying to follow a strategy of opposing polarization and seeking compromise—for example, by toning down the anti-Islamist, or, later, anti-Erdoğan rhetoric—often served to legitimize AKP authoritarianism and underhanded political tactics that defied democratic norms. But trying to develop its own polarizing-cum-transformative politics to bring down the government often ended up hardening the AKP camp even further.

For example, when attempting to prevent the executive presidential system the AKP had proposed, whenever the opposition focused on the system's institutional flaws and authoritarian loopholes, they persuaded their own voters but failed to dent the progovernment voters' personalized trust in Erdoğan. When they tried to chip away at the trust between Erdoğan and his supporters by targeting his personality and alleged corruption, they again ended up strengthening the progovernment bloc, which closed ranks to protect their leader, and they subjected themselves to the criticism that they were focusing on personality and not proposing alternative policies.

Ninth, similar to cases such as Thailand and the Philippines (Slater and Arugay 2018), the political and bureaucratic elites contributed to the development of pernicious polarization when they tried to remove or discipline the AKP by using strategies that stretched constitutional boundaries—even when these were aimed at punishing the AKP's own transgressions. The opposition also missed opportunities to reform democratic institutions based on cooperation with the AKP at critical junctures.

Tenth, forced into a pro-status-quo position to obstruct the AKP's polarizing-cum-transformative politics, opposition parties failed to reinvent themselves as prochange actors with new discourses, programs, and organizational forms (Somer 2007 and 2014b; Kumbaracıbaşı 2009; Ayan Musil 2014). With the opposition now including those who were non-Islamist center-right, doing so could have reestablished the electoral balance of power with the AKP, compelling the latter to act more democratically (LeBas 2011; Somer 2017).

In the end, these mechanisms locked the AKP, its rivals, and potential bridge-makers in a downward spiral of authoritarian politics and democratic erosion. The more polarizing politics proved effective, the more it took control of politics, required more of itself, and weakened democracy.

Until 2014 or so, pernicious polarization was likely preventable. One historical-institutional, one political-economic and organizational, and one agentic facilitating factor seem to have undermined this possibility. Polarization built on the mutually exclusive Islamist and secularist narratives of the formative rift (Somer 2010a). These could be compared with ethnic and national "foundational myths," which enhance pernicious consequences when they become the basis of polarization (LeBas and Munemo, this volume). Polarizing-cum-transformative politics generated powerful stakeholders in the media, business, and "GONGO society," i.e., NGOs sponsored or at times directly organized by the government or the governing party, that had political-economic interests in the continuation of polarized politics. Opposition actors performed poorly in uniting and renewing themselves, due to limitations of power politics and ideology, personal shortcomings of self-restraint and talent, insufficient comprehension of the dynamics of polarizing-cum-transformative politics and, thus, an inability to develop novel strategies to control and redirect these dynamics for the purposes of democratic revival.

Notes

1. In both elections, Erdoğan's rivals shared a strongly anti-Erdoğan platform but the vote was divided between several candidates so his closest opponent got 38.4 and 30.6 percent of the votes in 2014 and 2018, respectively.

2. All of the above official figures of the High Electoral Board (YSK) obtained from http://www.ysk.gov.tr.

3. In some periods, political groups such as communists were also treated similarly.

4. The Dalton (2008) index had fallen to a relative low of 2.34 after reaching an apex of 3.55 during the 1990s. It rose to 3.20, 5.26 and 6.21 in 2007, 2011, and 2015, respectively (Erdogan and Uyan Semerci 2018, 39).

5. In April 2016, the highest appeal court overturned all the convictions for reasons including "fabricated evidence." "Turkey Ergenekon: Court quashes 'coup plot' convictions." BBC News, April 21, 2016. http://www.bbc.com/news/world-europe-36099889.

6. For example, the newspaper *Radikal*, which became digital in 2014 and discontinued in 2016.

7. See in particular chapter 5 by Pelin Ayan Musil and chapter 2 by Tosun, Tosun and Gökmen.

8. For a more general argument for authoritarian settings, see Svolik (2012).

References

Arato, Andrew. 2010. The constitutional reform proposal of the Turkish Government: The return of majority imposition. *Constellations* 17 (2): 345–50.

Ayan Musil, Pelin. 2014. Emergence of a dominant party system after multipartyism: Theoretical implications from the case of the AKP in Turkey. *South European Society and Politics* 20 (1): 71–92.

Aydın-Düzgit, Senem, and Evren Balta. 2018. When elites polarize over polarization: Framing the polarization debate in Turkey. *New Perspectives on Turkey* 59:109–33.

Aytaç, S. Erdem. 2014. Distributive politics in a multiparty system: The conditional cash transfer program in Turkey. *Comparative Political Studies* 47 (9): 1211–37.

Aytaç, S. Erdem, Ali Çarkoğlu, and Kerem Yıldırım. 2017. Taking sides: Determinants of support for a presidential system in Turkey. *South European Society and Politics* 22 (1): 1–20.

Berkes, Niyazi. 1998. *The development of secularism in Turkey*. New York, NY: Routledge.

Bermeo, Nancy. 2016. On democratic backsliding. *Journal of Democracy* 27 (1): 5–19.

Bilali, Rezarta, Yeshim Iqbal, and Ayşe Betül Çelik. 2018. The role of national identity, religious identity, and intergroup contact on social distance across multiple social divides in Turkey. *International Journal of Intercultural Relations* 65 (April): 73–85.

Bilgin, Hasret Dikici. 2018. Social conflicts and politicized cleavages in Turkey. In *Party politics in Turkey: A comparative perspective*, eds. Sabri Sayarı, Pelin Ayan Musil, and Özhan Demirkol, 179–95. New York, NY: Routledge.

Bozdoğan Sibel, and Reşat Kasaba, eds. 1997. *Rethinking modernity and national identity in Turkey*. Seattle, WA: University of Washington Press.

Çarkoğlu, Ali. 2008. Ideology or economic pragmatism? Profiling Turkish voters in 2007. *Turkish Studies* 9 (2): 317–44.

Cizre, Umit, and Joshua Walker. 2010. Conceiving the new Turkey after Ergenekon. *The International Spectator: Italian Journal of International Affairs* 45 (1): 89–98.

Daloğlu, Tülin. 4 March 2009. The decline of freedom of expression in Turkey. *The Washington Times*. Available from http://www.tulindaloglu.com/en/2009/02/27/the-decline-of-freedom-of-expression-in-turkey.

Demiralp, Seda. 2012. The odd tango of the Islamic Right and Kurdish Left in Turkey: A peripheral alliance to redesign the centre? *Middle Eastern Studies* 48 (2): 287–302.

Diamond, Larry. 2015. Facing up to the democratic recession. *Journal of Democracy* 26 (1): 141–55.

Erdogan, Emre. 2016. *Turkey: Divided we stand*. Washington, DC: German Marshall Fund.

Erdogan, Emre, and Pınar Uyan Semerci. 2018. *Fanus'ta Diyaloglar: Türkiye'de Kutuplaşmanın Boyutları (Dialogues in Bell Glass: The Dimensions of Polarization in Turkey)*. Istanbul: Bilgi Üniversitesi Yayınları.

Esen, Berk, and Sebnem Gumuscu. 2016. Rising competitive authoritarianism in Turkey. *Third World Quarterly* 6597 (February): 1–26.

Esen, Berk, and Sebnem Gumuscu. 2017. A small yes for presidentialism: The Turkish constitutional referendum of April 2017. *South European Society and Politics* 22 (3): 303–26.

Freedom House. 2018. Turkey. Freedom in the World 2018. Washington, DC: Freedom House.

Grigoriadis, Ioannis N. 2014. Turkey's foreign policy activism: Vision continuity and reality checks. *Southeast European and Black Sea Studies* 14 (2): 159–73.

Gumuscu, Sebnem. 2016. The clash of Islamists: The crisis of the Turkish state and democracy. *Pomeps Studies* 22:6–11.

Gürakar, Esra Çeviker. 2016. *Politics of favoritism in public procurement in Turkey: Reconfigurations of dependency networks in the AKP era*. New York, NY: Palgrave Macmillan.

Hale, William M., and Ergun Özbudun. 2010. *Islamism, democracy and liberalism in Turkey : The case of the AKP*. New York, NY: Routledge.

Heper, Metin. 1992. The strong state as a problem for the consolidation of democracy: Turkey and Germany compared. *Comparative Political Studies* 25 (2): 169–94.

Higgings, Andrew. 23 February 2009. Turkish mogul butts heads with premier. *Wall Street Journal*.

Huntington, Samuel P. 1996. *The clash of civilizations and the remaking of world order*. New York, NY: Simon & Schuster.

Jenkins, Gareth. 2011. Ergenekon, Sledgehammer, and the politics of Turkish justice: Conspiracies and coincidences. *MERIA* 15 (2).

Kalaycıoğlu, Ersin. 2012. Kulturkampf in Turkey: The constitutional referendum of 12 September 2010. *South European Society and Politics* 17 (1): 1–22.

Kaya, Ayhan. 2014. Islamisation of Turkey under the AKP rule: Empowering family, faith and charity. *South European Society and Politics*, 1–23.

Kinzer, Stephen. 2008. *Crescent and star: Turkey between two worlds*. New York, NY: Farrar Straus & Giroux.

KONDA. 2017. Konda barometer. Istanbul. Available from http://konda.com.tr/en/konda-barometer/.

Kumbaracıbaşı, Arda Can. 2009. *The Turkish politics and the rise of the AKP: Dilemmas of institutionalization and leadership strategy*. Oxon: Routledge.

Kuru, Ahmet, and Alfred Stepan. 2012. *Democracy, Islam, and secularism in Turkey*. New York, NY: Columbia University Press.

Kutay, Acar. 2018. Carl Schmitt and struggles over the political decision in Turkey. Working Paper, University of Copenhagen.

Lancaster, Caroline. 2014. The iron law of Erdogan: The decay from intra-party democracy to personalistic rule. *Third World Quarterly* 35 (9): 1672–90.

Lauka, Alban, Jennifer McCoy, and Rengin B. Firat. 2018. Mass partisan polarization: Measuring a relational concept. *American Behavioral Scientist* 62 (1): 107–26.

LeBas, Adrienne. 2011. *From protest to parties: Party-building and democratization in Africa*. Oxford: Oxford University Press.

Mardin, Şerif. 1973. Center-periphery relations: A key to Turkish politics. *Daedalus* 102 (1): 169–90.

Mardin, Şerif. 2006. *Religion, society, and modernity in Turkey*. New York, NY: Syracuse University Press.

McCoy, Jennifer, Tahmina Rahman, and Murat Somer. 2018. Polarization and the global crisis of democracy: Common patterns, dynamics, and pernicious consequences for democratic polities. *American Behavioral Scientist* 62 (1): 16–42.

Ocakli, Feyyaz. 2015. Notable networks: Elite recruitment, organizational cohesiveness, and Islamist electoral success in Turkey. *Politics & Society* 43 (3): 385–413.

Öktem, Kerem. 2011. *Angry nation: Turkey since 1989*. London: Zed Books.

Öktem, Kerem, and Karabekir Akkoyunlu, eds. 2017. *Exit from democracy: Illiberal governance in Turkey and beyond*. London: Routledge.

Öniş, Ziya. 2012. Turkey and the Arab Spring: Between ethics and self interest. *ISSI Strategic Studies* 30 (3): 23–32.

Öniş, Ziya. 2007. Conservative globalists versus defensive nationalists: Political Parties and paradoxes of Europeanization in Turkey. *Journal of Southern Europe and the Balkans* 9 (3): 247–61.

Ozbudun, Ergun. 1981. The Turkish party system: Institutionalization, polarization, and fragmentation. *Middle Eastern Studies* 17 (2): 228–40.

Ozbudun, Ergun. 2007. Democratization reforms in Turkey, 1993–2004. *Turkish Studies* 8 (2): 179–96.

Ozbudun, Ergun. 2014. AKP at the crossroads: Erdoğan's majoritarian drift. *South European Society and Politics* 19 (2): 155–67.

Sarfati, Yusuf. 2017. How Turkey's slide to authoritarianism defies modernization theory. *Turkish Studies* 18 (3): 395–415.

Sayarı, Sabri, Pelin Ayan Musil, and Özhan Demirkol, eds. 2018. *Party politics in Turkey: A comparative perspective*. New York, NY: Routledge.

Slater, Dan. 2012. Strong-state democratization in Malaysia and Singapore. *Journal of Democracy* 23 (2): 19–33.

Slater, Dan. 2013. Democratic careening. *World Politics* 65 (4): 729–63.
Slater, Dan, and Aries A. Arugay. 2018. Polarizing figures: Executive power and institutional conflict in Asian democracies. *American Behavioral Scientist* 62 (1): 92–106.
Somer, Murat. 2001. Cascades of ethnic polarization: Lessons from Yugoslavia. *The ANNALS of the American Academy of Political and Social Science* 573:127–51.
Somer, Murat. 2007. Moderate Islam and secularist opposition in Turkey: Implications for the world, Muslims and secular democracy. *Third World Quarterly* 28 (7): 1271–89.
Somer, Murat. 2010a. Democratization, clashing narratives, and "twin tolerations" between Islamic-conservative and pro-secular actors. In *Nationalisms and politics in Turkey: Political Islam, Kemalism and the Kurdish issue*, eds. Marlies Casier and Joost Jongerden, 28–47. London: Routledge.
Somer, Murat. 2010b. Media values and democratization: What unites and what divides religious-conservative and pro-secular elites? *Turkish Studies* 11 (4): 555–77.
Somer, Murat. 2014a. Moderation of religious and secular politics, a country's "centre" and democratization. *Democratization* 21 (2): 244–67.
Somer, Murat. 2014b. Theory-consuming or theory-producing? Studying Turkey as a theory-developing critical case. *Turkish Studies* 15 (4): 571–88.
Somer, Murat. 2016. Understanding Turkey's democratic breakdown: Old vs. new and indigenous vs. global authoritarianism. *Journal of Southeast European and Black Sea* 16 (4): 481–503.
Somer, Murat. 2017. Conquering versus democratizing the state: Political islamists and fourth wave democratization in Turkey and Tunisia. *Democratization* 24 (6): 1025–43.
Somer, Murat, and Jennifer McCoy. 2018. Déjà vu? Polarization and endangered democracies in the 21st century. *American Behavioral Scientist* 62 (1): 3–15.
Svolik, M. W. 2012. *The politics of authoritarian rule*. Cambridge: Cambridge University Press.
Svolik, Milan W. 2014. Which democracies will last? Coups, incumbent takeovers, and the dynamic of democratic consolidation. *British Journal of Political Science* 45 (4): 715–38.
Stepan, Alfred, ed. 2009. *Democracy in danger*. Baltimore, MD: The Johns Hopkins University Press.
Tait, Robert. 31 July 2008. Turkey's governing party avoids being shut down for anti-secularism. *Guardian*. Available from https://www.theguardian.com/world/2008/jul/30/turkey.nato1.
Tepe, Sultan. 2005. Turkey's AKP: A model "muslim-democratic" party? *Journal of Democracy* 16 (3): 69–82.
Toprak, Binnaz, İrfan Bozan, Tan Morgül, and Nedim Şener. 2008. *Türkiye'de Farklı Olmak (Being different in Turkey)*. Istanbul: Boğaziçi Üniversitesi Yayınları.
Tuğal, Cihan. 2009. *Passive revolution: Absorbing the Islamic challenge to capitalism*. Stanford, CA: Stanford University Press.
Yavuz, Hakan M., and Bayram Balcı, eds. 2018. *Turkey's July 15th coup: What happened and why*. Salt Lake City, UT: University of Utah Press.
Yavuz, M. Hakan. 2009. *Secularism and Muslim democracy in Turkey*. Cambridge: Cambridge University Press.
Yeşil, Bilge. 2016. *Media in Turkey: The origins of an authoritarian neoliberal state*. Urbana, IL: University of Illinois Press.
Yılmaz, Afife Yasemin. 2017. Türkiye'de Donan Siyasetin Şifreleri (The Codes of Turkey's Frozen Politics). Istanbul: KONDA.
Yörük, Erdem, and Murat Yüksel. 2014. Class and politics in Turkey's Gezi protests. *New Left Review* 89:103–23.

Polarization, Participatory Democracy, and Democratic Erosion in Venezuela's Twenty-First Century Socialism

By
MARÍA PILAR
GARCÍA-GUADILLA
and
ANA MALLEN

This article analyzes the emergence and consolidation of political polarization in Venezuela during the so-called Bolivarian Revolution, led by Hugo Chávez and his successor Nicolás Maduro from 1999 to 2018. We also examine the conditions under which polarization in Venezuela became pernicious, and contributed to erosion of democracy. Given the underlying class cleavages that were associated with pro- and anti-*Chavista* identities, we argue that the central dimension of polarization began with a political-ideological rift around competing concepts of democracy—participatory and representative, the rights that each vision privileged (individual civil and political rights vs. collective social and economic rights), and the interpretation of participatory democracy as a complement or substitute for representative democracy. As a result, the inclusion of representative and participatory models of democracy in the 1999 Bolivarian constitution failed to deepen democracy. Instead, they came to be seen as mutually exclusive or incompatible. The result was a polarized democracy that became increasingly authoritarian.

Keywords: polarization; participatory democracy; polarized democracy; Venezuela; twenty-first-century socialism

Venezuela represents an extreme case of polarization that we will define as pernicious,[1] exclusionary and, more recently, fragmented. Following Anderson (1983), Fraser (1992), Habermas (2000), Horkheimer and Adorno (2002), and Warner (2005), we understand polarization as part of the public sphere, where antagonistic political narratives are exacerbated to such a degree that they act as prisms through which all forms of public social interaction are interpreted.

María Pilar García-Guadilla is a professor of political and urban sociology at the Universidad Simón Bolívar, Venezuela. She specializes in social movements, popular organizations, and democracy from below. Her most recent book is, Venezuela Polarized Politics: The Paradox of Direct Democracy under Chávez (*Lynne Rienner 2017), coauthored with Ana Mallen.*

DOI: 10.1177/0002716218817733

Polarization implies two conflicting forces or groups (divided by social class, political ideologies, or other characteristics) that are usually opposites; that is, groups that hold values, principles, interests, and ideologies that are perceived as incompatible and exclusionary. In this context, rational debate based on shared constitutional principles seems impossible because there are no common values and interpretations through which to engage in dialogue and conciliation. The differences between the groups tend to stimulate conflict and make it difficult to achieve the ideological, political, and social consensus needed for democratic governability. In the extreme form of polarization, where principles, interests, and/or ideologies are perceived as antagonistic, attempts to eliminate or suppress the "other," frequently considered an enemy, may justify exclusion and the use of violence (Mallen and García-Guadilla 2017; McCoy, Rahman, and Somer 2018; Lozada 2002).

Polarization in Venezuela's Participatory Democracy

Mallen and García-Guadilla (2017) define the polarization that took place in Venezuela under the presidency of Hugo Chávez (1999–2013) as "a state of heightened tension between citizens, whose very subjectivity [was] subsumed under their perceived political affiliation" (p. 4). From 2001 to 2018, tensions and conflicts from polarization became so severe that "all forms of public social interaction [were] interpreted through antagonistic political narratives" (p. 5). In other words, political identities became social identities, with all of the accompanying dynamics of intergroup conflict in which group members trust and like their own group but distrust and dislike the "other" group.

Polarization has been linked to poverty and social exclusion (Chakravarty 2009; Knox and Pinch 2010; Moulaert, Rodriguez, and Swingedouw 2003) and to heightened social class cleavages (García-Guadilla 2003, 2007; Ellner 2003). It has also been associated with the transition from authoritarian regimes to representative democracy, as in Turkey, the Arab Spring countries, and Hungary after the disintegration of the Soviet Union (Agh 2012; McCoy, Rahman, and Somer 2018). Somer and McCoy (2018) have pointed out three theoretical possibilities in the relationship between democracy and polarization: polarization

Ana Mallen has researched Venezuelan politics for 15 years and has worked with communities in Mexico, the United States, and Venezuela. She coauthored the book, Venezuela Polarized Politics: The Paradox of Direct Democracy under Chávez *(Lynne Rienner 2017), with María Pilar García-Guadilla.*

NOTE: The empirical information for analyzing polarization in Venezuela comes from numerous databases, documents, interviews, and other primary and secondary material that were collected for the research project, *Participatory democracy and the constitutionalization of new citizenship and rationalities: Social actors and sociopolitical conflict in Venezuela under Chávez*, FONACIT-USB (2001–2012). This research project was coordinated by María Pilar García-Guadilla. Additional databases were used for 2013–2018 (GAUS-USB 2013-20118). The theorization and conceptualization of polarization are based on Mallen and García-Guadilla (2017).

contributing to the deterioration of democracy, polarization resulting from democratic crisis, and the more positive outcome of polarization contributing to democratic deepening (p. 3).

Despite Venezuela's historic high levels of poverty, social inequality, and social class differences, the country did not suffer class warfare or overt polarization before President Hugo Chávez came to power (Naim and Piñango1984); neither did polarization occur during the transition from the Perez Jiménez dictatorship to liberal-representative democracy in 1958. As we explain, polarization in Venezuela materialized with Hugo Chávez's rise to power and the incorporation of participatory democracy in the Bolivarian Constitution of 1999. The constitution defines democracy as "participatory and protagonist," as well as "representative," with the aim of including the previously excluded sectors of society. It excluded the previously dominant groups (mainly the middle and upper classes), who then became the political opposition. Polarization is thus associated with the ambiguous constitutional definition of democracy, with the relationship between representative and participatory democracy and the singular, rather than plural, concept of the people as the constitutional authority (the "sovereign").

Other interrelated socioeconomic, institutional, political-ideological, and socio-psychological contributing factors included: high levels of poverty and social inequity; Chávez's Bolivarian revolutionary vision, which was incompatible with the existing liberal regime; President Chávez's identification of the popular sector as the source of constitutional authority and his emphasis on including this group while excluding the middle and upper classes; and, finally, attempts by both groups to create exclusionary dominant narratives to explain social reality where the other group was identified as the enemy.[2]

The Socio-Political Context of Venezuela's Polarization: 1958–2018

Venezuela's longest experience with democracy began after the coup d'état against the military dictator Pérez Jiménez in 1958. In its aftermath, political parties, the economic elite, the military, the trade unions, and the church entered into the Pact of Punto Fijo, assuring gradual reform and a model of social peace based on broad distribution of oil revenues (López Maya, Calcaño, and Maingón 1989). The resulting Venezuelan Constitution of 1961 outlined a liberal-representative democracy where the only democratic exercise was voting for the president.[3] According to Rey (1991) and Romero (1997), participation in the election of regional and local authorities or other forms of participation were excluded from the political process for the sake of the fledgling democracy's political stability. By the end of the 1980s, with oil revenues falling and the national debt rising, this political agreement could not ensure "consensus and stability," and the political alliances were broken. Moreover, in 1989, the acute oil-related economic crisis led the government of Carlos Andrés Perez to apply neoliberal macroeconomic adjustment policies that caused widespread riots and political instability, with high costs for the legitimacy of the entire political party system, which the popular sector viewed as broadly collusive.

In December 1998, Lieutenant Colonel Hugo Chávez, a political outsider, was elected as President of Venezuela, representing the final breakdown of the Pact of Punto Fijo, which had lasted for 40 years (1958–1998). He entered politics espousing an anti-neoliberal discourse and adopting an agenda that blamed capitalism and neoliberal economic austerity measures for poverty, social inequality, and even polarization. Like his predecessors, Chávez promised to use oil benefits to end poverty and to include the excluded sectors of society. But he also promised to reform the democratic process to reduce the influence of the corrupt elite, whom he blamed for Venezuela's ills. Once elected, in February 1999, he convoked a constituent process to draft a new constitution, which was approved via referendum in December 1999. The resulting Bolivarian Constitution embodied the concept of democracy as "protagonist and participatory" and included the previously ignored and marginalized urban and rural poor sectors,[4] aiming to transform them from recipients to protagonists in the government's decision-making process.

After Chávez's death in 2013, his successor, the uncharismatic President Nicolas Maduro, tried unsuccessfully to fulfill Chávez's final mandate, known as the "Rudder's Coup" (*Golpe de Timón*; Chávez 2012): to strengthen the Bolivarian revolution by establishing the Communal State—the government's model of direct democracy. The new order was to comprise communal councils promoted by President Chávez that, in aggregate, would form communes. In turn, communes would form federations, confederations, and communal cities. These new forms of citizen organization, as well as social welfare programs, received direct funding from the government. After Chávez died, the decline of oil prices, widespread corruption, high rates of inflation, and the inefficiency and failure of President Maduro's anti-neoliberal economic policies resulted in a decline in social welfare programs and hindered the implementation of the Communal State.[5] Poverty increased (ENCOVI 2017), and even the popular sectors were excluded from the basic food program (*bolsas CLAPS*) if they did not ideologically align with the regime. Managed by the military and the government's political party, PSUV, these programs accentuated the citizenry's dependence on the government to meet basic needs.

After Maduro's election to the presidency in 2013, the political opposition was divided over whether to pursue insurrectional or electoral strategies to achieve its objective of regime change. The opposition's success in the December 2015 legislative election for the National Assembly, in which they gained a supermajority of representatives, prompted President Maduro to govern by decree. The National Assembly responded by protesting the laws and regulations that resulted from Maduro's decrees. The opposition also collected signatures to hold a recall referendum against President Maduro in 2016, an effort that was eventually blocked by the National Electoral Council (CNE) at the end of that year. Massive new protests broke out in April 2017 after the Supreme Court nullified the National Assembly's authority. In response, the Maduro government cracked down on the civilian protestors, arresting hundreds and using lethal force that resulted in more than 100 deaths.

In a procedure considered unconstitutional by the opposition, Maduro convened a new Constituent Assembly that superseded the authority of all levels and branches of government, including the National Assembly, governors, and local mayors. Its stated purpose was to draft guidelines for a more radical constitution that redirected the revolution toward the Communal State. In practice, the Constituent Assembly, installed on August 4, 2017, assumed de facto power and made all the country's important political decisions, following Maduro's dictates.

The economic crisis also led to what the opposition called "a humanitarian crisis"—resulting from hyperinflation and a severe scarcity of food, medical supplies, electricity, water, transportation, and other basic and social infrastructural services—that affected both the popular sectors and the middle class. Street protests multiplied as the popular sectors demanded access to food, medicine, and basic services.[6] The government responded with further repression and grew increasingly authoritarian (PROVEA 2014b, 2017; OVCS 2014, 2017).

How Polarization Emerged and Disrupted Democracy in Venezuela (1999–2018)

To explain the emergence, consolidation, deepening, fragmentation, and attenuation of polarization, we analyze various cycles of mass mobilizations after the ratification of the 1999 Bolivarian Constitution. Supporters and detractors of the twenty-first-century socialist model each used mass mobilization as the strategy, aiming to demonstrate that they represented the numerical majority, and, therefore, the constitutional sovereign.

The constituent process of 1999: Seeds of polarization[7]

This first cycle of mobilization extended from February 1999, when Chávez assumed the presidency and called for a Constituent Assembly, to December 2001, when the opposition took to the streets to protest the enabling laws decreed by Chávez.[8] The 1999 Bolivarian Constitution that resulted was one of the few points of consensus among Venezuelan citizens of different ideological positions, if not the only one.

Chávez's revolution interpreted "constituent power" to be embodied by the "people"—its sole source of authority. The elected Constituent Assembly not only had the power to write a new constitution but also authority above all "constituted" powers, including the existing legislature and judiciary. Chávez's first constituent process was nonpolarized, inclusive, participatory, and institutional; it included diverse organizations, institutions, and citizens. As a result, the 1999 Bolivarian Constitution reflects political-ideological differences (García-Guadilla and Hurtado 2000). Despite these differences, the constitution defines the government's source of power as the unitary "people" (el pueblo), rather than employing the liberal democratic concept of pluralism, where competing individual interests coincide. This view of the people as a homogenous whole would become the primary source of polarizing political-ideological conflicts (García-Guadilla 2003; García-Guadilla and Mallen 2013).[9]

One of the first polarizing conflicts in fact involved the definition of the *constitutional sovereign*, or source of constitutional authority, and how to best interpret the will of the people. In the 1999 National Constituent Assembly, the *sovereign* was defined as a unitary, indivisible mandate, rather like Rousseau's concept of a singular and unequivocal "general will." In contrast to the 2008 Ecuadorian and 2009 Bolivian constitutions, Venezuela's constituent members defined themselves as representing the will of the people, as opposed to the will of different regions; ethnic groups; or religious, social, economic, and political interests.[10]

As a result, when implementing inclusive public policies, President Chávez associated the sovereign—the source of constitutional authority—with only the previously excluded popular sectors (*el Pueblo*), as he in turn excluded the middle and upper class. By legitimizing participatory democracy as the voice of this sovereign, and as the chosen mechanism to achieve legitimacy, the government increased the potential for confrontation and eventually polarization. Under these new rules of the game, supporters and detractors of the regime tried to appropriate and represent this unique sovereign to legitimize their demands, ignoring the legitimate claims of their opponents. Increasingly, the two self-defined "sovereigns," whom we will call the *Chavistas* and the opposition, took their fight for dominance and representation of the people to the streets in the form of massive mobilizations.

The Bolivarian Constitution included both representative and participative models of democracy but did not specify the mechanisms for their coexistence and implementation. In practice, this ambiguity led to two, mutually exclusive, models of democracy. One was the liberal democratic model of representation, supported by the opposition; the other, supported by *Chavistas*, was the radical or "communal" model based on a participatory-protagonist framework. The model of "liberal" democracy was based on Pact of Punto Fijo. In addition to favoring representation over participation, this model emphasized individual civil and political rights. In contrast, the radical or communal democracy proposed by Chávez privileged direct citizen participation and collective, socioeconomic, and cultural rights. Polarized conflict emerged from the need to resolve disputes concerning constitutional rights since the opposition tended to privilege representative democracy and interpreted participatory democracy as its complement, while *Chavismo* favored participatory democracy and attempted to replace representation with direct participation through institutions based on collective decision-making (García-Guadilla 2003).

The enabling laws (2001–2004) and the coup d'état: The emergence and consolidation of antagonistic polarization

In December 2001, violent protests broke out against the enabling laws; they lasted until 2004, when the opposition lost the recall referendum to remove President Chávez from power. This period can be characterized as polarized, exclusionary, nonparticipatory, and subversive.

After the Bolivarian Constitution of 1999 was approved via referendum, the National Assembly attempted to develop, alongside the citizenry, the judicial body to institutionalize it. Due to the difficulties and delays in drafting the laws through participatory mechanisms and differences in the interpretation of representative and participatory democracy, President Chávez decreed the forty-nine so-called enabling laws (*Leyes Habilitantes*), which included the Land and Agrarian Development Law and the Law of Hydrocarbons.

The opposition claimed that the enabling laws embodied an interpretation of democracy different from the one laid out in the constitution, and that the laws contradicted liberal democratic values; the laws were perceived by the opposition as benefiting the poor sectors exclusively and disadvantaging traditional class interests and privileges. The opposition mobilized against the laws using both constitutional and insurrectional mechanisms to demonstrate their discontent and prove their numerical superiority through mobilizations and protests.[11]

Chávez's supporters also mobilized in favor of the laws, because they thought that they would benefit from them. As a result, two polarized groups of citizens were formed (the opposition and Chávez's supporters) that, since December 2001, have continuously competed both constitutionally and extraconstitutionally to defend their values, interests, identities, and contrasting sociopolitical projects.[12] Initially, both groups conducted peaceful marches and organized parallel street protests with their own slogans, banners, and songs. But they began to clash violently when each group tried to take over symbolic public spaces that the other group considered to be its own territory.

From 2001 to 2003, the opposition used subversive strategies, beginning with the *guarimbas* (street protests including barricades and burning tires to impede pedestrian and vehicular passage). In April 2002, they perpetrated a failed coup d'état and a failed general strike that lasted from December 2002 to February 2003, both aiming to remove Chávez from power.

As the polarizing conflicts gained visibility through the media, they extended into the societal sphere and encouraged the rise of territorial and spatial divisions that would eventually reconfigure the capital city of Caracas into polarized public spaces and ghettos (García-Guadilla 2003; García-Guadilla and Mallen 2013). This process transformed previously existing class differences into outright class conflicts, giving way to antagonistic differences or what McCoy, Rahman, and Somer (2018) define as "pernicious polarization." These differences also materialized into two opposing social images associated with ideological position, social class, and place of residence, which manifested as polarized and antagonistic narratives about the "other" as the "enemy."

The recall referendum, the student movement for "freedom" and the constitutional reform (2004–2012): New subjects and spaces for depolarization?

This period can be described as ideologically polarized but participatory and institutional. It began when the opposition again took the constitutional path and voiced its discontent and grievances against the government through existing mechanisms of representative and participatory democracy: the recall referendum against President Chávez in 2004, and the elections for president in 2006 and 2012, governors in 2008 and 2012, local mayors in 2008 and 2013, and the legislature in 2005 and 2010. The period ended with President Chávez's call to radicalize the revolution toward the communal state, and with his death in 2013.

After losing the recall referendum against Chávez in 2004, the opposition began to focus on confronting the government through marches and other constitutional forms of protest. One of the most representative conflicts was the protest against the May 2007 "closure" (according to the opposition) or the "nonrenewal" (according to the government) of the broadcast license held by the media outlet RCTV, one of the oldest and most important television stations identified with the opposition.[13] The government's decision to revoke RCTV's license motivated high school and university students to mobilize in protest, for the first time in almost two decades, against the alleged violation of freedom of speech. The government, for its part, mobilized Bolivarian students belonging to newly created public universities. In this context, the Students for Freedom movement proposed a "depolarized" dialogue with the Bolivarian students. The olive branch ultimately failed because the students could not engage in dialogue without making reference to the polarized representations about the "other" (García-Guadilla and Mallen 2010).

Also in 2007, the opposition conducted peaceful marches and other forms of protest against Chavez's proposal to reform the constitution. The proposed reform favored replacing representative democracy with participatory or direct democracy at the local and regional levels, and implicitly attempted to radicalize the revolution by institutionalizing new forms of geopolitical and socioeconomic organization known as the communal state. While the government and Chávez himself campaigned for the constitutional reform, university students who were opposed to such a reform, and who were already organized from their previous resistance over RCTV, banded with opposition parties. The "No" campaign succeeded, and the constitutional reform was rejected in a referendum.

Unlike the prior period of hyperpolarization, mobilizations against the closure of RCTV and against the constitutional reform of 2007 were conciliatory in their approach and did not question the legitimacy of the government. Moreover, in the case of the constitutional reform, both defenders and challengers generally agreed to use the mechanisms of participatory democracy (i.e., a referendum) to decide whether to approve it.

Despite the voters' rejection of the constitutional reform, the government decided to approve many of its proposals through its majority in the National Assembly, which was controlled by the governing party after the opposition had boycotted the 2005 election. Many of the proposed reforms were incorporated into the so-called popular power laws—the Law of the Communes, the Law of the People's Power, the Law of Public and Popular Planning, the Law of Social Accountability, the Law of the Communal Economic System, and the Law on Communal Councils.[14] These popular power laws focused on giving the popular sectors mechanisms for direct citizen participation. They deepened polarization, since the Socialist Development Economic and Social Plan of the Nation

2013–2019, based on such laws, was intended to radicalize the revolution by emphasizing collective rights and direct democracy over individual rights and representative democracy.

Attenuated polarization, fragmentation of the poles, and increasing authoritarianism (2013–2018)

The current period began with the death of Hugo Chávez and the arrival of Nicolas Maduro to power through special elections in 2013. It can be characterized by the use of institutional and subversive strategies, the attenuation of the social substrata of political polarization, and the fragmentation of both poles. In addition, conflicts between the government and the political opposition were accentuated by an acute economic and political crisis that resulted from falling oil prices, high levels of corruption, increased authoritarianism, and the criminalization of protests, among other factors. In this context of this crisis, the government accentuated the clientelist practices and excluded nonsupporters from receiving benefits.

During this period, the opposition frequently used the mechanisms of participatory democracy to demand regime change, i.e., Maduro's resignation or early departure. They mobilized through both peaceful and violent street protests, particularly in the years between 2014 and 2017.[15] In 2016 they also initiated a recall referendum against Maduro, which was delayed and then blocked by the National Electoral Council in October of that year. While the popular sectors mobilized primarily around basic needs (food, medicine, and basic services such as water, electricity, gas, and transportation), the middle and upper classes protested for political change. As the lack of food and medicine became critical, the middle class at times joined the popular sectors in these protests; as a result, the social substrata of political and ideological polarization attenuated but did not disappear completely.

The opposition was divided about using the mechanisms of representative democracy to achieve their goal of removing Maduro and his party from power. In particular, because of the restrictions on candidates and parties and the inequitable conditions imposed unilaterally by President Maduro, much of the opposition questioned participation in the regional and local elections of 2017 and the presidential elections of 2018. The result was a high rate of electoral abstention and doubts about using representative democracy as a means to resolve conflicts. On the other hand, the economic crisis, high inflation, and the government's growing use of economic policies and social programs to benefit only loyal partisans increased poverty and exclusion for ideological reasons.[16] Moreover, in addition to the exclusion of the opposition, the cooptation of the network of popular-sector social organizations, such as the communal councils, increased as a result of exclusionary partisan practices and military control of new social programs. The economic and political crisis (called a "humanitarian crisis" by the opposition) also contributed to a lessening of societal polarization, as all social groups were affected by the scarcity and high prices of food and medicine, the deterioration of basic services such as potable water and electricity, the lack of domestic gas and public transportation, and high rate of inflation. In this period, the opposition fragmented over disagreements on how to force political change to deal with the Maduro government's increased authoritarianism, corruption, and lack of accountability.[17]

One of the first events of this period, in 2014, involved the failed protests known as *La Salida* (the Exit), which emerged from divisions within the opposition. The *La Salida* protests began in February 2014, promoted mainly by two opposition political parties: *Voluntad Popular*, led by Leopoldo López, and VENTE, led by María Corina Machado; they lasted four months. The protesters, mainly young students, rejected President Maduro's legitimacy and hoped to force him to resign. This "insurrectional" strategy resulted in a high number of deaths, injuries, and arrests due to severe repression by the police and the uncontrolled violent government-allied gangs known as the *Colectivos* (PROVEA 2014; OVCS 2014). *La Salida* also divided the opposition, represented in the Democratic Unity Roundtable (*Mesa de la Unidad Democrática*), over the timing, objectives, and strategies of the protests, such as the use of violent *guarimbas* versus electoral mobilization.

In 2015, for the first time since Chávez came to power, the opposition won a majority in the National Assembly, legitimizing the use of the mechanisms of representative democracy. This victory brought temporary relief in the confrontation between the representative and participatory concepts of democracy—one of the underlying cleavages of polarization. President Maduro's response to the opposition's majority in the National Assembly was to convene the Communal Assembly (*Parlamento Comunal*), a parallel popular entity not mentioned in the Constitution but included in the popular power laws. Its main purpose was to replace the National Assembly and counteract its representative power with "protagonist participatory democracy."[18] The Communal Assembly was unable to settle the differences among its members, however, and soon fell apart. Consequently, President Maduro asked the Supreme Court for extraordinary powers to govern by decree, sidelining the National Assembly.

Their supermajority in the National Assembly was interpreted by the opposition as a mandate to incarnate the will of the sovereign. As part of its political strategy, the opposition activated the mechanisms of participatory democracy by calling for a recall referendum against President Maduro in 2016. Nonetheless, this referendum was suspended by the government. Given the National Assembly's belligerence, Maduro pressured the Supreme Court to neutralize it and to postpone the 2016 December election for governors for fear of an opposition win. In late March 2017, the Supreme Court went further, holding the National Assembly in contempt and eviscerating its legislative capacity. This act generated massive, daily protests from April through July 2017, which were harshly repressed and territorially polarizing.[19] Most of these protests were confined to the municipalities where the opposition held a majority. When protests attempted to cross the politically defined borders into "prohibited" areas of the cities, severe repression by police occurred and more than 100 people were killed.

In the middle of these conflicts, President Maduro ordered a new Constituent Assembly election to be held on July 30, 2017, and the opposition called a hasty and successful public consultation (*Consulta Popular*) against it on July 16, 2017. The opposition considered the convoking of a Constituent Assembly as unconstitutional and illegitimate, and boycotted the vote. The election process also garnered widespread international criticism. Despite these objections, the government installed the Constituent Assembly, which served as a parallel institution to the National Assembly and asserted its authority over the Assembly, similar to the supreme authority granted the 1999 Constituent Assembly. Conflicts once again evolved between representative and participative institutions, as most of the functions that constitutionally corresponded to the National Assembly were transferred to the Constituent Assembly, dominated by Maduro's allies.

Beginning in 2015, the United States led an international movement to impose sanctions on individual government officials for their alleged human rights abuses and corruption, followed by financial sanctions that restricted the government's ability to refinance its debt after August 2017 (Ramsey 2018). Given the high degree of polarization and political conflict amid a social and economic crisis, in 2016 and 2017 the international community also intervened to facilitate a dialogue between the government and opposition.

After several failed attempts at dialogue, a new round of mediation began in December 2017, hosted by the government of the Dominican Republic and assisted by five "friendly" countries chosen by both sides in the conflict. One of the main points of discussion was electoral conditions for the constitutionally mandated presidential election in 2018. As the talks began to falter, in January 2018 President Maduro rejected the opposition's conditions and unilaterally ordered early presidential elections to be held on May 20, 2018.[20] The opposition fractured once again. Most political parties that were part of the Mesa de la Unidad Democrática decided not to participate, but a group of smaller parties backed an opposition candidate, Henri Falcón. The result was a high rate of abstention, a questionable victory for Maduro in a compromised electoral process, and the narrowing of representative and participatory spaces to resolve conflicts.

The consequences of the highly contentious polarization for the democratic regime were profound. The progressive elimination of spaces for peaceful protest and electoral contestation of power, along with the severe erosion of the separation of powers and the failure to protect universal rights, led many analysts to identify the Venezuelan regime as authoritarian by 2017 (Mancini 2014; Magdaleno 2018). The fear of retribution if they were to lose power presumably led the Maduro government to seek to retain power at all costs. On the other side, the lack of access to democratic mechanisms led some in the opposition to call for nondemocratic actions to remove the regime, following the pattern of democratic erosion in polarized contexts described by McCoy, Rahman, and Somer (2018).

The Nature of Venezuela's Pernicious Polarization and Its Consequences for Democracy

Based on Somer and McCoy (2018)'s three possible relationships between democracy and polarization, the Venezuelan experience indicates that the relationship between democracy and polarization, as well as the definition of polarization as *pernicious* or *benign*, depends on the following interdependent and contributing factors.

First, a divided and incompatible interpretation of democracy became the explicit boundary line between the two camps in Venezuela, activating ideological and political polarization. The constitutional inclusion of two models of democracy, representative and participatory, and their interpretation as mutually exclusive or incompatible when it came to resolving disputes, led to polarization. The old elite and the middle and upper classes largely interpreted democracy as liberal-representative, while followers of President Chávez, who belonged mainly to the popular sectors, interpreted it as participatory or as a way to achieve inclusion and socioeconomic rights. As a result, disputes involving rights derived from one or the other model of democracy emerged as polarized conflicts. On the other hand, according to the Bolivarian Constitution, the model of participatory democracy presumed a major change in constitutional authority (from the individual to the collective *Pueblo*) and stressed competing rights (the defense of liberal rights versus socioeconomic and cultural rights). This facilitated the emergence of two types of subjects who polarized around the defense of competing rights.

A singular, nonpluralistic definition of the source of constitutional authority (the "sovereign") tends to encourage polarization because it does not incorporate a multiplicity of interests, identities, and values. The constitutional definition of a unique and unified sovereign in the Bolivarian Constitution and its empirical identification with the popular sectors, at the expense of the middle and upper-classes, led to polarized conflicts between the two ideologically opposed groups that sought to represent the sovereign.

Second, a necessary but not sufficient condition to trigger open polarization was the prior existence of an underlying cleavage—in this case, high levels of poverty and socioeconomic inequality that revealed previously concealed social class polarization. Despite the absence of an open class struggle, Hugo Chávez's discourse and the institutionalization of participatory democracy made explicit, and may have exacerbated, the existing social-class cleavage underlying the hidden polarization, as García Guadilla (2007, 2003) and Ellner (2003) have demonstrated.

The consequences of political-ideological polarization over the concept of democracy had logical consequences for the practice of democracy itself. In participatory democracy, the public space is privileged by political contenders to legitimate their competing sociopolitical projects and agendas. In practice, the social mobilization in public spaces of detractors and supporters of the *Chavista* project, who competed to be recognized as "the constitutional sovereign," led to violent physical confrontations and fostered the creation of exclusionary spaces, narratives, and images about the "other." Further, Stavrakakis (2018) stresses that populism can threaten democracy and set off pernicious polarization depending on whether it is inclusionary or exclusionary. One of the characteristics of Venezuela's populism as it has developed in its second decade is its nominal inclusionary narrative of sharing economic and political resources with previously excluded sectors, coexisting with its actual exclusionary character (García-Guadilla 2018) that nourishes pernicious polarization. Particularly under President Maduro, most public policies are directed to include only those popular sectors allied ideologically with the government. Those not allied are excluded due to the scarcity of resources to feed populism. The middle and upper classes, who are associated with the opposition, are also excluded and considered not as a political adversary, but as the enemy to be eradicated through authoritarian decrees.

In Venezuela, the institutionalization of participatory democracy activated a form of polarization that went beyond the political realm and extended into everyday social interaction. In the presence of previous high levels of poverty and social inequity and exclusion, and of two ideologically antagonistic competing sociopolitical projects, participatory democracy could not produce a more democratic regime. Moreover, Venezuela's conflict assumed the shape of an existential struggle, whose success was perceived by the citizenry as vital for the survival of their definition of democracy, their worldview, and their way of life.

In the short run, mild forms of political-ideological polarization may deepen democracy, as McCoy, Rahman, and Somer (2018) argue. But the Venezuelan case demonstrates that under high levels of poverty and social inequality, and with two antagonistic sociopolitical projects, more benign forms of polarization are not likely; instead, a severe or pernicious form of polarization that disrupts democracy will emerge.

Consequently, some of the requisites to avoid the emergence of pernicious polarization are: to reduce poverty and social inequality, maintain a certain degree of ideological compatibility between the two opposing sociopolitical projects and their expression in a clear constitutional framework that reflects plurality, and design participatory public policies in which all citizens, regardless of their differences, feel included.

Notes

1. The term "antagonistic" polarization, based in Schmitt's (1996) clear notion of antagonism, implies that one ideological pole excludes "the other" whose adherents are considered the enemy, not merely an adversary. The term can be equated with "pernicious polarization" proposed by McCoy and Rahman (2016).

2. Mallen and García-Guadilla (2017) have pointed out that the reasons frequently mentioned by scholars to explain polarization in Venezuela such as the high levels of poverty and social inequities, class cleavages (García-Guadilla 2003, 2007; Ellner 2003), or President Chavez's confrontational and divisive discourse (Madriz 2000, Molero de Cabeza 2002, Bolívar 2008) are important contributing factors; nonetheless, they "cannot fully account for a polarization so severe that the discourse and actions of individual citizens, and of organized communities, are reduced to their perceived political affiliation" (p. 3).

3. Under much of the previous *Punto Fijo* regime, citizens did not vote for governors or mayors as these were selected by the winning party. In addition, participation in decisions-making, even at the local level, was very limited.

4. As in the previous *Punto Fijo* regime, Chávez's concept of "twenty-first-century socialism" relied on Venezuela's oil sector to sustain the social programs or *Misiones* aimed to achieve socioeconomic inclusion and to finance the network of social organizations designed for participatory democracy.

5. Poverty levels and social inequality rates oscillated beyond 50 percent in Venezuela when Chávez won the presidency. Poverty decreased to 23.6 percent from 2004 to 2012. With the fall of oil prices, poverty levels increased again after 2012 and by February 2018, reached as high as 61 percent, according to the Survey of Living Conditions (ENCOVI 2017) that was carried out by various Venezuelan universities.

6. While we focus our analysis on the mobilizations of the opposition against the government, it should be noted that throughout the period analyzed, there were also mobilizations and marches in favor of the government. In these cases, the government granted permission to march to its followers and banned the opposition from occupying symbolic places, often resulting in territorial polarization and violent confrontations between the two groups.

7. This section builds and borrows from García-Guadilla (2003) and García-Guadilla and Mallen (2012, 2013) and Mallen and García-Guadilla (2017).

8. The Venezuelan constitutions of 1961 and 1999 allowed the legislature to delegate legislative powers to the president under certain conditions. Chávez took advantage of the more lax conditions in the 1999 constitution to encourage such delegation, and used that authority at various points to legislate by decree with "enabling laws."

9. Similarly, in Egypt during the Arab Spring, the lack of shared common visions and principles around the definition of sovereign authority in the proposed new constitutions could partially explain the failure of the transition from an authoritarian to a democratic government.

10. The constitutions of Ecuador of 2008 (Muñoz 2008) and Bolivia of 2009 (Mendoza 2013), two countries with deep indigenous roots that identified with the twenty-first-century socialism movement, recognized the State as a multi- or plural-nation. Plural nationality implies State recognition and inclusion as equals of different ethnic, cultural groups, or "nations", and their self-determination. In contrast, the Venezuelan Constitution of 1999 stated that the indigenous population constitutes a *Pueblo* (a people) and not a Nation. Consequently, although the customs and culture of the indigenous *Pueblos* should be respected, they must adhere to the notion of "majority" implied in the term "the sovereign" to resolve conflicts with the State.

11. Even though the education law was not part of the enabling laws, the first citizen mobilizations in 2001 protested a government draft of the law of education. Teachers and parents objected that the law had not been drafted through participatory means (Mallen 2003; López Maya 2005).

12. Through numerous marches and street protests, the opposition defended individual rights such as freedom of expression or private property, while the government and its supporters argued the need to limit such rights, proposing the possibility of expropriating private property based on the notion of public utility and to give priority to collective socioeconomic and cultural rights (García-Guadilla and Mallen 2013).

13. The private media, identified with the political opposition, supported the massive mobilizations during the 2002–2007 period and behaved as a political party. For its part, the government also displayed partisan behavior through an initially small public media. Due to the important role that media have in disseminating information, the government gradually increased control over critical media. It seized direct control of media licenses, financed the establishment of government-friendly media outlets, or intimidated media outlets and journalists friendly to the opposition to self-censor (Mallen and García-Guadilla 2017).

14. Despite the claims of the opposition that these laws were unconstitutional, they were approved by the majority the government held in the Congress.

15. See the reports of the Venezuelan Observatory of Social Conflicts, https://www.observatoriodeconflictos.org.ve/sin-categoria/conflictividad-social-en-venezuela-en-el-primer-trimestre-de-2018. See also, *Informe Anual* (PROVEA 2014, 2017).

16. Access to social programs such as the so-called *Bolsas de Alimentación* (Bags of Food) distributed by CLAPS (*Comités Locales de Abastecimiento y Producción*), required political registration through a new identity card system—the *Carnet de la Patria*—managed by the governing PSUV party.

17. The government appeared united, but in fact, internal critics were simply expelled or jailed on alleged corruption charges. These internal criticisms accused Maduro and his team of corruption and failure to follow the legacy of Chávez.

18. Although based on the communal law, the Communal Assembly did not have constitutional support since the constitutional reform referendum that included it, was defeated in 2007.

19. See, PROVEA (2017) and OVCS (2017).

20. The conditions were the postponement of the early electoral timetable, the release of the political leaders from prison, the removal of the disqualification attached to the main leaders and political parties, and the acceptance of humanitarian aid to alleviate shortages of food, medicine, and other basic goods.

References

Agh, Attila. 2012. The socioeconomic crisis and social polarization in Hungary: The paradoxes of the European integration process. In *Politische Kultur in (Südost-)Europa*, ed. Sonja Schuler, 59–85. Munich: Verlag Otto Sagner.

Anderson, Benedict. 1983. *Imagined communities*. London: Verso.

Bolívar, Adriana. 2008. "Cachorro del imperio" versus "cachorro de Fidel": los insultos en la política latinoamericana. *Discurso y Sociedad* 2:1–38.

Chakravarty, Satya R. 2009. *Inequality, polarization and poverty*. In *Economic studies in inequality, social exclusion and well-being*, ed. Jacques Sibler. New York, NY: Springer.

Ellner, Steve. 2003. Introduction: The Search for Explanations. In *Venezuelan politics in the Chávez era: Class, polarization, and conflict*, eds. Steve Ellner and Daniel Hellinger, 7–25. Boulder, CO: Lynne Rienner.

Encuesta sobre Condiciones de Vida (ENCOVI). 2017. Available from: https://www.ucab.edu.ve/wp-content/uploads/sites/2/2018/02/ENCOVI-2017-presentaci%C3%B3n-para-difundir-.pdf.

Fraser, Nancy. 1992. Rethinking the public sphere: A contribution to the critique of actually existing democracy. In *Habermas and the public sphere*, ed. Craig Calhoun, 109–42. Cambridge, MA: MIT Press.

García-Guadilla, María Pilar. 2018. The incorporation of the popular sector and social movements in Venezuelan twenty-first-century socialism. In *Reshaping the political arena in Latin America: From resisting neoliberalism to the second incorporation*, eds. Eduardo Silva and Federico Rossi, 60–77. Pittsburgh, PA: University of Pittsburgh Press.

García-Guadilla, María Pilar. 2007. Social movements in a polarized setting: Myths of Venezuelan civil society. In *Venezuela: Hugo Chávez and the decline of an exceptional democracy*, eds. Steve Ellner and Miguel Thinker-Salas, 140–54. Lanham, MD: Rowan & Littlefield Publishers.

García-Guadilla, María Pilar. 2003. Civil society: Institutionalization, fragmentation, autonomy. In *Venezuelan politics in the Chavez Era: Class, polarization and conflict*, eds. Steve Ellner and Daniel Hellinger, 179–96. Boulder, CO: Lynne Rienner

García-Guadilla, María Pilar, and Ana Mallen. 2013 A rude awakening: The underside of Venezuela's civil society in the time of Hugo Chávez. *Politeja* 24:141–62.

García-Guadilla, María Pilar, and Ana Mallen. 2012. El momento fundacional de la Venezuela Bolivariana; el problema de la legitimidad de la Asamblea Nacional Constituyente Venezolana de 1999. *POLITEIA* 49 (35): 65–98.

García-Guadilla, María Pilar, and Ana Mallen. 2010. El movimiento estudiantil venezolano: Narrativas, polarización social y públicos antagónicos. *Cuadernos del CENDES* 27 (73): 71–95

García-Guadilla, María Pilar, and Mónica Hurtado. 2000. Participation and constitution making in Colombia and Venezuela: Enlarging the scope of democracy. Paper presented at the XXII International Congress of the Latin American Studies Association. Available from http://lasa.international.pitt.edu/Lasa2000/Garcia-Guadilla-Hurtado.PDF.

Golpe de Timón (Chávez 2012): Documento: palabras del Presidente Hugo Chávez. Colección Claves. Correo del Orinoco. Available from https://prensapcv.wordpress.com/2015/10/06/documento-golpe-de-timon-palabras-del-presidente-hugo-chavez.

Habermas, Jurgen. 2000. *The structural transformation of the public sphere*. Cambridge, MA: MIT Press.

Horkheimer, Max, and Theodor W. Adorno. 2002. *The culture industry: Enlightenment as mass deception*, in *dialectic of enlightenment*. Stanford, CA: Stanford University Press.

Knox, Paul, and Steven Pinch. 2010. *Urban social geography*, 6th ed. New York, NY: Prentice Hall.

López Maya, Margarita. 2005. *Del Viernes Negro al Referendo Revocatorio*. Caracas: Alfadil.

López Maya, Margarita, Luis Gómez Calcaño, and Thaís Maingón. 1989. *De Punto Fijo al Pacto Social: Desarrollo y Hegemonía en Venezuela (1958–1985)*. Caracas: Fondo Editorial Acta Científica Venezolana.

Lozada, Mireya. 2002. Violencia política y polarización social: desafíos y alternativas [A dialogue for social inclusion and analysis for democracy]. Conference paper presented at the Center for Latin American Studies Rómulo Gallegos, Caracas.

Madriz, María Fernanda. 2002. La noción de pueblo en el discurso populista en. In *Revista Latinoamericana de Estudios del Discurso* 2 (1). Asociación Latinoamericana de Estudios del Discurso (ALED). Caracas: Universidad Central de Venezuela.

Magdaleno, John 2018. Escenarios en la encrucijada venezolana. *Nueva Sociedad* 274:152–64.

Mallen, Ana. 2003. El Caso de la Asamblea Nacional de Educación. Paper presented at the annual conference of the Latin American Studies Association, Dallas, Texas. March 27–29.

Mallen, Ana, and María Pilar García-Guadilla. 2017. *Venezuela's polarized politics: The paradox of direct democracy under Chávez.* Boulder, CO: Lynne Rienner Publishers.

Mancini, Yanina. 2014. Cómo conviven las tendencias autoritarias y democráticas en Venezuela y Bolivia? Carta Informativa de la Junta de Estudios Históricos de La Matanza. Argentina: Universidad de La Matanza.

McCoy, Jennifer, and Tahmina Rahman. 2016. Polarized democracies in comparative perspectives: Towards a conceptual framework. Paper presented at International Political Science Association Conference, Poznan, Poland, July 26.

McCoy, Jennifer, Tahmina Rahman, and Murat Somer. 2018. Polarization and the global crisis of democracy: Common patterns, dynamics, and pernicious consequences for democratic polities. *American Behavioral Scientist* 62 (1): 16–42.

Mendoza, Julieta. 2013. El Estado Plurinacional de Bolivia. *Concepts* no 1: 58–68. Available from http://espaciostransnacionales.org/wp-content/uploads/2014/10/6-Estado-plurinacional1.pdf.

Molero de Cabeza, Lourdes. 2002. El personalismo en el Discurso Político Venezolano. Un Enfoque Semántico y Pragmático, *Convergencia* 9 (29). Toluca: Universidad Autónoma del Estado de México.

Moulaert, Frank, Arantxa Rodriguez, and Eric Swingedouw. 2003. *The globalized city: Economic restructuring and social polarization in European cities.* Oxford: Oxford University Press.

Muñoz, Francisco. 2008. La Plurinacionalidad en la nueva Constitución, ILDIS-La Tendencia, Quito.

Naím, Moisés, and Ramón Piñango 1984. *El caso Venezuela: una ilusión de armonía.* Caracas: IESA.

OVCS. 2014. Conflictividad social de Venezuela en el primer semestre de 2014. Available from https://www.observatoriodeconflictos.org.ve/tendencias-de-la-conflictividad/conflictividad-social-en-venezuela-en-2017.

OVCS. 2017. Conflictividad social de Venezuela 2017. Available from https://www.observatoriodeconflictos.org.ve/tendencias-de-la-conflictividad/conflictividad-social-en-venezuela-en-2017.

PROVEA. 2014. *Informe Anual 2014* (Informe Anual sobre Derechos Humanos en Venezuela) Caracas. Available from https://www.derechos.org.ve/informe-anual/informe-anual-enero-diciembre-2014.

PROVEA. 2014. Boletín Internacional sobre Derechos Humanos. Edición No 19". Febrero 2014.

PROVEA. 2017. *Informe Anual 2017.* (Informe Anual sobre Derechos Humanos en Venezuela) Caracas. Available from https://www.derechos.org.ve/informe-anual/informe-anual-enero-diciembre-2017.

Ramsey, Geoff. 2018. Assessing the use of targeted sanctions on venezuelan officials and elites. Washington, DC: Washington Office on Latin America. Available from https://venezuelablog.org/assessing-use-targeted-sanctions-venezuelan-officials-elites (accessed June 22, 2018).

Rey, Juan Carlos. 1991. La democracia venezolana y la crisis del sistema populista de conciliación. *Revista de Estudios Políticos*, 553–78.

Romero, Anibal. 1997. Rearranging the deck chairs on the Titanic: The agony of democracy in Venezuela. *Latin American Research Review* 32 (1): 7–36.

Somer, Murat, and Jennifer McCoy. 2018. Dejá vu? Polarization and endangered democracies in the 21st century. *American Behavioral Scientist* 62 (1): 3–15

Stavrakakis, Yannis. 2018. Paradoxes of polarization: Democracy's inherent division and the (anti-) populist challenge. *American Behavioral Scientist* 62 (1): 43–58

Schmitt, Carl. 1996. *The Concept of the political.* Chicago, IL: University of Chicago Press.

Warner, Michael. 2005. *Publics and Counterpublics.* New York, NY: Zone Books.

The Political Nature of Ideological Polarization: The Case of Hungary

By
FEDERICO VEGETTI

Polarization in Hungary is one of the most severe cases in Europe. It is predominantly elite-driven, and determined mostly by the antagonistic confrontation between the parties. Left and Right blocs oppose each other in a struggle where the loser is completely denied any influence on policymaking. The two blocs endorse opposing views on socio-cultural policies, but this division emerged as a consequence of the rhetoric and coalitional choices of parties, more than from the societal divisions that they ostensibly represent. Moreover, while the perceived ideological distance between party blocs is wide, the actual programmatic differences in the parties' economic and social policy stances are modest. This article draws on a broad range of sources to describe the process of polarization in Hungary after the fall of communism. I discuss how a polarizing style of political competition can lead to a politically divided society and, over the long run, to democratic erosion.

Keywords: Hungary; political polarization; Left–Right; ideology; illiberal democracy

Hungary transitioned to democracy in 1989, and by 1998 the cleavages that cut through the nascent multiparty political system had become perfectly bipolar, with all major parties belonging to either the "Left" or the "Right." But the classic economic ideological measures, such as the role of the market versus government regulation in the economy, do not define the Left–Right scale in Hungary. Instead, Hungarian parties are polarized on cultural and symbolic issues, such as religion, nationalism–cosmopolitanism and, more recently, immigration, and they define Left–Right in those terms. The two party blocs emerged due to a

Federico Vegetti is a postdoctoral researcher at the University of Milan (Italy). From 2013 to 2018 he was a research fellow at the Central European University in Budapest, where he learned about polarization in Hungary first hand.

Correspondence: vegetti.fede@gmail.com

DOI: 10.1177/0002716218813895

ANNALS, *AAPSS*, 681, January 2019

consistent pattern of coalition formation among parties, which never bridged the Left–Right divide. Moreover, the perceived ideological distance between blocs is inflated by antagonistic and delegitimizing actions and rhetoric that characterize interaction between the opposing camps.

This article describes the contours of party politics in Hungary, focusing on the resurgence of polarization from 2002 to 2010 and its essential stability through 2018. It shows that the high degree of party ideological polarization perceived by Hungarian citizens does not correspond to large programmatic differences between parties. I argue that the perceived *ideological* conflict has *political* origins, and that the winner-take-all logic produced by institutional rules, combined with psychological elements of the us-versus-them discourse employed by the parties, provides perverse incentives for de-democratization.

According to Freedom House, Hungary is the only European Union (EU) member country that shows a significant decline in its aggregate Freedom Score over the past 10 years (see Freedom House 2017a). The V-Dem Liberal Democracy Index for Hungary has been falling since 2010, and it is now the lowest among EU-member countries (see Coppedge et al. 2018). As the ruling party Fidesz further concentrates power, its leader, Viktor Orbán, is moving the country toward an openly illiberal democratic system, weakening checks and balances and press freedoms, and changing rules for electoral advantage—the early stages of what countries like Turkey and Venezuela have gone through.

The Nature of Polarization in Hungary

The extent of political polarization in any given country can be understood through either of two perspectives. The *wide range* view holds that polarization is a matter of differentiation of the policy supply: in this case, the choices offered to citizens are as wide as the policy ground covered by the political parties (Dalton 2008). This view tends to focus on positive implications of polarization, such as increased electoral competitiveness and mobilization. One example of this model is Switzerland, where Lachat (2011) shows that party polarization is associated with greater importance of substantive policy considerations for citizens' vote choice. The *entrenchment* view, on the other hand, argues that polarization implies concentration of the policy supply around two poles, with little room for a middle ground (McCarty et al. 2006; McCoy, Rahman, and Somer 2018). Scholars taking this perspective have found that voters in polarized polities are more partisan, less likely to switch between parties over time, and more biased in their political evaluations and opinions (Druckman, Peterson, and Slothuus 2013; Smidt 2017; Vegetti 2014). While the wide range view looks at the global divergence between actors and preferences, the entrenchment perspective emphasizes local convergence: namely the alignment of actors and preferences along a single conflict dimension. When polarization follows this pattern, between-group alienation and within-group concentration are likely to reinforce each other and lead to conflict (DiMaggio, Evans, and Bryson 1996). Hungarian politics is a textbook example of entrenched polarization.

FIGURE 1
Perceived Left–Right Party Polarization in European Countries, 2004–2014

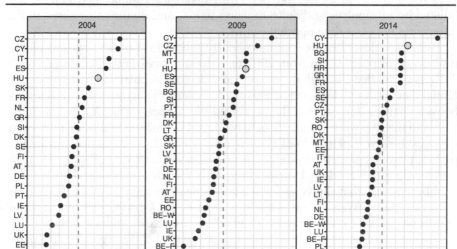

SOURCE: European Elections Studies (Egmond et al. 2009; Schmitt et al. 2009, 2016).
NOTE: Dashed lines are the year means.

The structure of political divisions in Hungary is summarized by a single, dominant Left–Right divide (Körösényi 1999; Palonen 2009; Todosijević 2004). Looking at that indicator with the available data, it is evident that (1) Hungary is one of the most polarized polities in Europe, and (2) the ideological polarization of Hungarian parties has been growing since the late 1990s. Figure 1 shows how polarized Hungarian citizens perceived their own party system to be, compared with other European citizens, in 2004, 2009, and 2014.[1]

Since it joined the EU, Hungary has climbed the ladder from the fifth to the second most polarized political system in the union, behind only Cyprus; although the absolute value and distance from the average in each year have not changed over time. Figure 2 offers a wider time perspective, including three observations made around national elections in 1998, 2002, and 2006.[2] As the figure shows, there is a substantial difference between national and European parliamentary elections with respect to party polarization. In national elections, party polarization has grown about 0.28 points between 1998 and 2006, more than a quarter of the entire scale. In European elections, polarization is lower on average and remains fairly stable over time.

The observed difference between national and European elections comes mostly from different distributions of votes. Between 1990 and 2010, Hungarian parliamentary elections were contested with a two-round dual-ballot system, where 176 members of the national assembly were elected through district ballots, 152 members were seated from party lists in 20 territorial units through

FIGURE 2
Perceived Left–Right Party Polarization in Hungary in National
and European Elections, 1998–2014

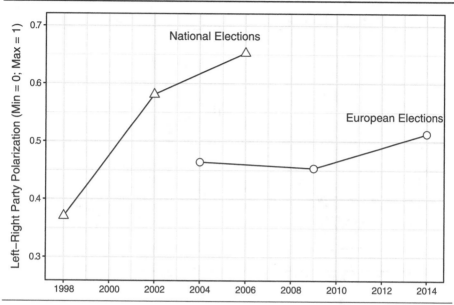

SOURCE: CSES (2015a, 2015b); Comparative National Elections Project (CNEP), https://u
.osu.edu/cnep.

proportional rule, and 58 seats were allocated from national compensation lists
(see Benoit 1996).[3] While European elections are held under a pure proportional
rule, the majoritarian component of the Hungarian electoral system is likely to
have affected both party competition, by providing incentives for smaller parties
to merge or form alliances with larger parties (Tóka 1995), and voting behavior,
by causing voters to concentrate in larger parties (Blais and Carty 1991). In fact,
scholars tend to agree that the mechanics of the electoral system, and the incentives they provide to party competition, played an important role in reducing the
number of parties and promoting a bipolar structure of competition over the first
decade after democratization (see Enyedi 2006; Tóka and Popa 2013). In
Hungary, two party blocs, one on the Left and one on the Right, have dominated
the political arena since the end of the 1990s. However, whereas parties in two-
party systems are commonly expected to converge toward the center (see Downs
1957), the ideological distance between the Left and Right parties is high and
growing.

What is the nature of the observed polarization? According to Fortunato,
Stevenson, and Vonnahme (2016), the Left–Right schema helps citizens to deal
with the complexity of politics by providing information both about parties' policy
positions and about probable patterns of coalition formation. In other words, next
to a substantive policy content, ideological labels contain a relational component

FIGURE 3

Polarization of the Party Platforms on Economic and Socio-Cultural Issues in
Hungary and EU Countries, 2004–2014

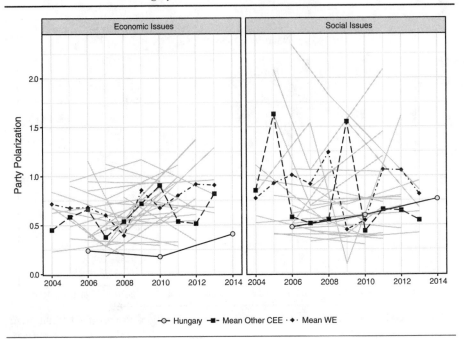

SOURCE: Manifesto Project (Volkens et al. 2015).

that tells citizens about which political groups the different parties belong to (see
also Arian and Shamir 1983).

In Hungary, socio-structural cleavages such as class have had little bearing on
political divisions (Enyedi 2005, 2006; Tóka 1998; Tóka and Popa 2013). Likewise,
the striking perceived party differences on the Left–Right scale are not reflected
in equally large policy differences. This can be seen by looking at party platforms
coded by the Manifesto Project (Volkens et al. 2015). Figure 3 shows the level of
polarization between party programs on economic and socio-cultural issues.[4]

The figure focuses on the same time period and compares the same countries
as Figure 1. However, it tells a different story. First, Hungarian parties are the
least polarized in Europe with respect to economic policies. This is explained by
the highly reformist consensus of the postcommunist parties in Hungary, which
promptly embraced market capitalism right after the transition (Kitschelt et al.
1999; Markowski 1997). Second, Figure 3 shows that on the socio-cultural policy
dimension, which includes law and order, multiculturalism, and national way of
life, Hungarian parties are slightly more polarized than they are on economic
issues. In fact, scholars have repeatedly stressed that the relevant dimension of
substantive political conflict in Hungary is cultural (Enyedi 2006; Körösényi
1999; Markowski 1997; Tóka and Popa 2013). This can also be seen by looking at

FIGURE 4
Party Polarization on Economic, Social, and Cultural Issues as Assessed by
Country Experts in Hungary 2014

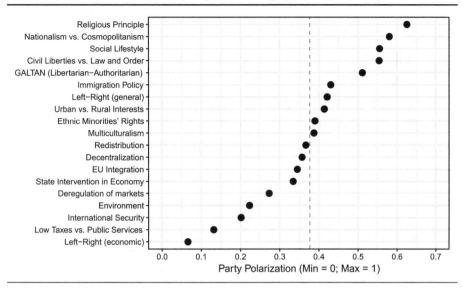

SOURCE: Chapel Hill Expert Survey (Polk et al. 2017).
NOTE: Dashed line is the grand mean.

political experts' ratings of the parties on different policy issues (Polk et al. 2017). Figure 4 shows party polarization in Hungary, as computed in the usual way, on a wide range of policies. It is clear from the figure that experts perceive Hungarian parties to be very much divided on cultural and symbolic matters, most notably on religion and national versus cosmopolitan views, and very little on economic ones.

But if parties' programmatic differences are limited, why is the socio-cultural dimension regarded as so important? This division may be rooted in the clash between *urbánus* (urban) and *népi* (folk) ideologies, which emerged in the period between world wars as a controversy among intellectuals and resurfaced among dissidents in communist times (Nagy 2017). However, two other underlying cleavages are equally represented in the cultural divide among Hungarian parties. One is the *religious-secular* cleavage, the most relevant in Figure 4. The other is the *political class* cleavage, a postcommunist version of the class cleavage dividing workers and members of the *nomenklatura* (Körösényi 1999). These cleavages did not overlap initially. Their activation, overlap, and mapping onto the Left–Right divide followed from a process of simplification of the political system that was determined by party agency.

As mentioned earlier, an important function of Left–Right labels is to help citizens form expectations about which parties are likely to form coalitions together (Fortunato, Stevenson, and Vonnahme 2016). This function, often overlooked by scholars of politics, is made possible by the Left–Right labels' relatively abstract nature. According to Arian and Shamir (1983), these are just "cues" used by parties to discuss political matters. They may be filled with policy content if they are used to define policy alternatives, or with relational content if they are used to define political groups and relations. When parties emphasize or downplay their differences with other parties over the issues, these will be captured by Left–Right distinctions. Likewise, if the interaction between parties is characterized by aggressiveness and unwillingness to cooperate, the perception of Left-Right polarization will be heightened.

Two elements of party behavior in Hungary contributed over time to the definition of Left–Right conflict in cultural terms and to the perception of polarization. One is the *coalitional behavior* of the parties, and the other is the *style of interaction* among them. The following fact illustrates the first element: from 1994 until at least 2018, Hungary has never had a coalition at the national level bridging the Left–Right divide. In other words, in Fortunato, Stevenson, and Vonnahme (2016)'s language, the Left–Right divide predicts perfectly which coalitions are likely to be formed. Second, the two blocs interact with each other in a fairly aggressive way, a style that Enyedi (2016b) calls "populist polarization." In general, populist rhetoric involves (1) a Manichean worldview, where politics is a struggle between good and evil; (2) a view of the people as homogeneous and fundamentally good; and (3) a view of the elites as the cause of all evils (see Mudde 2004). In Hungary, these elements are central to party rhetoric (Enyedi 2016b; Palonen 2009), especially on the Right (Enyedi 2016a). However, this state of affairs did not come about immediately after the democratic transition; it took about a decade to emerge.

The Boiling Frog: Dynamics of Polarization in Hungary

Hungary's transition to democracy from communist rule happened peacefully in October 1989, following one of the less rigid regimes in the region (Herman 2016). The first two elections brought the same six parties to parliament: the Hungarian Socialist Party (MSZP), heir of the Hungarian communist party; the national-conservative Hungarian Democratic Forum (MDF); the Independent Smallholders' Party (FKGP); the Christian-conservative Christian Democratic People's Party (KDNP); the liberal Alliance of Free Democrats (SZDSZ); and the liberal youth party FIDESZ led by Viktor Orbán.

In the first election, in 1990, party competition was structured around three poles: socialists, Christian-nationalists, and liberals (Körösényi 1999). This structure derived from two cross-cutting cleavages among parties. One was the religious-cultural divide, with the socialists on one side, the Christians and nationalists on the other, and the liberals in the middle. The other was the divide over anticommunism, which had the socialists on one side, the liberals with the smallholders on the other, and the Christians and nationalists spread in the middle (Enyedi 2006; Körösényi 1999). Mass electoral preferences did not reflect any strong socio-structural pattern (Tóka 1998). The election was won by the conservative MDF, which chose to form a Christian-nationalist government with FKGP and KDNP. This coalition was neither the only one possible nor the most obvious (Tóka and Popa 2013): MDF could have formed a government with SZDSZ and FIDESZ, to emphasize promarket policies and discontinuity from the communist past; or with MSZP, to emphasize continuity and social responsibility. Instead, by allying with KDNP and FKGP, the party gave the coalition a traditionalist identity, emphasizing the primacy of that religious-cultural cleavage over the others.

The election of 1994 completed the process of simplification of the political conflict space. The Christian-nationalist coalition experienced a dramatic loss of popularity over the previous legislature, leading to a victory of the communist-successor party MSZP. This result split the liberal camp in two. While SZDSZ joined the socialists in government, FIDESZ refused to cooperate with the ex-communists and remained in the opposition. Both parties were arguably motivated by opportunities within the Left and Right camps, as well as by the majoritarian incentives provided by the electoral system. SZDSZ agreed with MSZP on promarket reforms and privatization, and seized the opportunity to influence policymaking from within the Left bloc (Grzymala-Busse 2001). FIDESZ, on the other hand, took the opportunity offered by the Right bloc's weakness and began moving decisively rightward, changing its image from a liberal youth party to a conservative people's party (Enyedi 2005; Körösényi 1999). Consequently, FIDESZ began adopting language and symbols typical of the traditionalist Right, while becoming increasingly pro-state on economics (Enyedi 2006). By 1998, FIDESZ was the Right-bloc frontrunner and managed to win the election, forming a right-wing government together with FKGP and MDF.

Though the socio-cultural dimension had emerged as the most important determinant of the party blocs' ideological identity, the actual party platforms were not very polarized in terms of their socio-cultural positions. As Figure 5 shows, the FIDESZ's policy platform became more socially conservative between 1998 and 2002, but all parties made a similar shift, including MSZP, which in 2002 appeared to be even more conservative than FIDESZ on social issues. Indeed, as Figure 6 shows, between 1990 and 1998 polarization on social issues reflected in party manifestos dropped greatly. It started growing again in 2002, and by 2014 had almost reached the peak of the early 1990s. A similar party system-wide shift occurred on economic policies, although in this case from Right to Left, but economic polarization never reached the heights of the 1990s.

Party manifestos do not necessarily reflect the policies that parties will implement in practice. However, they are supposed to capture the policy content that parties use to campaign, in terms of both constraining the candidates and shaping the branding material supplied to voters (Eder, Jenny, and Müller 2017). In this respect, the official policy positions that Hungarian parties express in the economic and social domains are not severely polarized. However, from the end of the 1990s, parties' *rhetoric* became increasingly combative, starting from the Right camp.

FIGURE 5
Positions of Four Hungarian Parties on Economic and Social Issues, 1990–2014

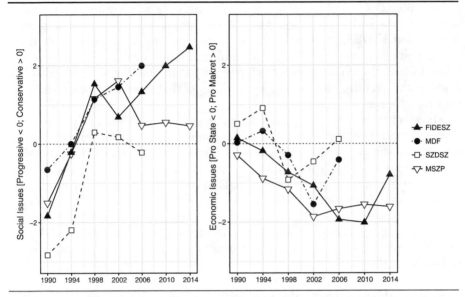

NOTE: From 2006 the positions of FIDESZ refer to the FIDESZ/KNDP coalition.
SOURCE: Volkens et al. (2015).

The Left-liberal coalition won the 2002 election. FIDESZ, under Viktor Orbán's leadership, strongly condemned the result, accusing MSZP of rigging the vote and denying the legitimacy of a "state" that had left the "nation" (i.e., the people) in the opposition (Müller 2011). The party also initiated a network of civil organizations, called "civic circles," that started coordinating both political and nonpolitical activities, such as mass demonstrations, petitions, blood donations, and fundraising campaigns (Enyedi 2005). Finally, its rhetoric became distinctly more populist, attacking political elites, banks, and multinationals, and taking on an even stronger emphasis on national symbols (Palonen 2009).

Political parties commonly try to distinguish themselves from one another with some degree of "us-versus-them" rhetoric. But in a polarized context, discourse tends to focus on the *who* rather than the *what* of politics (Stanley 2008). In this type of discourse, what most essentially defines *us* is that we are *not them* (Palonen 2009; McCoy, Rahman, Somer 2018). In Hungary, this is reflected in the way citizens place parties on the Left–Right dimension. As Figure 7 shows, between 1998 and 2002, Hungarian voters perceived a radical shift of all parties toward the extremes of the Left–Right scale, even though, as Figure 5 shows, MSZP's 2002 program on social issues was even more conservative than FIDESZ's, and the distance of the two parties on economic issues had not grown substantially. However, as the symbolic conflict between the Left and Right blocs grew, the divide between the Left and Right parties became more prominent. This was perceived by the citizens as a rise in ideological polarization.

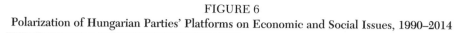

FIGURE 6

Polarization of Hungarian Parties' Platforms on Economic and Social Issues, 1990–2014

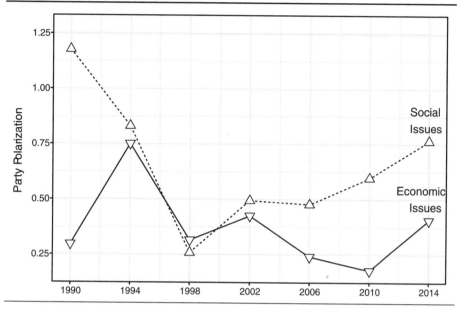

SOURCE: Volkens et al. (2015).

The trajectories of MDF and KDNP in Figure 7 also support this argument. The respondents' perception of a switch between ideological Left and Right of the two parties is more determined by being part of the in-group or out-group with respect to FIDESZ, than by actual policy shifts. MDF had a more socially conservative platform than FIDESZ in all years except 1998. However, Figure 7 shows, starting in 2004, Hungarian citizens began placing the party further and further to the Left until the last observed election in 2009 (the party was dissolved in 2011), when they placed it directly to the Left of center. In fact, in 2002 MDF ran a joint electoral list with FIDESZ, but refused to do so in the following elections. Though MDF never identified itself as a Left-wing party, its interaction with FIDESZ became increasingly adversarial.

KDNP's trajectory was just the opposite. In every election since 2006, the party has run in a joint list with FIDESZ. However, in 2002 the party ran in a list with other centrist parties, called *Centrumpárt*. KDNP was not on the Left in 2002, but the fact that it was out of the Right-wing bloc was enough for respondents to place it there.

The parties' "us-versus-them" logic, combined with symbolic use of Left–Right labels, created an informational environment where perceived party ideological distances are a function of the degree of their membership in the same group. Parties belonging to different blocs are assumed to be very distant to each other ideologically, even when their policy differences are not so great. Moreover, a very stable pattern of coalition formation, without any party ever bridging the

FIGURE 7
Left-Right Positions of Parties in Hungary as Perceived by the Citizens, 1998–2014

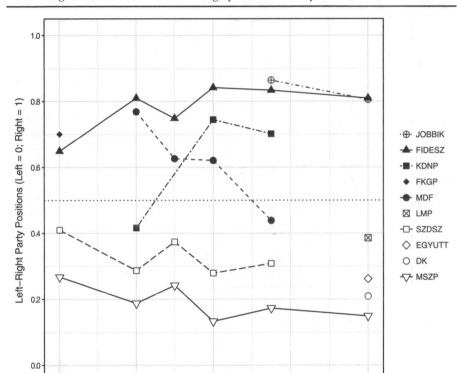

SOURCE: CSES (2015a, 2015b), CNEP, Schmitt et al. (2009, 2016).

Left-Right divide, contributed to the definition of the party system's two-bloc configuration.

A crucial feature of the interaction between blocs that keeps this narrative going is a lack of *institutional consensus*; that is, the failure of one bloc to accept the other as a legitimate political interlocutor (Baylis 2012). This can be partly explained by the all-or-nothing nature of majoritarian parliamentary systems, where broad agreement and compromise are not needed for effective governance. In Hungary, elections had become high-stakes affairs: losing the elections means being excluded not only from office, but from the entire political regime (Enyedi 2016b). Government and opposition disagree by default and systematically refuse to support each other's legislative initiatives (Lengyel and Ilonszki 2010), mostly because governments do not need the opposition to pass legislation.

Such winner-take-all logic implies that parties are generally more anxious about the possibility of electoral defeat, since defeat implies losing any chance to influence decision-making. As a consequence, parties exploit all means to secure their own victory. One example is the diffuse tendency to outbid opponents on fiscal issues during electoral campaigns. This practice has inflated government spending over time, increasing state indebtedness and producing large budget deficits (Lengyel and Ilonszki 2010). Additionally, parties in Hungary persistently question each other's legitimacy, refuse to speak with political rivals, and deny the integrity of the elections they lose. The accusations differ between blocs. As Körösényi (2013) notes, "The Hungarian right has called into question the *national* commitment of the left and the left the *democratic* commitment of the right" (p. 16, emphasis in original). As FIDESZ accuses MSZP governments of serving the international elites against the interests of the Hungarian people, MSZP accuses FIDESZ governments of failing to respect democratic pluralism. This rhetoric fits well with the populism-elitism divide and has little to do with policy differences.

All these elements came together in 2006. After four years of MSZP government, and after a campaign very much focused on fiscal outbidding, voters kept the Left-liberal coalition in power. However, events that occurred in the years following the election undermined the Left bloc's popularity for many years afterward. First, the government introduced harsh austerity measures to tackle large state deficits that had been accumulating since the previous legislature (Sitter and Batory 2006; Tóka and Popa 2013). Second, the press brought to public attention several corruption scandals involving MSZP and SZDSZ officials over the entire term. (Bíró Nagy, and Róna 2012; Müller 2011). Finally, in a country where symbols are central to politics, one particular event had a strong impact on the government's perceived legitimacy. A few months after the election, a recording of a speech given by socialist prime minister, Ferenc Gyurcsány, to his own party members leaked on the national radio. Using strong language, the PM admitted to having "lied in the morning, at noon and at night" about the true state of the Hungarian economy to win the elections.[5] The rationale of Gyurcsány's speech was to persuade his own party's delegates that the government had to deal with state finances and introduce policies to correct past misdoings. But the speech was received as a betrayal of the Hungarian people perpetrated by a government whose priority was to serve private interests (Müller 2011). Over the following weeks, FIDESZ, as well as other extreme Right-wing groups, organized demonstrations and other protest events in Budapest, some of which were harshly suppressed by the police (Harper 2006). Despite repeated demands by the opposition, Gyurcsány refused to resign. But soon, with the global economic crisis, the consequences of economic mismanagement arrived. In 2008 the government accepted a rescue package from the IMF and initiated cuts to social and unemployment benefits. Gyurcsány eventually stepped down in 2009, leaving the lead to a caretaker government under which both austerity measures and corruption scandals continued.

The next election in 2010 yielded a landslide victory for FIDESZ, which obtained 53 percent of the votes. MSZP's support dropped by more than half, and SZDSZ and MDF disappeared from parliament. The election also brought two new parties into the political arena: the green "politics can be different" (LMP) party and the far-Right Jobbik. This reshuffling increased the overall fragmentation of the party system. LMP and Jobbik's unwillingness to enter a coalition with the largest parties in their respective blocs introduced within-bloc competition that disrupted the trend of previous years toward a two-party system. However, it did not undermine the existing cleavage structure, which remained centered on the conservative and liberal camps (Tóka and Popa 2013).

Because Hungary's electoral system gives disproportionate representation to the majority party, FIDESZ's 53 percent of the vote translated into a supermajority of more than two-thirds of the seats in parliament. This granted FIDESZ the power to make a number of important institutional changes, including amending the Hungarian constitution. During its first two years in power, the government made several changes to the system of checks and balances with the aim of enhancing its own power. These included neutralizing the Constitutional Court, appointing FIDESZ members to the Election Commission, electing a new president, and putting the media under government control by appointing loyalists to the newly established Media Authority and Media Council (Bánkuti Halmai, and Scheppele 2012; Herman 2016; Müller 2011). Indeed, following the regulatory changes initiated in 2010, Hungary now falls among the most restrictive in Europe in terms of freedom of press (Freedom House 2017b). Additionally, the government made two critical changes to electoral law. First, it increased the share of parliamentary seats elected in single-member districts, making the system even more disproportional. Second, it changed the boundaries of the electoral districts to FIDESZ's advantage (see Scheppele 2014; Szigetvári, Tordai, and Vető 2011).

In the elections of 2014, the opposition was highly fragmented. On the Right, Jobbik presented itself as an alternative to FIDESZ, offering a more extreme version of the same rhetoric (Bartlett et al. 2012). On the Left, MSZP and other smaller parties (two of which, Együtt and DK, splintered from MSZP after 2010) formed the coalition Unity, hoping to be competitive against FIDESZ in the new single-member districts, while LMP ran independently. FIDESZ still won the election, again obtaining two-thirds of parliamentary seats. Jobbik became the second largest party in the country. The entire Left camp obtained only slightly more than 30 percent of the votes, scattered among four parties. The situation remained much the same in the 2018 election, with FIDESZ increasing its support even further, and the Left-wing opposition becoming weaker and more fragmented than it had been.

Consequences for Democracy: Electorate Immobilism and Illiberal State

Though the party landscape has changed dramatically since the 1990s, electoral politics in Hungary seems to be constantly moving toward a state of affairs in which elections are a mere count of who is willing to turn out to support their own in-group. This process was in place until 2006, took a temporary pause with the demise of the Left camp, and started again afterward. We can see this process by looking at aggregate electoral volatility over time. Figure 8 shows two types of volatility, as proposed by Powell and Tucker (2014).[6]

FIGURE 8
Aggregate Electoral Volatility in Hungary, 1994–2018

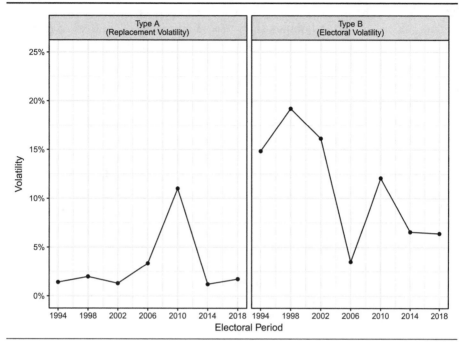

NOTE: Party vote shares in each year are weighted for turnout.

Type A, or *replacement* volatility, is the variability produced by the disappearance of old parties and the appearance of new ones. The peak in 2010 reflects the shakeup of the party system caused by the arrival of Jobbik and LMP. Before and after that, the system looks remarkably stable, with less than 5 percent of votes being moved from old to new parties.[7] Type B volatility is the *change in vote shares* of existing parties, and reflects the variability in aggregate support among stable parties from one election to another. This trend matches the events described in the previous section fairly well. The rise of FIDESZ as the frontrunner of the Right bloc between 1994 and 1998 produced an all-time high in volatility in 1998, with almost 20 percent of aggregate vote share changing among existing parties. The entrenchment of the conflict after 2002's reorganization of FIDESZ's civic base is reflected in an entrenchment of party support in 2006, which changed less than 5 percent on aggregate. The spectacular collapse of the Left after the 2006–2010 legislature, which produced a decrease of almost 25 percent of the vote share for MSZP and a 10 percent rise for FIDESZ, is captured by a peak of volatility in 2010. However, from 2014, with the new system of electoral constraints in place for the opposition, the gerrymandering of districts, and the increased disproportionality of the system, party support seems to be headed toward another period of entrenchment.

Electoral immobilism is matched at the societal level by the penetration of political "bloc identity" in several aspects of social life. As Lengyel and Ilonszki (2010) describe it, "there are magazines for dog-keepers, bird-watchers, fishing anglers and many other hobbies that voice Right-wing or Left-wing political views. It has been found that instead of discussing their monthly rents and other housing issues, tenants and owners of condominiums use political labels to denounce each other in meetings" (p. 165). This resembles what Iyengar and Westwood (2015) observe in the United States, another well-known case of entrenched political polarization, and the process of political polarization extending into social relations as political identity becomes social identity, described by McCoy, Rahmin, and Somer (2018).

This type of severe political and societal polarization has pernicious consequences for democracy. In the Hungarian case, the governing party FIDESZ, with the apparent support of its voters, appears to have moved from viewing competitors as normal electoral adversaries to seeing them as enemies to be eliminated from the political scene—the type of pernicious outcome described by McCoy, Rahman, and Somer (2018). When political differences turn into a Manichean conflict between good and evil, it is common to see the winner excluding the loser from any position of power and using every possible means to prevent it from being a threat in the future. In this situation, it is not unlikely that the loser will start questioning the legitimacy of the institutions that allow the winner to win and stay in power. As a result, citizens may grow increasingly cynical about official politics, which they see as a self-referential power game that has nothing to do with the actual problems of the country.

In July 2014, Viktor Orbán gave a speech in front of an audience of ethnic Hungarians in Băile Tuşnad, Romania, which generated a stir among the international press. In the speech, the prime minister clearly stated his goal to turn Hungary into an "illiberal state," a system that "does not reject the fundamental principles of liberalism such as freedom … but it does not make this ideology the central element of state organization, but instead includes a different, special, national approach."[8] While these words leave a lot of room for interpretation, the actions that the FIDESZ government has been taking have indeed undermined the liberal-democratic features of the Hungarian political regime. The reforms begun by Orbán's FIDESZ government in 2010, and continued after 2014, appear to be engineered to give it a strong electoral advantage over its competitors in a nonlevel playing field, in a way that increasingly resembles "competitive authoritarian" regimes rather than electoral democracies (Levitsky and Way 2010). Hungary has a strong governing party holding two-thirds of parliamentary seats, a media environment hostile to voices that are not progovernment, and a political discourse heavily focused on topics like immigration and national identity, where opposition forces are often accused of pursuing foreign interests. All of this is tied to the specific polarizing rhetoric that Hungarian parties, more notably on the Right, have been using since the turn of the century in 2000. The current disproportionate electoral system produces results that are even more unrepresentative than the previous one, increasing the gap between winners and losers, and thus actually increasing the incentives for the incumbent to stay in power.

The opposition, on the other hand, has failed as of 2018 to coalesce into a strong counter-mobilization capable of challenging FIDESZ's grip on power. In the April 2018 elections, the opposition split and FIDESZ won 49.3 percent of the votes and 133 seats in parliament, giving Orbán his third term as prime minister since 2010, and his fourth overall, with another supermajority of two-thirds of parliament. Moreover, with a 70 percent turnout, the government can claim full electoral legitimacy. These results are due at least in part to FIDESZ's management of the immigration issue, which became visible in Hungary in summer 2015, at the peak of the refugee crisis, when thousands of asylum-seekers entering Hungary from the Balkans flocked together around the Budapest central train station for several days. Since then, Orbán's discourse has increasingly focused on immigration, in a trend that appears to be increasingly common among European Right-wing parties. However, while anti-immigration positions are gaining momentum all over Europe only recently, the success of FIDESZ's nationalist rhetoric has its roots in a process of successful management of political polarization that has lasted for two decades.

Notes

1. Following a conventional approach in the literature (e.g., Dalton 2008), party polarization is calculated by weighting each party's ideological extremity by its relative vote share. The measure is further normalized to range between 0 and 1. See the online appendix for a description of the data and the formula used to compute polarization.

2. As of early 2018, 2006 is the last year where national electoral data are available for Hungary.

3. The compensation mechanism is a complex system aimed at increasing the proportionality of the seat distribution by employing surplus votes for candidates in single member districts that did not win the contest. See Benoit (1996) for a detailed description of the system. In 2012, the electoral law was changed to a one-round mixed system with a prevalence of single-member districts, still proving largely majoritarian. See Nagy (2015).

4. The choice of categories corresponding to economic Left and Right is based on Benoit and Laver (2007). The categories included in the social dimension have been modified to cover issues that are more relevant for the cultural cleavage in Hungary, like multiculturalism, internationalism, and traditional morality. See the online appendix for the list of categories that have been used. Party positions have been obtained using Lowe et al. (2011)'s method, and have no theoretical end points, hence the values of polarization in Figure 3 are not normalized between 0 and 1.

5. An English translation of the speech is available from https://en.wikipedia.org/wiki/Őszöd_speech.

6. See the online appendix for the results of all elections from 1990 to 2014. To limit the distortions produced by different voting populations between different years, vote shares have been normalized by the year turnout.

7. Replacement volatility is supposed to be the most prevalent among new democracies in Central-Eastern Europe, although in Hungary this does not seem to be the case. Note that the values displayed here, albeit based on the same formula proposed by Powell and Tucker (2014), are different from the values in the data provided by the authors (which end in 2006). However, Powell and Tucker (2014)'s data appear problematic at face value: between 1994 and 2006, Type B volatility is constantly declining, although the surge in FIDESZ' support and drop in SZDSZ' and MDF's support in 1998 should be reflected in higher volatility on that year compared with 1994. Moreover, Type A volatility in Powell and Tucker (2014)'s data has a peak of about 16 percent in 2002, double as much as in 1998 and 2006, despite no large parties appearing or disappearing in that year.

8. See the full English translation of the speech on the official website of the Hungarian Government: http://www.kormany.hu/en/the-prime-minister/the-prime-minister-s-speeches/prime-minister-viktor-orban-s-speech-at-the-25th-balvanyos-summer-free-university-and-student-camp (retrieved on July 16, 2018).

References

Arian, Asher, and Michal Shamir. 1983. The primarily political functions of the Left-Right continuum. *Comparative Politics* 15 (2): 139–58.

Bánkuti, Miklós, Gábor Halmai, and Kim Lane Scheppele. 2012. Disabling the constitution. *Journal of Democracy* 23 (3): 138–46.

Bartlett, Jamie, Jonathan Birdwell, Péter Krekó, Jack Benfield, and Gabor Gyori. 2012. *Populism in Europe: Hungary*. New York, NY: Demos.

Baylis, Thomas A. 2012. Elite consensus and political polarization: Cases from Central Europe. *Historical Social Research / Historische Sozialforschung* 37.1 (139): 90–106.

Benoit, Kenneth. 1996. Hungary's "two-vote" electoral system. *Representation* 33 (4): 162–70.

Benoit, Kenneth, and Michael Laver. 2007. Estimating party policy positions: Comparing expert surveys and hand-coded content analysis. *Electoral Studies* 26:90–107.

Bíró Nagy, András., and Dániel Róna. 2012. Freefall - Political agenda explanations for the Hungarian Socialist Party's loss of popularity between 2006–2010. Working Papers in Political Science. Institute for Political Science, MTA Centre for Social Sciences. Available from http://politologia.tk.mta.hu/uploads/files/archived/7790_2012_5_wp.pdf.

Blais, André, and R. Kenneth Carty. 1991. The psychological impact of electoral laws: Measuring Duverger's elusive factor. *British Journal of Political Science* 21 (1): 79–93.

Coppedge, Michael, John Gerring, Carl Henrik Knutsen, Staffan I. Lindberg, Svend-Erik Skaaning, Jan Teorell, David Altman, Michael Bernhard, Steven M. Fish, Agnes Cornell, et al. 2018. V-Dem Country-Year Dataset 2018. Varieties of Democracy (V- Dem) Project. Available from https://doi.org/10.23696/vdemcy18.

CSES. 2015a. The Comparative Study of Electoral Systems. CSES MODULE 1 FULL RELEASE [dataset]. doi:10.7804/cses.module1.2015-12-15.

CSES. 2015b. The Comparative Study of Electoral Systems. CSES MODULE 2 FULL RELEASE. [dataset]. doi:10.7804/cses.module2.2015-12-15.

Dalton, Russell J. 2008. The quantity and the quality of party systems. Party system polarization, its measurement, and its consequences. *Comparative Political Studies* 41 (7): 899–920.

DiMaggio, Paul, John Evans, and Bethany Bryson. 1996. Have Americans' social attitudes become more polarized? *American Journal of Sociology* 102 (3): 690–755.

Downs, Anthony. 1957. *An economic theory of democracy*. New York, NY: Harper and Row.

Druckman, James N., Erik Peterson, and Rune Slothuus. 2013. How elite partisan polarization affects public opinion formation. *American Political Science Review* 107 (1): 57–79.

Eder, Nikolaus, Marcelo Jenny, and Wolfgang C. Müller. 2017. Manifesto functions: How party candidates view and use their party's central policy document. *Electoral Studies* 45:75–87.

Enyedi, Zsolt. 2005. The role of agency in cleavage formation. *European Journal of Political Research* 44 (5): 697–720.

Enyedi, Zsolt. 2006. The survival of the fittest: Party system concentration in Hungary. In *Post-communist EU Member States: Parties and party systems*, ed. Susanne Jungerstam-Mulders, 177–202. Aldershot, UK: Ashgate.

Enyedi, Zsolt. 2016a. Paternalist populism and illiberal elitism in Central Europe. *Journal of Political Ideologies* 21 (1): 9–25.

Enyedi, Zsolt. 2016b. Populist polarization and party system institutionalization: The role of party politics in de-democratization. *Problems of Post-Communism* 63 (4): 210–20.

Fortunato, David, Randolph T. Stevenson, and Greg Vonnahme. 2016. Context and political knowledge: Explaining cross-national variation in partisan Left-Right knowledge. *The Journal of Politics* 78 (4): 1211–1228.

Freedom House. 2017a. Freedom in the World, 2017. Available from https://freedomhouse.org/report/freedom-world/freedom-world-2017.

Freedom House. 2017b. Freedom of Press Report 2017: Hungary. Available from https://freedomhouse.org/report/freedom-press/2017/hungary.

Grzymala-Busse, Anna. 2001. Coalition formation and the regime divide in new democracies: East Central Europe. *Comparative Politics* 34 (1): 85–104.

Harper, Krista. 2006. Two Hungarian uprisings: 1956 and 2006. *Anthropology of East Europe Review* 24 (2): 4–5.

Herman, Lise Esther. 2016. Re-evaluating the post-communist success story: Party elite loyalty, citizen mobilization and the erosion of Hungarian democracy. *European Political Science Review* 8 (2): 251–84.

Iyengar, Shanto, and Sean J. Westwood. 2015. Fear and loathing across party lines: New evidence on group polarization. *American Journal of Political Science* 59 (3): 690– 707.

Kitschelt, Herbert, Zdenka Mansfeldova, Radoslaw Markowski, and Gábor Tóka, eds. 1999. *Postcommunist party systems: Competition, representation, and inter-party cooperation.* New York, NY: Cambridge University Press.

Körösényi, András. 1999. *Government and politics in Hungary.* Budapest: Central European University Press.

Körösényi, András. 2013. Political polarization and its consequences on democratic accountability. *Corvinus Journal of Sociology and Social Policy* 4 (2): 3–30.

Lachat, Romain. 2011. Electoral competitiveness and issue voting. *Political Behavior* 33 (4): 645–63.

Lengyel, György, and Gabriella Ilonszki. 2010. Hungary: Between consolidated and simulated democracy. In *Democratic elitism: New theoretical and comparative perspectives,* eds. Heinrich Best and John Higley, 153–72. Leiden: Brill.

Levitsky, Steven, and Lucan A. Way. 2010. *Competitive authoritarianism: Hybrid regimes after the Cold War.* Cambridge: Cambridge University Press.

Lowe, Will, Kenneth Benoit, Slava Mikhaylov, and Michael Laver. 2011. Scaling policy preferences from coded political texts. *Legislative Studies Quarterly* 36 (1): 123–55.

Markowski, Radoslaw. 1997. Political parties and ideological spaces in East Central Europe. *Communist and Post-Communist Studies* 30 (3): 221–54.

McCarty, Nolan, Keith T. Poole, and Howard Rosenthal. 2006. *Polarized America: The dance of ideology and unequal riches.* Cambridge, MA: MIT Press.

McCoy, Jennifer, Tahmina Rahman, and Murat Somer. 2018. Polarization and the global crisis of democracy: Common patterns, dynamics, and pernicious consequences for democratic polities. *American Behavioral Scientist* 62 (1): 16–42.

Mudde, Cas. 2004. The Populist Zeitgeist. *Government and Opposition* 39 (4): 542–63.

Müller, J.-W. 2011. The Hungarian tragedy. *Dissent Magazine,* 5. Available from https://www.dissentmagazine.org/article/the-hungarian-tragedy.

Nagy, Attila T. 2015. Hungarian electoral system and procedure. Centre for Fair Political Analysis. Available from http://www.meltanyossag.hu/content/files/Hungarian%20electoral%20system%20and%20procedure.pdf.

Nagy, Zsolt. 2017. *Great Expectations and interwar realities: Hungarian cultural diplomacy, 1918–1941.* Budapest: Central European University Press.

Palonen, Emilia. 2009. Political polarisation and populism in contemporary Hungary. *Parliamentary Affairs* 62 (2): 318–34.

Polk, Jonathan, Jan Rovny, Ryan Bakker, Erica Edwards, Liesbet Hooghe, Seth Jolly, Jelle Koedam, Filip Kostelka, Gary Marks, Gijs Schumacher, et al. 2017. Explaining the salience of anti-elitism and reducing political corruption for political parties in Europe with the 2014 Chapel Hill Expert Survey data. *Research & Politics* 4 (1): 1–9.

Powell, Eleanor Neff, and Joshua A. Tucker. 2014. Revisiting electoral volatility in post- communist countries: New data, new results and new approaches. *British Journal of Political Science* 44 (1): 123–47.

Scheppele, Kim Lane. April 2014. Legal but not fair (Hungary). Available from https://krugman.blogs.nytimes.com/2014/04/13/legal-but-not-fair-hungary.

Sitter, Nick, and Agnes Batory. 2006. Europe and the Hungarian elections of April 2006. Election Briefing No. 28. Sussex European Institute. Available from https://www.sussex.ac.uk/webteam/gateway/file.php?name=epern-election-briefing-no-28.pdf&site=266.

Smidt, Corwin D. 2017. Polarization and the decline of the American floating voter. *American Journal of Political Science* 61 (2): 365–81.

Schmitt, Hermann, Sebastian Adrian Popa, Sara B. Hobolt, and Eftichia Teperoglou. 2016. European Parliament Election Study 2014, Voter Study, First Post-Election Survey. DOI:10.4232/1.12628.

Schmitt, Hermann, Stefano Bartolini, Wouter van der Brug, Cees van der Eijk, Mark Franklin, Dieter Fuchs, Gabor Toka, Michael Marsh, and Jacques Thomassen. 2009. European Election Study 2004. 2nd ed. DOI: 10.4232/1.10086.

Stanley, Ben. 2008. The thin ideology of populism. *Journal of Political Ideologies* 13 (1): 95–110.

Szigetvári, Viktor, Csaba Tordai, and Balázs Vető. 2011. Beyond democracy—The model of the new Hungarian parliamentary electoral system (Part 2) (Haza és Haladás Közpolitikai Alapítvány). Available from https://lapa.princeton.edu/hosteddocs/hungary/Beyond%20democracy%20-%2027%20Nov%20 2011.pdf.

Todosijević, Bojan. 2004. The Hungarian voter: Left–Right dimension as a clue to policy preferences. *International Political Science Review* 25 (4): 411–33.

Tóka, Gábor. 1995. *Seats and votes: Consequences of the Hungarian election law. The 1990 elections to the Hungarian National Assembly*, ed. Gábor Tóka. Berlin: Sigma.

Tóka, Gábor. 1998. Party appeals and voter loyalty in new democracies. *Political Studies* 46 (3): 589–610.

Tóka, Gábor, and Sebastian Adrian Popa. 2013. Hungary. In *Handbook of political change in Eastern Europe*, 3rd ed., eds. Sten Berglund, Joakim Ekman, and Franklin H. Aarebrot. Cheltenham: Edward Elgar Publishing Ltd.

Vegetti, Federico. 2014. From political conflict to partisan evaluations: How citizens assess party ideology and competence in polarized elections. *Electoral Studies* 35:230–41.

Volkens, Andrea, Pola Lehmann, Theres Matthieß, Nicolas Merz, Sven Regel, and Annika Werner. 2015. The Manifesto Data Collection. Manifesto Project (MRG/CMP/MARPOR). Available from https://manifesto-project.wzb.eu.

Poland: A Case of Top-Down Polarization

HUBERT TWORZECKI

Poland represents a surprising case of democratic backsliding since the return to power of the PiS party in
2015, given that positive conditions associated with
democracy are present—consistent strong per capita
economic growth since 1989, moderate inequality, rising wages, strong preference for democracy, high levels
of happiness, and a parliamentary system with proportional representation. The lack of strong underlying
cleavages indicates the polarization was not bottom up.
Instead, this article argues that polarization was driven
from the top down by a segment of the political class
that donned the cloak of radical populist anti-establishmentarianism to gain popular support, win an election,
and rewrite the constitutional rules of the game to its
own benefit. The Polish case points to the importance
of elite cues, and especially the pernicious consequences of system-delegitimizing rhetoric, creating
distrust in the media and institutions.

Keywords: Poland; democratic backsliding; top-down
polarization

Since the elections of 2015, Poland has
joined the ranks of countries experiencing
democratic backsliding. It was a process driven
from the top down by a segment of the political
class that donned the cloak of radical populist
anti-establishmentarianism to gain popular
support, win an election, and rewrite the constitutional rules of the game to its own benefit.
Put differently, Poland's democratic backsliding
story is essentially one of "establishment insiders 'breaking bad,'" to borrow a phrase from
Hanley and Dawson (2017). As argued by

Hubert Tworzecki is an associate professor of political
science at Emory University. His research interests
include political parties, elections, and voting in new
democracies. He is the author of Learning to Choose:
Electoral Politics in East-Central Europe *(Stanford*
University Press 2002), Parties and Politics in Post-
1989 Poland *(Westview Press 1996)*, *as well as numer-*
ous journal articles.

Correspondence: htworze@emory.edu

DOI: 10.1177/0002716218809322

ANNALS, *AAPSS*, 681, January 2019

97

Tworzecki and Markowski (2017), having won by a twist of domestic and international circumstances unlikely to be repeated, The Law and Justice Party (PiS) set about changing the rules so it could carry out what it called an "exchange of elites" (i.e., rewarding its activists and supporters in a tidal wave of patronage and clientelism) with both permanence and impunity. In terms of the three patterns described in McCoy, Rahman, and Somer (2018), Poland therefore fits in the category of democratic erosion under new elites.

Although Poland is routinely mentioned in journalistic accounts and academic studies as one of many cases of backsliding or outright breakdown, in important ways it stands apart from the rest. Indeed, the puzzle presented by Poland is that it appears to contradict decades of accumulated political science research on transitions to and from democracy in that it lacks any of the major risk factors identified by previous literature, such as persistent economic dysfunction, crippling racial or ethnic divisions, polarizing winner-take-all institutions (e.g., presidentialism or single-member-district elections), or pernicious international entanglements (e.g., trade dependence on nondemocracies).

The Puzzle of Poland's Democratic Erosion (2015–18)

Contrary to the expectations of theories that associate risks to democracies with low incomes,[1] inequality (Acemoglu and Robinson 2005; Boix 2003), or poor economic performance (Kapstein and Converse 2008; Svolik 2013; Bernhard, Reenock, and Nordstrom 2003), Poland has seen its per capita GDP increase by 4.1 percent per year since 1989—a remarkable record, matched in the middle/high income country category only by South Korea (Piatkowski 2018). Economic inequality in Poland is moderate by European and low by global standards,[2] *oligarchization* is a nonissue (the ratio of billionaire wealth to GDP, at 1.3 percent, is among the lowest in the world; see Brzeziński 2017), unemployment is in single digits, and incomes have not stagnated, as in some democracies, but risen steadily, if unevenly, across the board.[3] Nevertheless, perceptions of inequitable distributions of material gain have created a type of legitimacy deficit for the post–Cold War system, ably exploited by rising populist parties as described here.

Poland's membership in the European Union (EU) and dependence on trade and investment from other EU member states should have resulted, in line with "linkage and leverage" theories (Levitsky and Way 2006), in significant pressure on elites to maintain the liberal-democratic package of popular accountability, transparency, and rule of law.

On the political/institutional side, Poland should have been safe from anyone's authoritarian ambitions thanks to a parliamentary system[4] and a proportional electoral law, both of which should have—at least in theory—discouraged the kind of zero-sum politics characteristic of presidentialism, especially when combined with single-member district legislative elections (Mainwaring and Shugart 1997). Furthermore, Poland's constitution features a comprehensive set of checks and balances, along with both domestic (Constitutional Tribunal, truly independent Central Bank) and external (the European Union) constraints on the power of raw majoritarianism.

In terms of actual political practice, between 1989 and 2015, Poland's parliamentary elections have resulted in seven peaceful handovers of power (including to and from the communist successor party), which, in view of "habituation"[5] theories should have given the political elite plenty of time to internalize democratic norms, or, alternatively, in view of "institutional stickiness" theories, should have been plenty of time for the emergence of system-stabilizing, self-reinforcing dynamics (Pierson 2004, 10). Indeed, at 26 years old, Poland's democracy should not have been fragile in view of the expected impact of time on democratic survival.[6]

Last, surveys of the Polish public in the run-up to the 2015 elections showed very high levels of happiness and satisfaction with life,[7] and a strong preference for democracy over any other political system (76 percent), positive evaluations of democratic performance (59 percent), and no evidence of any significant shift in these attitudes compared with previous years (Markowski and Kotnarowski 2016; Markowski and Tworzecki 2016).

Despite these highly favorable circumstances, after the elections of 2015 Poland experienced a period of unprecedented political turmoil. PiS, having won the presidency and majorities in both chambers of parliament (a slim 51 percent of seats in the lower house, based on winning just under 38 percent of the popular vote),[8] almost instantly embarked on an agenda of far-reaching systemic change. Lacking the two-thirds of majority needed to change the constitution outright, as Hungary's government had done several years earlier, PiS sought to accomplish the same goal through ordinary legislation. When the Constitutional Tribunal objected, its rulings were ignored until it could be packed with government supporters, some of whom were sworn in by the president—a strong partisan of PiS himself, who made no effort to stand in the government's way—in a rushed, middle-of-the-night ceremony. The national legislature was likewise turned into a rubber-stamp body through routine side-stepping of parliamentary procedure.[9]

On the executive side, the offices of the president and prime minister were reduced to mere decorations, while actual decision-making power came to be exercised extra-constitutionally by the PiS party chairman, Jarosław Kaczyński. Kaczyński—who had previously served as prime minister in a PiS-led coalition government during 2005–2007—was technically only an ordinary member of the lower house of parliament, but he was routinely referred to by his subordinates as *Naczelnik* (leader)—the informal title once held by Poland's father of independence, Józef Piłsudski, who became the country's authoritarian strongman during the interwar years (1926–35).

Effectively freed from constitutional constraints, the new government pushed through a flurry of laws aimed at undermining the independence and oversight functions of the judiciary, bringing nongovernmental organizations (NGOs) and commercial media to heel through restrictive regulatory measures, limiting citizens' freedoms of speech and assembly, increasing the government's surveillance powers, restricting property rights (e.g., the ability to freely dispose of privately owned farmland), and changing the civil service law to remove merit criteria for appointments so as to be able to fill state jobs with party loyalists.[10] The government also made a number of potentially troubling changes to electoral laws and to institutions responsible for the conduct of elections (Marcinkiewicz and Stegmaier 2018).

Along the way, these extra-constitutional actions were accompanied by a propaganda offensive in state-owned and private, progovernment media outlets that eerily mimicked both the style and substance of the Kremlin's messaging in Putin's Russia: delegitimizing parliamentary and civic opposition as enemies and traitors, while stoking xenophobia and ethnic nationalism, with particular hostility directed toward liberal-democratic values and toward the European Union as their institutional embodiment (Chapman 2017).

Simultaneously, however, in what were some of the largest downwardly redistributive transfers of the post-1989 period, the PiS government introduced a new tax-free child subsidy, brought in a free prescription drug benefit for the elderly, and reduced the retirement age raised by the previous governing coalition. And even though it continually stressed its anticommunism, time and again the government made a nod in the direction of those nostalgic for the days of a command economy, criticizing the sell-off of state-owned enterprises and collective farms during the privatizations of the 1990s, and signaling its commitment to the idea that the state should once again oversee economic development and take upon itself the burdens of providing citizens with employment, housing, and child-care.[11] Critical voices, both among opposition elites and segments of the public (particularly the urban middle classes) concerned about the economic consequences of these policies, were dismissed as mere protestations of those who had to give up their "place at the trough" in favor of people victimized and left behind during the post-1989 transition to a market-based economy.

In the nearly three years that have elapsed since the 2015 election, Polish society has remained deeply conflicted about these developments. Surveys continue to show that strong majorities support the government's downwardly redistributive social programs, but majorities almost as large recognize that it does not follow the rule of law.[12] Likewise, even though PiS still—as of mid-2018—retains a strong lead in the polls,[13] its support has shrunk back to the same <40 percent level it had received in the 2015 election, which, given Poland's history of roughly 50 percent turnouts, may be interpreted as <20 percent of the total electorate, or somewhere between 5.1 and 5.7 million voters (Markowski 2018). Put another way: the generous social programs brought the governing party no great popularity gains over its election result; but then its takeover of the judiciary and attempts to curtail various rights and liberties did not result in significant losses.

So if "PiS did not appear out of nowhere" (as many Polish political commentators are fond of saying), if the country's democratic backsliding has its root causes stretching back many years, what are they? There are a number of possible explanations, including on the demand-side, the supply-side, and various combinations of both. Taking a cue from recent American literature (Abramowitz 2010; Webster and Abramowitz 2017; Mason 2018; Grossmann and Hopkins 2016), this article takes up the proposition that the key mechanisms at work in Poland have been asymmetric polarization at the elite level (meaning that one major party—PiS—broke with the prevailing liberal-democratic consensus and moved toward ever more extreme positions), resulting in polarization at the level of the electorate. Examining both aspects of the story is beyond the scope of this article, and therefore the empirical analyses that follows focuses on the mass level; however, the next section gives a brief synopsis of how and why one party reneged on its commitment to the democratic rules of the game and embraced the idea of an antisystemic revolt.

Polarization among the Elites

The elections of 2015, which precipitated Poland's turn of democratic backsliding, may be viewed as the final act in the evolution of the country's second postcommunist party system. The first system, which lasted from 1989 until 2005, pitted the Democratic Left Alliance (SLD)—the modernized heirs of the former Communist Party—against the diverse heirs of the oppositional Solidarity Movement. The SLD featured broad elite consensus on key issues, including the overall goal of "westernization," understood as building up the institutional framework of liberal democracy and a market-based economy.

By the early 2000s, however, amid an economic slowdown and anxieties related to Poland's approaching EU accession date, there were signs that the party system was about to undergo significant changes. Chief among these were the gradual unraveling of the SLD in the wake of corruption scandals and the rise of populist, anti-establishment parties of various stripes.[14] This turn of events paved the way for the emergence of a second party system oriented along a new axis of "liberalism vs. solidarism," which pitted the beneficiaries of the post-1989 economic and political transformation against those who felt that they had experienced a decline in their economic well-being or their social esteem (Markowski 2006).

Two new parties, both created in 2001, were in the forefront of this transformation: PiS and the Civic Platform (PO). Although at first ideological and programmatic differences between them were small (both positioned themselves as center-right, and it was widely assumed that they would form a PO-PiS coalition government after the next elections), in the years that followed, they positioned themselves on opposing sides of this new cleavage. Specifically, the PO kept a center-right stance, directing its message to more economically prosperous individuals who were generally content with the direction and socioeconomic consequences of the post-1989 transformation. By contrast, having invented and popularized the "liberalism vs. solidarism" discourse during the 2005 election campaign, PiS set about questioning not only the distributive consequences of the transformation, but also increasingly the entire post-1989 liberal-democratic political order itself. Directing its message to culturally traditionalist (Catholic church-goers) and economically hard-pressed voters, PiS advocated systemic change in the direction of ethno-religious majoritarianism. It produced in 2005 and 2010 two complete drafts of a new constitution that, in addition to enshrining national-Catholicism as the de facto state ideology, would have centralized power in the hands of an executive presidency virtually unconstrained by institutional checks and balances.[15]

After winning both the presidency and the plurality of parliamentary seats in the 2005 elections, PiS formed a coalition government with two small populist parties on the right and the left (LPR and Self-Defense). Unhappy with having to depend on their support, PiS set about to co-opt or neutralize these small parties' leaders and absorb their electorates. In early elections in 2007, however, PiS lost to the PO and spent the next eight years in opposition.[16]

It was during those eight years that PiS became more and more radical in its rejection of the status quo. This radicalization happened for two main reasons. The first had to do with incentives created by the cultural prominence of authoritarian ideologies, principally the aforementioned 1930s-style national Catholicism—a type of integral nationalism that had never been discredited in East-Central Europe in the same way it had been in the postwar West. This ideology was bolstered by its embrace from powerful societal actors (namely Poland's Catholic Church, which with the passage of time became ever more reactionary) willing to join PiS to carry out a "cultural counterrevolution"[17] aimed at reversing the emancipatory trends initiated by the fall of communism and restoring something resembling the hierarchical social order of a century earlier. In a country where almost 40 percent of the population attends religious services at least weekly, and where hardly a week goes by without a public pronouncement by a senior clergyman likening liberalism to "soft totalitarianism" and parliamentary democracy to a "dictatorship of materialism,"[18] the impact of this alliance should not be underestimated. In particular, it has the potential for systematically undermining popular support for liberal-democratic values and institutions.

The second reason for the PiS radicalization had to do with internal politics of autocratically run political parties. While it is true that many Polish parties have long suffered from institutional underdevelopment and internal democratic deficits, PiS was an extreme case, fitting Panebianco's (1988, 147) definition of a *charismatic party* in which there exists "total symbiosis between the leader and the organizational identity." Indeed, one could go further and argue that, due to the extent of this symbiosis, PiS was not so much an "organization" (a term that implies a degree of institutionalization and depersonalization), but rather the private domain of its chairman,[19] a type that some literature refers to as a *personal party*—one held together only by the founder's authority (McDonnell 2016, 723). Consequently, although for a few years after its founding in 2001—when it was still a moderate, mainstream party—PiS could accommodate within its ranks a number of moderate, mainstream politicians with national reputations of their own, afterwards it became clear that Mr. Kaczyński insisted on treating the party as his personal property, the party was subjected to a process of negative selection, shedding its best and brightest and replacing them with more "plebeian" cadres— people with little to lose and potentially much to gain from a fundamental transformation of the social, economic, and political orders in a manner that would discount meritocratic criteria in favor of political patronage and clientelism.

In the years that followed, these politicians advanced the party through ideological outbidding, knocking out rivals in "purity tests" and engaging in displays of fervent loyalty to the leader. The result was radicalization, leader cult reminiscent of a religious sect, and ultimately full-blown authoritarianism not just in the party's internal politics, but in its relationship with the voter base and its approach to constitutionalism and the rule of law. After President Lech Kaczyński (the twin brother of PiS leader Jarosław) died in 2010 in an airplane crash in Smolensk, Russia, these trends only accelerated, and PiS became a kind of quasi-church with its own martyr (the dead president), its dogma (belief that the crash was the result of a conspiracy between the Kremlin and the president's domestic enemies), its special rituals (monthly processions through the center of Warsaw to commemorate the president's death), and its prophet-leader Jarosław on a mission to take the suffering nation to the promised land.

To be clear, seeking to change the constitution by itself (assuming, of course, that PiS had won a sufficiently large majority to do this according to the rules) would fall well within the confines of normal democratic politics; however, with the passage of time, the party's other positions became much more pernicious in the sense of making a systematic effort to delegitimize existing institutions (including elections), sow mistrust by normalizing conspiracy theories, and flood the news environment with false information. Through its aligned media outlets (including Church-owned ones), PiS and its allies in the media sought to create an alternative reality in which pre-2015 Poland was portrayed not as an economically thriving democracy, but as a country "in ruins" where elites lived the high life while the people suffered, election results were falsified, corruption and lawlessness were rampant, non-PiS media outlets could not be trusted, dissent was repressed, and protesting workers risked being shot by the police.

Polarization among the Electorate

Poland's polarization, then, has been asymmetric: the PiS moved toward an extreme position of reneging on its commitment to respect the constitution, while its main rival (PO) did not change its position and remained a broadly centrist mainstream party. To what extent did this asymmetric polarization on the part of one political party translate into polarization at the level of the general electorate? Might Poland have witnessed a process similar to the one described by Svolik (2017, 1) in the case of Venezuela, whereby "voters in polarized societies are … willing to trade off democratic principles for partisan interests"? The answers are far from obvious. PiS' internal culture of unquestioning obedience to the leader meant that it was capable of toning down its radicalism temporarily, whenever he commanded it, as happened in the 2015 election campaign. Indeed, in the early days of the campaign, especially during the presidential contest, the party's most controversial figures, including Mr. Kaczyński himself, largely withdrew from public view and the presidential campaign was dominated by ordinary issues (old age pensions, child support policies, etc.).

Then again, the tone of the parliamentary campaign that followed a few weeks later had a much harsher edge, with leading PiS figures saying manifestly untrue things like "GDP growth is mainly on paper, Poles are getting poorer, the middle class is disappearing" (Cienski 2015). In addition, PiS instrumentalized the Middle Eastern refugee crisis, presenting it as a multifaceted threat to physical security (in the words of top PiS figures, the refugees would not only bring

FIGURE 1
Electorate Demographics

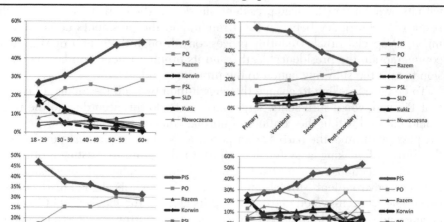

SOURCE: October 25, 2015 parliamentary election; IPSOS exit poll data.
NOTE: Percent of vote for a given party in a given category: age, education, urbanization, job-type.

"diseases and parasites," but also "blow up Polish infants"), to identity and sacred values (they would "turn churches into lavatories"), and to economic well-being (they would compete with locals for welfare payments, housing subsidies, etc.) (Wasik and Foy 2015). This was clearly about firing up the base, not about appealing to moderate voters.

When it was all over, PiS won the plurality (37.6 percent) of votes, while the incumbent PO-PSL coalition came in second with the combined total of 29.2 percent. The exit polls (Figure 1) showed that, as expected, PiS did best among its core electorate of older, rural, less-educated voters employed in less-skilled occupations; however, it won pluralities in virtually all socioeconomic categories. The only exception was among those employed in managerial positions—PiS tied with PO. A new party, called Nowoczesna (Modern), tried to offer a sharply defined liberal alternative to PO's centrist blandness, and succeeded in winning 7.6 percent of votes, but even among its core target of urban professionals it lagged far behind PiS and PO.[20] Notably, in the 18–29 age category the two largest parties (i.e., PO and PiS) did the worst, and the two small antisystem parties registered their strongest showing. These two were "Kukiz'15," an anarchistic-flavored right-populist party started by a former punk rocker Pawel Kukiz; and "Korwin," an odd libertarian-monarchist outfit led by the provocateur European Parliament member Janusz Korwin-Mikke, whose penchant for making bigoted statements got him suspended by the European Parliament in 2017 (Rankin 2017).

FIGURE 2
Predicted Probability of Voting for PiS vs. PO in 2015

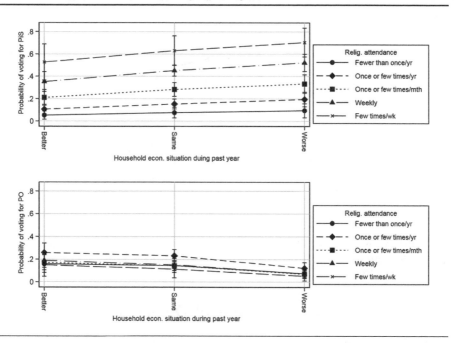

SOURCE: Polish National Election Survey data.

Put another way, if we look only at the three thicker lines in Figure 1 indicating "antisystem" parties (i.e., those that ran on a radical critique of the status quo combined with a call for fundamental systemic change), we could make the argument that the goal of dismantling the status quo was backed by a collection of social groups that included older individuals from traditionalist social settings (close-knit, religious, rural) voting for PiS with its old-fashioned national Catholicism, as well as younger persons from diverse backgrounds (and not necessarily with low socio-economic status) voting for the more eclectic populism of Kukiz'15 and Korwin. Conversely, supporters of the status quo were concentrated among the middle and older age groups, principally among the urban middle classes.

Since the exit poll asked neither about income nor religious attendance, it might be useful to supplement it by looking at relevant data from the postelection Polish National Election Survey (PGSW) to obtain a better purchase of whether economic anxieties (operationalized here as perception that the financial condition of the respondent's household had worsened over the previous year) or cultural factors (commitment to traditionalist, identity-reinforcing rituals, operationalized here as regular attendance at religious services) were more predictive of voting for the two largest parties, PiS and PO.[21] As Figure 2 reveals, religious attendance was more predictive of the vote than economic assessments, especially in case of PiS. These results are not surprising in view of other research

FIGURE 3
Positive and Negative Affective Partisanship

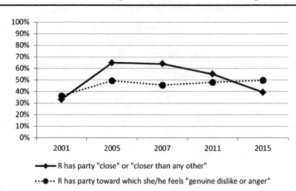

SOURCE: PGSW data.

on Polish voters (see, for example, Jasiewicz 2009), which had consistently shown that religiosity mattered more than economic circumstances.

Polarization and Erosion of Democratic Norms

It should be noted, however, that the picture presented above is suggestive more of social sorting than polarization.[22] So what specific evidence is there that in the run-up to 2015 the Polish public had become polarized in a way that made democratic backsliding possible in the manner described by McCoy, Rahman, and Somer (2018)? Specifically, was there a rise in 1) affective polarization, especially in the sense of negative partisanship where voters express more negative sentiment about opposing parties than positive sentiment about their own party, and 2) ideological polarization, in the sense of partisan divergence on evaluations of and normative commitment to democracy? McCoy, Rahman, and Somer (2018) hypothesize that growing affective polarization and the zero-sum perceptions associated with us-vs.-them politics will lead partisan supporters to tolerate illiberal behavior by their own party, and thus the erosion of democratic norms. The analyses that follow take up these questions by looking at successive waves (2001, 2005, 2007, 2011, 2015) of the PGSW, each of which was conducted in the immediate aftermath of a parliamentary election on a nationally representative random sample of respondents using face-to-face interviews.

Affective polarization: Sympathy and antipathy toward political parties

Let us consider first the question of affective polarization. Figure 3 shows that, in 2001, around a third of respondents mentioned a party that they considered in line with their beliefs, while roughly the same proportion said that there was a party toward which they felt "genuine dislike or anger." The graph shows a spike

FIGURE 4
Positive Affective Partisanship, by Vote in Parliamentary Election

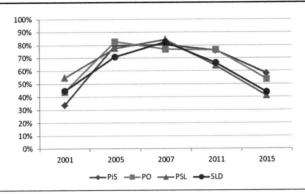

SOURCE: PGSW data.

FIGURE 5
Negative Affective Partisanship, by Vote in Parliamentary Election

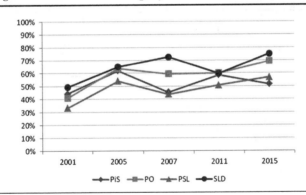

SOURCE: PGSW data.

in positive partisanship during 2005–07 followed by a small decline, while the level of negative partisanship from 2001 onward has remained much more flat.

But perhaps beneath these overall trends there were changes in the level of affective partisanship—of either the positive or negative variety—within specific party electorates?[23] This appears not to have been the case. As Figure 4 makes clear, positive partisanship rises pretty uniformly in the electorates of the four major parties in 2005–07, and then declines in all four, with just a slightly smaller decline among voters of the two largest parties (PiS and PO). With regard to negative partisanship (Figure 5), there are some differences among parties, but no steep rise in any one electorate, not even among PiS voters, despite all the angry rhetoric coming from that party's elites.

FIGURE 6
Affective Differential Plots

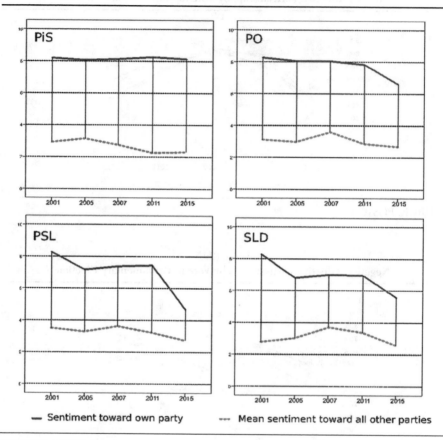

SOURCE: PGSW data.

Another way to examine the possibility that there might have been a rise in affective polarization is to consider how responses on "feeling thermometer" scales (i.e., how much the respondent likes a given party, on a scale from 0 to 10) have changed over the years. To do so, Figure 6 shows the "affective differentials," meaning differences between sentiments toward one's own party (solid lines) vs. the mean value of sentiments toward all other parties (dashed lines). It would appear that respondents for whom PiS was the party "close or closer than any other" (the top left of Figure 6) have remained much more steady in their positive feelings (the solid line in that top left graph is almost completely flat) than any of the others, whose positive sentiment have all declined. Further, the affective differential of PiS respondents (indicated by vertical range lines between solid and dashed lines) is not only the largest among the four partisan groups, but has increased over the years, while it has shrunk in the other three electorates. Put another way, uniquely among Polish parties, PiS appears to have

FIGURE 7
Democracy is Better Than Any Other System

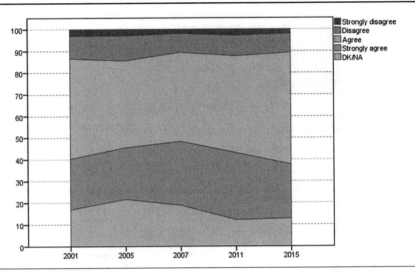

SOURCE: PGSW data.

succeeded in creating an electorate with a strong and lasting positive sentiment toward itself, and with a larger affective distance toward all of its competitors. Now, this was surely not the reason PiS decided to embark on a course of democratic backsliding, but it might have played some role in it its calculations, in that having a uniquely committed electorate gave its leaders the confidence that they might just get away with a brazen power grab.

Ideological polarization: Support for democracy

Let us turn now to examining the issue of prodemocratic sentiments more directly to see if a declining normative commitment among voters may be emboldening party leadership to violate democratic norms. The PGSW surveys contain one question that gauges respondents' commitment to democracy in the normative sense, as well as another question asking them to evaluate democracy's actual performance. The overall distributions of responses to these questions are shown in Figure 7 ("Is democracy better than any other system?") and Figure 8 ("Is democracy in Poland performing well?"). On the normative side, the data show a small and steadily shrinking proportion (to around 10 percent by 2015) of respondents who might be described as nondemocrats. By contrast, the prodemocratic "strongly agree" responses are consistently in the 30 percent range, while the "agree" category has grown from around 40 percent in 1997 to 60 percent in 2015 (so 90 percent support democracy as a system). On the evaluative "Is democracy in Poland performing well?" question, the responses are somewhat less enthusiastic, with a consistently small proportion (3–5 percent) of "strongly

FIGURE 8
Democracy in Poland is Performing Well

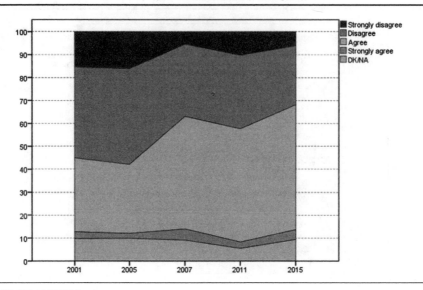

SOURCE: PGSW data.

FIGURE 9
Differences in Normative Commitment to Democracy, by Vote in Parliamentary Election

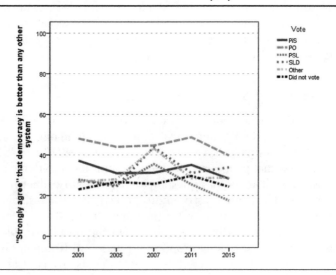

SOURCE: PGSW data.

agree" responses, but a steadily growing (to 55 percent in 2015) proportion of "agrees." At first glance then, these figures do not seem to indicate a democracy

FIGURE 10
Differences in Evaluations of Democratic Performance, by Vote
in Parliamentary Election

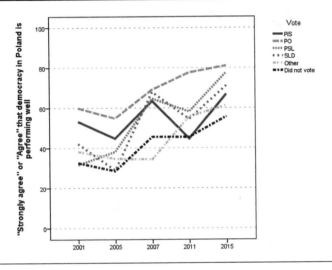

SOURCE: PGSW data.

in trouble, or a people who have lost faith in the political system and might be open to nondemocratic alternatives.

But what about the possibility that, over the years, these commitments and evaluations became intertwined with partisanship: that support for democracy increasingly became a partisan issue? Again, this does not appear to have been the case. According to Figure 9, although a partisan gap does exist among respondents on the question of whether democracy is preferable to any other system, it has not widened over time. Throughout the entire duration of the second party system (2001–2015), PO voters were ahead of PiS voters in supporting democracy by an 11–13 point margin.[24]

Sharper partisan differences are definitely visible in evaluations of democratic performance (Figure 10), especially between supporters of PO and PiS, where an almost 38-point gap opened in 2011, shrinking to about 17 percent in 2015. To be sure, there is plenty of research from other countries to the effect that partisanship affects people's evaluations of the state of the national economy, of whether the country is "on the right track," and of its undemocratic performance (see, for example, Pew Research Center 2017). And indeed, there is nothing terribly surprising—or out of line with findings from other countries—in that supporters of the party currently in opposition (as PiS had been from 2007 to 2015) would be more critical of the political system's performance than supporters of the party in power (as PO had been during the same period).

All in all then, it is a mixed picture: partisanship does matter for some things, but in terms of normative commitment to democracy as a system "better than any

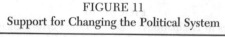

FIGURE 11
Support for Changing the Political System

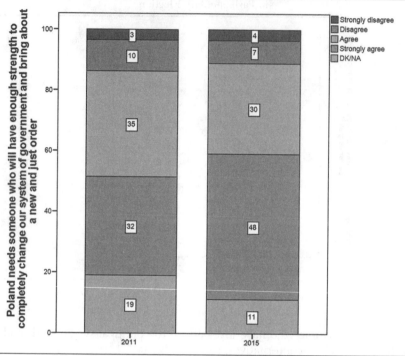

SOURCE: PGSW data.

other," these differences are not large, even where one would most expect to see them between supporters and opponents of the party (PiS) responsible for embarking on a course of democratic backsliding. More significant perhaps is the finding that both normative comments and performance evaluations of democracy are lowest among nonvoters, who are by far the largest group of the electorate given Poland's history of only around 40–50 percent turnouts in parliamentary elections.

There is still the possibility, though, that any survey question that contains some variant of the word "democracy" will inevitably pick up a large amount of social desirability bias associated with this system of government. Especially in face-to-face interviews, which is how all the PGSW studies were conducted, respondents likely feel reluctant to present themselves as skeptical or hostile to democracy. And besides, the new populists in Poland and elsewhere do not claim to be "antidemocratic"—they just understand the term differently, as a kind of simple majoritarianism—which means that a populist party supporter is not necessarily falsifying his or her preferences in claiming to be a committed democrat.

To get around this problem, and gauge the extent of support for systemic change in the Polish electorate, the 2011 and 2015 editions of the PGSW contained the question: "Do you agree or disagree that Poland needs someone who

FIGURE 12

Support for Changing the Political System, by Vote in Parliamentary Election

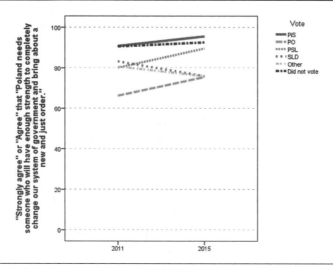

SOURCE: PGSW data.

will have enough strength to completely change our system of government and bring about a new and just order?" This wording consciously avoids the term "democracy," and although it hints at a strong leader ("someone who will have enough strength …"), it does so in a subtle way that does not necessarily imply a dictator who runs roughshod over parliament or does away with elections. However, the wording is explicitly asking about support for "completely changing" the system of government, so responses to it might be interpreted as indicating willingness to see major changes made to the constitutional status quo.

The breakdown of answers to this question (Figure 11) is quite striking, with nearly 78 percent of respondents in 2015 placing themselves in the "agree" or "strongly agree" categories—an 11-point increase from 2011. Broken down by parliamentary vote (Figure 12), an astonishing 96 percent of those who voted for PiS in 2015 expressed support for major systemic change, as did nearly the same proportion of those who did not go to the polls at all. There was a huge, 21-point gap in 2015 between the supporters of PiS and PO, but it is striking that more than 75 percent of PO's voters wanted systemic change as well, and this for the quintessential mainstream "status quo" party seeking a third term in office. What these results hint at, therefore, is not only partisan polarization on the question of maintaining vs. changing the political system, but a massive legitimacy deficit that spanned across partisan divides—including among nonvoters who, had they actually turned out in 2015, might have swayed the result even more in favor of PiS. Unfortunately, this exact question was not asked prior to 2011, so it is not possible to establish whether this sentiment had been as intense all along, or if it had spiked as a kind of spillover effect from the negative, system-delegitimizing rhetoric coming from PiS party elites from 2005 onward.[25]

Conclusion

Unraveling the puzzle of Poland's democratic backsliding will demand considerable analytical sophistication, with equal attention paid to the role of demand-side and supply-side factors. The results presented here offer initial indications of how popular opinion might have evolved in terms of rising demand for systemic change. Though perhaps surprising at first glance, they fit well with other findings that have been familiar to researchers of Polish and other postcommunist electorates for more than two decades: namely that the political systems—and, more broadly, new social orders (including economic and status hierarchies)—established in the wake of communism's collapse never gained moral approval in the sense of the social outcomes they produced being perceived as legitimate, just, and fair. For example, when asked to choose between the statements "Thanks to post-1989 reforms, everyone is better off" versus "A handful of rich people is getting richer and average people are getting poorer," the latter was picked by 88 percent of Polish respondents in 1992 (with some justification, since the early 1990s were a time of sharp economic contraction). But more astonishing in view of steadily rising incomes for all sectors over the next decades was the 2014 response to that same question: 79 percent of respondents answered again that the rich were getting richer and average people poorer.[26]

To be sure, so-called system justification sentiments are a double-edged sword: when they are very strong (i.e., when large majorities believe that social outcomes are just and fair, and that individuals have only themselves to blame for their failures), they may make it more difficult to address problems of inequality or discrimination (Jost and Hunyady 2005; Wakslak et al. 2007). But when they are very weak—as in the Polish case where perceived inequity is high—they may make it easier for opportunistic elites to tear down existing institutions on the promise of bringing about a new and just order.

Psychologists have long puzzled over the mechanisms through which these system-justifying beliefs are produced: whether they are internal, having to do with needs for reassurance and rationalization, or linked to observable societal processes of rising incomes or other measures of upward mobility, or perhaps result from elite cues and socialization into a political culture in which existing institutions and their outcomes are deemed by authority figures to be fair and legitimate. The Polish case seems to point to the importance of elite cues, and especially the pernicious consequences of system-delegitimizing rhetoric that may have contributed to resentment about perceived unfairness and thus support for an antisystem party like the PiS, despite economic progress and steadily rising levels of individual happiness and satisfaction with life.

Notes

1. Poland's per capita GDP in 2015 was almost twice that of Argentina in 1975—the level that had long been regarded as the threshold above which democracies did not break down (Przeworski et al. 2000; Przeworski 2008).

2. Poland's Gini coefficient of .31 is almost exactly at the European Union mean and far below that of Russia—or the United States for that matter (Novokmet, Piketty, and Zocman 2017); see http://ec.europa. eu/eurostat/tgm/table.do?tab=table&language=en&pcode=tessi190.

3. While incomes did grow fastest at the top (at an average of 4.2 percent per year since 1989 for the top 10 percent), there was also growth—albeit slower—among middle (1.5 percent per year for the middle 40 percent) and lower-income categories (1 percent per year for the bottom 50 percent) (Bukowski and Novokmet 2017).

4. Although popularly elected, Poland's presidency is nonexecutive, so the country is best classified as having a parliamentary rather than a semi-presidential system, and therefore "perils of presidentialism" (Linz 1990) arguments do not apply to it.

5. The idea that the passage of time works in democracy's favor through a "habituation" mechanism, first given wide currency by Rustow (1970), was later identified by Carothers (2002) as one of the core assumptions of the so-called transitions paradigm.

6. Contrary to the expectations of the early transitions literature, later research showed that "the risk of democratic breakdown actually increases with the passage of time, other things being equal, for what is usually the first several election cycles … If a democracy manages to survive into its early twenties, the risk of failure begins to decline with the passage of time as generally expected" (Ulfelder 2009, 30).

7. In the 2015 edition of the *Diagnoza Społeczna* survey (Czapiński and Panek 2015), 81 percent of respondents described their lives in positive terms (as very successful, successful, or mostly successful), following a steady increase from a low of 53 percent in the 1993 edition of the same survey.

8. This unusually high vote-seat disproportionality occurred because the United Left coalition failed to clear the threshold necessary to win parliamentary seats by a mere half of a percentage point. Poland's electoral law for the lower house of the national legislature is proportional, based on the d'Hondt formula, with a threshold of 5 percent for parties and 8 percent for coalitions. United Left ran as a coalition of the ex-communist Democratic Left Alliance and several other parties. It received 7.5 percent of votes and thus failed to enter parliament. This failure gave PiS its razor-thin parliamentary majority. For complete results and discussion of the 2015 elections see Tworzecki and Markowski (2015); Marcinkiewicz and Stegmaier (2016).

9. Post-2015, the national parliament began to operate in open disregard of both its constitutional role as a deliberative body (e.g., with PiS-appointed speakers of both chambers routinely limiting opposition members' speaking time to as little as one minute and penalizing them financially for going over the limit and/or turning off their microphones), as well as its own rules of procedure (e.g., by going around the so-called *vacatio legis* requirement, meaning time for reflection and public consultation before a bill may become a law, through the trick of bringing forth government legislative proposals as private members' bills) (Batory Foundation 2017).

10. For summaries of these developments see: U.S. Department of State (2017), Freedom House (2017b), Freedom House (2017a), European Commission for Democracy Through Law (Venice Commission) (2016), European Commission (2016), United Nations General Assembly (2017), United Nations General Assembly (2018), and Freedom House (2018).

11. The government's case for this set of economic politics is laid out in the report "Capitalism—The Polish Way" Polish Economic Institute (2018). For a critical outsider's take, see Orenstein (2018).

12. For example, according to an IPSOS survey from June 2016, 60 percent of respondents agreed with the statement that the new government, in contrast to the previous one, "cares more about the poor, the weak, the excluded," but only 44 percent agreed that it "respects the rule of law." See https://oko.press/ dobra-zmiana-minimalnie-wygrywa-pis-sie-troszczy/.

13. See https://en.wikipedia.org/wiki/Opinion_polling_for_the_next_Polish_parliamentary_election.

14. In accordance with commonly used definitions, the term *populist* is used here to describe anti-establishment parties that emphasize the divide between a homogenous, morally elevated people and a corrupt, unrepresentative elite. *Left-populists* typically make their case in economic terms (targeting the wealthy) in contrast to the ethnonationalism (and the targeting of outgroups) commonly invoked by *Right-populists* (Mudde and Kaltwasser 2013; Inglehart and Norris 2016).

15. As set out in the current 1997 Constitution, Poland's system of government may be described as parliamentarism with a directly elected, but nonexecutive and largely ceremonial presidency. By contrast, PiS's 2010 draft envisioned concentrating power in the hands of the president at the expense of the parliament and cabinet (e.g., the president would gain the ability to reject the parliament's candidate for prime

minister at his sole discretion), weakening judicial independence and the Constitutional Tribunal's power to declare laws unconstitutional (by requiring the Tribunal to reach verdicts by four-fifths majority), and introducing a provision that constitutionally guaranteed individual rights and liberties could be restricted by means of ordinary legislation in the name of the "common good." Unlike the 1997 Constitution, the draft lacked articles prohibiting discrimination (Art. 32), guaranteeing the rights and liberties of citizens (Art. 5), protecting freedom of the press (Art. 14), and prohibiting compulsory participation in religious practices (Art. 53).

16. PiS retained the presidency until Lech Kaczynski's death in a plane crash in 2010. Lech's twin brother and PiS chairman Jarosław Kaczynski ran as a candidate in the special presidential elections that followed later that same year, but lost to the Civic Platform's Bronisław Komorowski.

17. The goal of "cultural counterrevolution" was explicitly mentioned, for example, during a joint press conference between Hungary's Prime Minister Viktor Orbán and Poland's leader Jarosław Kaczyński on September 6, 2016 in Krynica, Poland. See: http://wpolityce.pl/polityka/307451-polska-i-wegry-oglaszaja-kontrrewolucje-kulturalna-debata-kaczynski-orban-w-krynicy.

18. For example, the headline-making statement in a homily delivered on June 24, 2018, by the head of the Polish Episcopate was that "Europe is becoming a place of soft totalitarianism." (http://fakty.interia.pl/polska/news-abp-gadecki-europa-staje-sie-miejscem-miekkiej-wersji-totali,nId,2598424).

19. The PiS statute (http://pis.org.pl/document/archive/download/122) gives the chairman unlimited power to suspend members' rights (including the right to participate in internal votes and other decision-making processes), as well as nearly exclusive power of initiative (nothing can happen without his say-so).

20. According to the same IPSOS exit poll, 71.4 percent of Nowoczesna's voters were former PO voters, so Nowoczesna's appearance on the political scene was one of the several reasons for PO's poor showing. Another reason was demobilization of PO's electorate: in the 2015 PGSW survey, among those who reported not having voted in the last election, the single largest group by far (at 17.5 percent) were former PO voters.

21. The predicted probabilities were calculated from multinomial logistic regression results, controlling for gender, age, education, and urban vs. rural place of residence.

22. Writing about the American case, Mason (2018, 18) defines social sorting as "increasing social homogeneity within each party, such that religious, racial, and ideological divides tend to line up along partisan lines."

23. Because the Polish party system still features plenty of "top-down" volatility, this analysis looks only at the four parties that, despite experiencing various ups and downs, have remained on the political scene continuously since the turn of the millennium: Law and Justice (PiS), Civic Platform (PO), Democratic Left Alliance (SLD), and the Polish Peasants' Party (PSL).

24. If considering both "strongly agree" and "agree" responses together, PO supporters were still ahead, but the PO-PiS gap was narrower, between 4 and 10 points.

25. No similar question was asked in the 2007 edition of PGSW; however, in previous years (1997, 2001, and 2005) there was a question with the following possible responses: "1. Our political system is good and does not need any changes; 2. Our political system is basically good and needs only small changes; 3. Our political system is not too good and needs many changes; 4. Our political system is not good and needs major changes." The total proportion of responses in favor of systemic change (answers 3 plus 4) increased from 50 percent in 1997, to 66 percent in 2001, to 74 percent in 2005. So on one hand there was an increase in 2005, but on the other hand there had been an upward trend even before then.

26. See CBOS research bulletin 31/2014, "Polacy o gospodarce wolnorynkowej," https://cbos.pl/SPISKOM.POL/2014/K_031_14.PDF.

References

Abramowitz, Alan. 2010. *The disappearing center: Engaged citizens, polarization, and American democracy.* New Haven, CT: Yale University Press.

Acemoglu, Daron, and James A. Robinson. 2005. *Economic origins of dictatorship and democracy.* Cambridge: Cambridge University Press.

Batory Foundation. 2017. Jakość procesu stanowienia prawa w drugim roku rządów Prawa i Sprawiedliwości. Available from http://www.batory.org.pl/upload/files/Programy%20operacyjne/Odpowiedzialne%20Panstwo/X%20Komunikat_OFL.pdf.

Bernhard, Michael, Christopher Reenock, and Timothy Nordstrom. 2003. Economic performance and survival in new democracies: Is there a honeymoon effect? *Comparative Political Studies* 36 (4): 404–31.

Boix, Carles. 2003. *Democracy and redistribution*, Cambridge studies in comparative politics. Cambridge: Cambridge University Press.

Brzeziński, Michał. 2017. Is high inequality an issue in Poland. Instytut Badań Strukturalnych. Available from http://ibs.org.pl/app/uploads/2017/06/IBS_Policy_Paper_01_2017_en.pdf.

Bukowski, Pawel, and Filip Novokmet. 2017. Inequality in Poland: Estimating the whole distribution by g-percentile, 1983–2015. Available from http://wid.world/wp-content/uploads/2017/11/Bukowski_Novokmet_WP_WIDworld_2017_21.pdf.

Campbell, Angus, Philip E. Converse, Warren E. Miller, and Donald E. Stokes. 1960. *The American voter*. New York, NY: Wiley.

Carothers, Thomas. 2002. The end of the transition paradigm. *The Journal of Democracy* 13 (1): 5–21.

Chapman, Annabelle. 2017. Pluralism under attack: The assault on press freedom in Poland. Freedom House. Available from https://freedomhouse.org/sites/default/files/FH_Poland_Report_Final_2017.pdf.

Cienski, Jan. 14 October 2015. The corbynization of Polish politics. Available from http://www.politico.eu/article/poland-election-duda-kopacz-parliament-kaczynski-belka/.

Czapiński, Janusz, and Tomasz Panek. 2015. *Diagnoza społeczna: Warunki i jakość życia Polaków*. Warsaw: Rada Monitoringu Społecznego.

European Commission. 2016. Commission recommendation regarding the rule of law in Poland. Available from http://europa.eu/rapid/press-release_MEMO-16-2644_en.htm.

European Commission for Democracy Through Law (Venice Commission). 2016. Opinions on Amendments to the Act of 25 June 2015 on the Constitutional Tribunal. Available from http://www.venice.coe.int/webforms/documents/default.aspx?pdffile=CDL-AD%282016%299001-e.

Freedom House. 2017a. Freedom in the world 2017: Populists and Autocrats—The dual threat to global democracy. Available from https://freedomhouse.org/sites/default/files/FH_FIW_2017_Report_Final.pdf.

Freedom House. 2017b. Nations in transit 2017: The false promise of populism. Available from https://freedomhouse.org/report/nations-transit/nations-transit-2017.

Freedom House. 2018. Nations in transit 2018. Available from https://freedomhouse.org/sites/default/files/NiT2018_Poland_0.pdf.

Grossmann, Matt, and David A Hopkins. 2016. *Asymmetric politics: Ideological Republicans and group interest Democrats*. Oxford: Oxford University Press.

Hanley, Seán, and James Dawson. 3 January 2017. Poland was never as democratic as it looked. *Foreign Policy*. Available from https://foreignpolicy.com/2017/01/03/poland-was-never-as-democratic-as-it-looked-law-and-justice-hungary-orban/.

Inglehart, Ronald F., and Pippa Norris. 2016. Trump, Brexit, and the rise of populism: Economic have-nots and cultural backlash. Faculty Research Working Paper Series, RWP16-026: Harvard University, Kennedy School.

Jasiewicz, Krzysztof. 2009. The past is never dead: Identity, class, and voting behavior in contemporary Poland. *East European Politics & Societies* 23 (4): 491–508.

Jost, John T., and Orsolya Hunyady. 2005. Antecedents and consequences of system-justifying ideologies. *Current Directions in Psychological Science* 14 (5): 260–65.

Kapstein, Ethan B., and Nathan Converse. 2008. *The fate of young democracies*.1st ed. Cambridge: Cambridge University Press.

Levitsky, Steven, and Lucan A. Way. 2006. Linkage versus leverage. Rethinking the international dimension of regime change. *Comparative Politics* 38 (4): 379–400.

Linz, Juan J. 1990. The perils of presidentialism. *Journal of Democracy* 1 (1): 51–69.

Mainwaring, Scott, and Matthew S. Shugart. 1997. Juan Linz, presidentialism, and democracy: A critical appraisal. *Comparative Politics* 29 (4): 449–71.

Marcinkiewicz, Kamil, and Mary Stegmaier. 2016. The parliamentary election in Poland, October 2015. *Electoral Studies*. DOI: 10.1016/j.electstud.2016.01.004.

Marcinkiewicz, Kamil, and Mary Stegmaier. 11 January 2018. Democratic elections in Poland face a new threat. Available from https://www.washingtonpost.com/news/monkey-cage/wp/2018/01/11/free-elections-in-poland-face-new-threats-from-a-new-electoral-reform-bill/.

Markowski, Radoslaw. 2018. Poparcie dla PiS w liczbach bezwzględnych spada. Available from https://wiadomo.co/prof-radoslaw-markowski-poparcie-dla-pis-w-liczbach-bezwzglednych-spada/.

Markowski, Radosław. 2006. The Polish elections of 2005: Pure chaos or a restructing of the party system? *West European Politics* 29 (4): 814–32.

Markowski, Radosław. 2008. The 2007 Polish parliamentary elections: Some structuring, still a lot of chaos. *West European Politics* 31 (5): 1055–1068.

Markowski, Radosław, and Michał Kotnarowski. 2 February 2016. Dlaczego zadowoleni wybrali partię niezadowolenia. *Polityka*.

Markowski, Radosław, and Hubert Tworzecki. 2 March 2016. Czar silnej ręki. *Polityka*.

Mason, Lilliana. 2018. *Uncivil agreement: How politics became our identity*. Chicago, IL: University of Chicago Press.

McCoy, Jennifer, Tahmina Rahman, and Murat Somer. 2018. Polarization and the global crisis of democracy: Common patterns, dynamics, and pernicious consequences for democratic polities. *American Behavioral Scientist* 62 (1):16–42.

McDonnell, Duncan. 2016. Populist leaders and coterie charisma. *Political Studies* 64 (3): 719–33.

Mudde, Cas, and Cristóbal Rovira Kaltwasser. 2013. Exclusionary vs. inclusionary populism: Comparing contemporary Europe and Latin America. *Government and Opposition* 48 (2):147–74.

Novokmet, Filip, Thomas Piketty, and Gabriel Zocman. 2017. From Soviets to Oligarchs: Inequality and property in Russia 1905-2016. NBER Working Paper No. 23712.

Orenstein, Mitchell A. 2018. Populism with socialist characteristics. Available from https://www.project-syndicate.org/commentary/socialism-and-populism-in-poland-by-mitchell-a--orenstein-2018-06.

Panebianco, Angelo. 1988. *Political parties: Organization and power*. New York, NY: Cambridge University Press.

Pew Research Center. 2017. Globally, broad support for representative and direct democracy. But many also endorse nondemocratic alternatives. Available from http://www.pewglobal.org/2017/10/16/globally-broad-support-for-representative-and-direct-democracy/.

Piatkowski, Marcin. 2018. *Europe's growth champion: Insights from the economic rise of Poland*. Oxford: Oxford University Press.

Pierson, Paul. 2004. *Politics in time: History, institutions, and social analysis*. Princeton, NJ: Princeton University Press.

Polish Economic Institute. 2018. Capitalism-The Polish way: The Socio-Economic Model of the European Union's 6th Biggest Economy.

Przeworski, Adam. 2008. Self-enforcing democracy. In *The Oxford handbook of political economy*, eds. Barry R. Weingast and Donald Wittman, 312–28. Oxford: Oxford University Press.

Przeworski, Adam, Michael E. Alvarez, José Antônio Cheibub, and Fernando Limongi. 2000. *Democracy and development: Political institutions and well-being in the world, 1950–1990, Cambridge studies in the theory of democracy*. New York, NY: Cambridge University Press.

Rankin, Jennifer. 14 March 2017. Polish MEP punished for saying women are less intelligent than men. *The Guardian*. Available from https://www.theguardian.com/

Rustow, Dankwart A. 1970. Transitions to democracy: Toward a dynamic model. *Comparative Politics* 2 (3): 337–63.

Svolik, Milan W. 2013. Learning to love democracy: Electoral accountability and the success of democracy. *American Journal of Political Science* 57 (3): 685–702.

Svolik, Milan W. 2017. *When polarization trumps civic virtue: Partisan conflict and the subversion of democracy by incumbents*. New Haven, CT: Department of Political Science, Yale University.

U.S. Department of State. 2017. *Poland 2016 human rights report*. Washington, DC: U.S. Department of State. Available from http://www.state.gov/j/drl/rls/hrrpt/humanrightsreport/index.htm?year=2016&dlid=265460.

Tworzecki, Hubert. 2002. *Learning to choose: Electoral politics in East-Central Europe*. Stanford, CA: Stanford University Press.

Tworzecki, Hubert, and Radosław Markowski. 3 November 2015. Did Poland just vote in an authoritarian government? *Washington Post*. Available from https://www.washingtonpost.com/news/monkey-cage/wp/2015/11/03/did-poland-just-vote-in-an-authoritarian-government/

Tworzecki, Hubert, and Radosław Markowski. 26 July 2017. Why is Poland's Law and Justice Party trying to rein in the judiciary? *Washington Post*. Available from https://www.washingtonpost.com/news/monkey-cage/wp/2017/07/26/why-is-polands-law-and-justice-party-trying-to-rein-in-the-judiciary/.

Ulfelder, Jay. 2009. *Forecasting democratic transitions and breakdowns*. Rochester, NY: Social Science Research Network.

United Nations General Assembly. 2017. *Draft report of the Working Group on the Universal Periodic Review: Poland*. New York, NY: UN. Available from https://www.upr-info.org/sites/default/files/document/poland/session_27_-_may_2017/a_hrc_wg.6_27_l.12.pdf.

United Nations General Assembly. 2018. *Report of the Special Rapporteur on the independence of judges and lawyers on his mission to Poland*. New York, NY: UN. Available from http://ap.ohchr.org/documents/dpage_e.aspx?si=A/HRC/38/38/Add.1.

Wakslak, Cheryl J., John T. Jost, Tom R. Tyler, and Emmeline S. Chen. 2007. Moral outrage mediates the dampening effect of system justification on support for redistributive social policies. *Psychological Science* 18 (3): 267–74.

Wasik, Zosia, and Henry Foy. 15 September 2016. Immigrants pay for Poland's fiery rhetoric. *Financial Times*. Available from https://www.ft.com.

Webster, Steven W., and Alan I. Abramowitz. 2017. The ideological foundations of affective polarization in the U.S. electorate. *American Politics Research* 45 (4): 621–47.

III. Democratic Careening and Gridlock

Polarization Without Poles: Machiavellian Conflicts and the Philippines' Lost Decade of Democracy, 2000–2010

By
ARIES A. ARUGAY
and
DAN SLATER

The Philippines' long democratic experience has been remarkably free of deeply politicized cleavages. Roman Catholicism as a hegemonic religion prevents religious polarization, ethnic identity fragmentation limits ethnic polarization, and weak parties forestall ideological or class polarization. Nevertheless, the country suffered a crisis of polarization during the short-lived Estrada presidency (1998–2001) and that of his successor, Gloria Macapagal-Arroyo (2001–2010). The severe conflict was a product of power maneuvers by anti-Estrada forces, followed by anti-Arroyo actors returning the favor, given her gross abuses of power. Echoing Machiavelli's famous distinction, the conflict pitted Estrada's *popoli* (the many) against Arroyo's oligarchic *grandi* (the few). This Machiavellian conflict ended with an oligarchic reassertion of Madisonian democratic rule through the electoral victory of Benigno Simeon Aquino III in 2010. We conclude the article by considering whether the populist challenge of current president Rodrigo Duterte (2016–) might spark a similarly destabilizing conflict in the years to come.

Keywords: polarization; elite conflict; democratization; people power; Philippines

For a diverse and sprawling archipelagic nation, the Philippines has long been remarkably free of deep political cleavages along class, religious, ethnic, or ideological lines. Though it is beset with a protracted Maoist-inspired communist insurgency and a

Aries A. Arugay is an associate professor of political science and holds the One University of the Philippines Professorial Chair in Comparative Democratization. He is also co-convenor of the Strategic Studies Program, Center for Integrative and Development Studies, University of the Philippines.

Dan Slater is a professor of political science and the Ronald and Eileen Weiser Professor of Emerging Democracies and director of the Weiser Center for Emerging Democracies (WCED) at the University of Michigan. He was previously a professor of political science and sociology for 12 years at the University of Chicago.

Correspondence: aries.arugay@upd.edu.ph

DOI: 10.1177/0002716218810385

ANNALS, *AAPSS*, 681, January 2019

Muslim secessionist movement in Mindanao, neither of these challenges has developed into polarized conflict in national politics. Unlike many of its counterparts in the postcolonial world, the Philippines' social diversity has never led to inherent antagonism between major ethno-linguistic communities often considered to be raw material for polarization. Religious polarization was prevented after more than three centuries of Spanish colonial rule securely placed Roman Catholicism as the nation's hegemonic religion (Gryzmala-Busse and Slater 2018). Its democratic regime—arguably Asia's oldest—has always been ruled by rival political dynasties that prevent the development of mass-based and ideologically driven political parties. Despite widespread poverty and steep inequality, Philippine democracy has never polarized along class or left-right ideological lines. Nor did the Philippines' one brutal experience with dictatorship for 21 years produce the kind of regime cleavage—an enduring divide between former opponents and proponents of the outgoing authoritarian regime—that can polarize young democracies. Rather than realizing the promise of people power after toppling the regime of Ferdinand Marcos in 1986, Corazon Aquino reinstalled the elitist and low-intensity democracy of the pre-Marcos years, and former authoritarian elites have remained comfortably in the fold (Gills and Rocamora 1992).

From a macro and comparative perspective, then, the Philippines stands out as a case where high social diversity and wrenching inequality have surprisingly coexisted with low political polarization. Social cleavages are not tempered in the political realm by their cross-cutting character; they are simply not the foundation for democratic competition. The lesson is that democratic transitions need not polarize a population into bitter warring camps defined by social cleavages, even when the social raw material for such polarization appears self-evident and democratic competition is deeply entrenched. But this is not to say that the Philippines has never suffered pernicious polarization. In this article, we take the absence of politicized formative rifts in the Philippines as a rare opportunity to trace polarized conflict to political instead of social foundations (Somer and McCoy, this volume).

Wherever social and economic explanations for a political dysfunction fail to pass muster, politics itself is usually the culprit. Our resolutely political account for pernicious polarization is grounded in our theory of the *Machiavellian conflict*. Inspired by the political realist's seminal ideas in the *Discourses*, this kind of conflict emanates from the friction between the institutions dominated by the *grandi* (great/few) and the *popoli* (people/many). In polarizing regime crises, warring factions comprising both the elites and the masses fight over which democratic institutions should have the final say and who will command them. Instead of reflecting and representing deep-seated class antagonism, these polarizing conflicts are fueled by clashing preferences over which institutions of accountability—those fostering inclusion versus those striving to ensure constraint—should take priority in times when their sovereign powers and political roles come into direct conflict. In other words, both sides in a Machiavellian conflict combine elites and masses in cross-class coalitions, although the populist camp typically generates an advantage among the masses while oligarchic forces draw more heavily from upper and middle classes. What generates Machiavellian conflict is not polarization between elites and masses per se, but a power struggle between the followers of a directly elected leader who wishes to rule in plebiscitary fashion, and those siding with actors trying to block him with every institutional weapon in the democratic arsenal.

The next section lays the conceptual groundwork for our theory of Machiavellian conflict and specifies how it differs from what we call Madisonian conflict. In brief, both types of conflict center on perceived abuses of executive powers, but Madisonian conflicts do not pit one side with a decisive advantage among the *popoli* against the other. We then build empirically upon the conceptual foundations that underpin our notion of Machiavellian conflict through a case study of the Philippines during its "lost decade" of democracy, 2000–2010. Finally, we consider whether the populist challenge of current president Rodrigo Duterte might spark a similarly destabilizing Machiavellian conflict in the years to come.

Conceptual Foundations of Machiavellian Conflicts

Polarization can worsen through mechanisms and processes that are institutional rather than ideological or sociological (Slater and Arugay 2018). Simply put, polarization does not require poles. To shed light on why, we should first explain what we mean by *oligarchy, populism, vertical accountability*, and *horizontal accountability*.

Oligarchy is among the most essential concepts in political science—as essential, if not as often invoked, as *democracy*. Unlike recent research that "runs against the grain of ordinary usage and a mountain of scholarship in the social sciences" by defining oligarchy strictly as "the politics of wealth defense by materially endowed actors" (Winters 2011, 7–8), we return to a canonical definition of oligarchy as rule by the few in a manner that diminishes democracy. Yet we add new substance by portraying oligarchy as a type of regime in which vertical accountability is weaker than horizontal accountability. By vertical accountability, we mean inclusion of the populace. By horizontal accountability, we mean constraints against excessive concentrations of executive power. There is no good reason to argue that either type of accountability is more essential to democracy than the other. But there is also no good reason to believe that developing one kind of accountability will necessarily lead to the development of the other. Quite the contrary: elites who are enveloped in regular, routine relations of mutual constraint have less incentive to mobilize the masses than those who are coping with severe elite conflict, and elites who are able to mobilize the masses are especially likely to reject constraints imposed by elites who lack such popular appeal.

If the underdevelopment of inclusion spells oligarchy, the underdevelopment of constraints points toward populism. Jansen (2011) defines *populism* as "any sustained, large-scale political project that mobilizes ordinarily marginalized social sectors into publicly visible and contentious political action, while articulating an anti-elite, nationalist rhetoric that valorizes ordinary people" (p. 82). The concept thus nicely captures both a ravenous appetite for mass (vertical) inclusion and an intense distaste for elite (horizontal) constraints. Populism swings the sword of vertical accountability at oligarchs; oligarchy uses horizontal accountability as a shield against populists.

When oligarchs and populists clash over whether democracy depends more on including the masses or constraining the ruler, we call it a *Machiavellian conflict*. In his *Discourses*, a treatise about the life and death of republics, Machiavelli offered concrete institutional solutions to counter the natural tensions that arise from the proclivity of the *grandi* (the few) to dominate and oppress the *popoli* (the people). He also explained that the *popoli* express their desire not to be oppressed by insisting on protecting their liberty from the *grandi*. According to Machiavelli, the story of any democratic republic centers on the balance of power between these two camps, and political conflicts escalate when each side insists on its exclusive right to solely control democracy's fate. Herein lies the key difference between Machiavellian and Madisonian conflicts. The latter represent a less severe sort of destabilization in which democracy polarizes over the proper use of presidential powers without leaving the fate of mass inclusion hanging in the balance.

Though we draw heavily on Machiavelli, we depart from his arguments in three interrelated ways. First, in our view, a Machiavellian conflict is a battle between potentially antagonistic blocs of diverse political actors and organizations instead of coherent socioeconomic classes. We veer away from the reductionist and deterministic power of class and instead focus on the forces that mold these blocs.

This brings us to our second point. In a Machiavellian conflict, the *grandi* and *popoli* are not neatly defined classes but instead cross-class or cross-sectoral political coalitions forged and mobilized by leaders who represent forces associated with either oligarchic constraint or populist inclusion. Rather than being driven purely by class cleavages, Machiavellian conflicts are politicized conflicts between constellations of political forces that represent mutually antagonistic visions of democracy. In other words, the *grandi* and *popoli* are just potential blocs. Somebody needs to do the politics to build them (De Leon, Desai, and Tugal 2015). Finally, a Machiavellian conflict transpires in competing institutions in which blocs emphasize their supreme legitimacy vis-à-vis other institutions. In a nutshell, a Machiavellian conflict features different blocs doing democracy in different ways, through different institutions.

In the case of the Philippines, a Machiavellian conflict between *popoli*-backed proponents of inclusion and *grandi*-led defenders of constraints occurred during the first decade of the twenty-first century. Although the specter of regime collapse loomed large in this decade of "democratic careening" (Slater 2013), democracy survived and stabilized when oligarchs reestablished solid control over Philippine politics with the election of Benigno Simeon Aquino III in 2010.

Machiavellian Conflict and Democratic Careening in the Philippines

The 1986 "people power" revolution that ousted Ferdinand Marcos appeared to be a major democratic breakthrough for the Philippines. The country's nonviolent transition from a highly personalized authoritarian regime was a notable

exception to democracy's third wave, consisting mostly of changes through negotiated pacts or violent ruptures (O'Donnell and Schmitter 1986). True to form,
the sultanistic nature of the Marcos dictatorship foreshadowed the revolutionary
nature of the country's democratic transition (Linz and Stepan 1996). But, unlike
in Romania, Nicaragua, and Iran, the revolutionary overthrow of a sultanistic
regime in the Philippines was nonviolent and lacked a clear ideological imprint
(Schock 2005; Thompson 2004).

Political actors who espoused radical ideologies had little leverage, paving the
way for an eclectic opposition coalition that centered on the leadership of wid-
owed housewife turned opposition leader Corazon Aquino. How were she and her
allies able to outmaneuver a powerful communist movement and an even more
formidable military? As leader of the opposition and presidential contender,
Aquino commanded the crowds gathered in Epifanio de los Santos Avenue
(EDSA)[1] and also had the support of civil society groups that formed after her
husband's assassination in 1983 (Thompson 1995). Her coalition of forces was also
far more cohesive than the more ideologically inclined alternatives such as a factionalized military and an increasingly divided left movement (Lee 2009;
Rocamora 1994). This source of legitimacy prevented communists and the
military—the Philippines' extreme left and extreme right poles—from grabbing
power, since they both believed that Aquino could easily mobilize civil society
against them (Boudreau 2009; Mendoza 2009). Democracy was not only the great
compromise between a military junta and a socialist regime; it was the only familiar political framework acceptable for both Filipino elites and the masses.[2]

Democratic compromise was facilitated by a lack of formative rifts splitting the
Philippine citizenry into sharply divided camps. To some degree, such rifts are
absent because Catholicism unifies the vast majority of the population, swamping
more divisive potential lines of identification. As David Steinberg puts it,
"Philippine nationalism, the Philippine identity, the Filipinos' value system, and
the economic and social fabric of the society are all directly linked to the Roman
Catholic experience" (Steinberg 1982, 83). Churches with deep national influence tend not to lose their moral authority unless they pick sides in partisan battles, especially by siding with dictators when the public rises up to oppose them
(Grzymala-Busse 2015). The Philippine Catholic Church made no such misstep
(Youngblood 1990). Moreover, the Catholic-Muslim divide is irrelevant to
national politics since the Muslim minority is too geographically peripheral and
numerically overwhelmed to become a claimant or forge a cleavage at a national
scale. The upshot is that identity politics in the Philippines is remarkably muted,
despite the archipelago's considerable ethnic and linguistic variety as well as its
geographically fragmented populace.

While the Philippines' historic lack of formative rifts augured a nonpolarized
democracy, its mode of transition could easily have given rise to a regime cleavage
between Marcos regime stalwarts and opposition leaders. The 1986 EDSA
uprising ended authoritarian rule and restored democracy, but it also contained a
revolutionary promise. Instead of being transformed into a catalyst for institution-
building and deep democratization, however, people power started and ended in
the streets. Aquino and her oligarchic political coalition further restored a

"cacique democracy" (Anderson 1988), marred by elite dominance, patronage politics, and social injustice (Timberman 1991). Aquino's successor, Fidel Ramos, prioritized political stability and economic progress over addressing the democratic deficits found in the Philippine political system (Hutchcroft and Rocamora 2003). For almost two decades, the Philippine political arena had no dominant majority party driven by ideology, ethnicity, or any other social cleavage. Just like it was before martial law, post-1986 democracy was defined by the personality of the president as the ultimate dispenser of patronage propped up by factions of a "wild" oligarchy unbounded by power-sharing pacts or shared norms (Quimpo 2015). However, the oligarchy generally lent support to the courts, the legislature, and other institutions of horizontal accountability. In addition, it did not overtly undermine the press, curtail civil liberties, or stifle civil society's involvement in politics. But for the first decade-plus of restored democracy in the Philippines, oligarchy was the order of the day, and vertical accountability between the elected and the electors—in a word, inclusivity—was badly attenuated.

The rise of Estrada and the populist challenge

In 1998, Joseph Ejercito Estrada, a movie actor turned politician, was elected the 13th president of the Philippines, garnering 40 percent of the national vote. His victory invalidated the ever-reliable formula for winning the presidency—a strong and extensive political machinery and patronage network—by directly appealing to Filipino voters (Hedman 2001). In a state where parties are merely window dressing for political clans, Estrada challenged the oligarchy through a combination of sheer charisma and populist appeals that resonated among lower classes who formed more than 70 percent of the country's population.

Estrada also defied the mold of a typical Philippine president. In the past, the Filipino electorate conventionally chose between candidates who were well-educated, morally upright, politically pedigreed, and affluent. His background and track record were belittled by the country's upper classes but emphatically embraced by the poor masses. Intellectuals sympathetic to Estrada interpreted his rise as an indication that the *grandi's* grip over the country's politics was loosening (David 2001). Far from being a mere Marcos proxy seeking a return to exclusivist authoritarian rule, Estrada set his sights on redrawing the map of Philippine politics in a more deeply inclusivist democratic mold.

Estrada's populist domineering and the grandi's reaction

The newly elected president wasted no time, starting his administration by espousing proposals construed as highly contentious, unpopular, and potentially polarizing. For example, Estrada's proposal to move Marcos's body from a cemetery in Hawaii to the National Heroes Cemetery and bury him there with complete military honors was met with severe public criticism (Doronila 2001).

Further provoking his critics, the president flouted the idea of amending the 1987 Constitution. A product of the anti-dictatorship struggle, that charter largely represented the bare democratic consensus mostly shaped by the Filipino *grandi*. Estrada sought to eliminate the constitutional provisions protecting national patrimony by allowing foreigners to own land, extract resources, and compete equally with domestic business, a move that severely threatened oligarchic economic interests. Opposition quickly formed with the aid of civil society groups that rallied public opinion against the proposal. Declining approval ratings, accompanied by a massive mobilization of social forces led by former president Corazon Aquino, the Catholic Church, middle classes, and the political opposition, forced Estrada to scrap this project (Arugay 2004). These two instances highlight how Estrada's legitimacy, which came from the marginalized sectors of Filipino society, was beginning to be challenged by the displaced members of the country's postauthoritarian political establishment.

Populist leaders rarely maintain good relations with the media, though the media's attention often fuels their rise to prominence. Estrada loved, and was loved by, the local press until it started running negative stories about him, featuring unflattering photos on front pages and relentless criticism. Scorned by a media largely owned by the *grandi*, Estrada waged war against members of the press by punishing them for unfavorable reportage that included exposés about government irregularities (Coronel 1999).

Estrada's involvement in rent-seeking from illicit activities marked the peak of his executive domineering. He was allegedly receiving millions in kickbacks for allowing illegal gambling operations around the country (de Dios 2001). Opposition and civil society leaders used this allegation, made by the president's former ally, Governor Luis Singson, as a rallying point to demand accountability. The resulting public outrage changed the populist leader's fate for the worse.

Oligarchic reassertion and people power redux

The *grandi*-led coalition against Estrada was headed by political veterans from the 1986 People Power Revolution, such as Archbishop of Manila Jaime Cardinal Sin, considered the leader of the Catholic Church, and ex-president Corazon Aquino. These credible moral leaders revived the dormant and dispersed opposition led by Vice-President Gloria Macapagal-Arroyo. Previously weak and fragmented minority parties united to challenge Estrada's legitimacy. The extent of Estrada's alleged corruption also led some of his party mates to desert his coalition. All these factors contributed to a highly charged political atmosphere by October 2000, which some civil society groups used to their advantage. The formerly small anti-Estrada movement quickly swelled to a broad societal coalition (Arugay 2004). The stage was set for a confrontation between two blocs, with Estrada, the entire government apparatus, and his loyal mass supporters on one side; and Arroyo, middle-class civil society, Catholic groups, and progressive social movements on the other.

Estrada and Arroyo became the centripetal forces behind these two highly polarized blocs, neither of which was solely defined by an ideological, social, ethnic, religious, or class cleavage. Their first confrontation was in the streets of Manila, with each bloc occupying a major demonstration site. This instigated pendular mobilizations across the country.

The conflicting Arroyo and Estrada blocs competed for popular support. The Arroyo bloc, mostly comprising the country's *grandi*, represented only one segment of the country's dense and robust civil society. Estrada's government successfully elicited support from other segments. In one major rally, Estrada gave a fiery speech in which he accused the elites of conspiring to unseat him but also promised to face the corruption charges against him at an appropriate time and venue.

In this regard, civil society itself was politically divided between the two blocs. Those who harbored more liberal visions of democracy supported by the oligarchy were pitted against a more grassroots but less organized segment of civil society aiming to protect the electoral mandate of a president they put in power. The Arroyo bloc had, at least momentarily, the upper hand in mobilization, but Estrada still had the full support of the military and other political institutions. The top brass of the armed forces continued to respect Estrada's electoral mandate while recognizing that an emerging bloc of social and political actors was bent on challenging his legitimacy.

In Estrada's view, he was a victim of the *grandi's* penchant for opposing the people's leadership choices. He reduced the brewing polarization to a question of class, albeit portrayed in populist rather than Marxist or left-right terms. But this oversimplified the Machiavellian conflict. The allegations of corruption focused on Estrada's accumulation of wealth, real estate, and other assets for himself, his family, and cronies that could have been used instead to help his poor constituency. Estrada downplayed being subjected to horizontal accountability as he refused to address the allegations. In turn, he overemphasized his electoral mandate, presenting himself as the sole representative of the country' *popoli*.

The rival mobilizations had historical resonance with the polarized conflict between the Marcos and Aquino blocs that ended in the 1986 People Power uprising. This time around, however, democracy was careening rather than being restored. Both sides saw the other bloc as the enemy of democracy and their own bloc as democracy's saviors. Instead of class cleavages, the dichotomy centered on whose vision of democracy should triumph and which democratic institutions should prevail. In other words, Philippine democracy was deadlocked by two equally powerful political blocs insisting on their own version of democracy, with one skewed toward oligarchy while the other embraced populism (Slater and Arugay 2018).

These rival elite factions exaggerated a conflict that was likely not seen or felt across the country. An opinion survey conducted in October 2000 revealed that only 29 percent of the public thought Estrada should resign, while 44 percent believed he should remain in office (see Table 1).

The impasse in the streets led the Arroyo bloc, which had been increasing in density and strength by the day, to shift the site of struggle toward the country's institutions of horizontal accountability. Presidential impeachment is the most important mechanism of horizontal accountability in Philippine democracy. The implosion of Estrada's coalition in the House of Representatives paved the way for his impeachment and allowed the Senate to conduct a trial to determine whether the president was guilty of corruption.

TABLE 1
Opinion on Whether Estrada Should Resign

		Area/Region				Class		
	RP	NCR	Luzon	Visayas	Mindanao	ABC	D	E
Agree	29	32	29	40	19	41	31	19
Disagree	44	51	42	33	56	39	42	53
Don't know enough	26	18	30	27	25	20	27	28
Net agreement[a]	–15	–19	–13	+7	–36	+2	–11	–34

[a]For greater precision, net agreements (% Agree minus % Disagree) are first computed before figures are rounded off.
SOURCE: Social Weather Stations (SWS) survey conducted from October 26–30, 2000 (https://www.sws.org.ph/swsmain/artcldisppage/?artcsyscode=ART-20160105135957).
Luzon, Visayas, and Mindanao are the country's main island groups. RP: Republic of the Philippines (entire country); NCR: National Capital Region (NCR) (better known as Metro Manila).

The sheer stress and pernicious sociopolitical polarization engendered by the first ever presidential impeachment trial in Asia eventually led to institutional gridlock. The Senate, a twenty-four-member body, was itself polarized between Estrada and Arroyo factions, making it difficult to secure the two-thirds vote necessary to convict the president. The Filipino public patiently allowed this horizontal accountability mechanism to run its course until a critical point: when members of Estrada's bloc among the senator-jurors suppressed important evidence that directly linked the president to corruption. The impeachment process immediately unraveled: the Senate president resigned, while the prosecution team abruptly left the court's premises to show their common disgust. The resignation was a clear symbol of the breakdown of the impeachment process as the sole constitutional means to settle the Machiavellian conflict that had paralyzed the country (Doronila 2001).

The unraveling of the impeachment process showed that formal institutions designed to constrain executive power had failed within the context of a Machiavellian conflict. Both blocs, representing oligarchy and populism, respectively, mutually decided to withdraw from the only constitutional means of resolving the crisis. But rather than an outright military coup from the conservative right, a violent revolution by the communist left, or an *autogolpe*[3] by the incumbent government, the outcome followed a familiar path—a reinstatement of oligarchic-liberal order through people power (Thompson 2008).

Though led by social forces mainly drawn from the middle class, the second People Power uprising had a peculiarly eclectic class character (Rivera 2001), with significant representation from the organized segments of the poor and marginalized social sectors. Also, the popular outrage expressed in the demonstrations reverberated beyond "imperial Manila," sending ripples of discontent around the archipelago (Reyes 2001). What it shared with its predecessor in 1986 was the organized and nonviolent character of the protests, which civil society leaders thought was necessary to get rid of Estrada. A breakout of violence could not only rob "people power" of its legitimacy, it might also give the government the necessary justification to disperse the crowd or, worse, declare martial law (Hernandez 2001).

Apart from the dramatic display of collective action, the Arroyo bloc, with the help of civil society figures, brokered a seemingly solid coup coalition with Estrada's other political enemies, as well as with groups that had extensive links to the military and the judiciary. The armed forces and the Supreme Court are considered as historically powerful veto players in Philippine politics, and they proved to be critical chess pieces in an otherwise deadlocked game between the two poles. This extraconstitutional resolution to the Machiavellian conflict demonstrated how unelected veto players in Philippine politics can decisively shift the balance of power between oligarchic and populist forces in Philippine democracy.

The popoli's backlash against the grandi's coup

The January 2001 People Power revolt received praise at home but fierce criticism abroad. Many summarily judged Estrada's overthrow to be a "popularly supported coup" conjured by political elites, the military, and opportunist business groups against a duly elected executive (Mydans 2000). Though this nonviolent upheaval was deemed extra-constitutional, the leadership change it occasioned did not result in a breakdown of the democratic regime. In the face of captured and feeble political institutions, Estrada's opponents were seeking to restore the oligarchic liberal order through alternative means of seeking accountability (Arugay 2005).

Far from resolving political conflict, Estrada's ouster subjected the country to further political instability. Rather than "re-equilibrating" Philippine democracy, it opened the floodgates for contentious politics, a crackdown on political freedoms, weak institutions, and a politicized military (Hutchcroft 2008).

Among the violent episodes in this drawn-out Machiavellian conflict between defenders of Philippine oligarchic democracy and counter-elite challengers with populist tendencies was a massive protest of pro-Estrada supporters in May 2001. Though their short-lived uprising was brutally repressed by the military, it displayed the mobilizational power of the Filipino *popoli*, who felt aggrieved when their elected president was extra-constitutionally removed by the *grandi* (Garrido 2008).

This mobilization aiming to restore Estrada to power was led by displaced political elites who alluded to the conspiratorial nature of the populist leader's removal. From the popoli's view, Estrada's degrading treatment in the hands of the elites who toppled him compelled them to take action by reclaiming Philippine democracy in a way previously owned by the *grandi*: people power (Schaffer 2008).

The highly emotional nature of the protest turned the gathered crowd into an angry mob that stormed the presidential palace now occupied by Arroyo. With the backing of the armed forces, Arroyo deployed several thousand soldiers to protect her fragile government deficient in procedural legitimacy. A "state of rebellion" was officially declared, allowing for numerous warrantless arrests of members of the Estrada bloc who had incited the siege.

The violence revealed other variants of people power, whose narrative was dominated by its nonviolent version in 1986. Machiavelli's claim in the *Discourses* that the *popoli* rise up when they feel aggrieved and oppressed proved true. And, though Estrada turned out to be an ineffective populist, this popular backlash represented resentment and longing for another vision of democracy previously untapped by the country's *grandi*. For the masses who belonged to the Estrada bloc, his prosecution for corruption was an unfair and selective application of democratic accountability, since the deposed president was not the only corrupt politician in the country.

In a Machiavellian conflict, those representing populism also succumb to the pressures of elitist principles, as established in Michels' iron law of oligarchy.[4] The Estrada bloc was at best another faction of elites who wanted to wrest power from the oligarchs who dominated Philippine politics. The pernicious polarization that started with Estrada's populist challenge was not resolved by his removal. The extraconstitutional installation of Arroyo set off a series of events that intensified the conflict, emboldened all political actors, and further polarized the country around these hostile yet nonideological blocs. The collective action that aimed to restore Estrada also revealed the impurities associated with populist challenges. Because the challenger bloc lacked a coherent ideology or shared identity that could push for a meaningful alternative to oligarchic democracy, it also succumbed to the same elitist, undemocratic, and exclusionary features that fed into the resentment against Philippine democracy.

Oligarchic re-equilibration and Aquino's electoral victory

In a Machiavellian conflict, blocs that center on personalities tend to implode, possibly leading to the creation of new blocs within the old ones. The fate of the precarious Arroyo bloc hung in the balance during the president's attempt to gain electoral legitimacy during the 2004 presidential elections. In the end, Arroyo prevailed by a narrow margin in a bitter contest against a candidate who acted as Estrada's political proxy.

This electoral polarization represented continued gridlock between the opposing Estrada and Arroyo forces. Shortly after the violent repression of a pro-Estrada riot, Filipinos went to the polls for the 2001 senate elections. The campaign leading to the elections mirrored the lingering political divide as Arroyo's senatorial ticket (her party calling itself the People Power Coalition) went head to head against Estrada's political bloc, known as *Pwersa ng Masa* (Force of the Masses). The election, considered to be a referendum on the legitimacy of Arroyo's government, produced inconclusive results, as Estrada's candidates, one of whom was his wife, won four of the thirteen slots.

The elections did not fully recalibrate to a pre-Estrada elite democracy in the Philippines. On the contrary, the Arroyo administration continued to stand on shaky political foundations after a damning electoral fraud scandal. The resignation of several cabinet officials further inflamed Arroyo's crisis of authority, though it did not diffuse to other political institutions such as the military and the bureaucracy. Civil society, however, was unable to provide the mobilizational power to create a semblance of a new Machiavellian conflict. The extraconstitutional nature of Estrada's removal dissuaded some of them from embarking on a similar initiative against Arroyo (Tolosa 2009).

Attempts to stoke a Machiavellian conflict by conjuring an anti-Arroyo bloc proved futile. Though hugely unpopular, her government was politically strategic in coopting the country's weak institutions—military, legislature, civil society, church, judiciary, and bureaucracy. The anti-Arroyo coalition was best described as a hodgepodge of familiar forces that, for the most part, made strange bedfellows. It ultimately stagnated into a few disgruntled ex-Arroyo bloc members alongside the remnants of Estrada's bloc. Once on opposite sides of the political fence, the pro-Estrada forces and those responsible for his downfall were now part of a movement unified by a narrow goal—the removal of the beleaguered president by means fair or foul. The unwieldy alliance lacked a consensus on two significant components: a feasible alternative to Arroyo and an acceptable means of leadership change (Rocamora 2007).

The fragmented opposition showed political weakness in its inability to impeach Arroyo. It also resorted to soliciting the support of some military generals, but that effort likewise failed. The last serious attempt to destabilize Arroyo, in February 2006, failed because civil society groups could not effectively recruit protest participants. The coalition was unable to persuade the poor masses who once belonged to Estrada's *popoli* that this was also their fight. The drive to remove Arroyo appeared to be another intra-elite affair that had no direct value or consequence in the masses' daily lives (Abinales and Amoroso 2006).

Like the patterns Bermeo (2003) observed in Latin America, the noisy protests merely reflected polarization among the elites that did not necessarily translate to the larger public. The *popoli* who chose to join any of the competing blocs seemed tired from the battles between factions of the country's political class. The 2010 elections would constitute an oligarchic reconsolidation with the victory of former president Corazon Aquino's firstborn, Benigno Simeon, as president, largely due to his political pedigree rather than his competence or track record.

Conclusion and Prospects for Polarization under Duterte

The Philippines' long experience with democratic rule did not spare it from a decade of pernicious polarization at the turn of the century. This polarization was not driven by formative rifts along religious, social, or ethnic lines; nor did economic or ideological divides cleave the overwhelmingly Catholic country in two. Rather, democracy suffered a major setback when political conflict among warring elites led to mobilizations, institutional crises, and extraconstitutional attempts to transfer executive power. The period of 2000–2010 was a lost decade for Philippine democracy as it careened between outright collapse and successful consolidation. But unlike so many other polarized nations, the Philippines recalibrated its democracy after the *grandi* decisively triumphed with the election of one of Filipino oligarchy's own as president in 2010.

With formative rifts absent in the Philippines' long history as Asia's oldest republic, political polarization could arise along such lines. Thus the Philippines defies conventional wisdom, because polarized conflict there was mainly elite-driven and devoid of identity cleavages. Instead, it was a conflict between more established oligarchic forces and a populist challenge that emanated from a disgruntled set of political elites. The oligarchy's rejection of Estrada was the impetus for the Machiavellian conflict in which he used the *popoli* to rally against the *grandi* who deprived him of his rightful place in the country's political landscape. Relying on unbridled majoritarian impulses, Estrada maximized executive prerogatives. This threatened the *grandi*, who threw everything in their liberal arsenal against the populist president. In the end, they had to again invoke people power, an extraconstitutional device that nonviolently deposed the president but opened the floodgates for pernicious polarization.

Estrada's removal from power awoke the *popoli*, who mobilized for the leader's re-installment and refused to grant his successor any modicum of legitimacy. When the anti-Estrada pole, led by Arroyo, imploded in 2004, the *grandi* found themselves at war with one another. In the attempt to oust Arroyo, the *grandi* tried to use the aggrieved *popoli* against her, but to no avail. The continuation of the Machiavellian conflict did not result in Arroyo's removal, but her presidency will be best remembered as unstable, illegitimate, and less than democratic.

Thus in 2010, Philippine democracy returned to its oligarchic mold. But the previously dormant *popoli's* consciousness was revived with Rodrigo Duterte's ascension to the presidency in 2016. Considered a political maverick, this populist president has ruled without regard for checks on executive power, civil liberties, and other liberal instruments. His emphasis on law and order struck a chord among the Filipino majority, who blamed the oligarchic elite for the country's poor governance. This has opened up the possibility that relations between Duterte and opposition elites will descend into a Machiavellian conflict in the future. Duterte's government has already moved to undermine human rights and curb the powers of accountability institutions, including the removal of the Supreme Court's Chief Justice. However, the possibility of pernicious polarization largely depends on the extent to which politics will be defined by Duterte's *hubris* and the opposition's impatience (Arugay 2017). So far, Duterte has not mobilized his popular constituency against his political opponents in a manner similar to other populist leaders such as Hugo Chávez of Venezuela or Thaksin Shinawatra of Thailand. But if the *grandi* either cannot organize themselves in self-defense or cannot generate mass support to help them block the highly popular leader's power grabs, Philippine democracy might not just career as it did in the 2000s; this time, it might actually collapse.

Notes

1. The main highway linking the various cities and municipalities that make up Metro Manila and the site of the popular uprising against the Marcos dictatorship.

2. For Huntington (1991), democratization in the Philippines resembled an interrupted democracy pattern where the martial law regime was an authoritarian interlude between episodes of democratic rule from 1946 to 1971 and 1986 onwards. During the first period, two parties (Nacionalista Party and Liberal Party) took turns in governing the country.

3. A Spanish term meaning "autocoup" or self-coup.

4. This law states that all organizations, even those committed to democratic principles and norms, eventually succumb to the control of an elite few (Michels 1962).

References

Abinales, Patricio N., and Donna J. Amoroso. 2006. The withering of Philippine democracy. *Current History* 696:290–5.

Anderson, Benedict. 1998. Cacique democracy in the Philippines: Origins and dreams. *New Left Review* 169 (3): 3–31.

Arugay, Aries A. 2017. The Philippines in 2016: The electoral earthquake and its aftershocks. In *Southeast Asian affairs*, eds. Malcolm Cook and Daljut Singh, 277–96. Singapore: ISEAS Yusof Ishak Institute.

Arugay, Aries A. 2004. Mobilizing for accountability: Contentious politics in the anti- Estrada campaign. *Philippine Sociological Review* 52:75–96.

Arugay, Aries A. 2005. The accountability deficit in the Philippines: Implications and prospects for democratic consolidation. *Philippine Political Science Journal* 26 (49): 63–88.

Bermeo, Nancy. 2003. *Ordinary people in extraordinary times*. Princeton, NJ: Princeton University Press.

Boudreau, Vincent. 2009. Elections, repression and authoritarian survival in post- transition Indonesia and the Philippines. *Pacific Review* 22 (2): 233–53.

Coronel, Sheila S. 1999. Lords of the press. I: *The Investigative Reporting Magazine* 5 (2).

David, Randolf S. 2001. Erap: A diary of disenchantment. In *Between fires: Fifteen perspectives on the Estrada crisis*, ed. Amando Doronila, 148–79. Pasig: Anvil Publishing, Inc.

De Dios, Emmanuel S. 2001. Corruption and the fall. In *Between fires: Fifteen perspectives on the Estrada crisis*, ed. Amando Doronila, 43–61. Pasig: Anvil Publishing, Inc.

De Leon, Cedric, Manali Desai, and Cihan Tugal, eds. 2015. *Building blocs: How parties organize society*. Stanford, CA: Stanford University Press.

Doronila, Amando. 2001. *The fall of Joseph Estrada: The inside story*. Pasig: Anvil Publishing Inc.

Garrido, Marco. 2008. Civil and uncivil society symbolic boundaries and civic exclusion in metro Manila. *Philippine Studies* 56 (4): 443–65.

Gills, Barry, and Joel Rocamora. 1992. Low intensity democracy. *Third World Quarterly* 13 (3): 501–23.

Grzymala-Busse, Anna. 2015. *Nations under God: How churches use moral authority to influence policy*. Princeton, NJ: Princeton University Press.

Grzymala-Busse, Anna, and Dan Slater. 2018. Making Godly nations: Church-state pathways in Poland and the Philippines. *Comparative Politics* 50 (3): 545–64.

Hedman, Eva-Lotta E. 2001. The spectre of populism in Philippine politics and society: Artista, masa, eraption! *South East Asia Research* 9 (1): 5–44.

Hernandez, Carolina G. 2001.Reflections on the role of the military in people power 2. In *Between fires: Fifteen perspectives on the Estrada crisis*, ed. Amando Doronila, 67–77. Pasig: Anvil Publishing, Inc.

Hutchcroft, Paul. D. 2008. The Arroyo Imbroglio in the Philippines. *Journal of Democracy* 19 (1): 141–55.

Hutchcroft, Paul D., and Joel Rocamora. 2003. Strong demands and weak institutions: The origins and evolution of the democratic deficit in the Philippines. *Journal of East Asian Studies* 3 (2): 259–92.

Jansen, Robert. 2011. Populist mobilization: A new theoretical approach to populism. *Sociological Theory* 29 (2): 75–96.

Lee, Terence. 2009. The armed forces and transitions from authoritarian rule explaining the role of the military in 1986 Philippines and 1998 Indonesia. *Comparative Political Studies* 42 (5): 640–69.

Linz, Juan J., and Alfred Stepan. 1996. *Problems of democratic transition and consolidation: Southern Europe, South America, and post-communist Europe*. Baltimore, MD: Johns Hopkins University Press.

Mendoza, Amado Jr. 2009. "People Power" in the Philippines, 1983–86. In *Civil resistance and power politics: The experience of non-violent action from Gandhi to the present*, eds. Adam Roberts and Timothy Garton Ash, 179–96. Oxford: Oxford University Press.

Michels, Robert. 1962. *Political parties: A sociological study of the oligarchic tendencies of modern democracy*. New York, NY: Collier Books.

Mydans, Seth. 5 February 2000. Expecting praise, Filipinos are criticized for ouster. *New York Times*.

O'Donnell, Guillermo, and Philippe C. Schmitter. 1986. *Transitions from authoritarian rule: Tentative conclusions about uncertain democracies*. Baltimore, MD: Johns Hopkins University Press.

Quimpo, Nathan. 2015. Can the Philippines' wild oligarchy be tamed? In *The Routledge handbook of Southeast Asian Democratization*, ed. William Cas, 335–50. London: Routledge.

Reyes, Ricardo B. 2001. People power comes into the new millennium. *Political Brief* 9 (2): 1–30.

Rivera, Temario C. 2001. The middle classes and democratization in the Philippines: From the Asian crisis to the ouster of Estrada. In *The Southeast Asian Middle classes: Democratization and social change*, ed. Abdul Rahman Embong, 230–61. Kuala Lumpur: Universiti Kebangsaan Malaysia.

Rocamora, Joel. 2007. From regime crisis to system change. In *Whither the Philippines in the 21st century?* eds. Rodolfo Severino and Lorraine Carlos Salazar, 18–42. Singapore: Institute of Southeast Asian Studies.

Rocamora, Joel. 1994. *Breaking through: The struggle within the Communist Party of the Philippines*. Pasig: Anvil Publishing, Inc.

Schaffer, Frederic Charles. 2008. *The hidden costs of clean election reform*. Ithaca, NY: Cornell University Press.

Schock, Kurt. 2005. *Unarmed insurrections: People power movements in nondemocracies*. Minneapolis, MN: University of Minnesota Press.

Slater, Dan. 2013. Democratic careening. *World Politics* 65 (4): 729–63.

Slater, Dan, and Aries A. Arugay. 2018. Polarizing figures: Executive power and institutional conflict in Asian democracies. *American Behavioral Scientist* 62 (1): 92–106.

Steinberg, David Joel. 1982. *The Philippines, a singular and a plural place*. Boulder, CO: Westview Press.

Thompson, Mark R. 2008. People power sours: Uncivil society in Thailand and the Philippines. *Current History* 107 (712): 381–87.

Thompson, Mark R. 2004. *Democratic revolutions: Asia and Eastern Europe*. London: Routledge.

Thompson, Mark R. 1995. *The anti-Marcos struggle: Personalistic rule and democratic transition in the Philippines*. New Haven, CT: Yale University Press.

Timberman, David G. 1991. *A changeless land: Continuity and change in Philippine politics*. Singapore: Institute of Southeast Asian Studies.

Tolosa, Benjamin T. 2009. Framing the challenges of political empowerment and engagement: Ideational interventions for democratization since 2005. In *Agenda for hope: Democratizing governance*, eds. Agustin Martin G. Rodriguez and Teresita Asuncion M. Lacandula, 49–75. Quezon City: Ateneo de Manila University Press.

Winters, Jeffrey. 2011. *Oligarchy*. New York, NY: Cambridge University Press.

Youngblood, Robert. 1990. *Marcos against the church: Economic development and political repression in the Philippines*. Ithaca, NY: Cornell University Press.

United States: Racial Resentment, Negative Partisanship, and Polarization in Trump's America

ALAN ABRAMOWITZ
and
JENNIFER McCOY

Growing racial, ideological, and cultural polarization within the American electorate contributed to the shocking victory of Donald Trump in the 2016 presidential election. Using data from American National Election Studies surveys, we show that Trump's unusually explicit appeals to racial and ethnic resentment attracted strong support from white working-class voters while repelling many college-educated whites along with the overwhelming majority of nonwhite voters. However, Trump's campaign exploited divisions that have been growing within the electorate for decades because of demographic and cultural changes in American society. The 2016 presidential campaign also reinforced another longstanding trend in American electoral politics: the rise of negative partisanship, that is voting based on hostility toward the opposing party and its leaders. We conclude with a discussion of the consequences of deepening partisan and affective polarization for American democracy and the perceptions by both experts and the public of an erosion in its quality.

Keywords: polarization; Donald Trump; 2016 presidential election; political parties; realignment

Donald Trump's victory in the 2016 presidential election was one of the most shocking upsets in American electoral history. Perhaps more than any presidential candidate since George Wallace in 1968, and certainly more than any major party candidate in the past 60 years, Donald Trump's candidacy reinforced some of the deepest social and cultural

Alan Abramowitz is Alben W. Barkley Professor of Political Science at Emory University. As a specialist in American elections, voting behavior, and public opinion, he has authored or coauthored seven books, dozens of contributions to edited volumes, and more than 50 articles in political science journals. His most recent book is The Great Alignment: Race, Party Transformation and the Rise of Donald Trump *(Yale University Press 2018).*

Correspondence: polsaa@emory.edu

DOI: 10.1177/0002716218811309

divisions within the American electorate—those based on race and religion. Nevertheless, it was, in many ways, the natural outgrowth of the racial, cultural, and ideological realignment that has transformed the American party system and the American electorate since the 1960s. Divides between a shrinking white majority and fast-growing nonwhite minority; values, morality, and lifestyles; and views about the proper role and size of government have been mirrored in the political parties (Abramowitz 2018).

The movement of white working class voters from the Democratic camp to the Republican camp has been going on since at least 1964, when Lyndon Johnson firmly aligned the Democratic Party with the cause of civil rights for African Americans. The movement of white evangelicals and other religious conservatives has been going on since at least 1980, when Ronald Reagan and the Republican Party came out for the repeal of Roe v. Wade.[1]

These voter shifts and the Southern Democratic political party realignment in the 1970s and 1980s led to increased party polarization in the 1990s and 2000s as Americans sorted into more ideologically homogeneous political parties, perceived the parties as growing further apart on policies, and their representatives in Congress voted in more lock-step party unity roll-call votes (Campbell 2016; Pew Research 2016). Within the electorate, the growing affective polarization (sympathy to the in-party and antipathy toward the out-party) accelerated after Barack Obama was elected in 2008 as the first African American biracial president, giving voice to an underrepresented minority with a long history of discrimination.

Obama's presidency disappointed those who hoped that the United States had entered a postracial political era. Instead, political scientists determined that racial resentment, ethno-nationalism, and racial prejudice played a major role in predicting voting choice among whites in the next two presidential elections, costing Obama votes in his second election in 2012 and lending votes to Trump in 2016 (Abramowitz 2016; Knuckey and Kim 2015; Morgan and Lee 2017; Tesler 2016).

Obama's election also spurred a counter-mobilization of white, conservative, and evangelical voters in the Tea Party movement. The early Tea Party movement expressed anger and resentment at the distributive injustice of welfare programs for "undeserving" immigrants, minorities, and youth, while favoring entitlement programs like Social Security and Medicare for "hard-working" Americans (Skocpol and Williamson 2016).

Six years later, the reaction to the growing racial, ethnic, religious, and gender diversity of the American electorate produced a surprising win for Donald Trump, whose campaign rhetoric was starkly polarizing and anti-establishment, dividing the country between "Us"—the "real" Americans who hungered for a return to an idealized past when industrial jobs provided for upward mobility and

Jennifer McCoy is a professor of political science at Georgia State University. As a specialist in comparative politics and democratization, she has coordinated international research on political polarization and democratic consequences. Her most recent book is International Mediation in Venezuela *(with Francisco Diez; United States Institute of Peace 2011).*

white males were in charge in the workplace and the family, and "Them"—the immigrants, minorities, and liberal elites who had wrought an "American carnage."[2] Trump's victory spawned another grass-roots counter-mobilization, this time on the Left and among college-educated women, who marched and ran for political office in massive numbers.

The U.S. story thus reflects the dynamics of severe polarization laid out in the introduction to this volume and in McCoy, Rahman, Somer (2018). The empowerment of new minority groups in the form of Barack Obama's election reinforced a sense of loss and disempowerment by white working-class voters whose economic base was shifting in a globalized economy and whose previously dominant social status was being challenged by the growing diversity of the country in terms of race and ethnicity, gender roles, and sexual orientation. Their sense of injury and injustice was exploited by Trump, who employed a populist polarizing message casting blame on the "nefarious" Washington elites working against the "virtuous" people, giving permission to his supporters to express their resentment and anger even, at times, in violent ways at some of his campaign rallies. As an outsider candidate, Trump masterfully articulated and reinforced the existing divides in the electorate, but did not create them. He appealed to the camp who viewed the effects of the demographic and social changes of the last half-century as mostly negative, as opposed to those in the other camp who viewed them positively (Abramowitz 2018).

Deepening racial, cultural, and ideological divides within the American electorate and the dramatic increase in negative affect toward the opposing party and its leaders made it possible for Donald Trump to win the 2016 presidential election despite having the highest negatives of any major party nominee in the history of public opinion polling. Trump first won the Republican nomination over the opposition of virtually the entire GOP establishment by playing to the anger and frustration of a large segment of the Republican electorate with the party's leaders for not delivering on campaign promises to reverse the policies of Barack Obama—promises that were clearly not realistic to begin with. That anger and frustration was fueled by alarm over changes in American society and culture, including, especially, the growing visibility and influence of racial and ethnic minorities (Ingraham 2016).

In the Republican primaries, Donald Trump's reputation as the nation's most prominent advocate of birtherism[3] (Barbaro 2016), his attacks on Mexican immigrants and Muslims and his promise to "make America great again" by renegotiating trade deals and bringing back lost manufacturing jobs resonated most strongly with white, working-class voters. However, the appeal of his message was by no means limited to the economically marginalized. Many relatively affluent whites found Trump's promise to reverse Barack Obama's policies and his attacks on the Washington political establishment appealing (Silver 2016). At the same time, however, Trump's racist, xenophobic, and misogynistic comments, as well as his attacks on the media and on leaders of both major parties turned off a large number of voters, especially racial minorities and college-educated white women. Even after winning the Republican nomination, Trump's unfavorable ratings remained far higher than his favorable ratings (Lauter 2016).

Two powerful trends affecting the American electorate further contributed to Donald Trump's rise and to his eventual victory in the 2016 presidential election: the politicization of racial resentment among white voters, especially among white working-class voters, and the rise of negative partisanship. Both of these trends reflected the transformation of the American party system in the twenty-first century due to the growing alignment of partisanship with race, religion, and ideology. The resulting political polarization reflected greater sorting of the electorate into more attitudinally homogeneous parties and exhibited the characteristics of severe polarization described by McCoy and Somer in the introduction to this volume: growing affective polarization, ethnocentrism (predisposition to divide society into Us vs. Them groups), social intolerance of out-groups, and unwillingness to cooperate and compromise.

Trump's Populist Appeal: Economic Discontent, Racial Resentment, and the Revolt of the White Working Class

According to the 2016 national exit poll (CNN 2016),[4] Donald Trump won the white vote by about 20 percentage points, almost the same margin as Romney. However, the exit poll data show that there were shifts in opposing directions among white voters. According to the data in Table 1, Republican support rose among white men but fell among white women. Trump's well publicized misogynistic comments bragging about inappropriate sexual advances on the notorious Hollywood Access tapes and accusations of sexual assault by various women undoubtedly contributed to his problems with female voters. Nevertheless, Trump still managed to outpoll Hillary Clinton by 9 percentage points among white women according to the national exit poll. Moreover, Trump made up for his losses among white women by outperforming Mitt Romney and defeating Hillary Clinton by close to a two to one margin among white men.

The opposing swings among white college graduates and nongraduates in Table 1 are even more striking than the opposing swings among white women and men. Among white college graduates, according to the national exit poll, Trump's three-point margin was the smallest in decades, and far smaller than Mitt Romney's 14-point margin in 2012. Among white voters without college degrees, however, Trump's 37-point margin was much greater than Romney's already impressive 25-point margin.

Related to the education divide, the exit polls showed that, among white voters, the class divide was also much larger than the gender divide. Trump defeated Clinton by 61 percent to 34 percent among white working-class women, and by a remarkable 71 percent to 23 percent among white working-class men. In contrast, Trump's margin among white male college graduates was a much narrower 53 percent to 39 percent and he lost to Hillary Clinton among white female college graduates by 51 percent to 44 percent.

White working-class voters have been moving toward the Republican Party since at least the 1970s, but the shift toward Donald Trump in 2016 was truly

TABLE 1

Change in Republican Margin among White Voter Groups between 2012 and 2016

Voter Group	Republican Margin in		
	2012	2016	Change
Male	+ 27	+ 31	+ 4
Female	+ 14	+ 9	− 5
College Grads	+ 14	+ 3	− 11
Non-Grads	+ 25	+ 37	+ 12

remarkable. While the size of this group has been shrinking for decades, it continues to make up a large share of the American electorate, especially in the key swing states in the Northeast and Midwest. This shift made Donald Trump's narrow victories in Michigan, Pennsylvania, and Wisconsin possible. A crucial question for anyone trying to understand the results of the 2016 election, therefore, is why Donald Trump's candidacy was so appealing to a large number of white working-class voters even as it repelled a large number of white college graduates along with the vast majority of nonwhite voters across the country.

Explanations for Donald Trump's appeal to white working-class voters have generally focused on two sets of factors. One explanation emphasizes the role of economic discontent and anxiety in fueling Trump's rise among this group. According to the economic discontent hypothesis, Trump's attacks on trade deals such as NAFTA and his promise to bring back manufacturing jobs appealed strongly to white working-class voters in small to medium-sized cities and rural areas that had been hard hit by the Great Recession and had not experienced as strong a recovery as larger metropolitan areas (Rasmus 2016; Hilsenrath and Davis 2016; Bell 2016). A second explanation emphasizes cultural factors in the roles of white racial resentment and ethno-nationalism. This hypothesis focuses on Trump's early embrace of birtherism, his explicit attacks on immigrants and Muslims, and his retweeting of messages and reluctance to disavow support from prominent white nationalist leaders and groups (Ingraham 2016; Yglesias 2016; Stone, Abramowitz, and Rapoport 2016, 8–10; Ball 2016).[5]

Of course, these two explanations are not mutually exclusive. Both may have some validity. Moreover, as Michael Tesler has argued, economic anxiety and discontent among white voters in 2016 appear to be closely connected to racial resentment. His analysis of survey data indicate that many white voters, especially those without college degrees, believe that racial minorities and immigrants have been favored by government policies while their own communities have been neglected, especially during the Obama years (Tesler 2016b). The Trump campaign explicitly connected these issues by arguing that illegal immigrants were taking jobs away from American citizens and reducing wages for American workers.

TABLE 2
Correlations of Racial Resentment Scale with Presidential Candidate Feeling
Thermometer Difference Ratings by Education among White Voters, 1988–2016

Year	All White Voters	College Grads	Not College Grads
1988	.205	.308	.175
1992	.275	.510	.157
2000	.247	.398	.154
2004	.398	.628	.261
2008	.485	.611	.416
2016	.636	.699	.549

NOTE: Feeling Thermometer Difference Ratings subtract the average feelings (scale of 0–100, from cool to warm) toward the Democratic candidate from the average feelings toward the Republican candidate.
SOURCES: American National Election Study Cumulative File and 2016 American National Election Study.

To sort out these competing explanations, we test the hypothesis that Trump's surge among white working class voters, compared with previous GOP presidential candidates, was due to his explicit appeal to white racial resentment and ethno-nationalism. Thus, Trump's campaign may have helped to politicize these attitudes, identifying them with a political party, especially among less educated white voters who tend to be less attentive to political campaigns and therefore less aware of differences between candidates on racial and other issues (Tesler 2016c). To test this hypothesis, we can compare the correlations between scores on the racial resentment scale and relative ratings of the Republican and Democratic presidential candidates on the feeling thermometer scale over time among white voters with and without college degrees. Table 2 displays these correlations for presidential candidates between 1988, when the American National Election Study (ANES) first began asking the questions in the racial resentment scale, and 2016. Data are not available for 2012 because the ANES survey did not include all four of the racial resentment items that year.

The results in Table 2 indicate that the sorting into political parties based on levels of racial resentment among white voters began well before 2016. As expected, these results also show that this relationship has consistently been stronger among white college graduates than among whites without college degrees. This is a typical finding due to greater attention to politics and higher information levels among college graduates than among the noncollege educated. In 2008, however, the presence of an African American presidential candidate on the ballot led to a sharp increase in the correlation between racial resentment and feeling thermometer ratings among white working-class voters. Data from the 2016 ANES indicate that Donald Trump's heavy emphasis on racial issues led to a further increase in the strength of this relationship, especially among white voters without college degrees. In terms of shared variance, the relationship between racial resentment and candidate feeling thermometer ratings was about 2.6 times stronger in 2016 than in 2004 among all white voters, but it was more than four times stronger among white working-class voters.

The findings in Table 2 reflect the fact that, over the past four elections, there has been a dramatic increase in support for Republican presidential candidates among the most racially resentful white working-class voters. In 2000, only 62 percent of working-class whites scoring high on racial resentment voted for George W. Bush over Al Gore. That percentage increased slightly to 68 percent in 2004 and 69 percent in 2008. In 2016, however, 87 percent of the most racially resentful white working-class voters supported Donald Trump over Hillary Clinton. In contrast, among the least racially resentful white working-class voters, the Republican share of the major party vote actually fell from 48 percent in 2000 and 41 percent in 2004 to 19 percent in 2008 and 24 percent in 2016.

Donald Trump's 2016 campaign included frequent appeals to white voters who were upset about economic trends such as stagnant wages and the loss of manufacturing jobs. What was most striking about Trump's campaign, however, was its explicit appeals to white resentment of the increasing visibility and influence of racial and ethnic minorities. Trump tried to connect these two issues by blaming economic problems on bad trade deals with countries such as Mexico and China, and competition for jobs from immigrants. Moreover, Trump's call for a ban on Muslims entering the United States sought to connect the issue of immigration to the threat of terrorism.

According to the 2016 exit poll, Trump's appeals to discontented white voters resonated most strongly among those without college degrees. The data from the 2016 ANES show the same pattern. According to the ANES data, Trump won 66 percent of the vote among white voters without college degrees, compared with only 44 percent of the vote among white college graduates. Moreover, the evidence displayed in Table 3 indicates that white voters without college degrees were much more likely to agree with key elements of Trump's campaign message than white college graduates.

The data in Table 3 show that, compared with college graduates, white voters without college degrees were much more likely to score high on measures of racial and ethnic resentment and misogyny.[6] They were also somewhat more likely to hold negative views of economic conditions, to view economic mobility as less possible than in the past, and to oppose free trade deals—although these differences were generally smaller and relatively few whites with or without college degrees were opposed to free trade agreements.

To compare the impact of racial and ethnic resentment with that of economic discontent, we conducted a multiple regression analysis of relative feeling thermometer ratings of Trump and Clinton among white voters, using the data from the 2016 ANES survey. Relative feeling thermometer ratings provide a more nuanced measure than the dichotomous vote choice question. However, these ratings strongly predict vote choice: only 3 percent of white voters rated Trump and Clinton equally on the feeling thermometer scale and 97 percent of those rating one candidate higher on the scale reported voting for that candidate. In addition to the measures of racial/ethnic resentment and economic discontent

TABLE 3

Political and Economic Attitudes of College and Non-College White Voters in 2016

	College Grads	Non-College
Mean FT Rating of Trump	31.0	50.1
Mean FT Rating of Clinton	42.6	31.7
High Racial Resentment	31%	50%
Anti-Immigration	27%	50%
High Misogyny	29%	51%
Anti-Gay Rights	26%	40%
Anti-Gun Control	39%	53%
National Economy Worse	23%	36%
Family Finances Worse	21%	30%
Little/No Econ Opportunity	28%	37%
Oppose Free Trade Deals	15%	27%
Economic Conservative	33%	41%

SOURCE: 2016 American National Election Study. FT: Feeling thermometer.

discussed above, we included several control variables in the regression analysis, including party identification, ideology, age, education, and gender. The results of the regression analysis are displayed in Table 4.

The variables included in the regression analysis explain 80 percent of the variance in relative feeling thermometer ratings of Trump and Clinton. After party identification, racial/ethnic resentment was by far the strongest predictor of relative ratings of Trump and Clinton—the higher the score on the racial/ethnic resentment scale, the more favorably white voters rated Trump relative to Clinton. The impact of the racial/ethnic resentment scale was much stronger than that of any of the economic variables included in the analysis, including opinions about free trade deals and economic mobility. Among the measures of economic discontent, ratings of the national economy had the strongest influence on feeling thermometer ratings of Trump and Clinton—the more negative the rating of the economy, the more positively white voters rated Trump relative to Clinton. Other measures of economic discontent had relatively weak effects.

After controlling for the other variables included in the regression analysis, the impact of education on relative ratings of Trump and Clinton completely disappears. In fact, the difference between white voters with and without college degrees in support for Trump is almost entirely explained by racial/ethnic resentment. Figure 1 displays the relationship between scores on the racial/ethnic resentment scale and support for Trump among white voters with and without college degrees.

The results in this figure show that there was a very strong relationship between racial/ethnic resentment and support for Trump regardless of education. Trump received almost no support among those scoring at the low end of

TABLE 4

Regression Analysis of Trump-Clinton Feeling Thermometer Ratings
among White Voters in 2016

Independent Variable	Beta	t-ratio	Significance
Age	−.026	−1.95	.05
Education	.003	0.25	
Family Income	−.001	−0.04	
Gender/Female	−.024	−1.81	.05
Republican Identification	.432	21.54	.001
R/E Resentment	.283	12.23	.001
Misogyny	.062	4.07	.001
Economic Conservatism	.040	1.73	.05
Anti-Gay Rights	.075	3.52	.001
Anti-Abortion	.022	1.30	
Anti-Free Trade	.052	3.74	.001
Financial Situation Worse	.031	2.04	.05
National Economy Worse	.135	7.97	.001
Econ Mobility Harder	.044	3.29	.001
Adjusted R^2 = .80			

NOTE: Dependent variable is Trump FT rating – Clinton FT rating. FT: Feeling thermometer; R/E racial/ethnic.
SOURCE: 2016 American National Election Study.

the scale, and almost unanimous support among those scoring at the high end of the scale. Moreover, there was almost no difference in support for Trump between white voters with and without college degrees after controlling for racial/ethnic resentment. White voters with high levels of racial/ethnic resentment voted overwhelmingly for Trump regardless of education, and white voters with low levels of racial/ethnic resentment voted overwhelmingly for Clinton regardless of education.

The results in Table 4 indicate that ratings of the national economy had a substantial impact on relative ratings of Trump and Clinton on the feeling thermometer scale by white voters after controlling for all the other predictors in the regression analysis, including racial/ethnic resentment. However, there was a close connection between racial resentment and economic discontent among white voters: the correlation between these two measures was a strong 0.53. Fifty percent of those scoring "very high" or "high" on the racial/ethnic resentment scale rated economic conditions as worse than one year earlier compared with only 6 percent of those scoring "low" or "very low" on the scale.

While these cross-sectional survey data do not make it possible to determine the direction of influence between these two variables, there are good theoretical reasons to believe that racial resentment has a stronger influence on economic discontent than economic discontent has on racial resentment. For one thing,

FIGURE 1
Percentage Voting for Trump by Racial/Ethnic Resentment among
College and Noncollege Whites in 2016

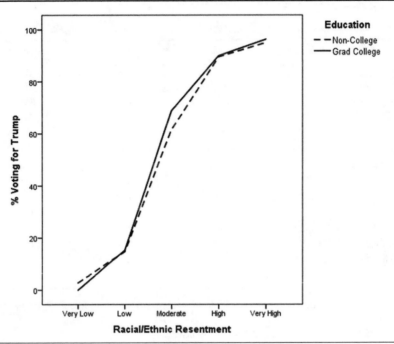

SOURCE: 2016 American National Election Study.

racial attitudes are generally more fundamental and stable at the individual level
than assessments of economic conditions, which can fluctuate considerably, even
over a relatively short time. Moreover, as discussed previously, the Trump campaign directly connected job losses for white workers with government policies
favoring the interests of nonwhites and immigrants.

Affective Polarization and Negative Partisanship in 2016

One of the most important developments in American public opinion over the
past 30 years has been the rise of affective polarization. Democrats and
Republicans are increasingly divided, not just in their policy preferences but also
in their feelings about the parties and their leaders. The main reason for this
growing divide has been the increasingly negative feelings that partisans hold
about the opposing party and its leaders (Iyengar and Westwood 2015). This has
given rise to the phenomenon of negative partisanship: large proportions of
Democrats and Republicans now dislike the opposing party and its leaders more
than they like their own party and its leaders. Dislike of the other side is so

strong, in fact, that even when partisans have reservations about their own party's candidate, they are very reluctant to cross party lines. The result, as we have seen, is that recent elections have been characterized by record levels of party loyalty and straight ticket voting (Abramowitz and Webster 2016).

The 2016 presidential election set new records for affective polarization and negative partisanship. Both major party nominees, Donald Trump and Hillary Clinton, had exceptionally high unfavorable ratings. According to the Gallup Poll, Trump had the highest unfavorable ratings of any presidential candidate in modern history with Clinton not far behind (Saad 2016b). However, this does not mean that most voters disliked both candidates. According to Gallup, only about one out of four Americans disliked both candidates (Newport and Dugan 2016). In fact, most Democratic voters had a favorable opinion of Clinton and most Republican voters had a favorable opinion of Trump. It is true that many Republican voters had reservations about Donald Trump and quite a few Democratic voters had reservations about Hillary Clinton. However, the vast majority of Republicans and Democrats strongly preferred their own party's nominee because they intensely disliked the opposing party's nominee (Saad 2016a).

Both Trump and Clinton experienced lengthy and divisive battles for their party's nomination. Clinton was viewed as a strong favorite from the outset but had to fend off a much stronger than expected challenge from the Left by Vermont Senator Bernie Sanders. Trump, in contrast, shocked almost everyone by winning the nomination rather easily over a crowded field of politically experienced Republican candidates. Even though he led in polls of Republican voters almost from the moment he announced his candidacy, Trump ended up winning less than half of the vote in the primaries. For both Clinton and Trump, therefore, one of the biggest challenges in the general election campaign was uniting their party by winning over voters who had supported other candidates in the primaries.

Despite the divisiveness of the Democratic and Republican nomination contests and their own high unfavorable ratings, in the end both Clinton and Trump largely succeeded in uniting their party's voters behind their candidacies in the general election. According to the national exit poll, the level of party loyalty in the 2016 presidential election was very similar to that in other recent presidential elections: almost 89 percent of Democratic identifiers and 88 percent of Republican identifiers voted for their own party's nominee. Only 8 percent of Democratic and Republican identifiers defected to the opposing party's nominee while 3 percent of Democratic identifiers and 4 percent of Republican identifiers voted for third party candidates. The key to both Trump's and Clinton's success in uniting their party's voters behind their candidacies was negative partisanship. Table 5 displays the average feeling thermometer ratings of Trump and Clinton by Democratic and Republican voters supporting different primary candidates in the 2016 ANES Pilot Study, which was conducted in late January, at the beginning of the presidential primary season. Among all Republican voters, Donald Trump received an average rating of 65 degrees on the feeling thermometer scale. Among all Democratic voters, Hillary Clinton received an average rating of 71 degrees on the feeling thermometer scale. These are rather mediocre ratings for presidential nominees from their own party's voters. In 2012, according to

TABLE 5
Affective Polarization in 2016: Average Feeling Thermometer Ratings of Clinton and
Trump by Party and Primary Candidate Preference

	Clinton	Trump	Difference
Identify/Lean Dem	70.9	18.9	+ 52.0
Favor Clinton	86.8	20.4	+ 66.4
Favor Sanders	55.5	13.6	+ 41.9
Identify/Lean Rep	12.5	65.0	- 52.5
Favor Trump	11.4	90.8	- 79.4
Favor Other	12.6	49.9	- 37.3

SOURCE: 2016 ANES Pilot Study

ANES data, Barack Obama received an average rating of 82 degrees from Democratic voters and Mitt Romney received an average rating of 72 degrees from Republican voters. However, ratings of the opposing party's candidate were far more negative in 2016 than in 2012. In 2012, according to ANES data, Barack Obama received an average rating of 29 degrees from Republican voters and Mitt Romney received an average rating of 28 degrees from Democratic voters. In 2016, Hillary Clinton received an average rating of only 12 degrees from Republican voters and Donald Trump received an average rating of only 19 degrees from Democratic voters.

The data in Table 5 show that, among both Democrats and Republicans, there was a large gap in feelings toward the party's nominee between voters who supported the nominee in the primaries and voters who supported other candidates in the primaries. Republican voters who supported Donald Trump in the primaries gave him an average rating of 91 degrees on the feeling thermometer while those who supported other candidates gave him an average rating of only 50 degrees—a gap of more than 40 degrees. Similarly, Democratic voters who supported Hillary Clinton in the primaries gave her an average rating of 87 degrees on the feeling thermometer, while those who supported Bernie Sanders gave her an average rating of only 58 degrees—a gap of almost 30 degrees.

Despite the very weak ratings of both party's nominees by those supporting other candidates in the primaries, the vast majority of these voters rated them more favorably than the opposing party's nominee. Eighty-eight percent of Sanders supporters rated Hillary Clinton higher than Donald Trump on the feeling thermometer and 82 percent of Republicans supporting candidates other than Donald Trump rated him higher than they rated Hillary Clinton. Only 8 percent of Democrats supporting Sanders rated Trump more favorably than Clinton and only 12 percent of Republicans supporting candidates other than Donald Trump rated Clinton more favorably than Trump. The reason for this is clear from the data in Table 5. Sanders' supporters actually disliked Donald Trump even more than Clinton supporters did; they gave Trump an average rating of only 14 degrees on the feeling thermometer. Similarly, Republicans supporting candidates other than Trump in the primary disliked Hillary Clinton almost as much as those supporting Trump; they gave Clinton an average rating of only 13 degrees on the feeling thermometer.

It is striking that the intensely negative feelings toward the opposing party's eventual nominee that we see in Table 5 were measured in late January 2016. This was long before Donald Trump and Hillary Clinton became their party's presidential nominees and began what would ultimately become, in the eyes of many political observers, one of the nastiest and most negative campaigns in modern political history.

According to these data, Democratic and Republican voters hardly needed to be persuaded to despise the opposing party's candidate. The large majority of Republicans strongly disliked Hillary Clinton and the large majority of Democrats strongly disliked Donald Trump long before the general election campaign began. It appears that for most Democratic and Republican voters, the general election campaign served mainly to reinforce the extremely negative feelings that they had held toward the opposing party's nominee even before the presidential primaries began.

Because of their intense dislike of the opposing party's nominee, even voters who had serious reservations about their own party's nominee were very reluctant to cross party lines. Donald Trump was an unacceptable choice for the vast majority of Democrats, even those who had supported Bernie Sanders in the Democratic primaries. Likewise, Hillary Clinton was an unacceptable choice for the vast majority of Republicans, even those who had supported candidates other than Donald Trump in the Republican primaries. In some ways, however, negative partisanship was more important on the Republican side in 2016. That is because, during and after the primaries, Republican elites had been far more divided than Democratic elites about their party's eventual nominee.

Looking Ahead: Polarization in the Age of Trump

Changing voting patterns in 2016 represented, in important ways, a continuation of the realignment of the American electorate that has been occurring since the 1970s. The most dramatic shift in voting patterns in the election involved the growing alignment of partisanship with education among white voters. White voters with college degrees shifted toward the Democratic Party while white voters without college degrees shifted toward the Republican Party. Donald Trump's candidacy clearly had something to do with this. Trump's campaign slogan, "Make America Great Again," was directed at white working-class voters hoping to turn back the clock to a time when people like them enjoyed greater influence and respect, rather than economic issues.

Like other populists with a savior message, in his campaign rhetoric, and even in his inaugural address, Donald Trump constantly painted a portrait of a nation in steep decline—decline that only he could reverse. Trump repeatedly claimed, without any evidence, that the unemployment rate in the United States was far higher than government statistics indicated, that rates of violent crime in the nation's inner cities were soaring, and that the quality of health care available to most Americans had deteriorated badly since the adoption of the Affordable Care Act. He also portrayed Islamic terrorism as a dire threat to the lives of ordinary Americans despite that very few Americans had actually been killed or injured in terrorist attacks by Islamic militants post-9/11 (Cassidy 2016; Kilgore 2017).[7]

According to an August 2016 survey conducted by the Pew Research Center, the large majority of Trump's supporters shared his dark vision of the condition and direction of the nation. Fully 81 percent of Trump supporters compared with only 19 percent of Clinton supporters believed that "life for people like them" has gotten worse in the past 50 years. Moreover, 68 percent of Trump supporters compared with only 30 percent of Clinton supporters expected life for the next generation of Americans to be worse than today (Pew Research Center 2016b).

The deep pessimism evinced by so many of Trump's supporters appears to be based largely on unhappiness with the nation's changing demographics and values. Trump's appeals to white racial resentment and ethnonationalism resonated with a large proportion of less-educated white voters who were uncomfortable with the increasing diversity of American society. Analyses using group status theory buttress the impact of this message as they show that threats to the status of the traditionally dominant group in the United States—white Christian males—by the increasingly multi-ethnic society and the perceived loss of American global dominance (Mutz 2018) helped to produce a cultural backlash similarly found in some European countries (Inglehart and Norris 2016).

Likewise, Trump's promise to appoint conservative judges who would limit the rights of gays and lesbians and curtail access to abortion appealed to religious conservatives upset with the growing liberalism of the American public on cultural issues. However, the same message that turned on a large number of white working-class voters, turned off an overwhelming majority of African Americans, Latinos, Asian Americans, and LGBT voters, along with many white college graduates, especially women, who benefited from, and welcomed, these changes. It thus deepened the polarization between the camp largely situated in the Democratic Party viewing the changes positively, and the camp aligning in the Republican Party viewing the changes negatively.

The president's behavior since his inauguration continues his strategy of polarization—identifying out-groups, especially immigrants, unfair trade agreements and defense alliances, and the "liberal" media and intellectuals as enemies of the people. He vilifies and ridicules his own critics from within the government, the society, or his own party. In turn, Democratic Party leaders have responded with increasingly harsh attacks on the president, including calls by some to begin impeachment proceedings. At the same time, negative feelings toward Mr. Trump have hardened among rank-and-file Democrats.

Consequences for democracy

Rising mistrust and, at times, hatred of the opposing party and its leaders may be one of the most dangerous consequences of growing partisan polarization. As McCoy, Rahman, and Somer (2018) note, when supporters of each party come to see both leaders and supporters of the other party not just as political rivals but as evildoers out to harm the nation, they are more likely to be willing to accept illiberal measures such as restrictions on freedom of expression or even the use of force against political opponents.

Partisan antipathy rose dramatically compared with 1994, when only 21 percent of Republicans and 17 percent of Democrats had highly unfavorable views of the other. By 2016, those figures had risen to 58 percent and 55 percent, respectively. Even more disturbing, roughly half of voters of each party say the other party makes them feel afraid, while those who say that the policies of the other party are so misguided they are a threat to the nation have risen rapidly. In 2016, 45 percent of Republicans viewed Democratic policies as a threat, up 8 points in just two years; 41 percent of Democrats viewed Republican policies as a threat, up 10 points in two years (Pew Research Center 2016).

Based on developments during the first 18 months of the Trump administration, there appears to be a strong likelihood that ideological conflict and partisan hostility will reach new heights during the Trump years. As a result, ideological polarization and negative partisanship are likely to remain major obstacles to efforts to work across party lines in government. Any such efforts will likely be greeted with deep suspicion by voters on both sides of the party divide, especially more attentive and politically active voters who vote in primaries to choose the party candidates. Republicans in Congress will be under intense pressure to use their majorities in the House and Senate to ram through key items on the Trump/GOP agenda without input from Democrats. Likewise, Democrats will be under intense pressure to use all the tools at their disposal, including the filibuster in the Senate for as long as it remains in place, to oppose the GOP/Trump agenda.

With very limited ability to resist congressional Republicans and Trump, Democrats and their liberal allies will likely turn increasingly to state governments under Democratic control and to the federal courts for assistance, as seen in the responses to President Trump's early executive orders. In an age of partisan hostility and conflict, the Trump years are likely to witness the most intense partisan hostility and conflict in modern American history. Given Trump's authoritarian inclinations, as seen in his attacks on the legitimacy of the news media, political opponents, the courts, and the electoral process itself, this is an especially worrisome development.

Polarization's impact on U.S. democracy has been primarily one of gridlock and careening as Republicans carried out an explicitly obstructionist strategy against the Obama administration, and Obama made use of unilateral executive orders to implement policy change. Subsequently, the Trump administration in its first year exhibited an evident bent to undo anything accomplished by Obama. The Republican-led Senate ended a practice of supermajority voting (filibuster and cloture) for Supreme Court appointments and attempted to enact major legislation without bipartisan consultation or support in 2017. Diminished tolerance of opposing views among political elites is also reflected in the degradation of respect for counter-arguments as indicated in a scale of 1–5 in which the United States fell from 4 to 3 (acknowledge but not value counterarguments) in

2013 and then to 2 (elites acknowledge the counterarguments only to degrade them and debase the individuals and groups who make such arguments) in 2016.[8]

Warning signs of another of our possible outcomes—democratic backsliding— emerged in the public's apparent tolerance of illiberal behavior by the new administration and some of its supporters in 2017. Violation of democratic norms in recent years, and especially since the election of Donald Trump, include the erosion of partisan restraint, presidential respect for freedom of the press, and the idea of a legitimate opposition (Levitsky and Ziblatt 2018).

Strong institutions have ensured executive constraint, particularly in the courts suppression of the early Muslim travel bans and separation of immigrant parents and children at the U.S. border. On the other hand, the Republican Party, with some exceptions, proved more an enabler than a constraint on the erosion of democratic norms as it upended bipartisanship and failed to counter the president's attacks on the independent judiciary and special counsel, as well as the media. The Democratic Party, under pressure from its own base, and in reciprocation for the Senate Republican majority refusal to schedule a vote on then-President Obama's Supreme Court nominee Merrick Garland in 2016, engaged in a tit-for-tat strategy to further the breakdown of bipartisan efforts at compromise, going for broke in filibustering Trump's Supreme Court nominee Neil Gorsuch. The filibuster provoked the Senate Republican leadership to use the "nuclear option" and end the 60-vote supermajority requirement to overcome filibusters for Supreme Court nominees. The Supreme Court battle extended the slow death of the filibuster begun in 2013 when Senate Democrats ended the 60-vote procedural vote for lower court nominees, in frustration at Republican blocking of Obama nominees.

This dramatic shift away from bipartisanship on important national decisions such as life-time judicial appointments is a product of deep polarization in which citizens and their elected representatives put partisan interests (my "team") above national interests. Thus, as Huq and Ginsburg (2017) note, even strong institutions and constitutional protections are vulnerable to regression. Scholars tracking assessments of political scientists indicate an increased risk of democratic backsliding and even breakdown (Democracy Threat Index 2018). Experts are asked to rank the threats to American democracy on a scale of 0 to 100 (complete democratic breakdown in next four years). From an average threat level in the mid-20s in first half of 2017, by August 2018 those assessments had raised to the high 30s. In substantive terms, this changed the assessment from Significant Violations atypical of a consolidated democracy, but that do not yet threaten breakdown, to Substantial Erosion with violations that signal significant erosion of democratic quality and warn of high potential for breakdown in the future. Not surprisingly, the largest threat was perceived in Political Leaders Rhetoric, followed by Executive Constraints and Treatment of the Media, but Respect for Elections emerged as a concern as well (Authoritarian Warning Survey 2018).

Another tracking survey of political science experts shows a continuous decline in the assessments of the quality of American democracy since 2015 (Brightline Watch 2018). Interestingly, the experts rated the quality slightly higher than the general public, who were more pessimistic about the quality of democracy. Ominously, however, a growing polarization in the public over those assessments

FIGURE 2
United States' Liberal Democracy Index: 1980–2017

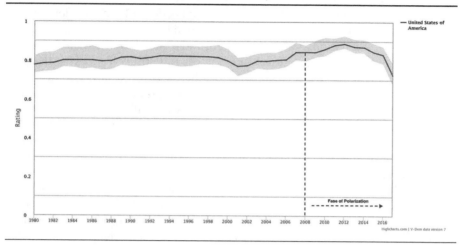

SOURCE: V-Dem data version 7.

became evident in July 2018: for the first time, Trump approvers saw an *improve-ment* in the quality, while Trump disapprovers saw a continuing *deterioration*, producing a new divergence in public opinion (Brightline Watch 2018).

Varieties of Democracy is a database that measures changes in more than 350 indicators of democracy worldwide since 1900. Figure 2 shows the lowest score on its Liberal Democracy Index for the United States since 1975. Though still relatively high, it fell in 2017 to 0.73 from a height of 0.83 on a scale of 0 to 1, with 1 as the strongest democracy score.[9]

The United States has survived periods of intense political polarization in the past. The deep hostility between Federalists and Democratic-Republicans in 1800 raised concerns about whether there could be a peaceful transition in party control of the presidency. A bloody Civil War over the institution of slavery between 1861 and 1865 posed a direct threat to the survival of the United States as a nation. Deep divisions over civil rights and the Vietnam War led to bloody confrontations in the streets and sharp divisions in the halls of Congress during the 1960s and 1970s. The nation even survived a president in Richard Nixon whose behavior threatened democratic norms and led to his eventual resignation under threat of impeachment.

Something feels different about the current period, however. In his sheer men-dacity and willingness to violate crucial democratic norms, apparently to protect himself and his family, Donald Trump appears to have gone beyond anything experienced during the Nixon years. Just as importantly, the rise of partisan polari-zation, hostility and mistrust has allowed Trump to maintain the support of the large majority of his own party's base and discouraged Republicans in Congress from acting as a check on many of his dangerous tendencies as long as they feel they need him to accomplish their policy objectives and maintain their own power.

On the other hand, there are some encouraging signs of functioning checks and balances. The Republican-led Congress tried, with limited success, to impose additional sanctions on Russia over the objections of the president, in the wake of evidence of Russian meddling in the 2016 elections (Philips 2018). The Senate came to the defense of U.S. citizens under attack by Russian President Putin, in the wake of Trump's apparent openness to Putin's offer during the July 2018 Summit to exchange interrogation rights (Schor 2018). Courts have weighed in to block some executive initiatives, while allowing others. A number of individuals within the Trump administration have shown a willingness to stand up to the president on issues such as Russian meddling and his requests to halt the Mueller investigation. And of course the Mueller probe itself continued despite the president's regularly stated desire to shut it down.

Most importantly, the American people will have an opportunity to render a verdict on the functioning of Congress and the administration in the 2018 midterm elections and, eventually, in the 2020 presidential election. If the midterm election results in a Democratic takeover of at least one chamber of Congress, as commonly happens in midterm elections, it will be widely viewed as a sharp rebuke of the president. A Democratic House or Senate would result in much more intense scrutiny and heightened oversight of the president and his administration, but also potentially an even greater gridlock. In the end, whether the decades-long deepening of polarization results in long-term damage to democratic norms and institutions or sparks a political reaction that ends up strengthening those norms and institutions may rest largely in the hands of the American electorate.

Notes

1. The following five paragraphs draw from McCoy, Rahman, and Somer (2018).

2. Donald Trump Speech Transcript from Inauguration as President. 2017. Available from https://www.news.com.au/finance/work/leaders/what-donald-trump-said-in-his-inauguration-speech/news-story/ebdd3cb77f0b2b385f8c663dbc724a7e.

3. "Birtherism" refers to a movement questioning the citizenship of Barack Obama. Donald Trump introduced the question into the national conversation in 2011. See Barbaro (2018).

4. Data for the national exit poll in 2016 were collected by Edison Research for the National Election Pool, a consortium of ABC News, The Associated Press, CBSNews, CNN, Fox News and NBC News.

5. For evidence that Trump's attacks on Mexican immigrants and Muslims were crucial to his support among Republican primary voters, see Rapoport, Abramowitz and Stone (2016); See also Ball (2016).

6. The measure of racial and ethnic resentment combines the traditional four-item racial resentment scale with six items measuring support or opposition to immigration. I combined these into one scale because the correlation between the racial resentment scale and the anti-immigration scale was a very strong 0.65. Moreover, a factor analysis of the 10 items indicates that they are measuring a single underlying dimension and the 10-item racial/ethnic resentment scale has a Cronbach's alpha of 0.87. The misogyny scale is based on three items measuring negative or hostile attitudes toward women.

7. For an analysis of Trump's inaugural address, see Kilgore (2017). Trump's Dark, Weird Inaugural Campaign Speech.

8. Varieties of Democracy. Variable graph. Accessed August 8, 2018. https://www.v-dem.net/en/analysis/VariableGraph/.

9. Ibid.

References

Abramowitz, Alan I. 2018. *The great alignment: Race, party transformation, and the rise of Donald Trump*. New Haven, CT: Yale University Press.

Abramowitz, Alan I. 2016. Donald Trump, partisan polarization, and the 2016 presidential election. Sabato's Crystal Ball. Available from http://www.centerforpolitics.org/crystalball/articles/donald-trump-partisan-polarization- and-the-2016-presidential-election.

Abramowitz, Alan I., and Steven Webster. 2016. The rise of negative partisanship and the nationalization of U.S. elections in the 21st century. *Electoral Studies* 41:12–22.

ANES Pilot Study. 2016. *ANES | American National Election Studies*. Available from https://electionstudies.org/project/anes-2016-pilot-study.

ANES Data Center. 2016. *ANES | American National Election Studies*. Available from https://electionstudies.org/data-center.

Authoritarian Warning Survey. 2018. Scholars on American democracy. Available from https://www.authwarningsurvey.com/survey.

Ball, Molly. 2016. Donald Trump and the politics of fear. *The Atlantic*. Available from https://www.theatlantic.com.

Barbaro, Michael. 20 January 2018. Donald Trump clung to 'birther' lie for years, and still isn't apologetic. *The New York Times*. Available from https://www.nytimes.com.

Bell, Torstein. 2016. The invisible economic catastrophe that Donald Trump spotted. New Statesman (blog). Available from https://www.newstatesman.com.

Bright Line Watch Survey Report: Wave 6. 2018. Bright Line Watch. Available from http://brightlinewatch.org/wave6/.

Campbell, James E. 2016. *Polarized: Making sense of a divided America*. Princeton, NJ: Princeton University Press.

Cassidy, John. 22 July 2016. Donald Trump's dark, dark convention speech. *The New Yorker*. Available from https://www.newyorker.com.

CNN. 2016. Election results: National exit polls. Available from http://www.cnn.com.

Collinson, Stephen. 17 January 2017. Tumult surrounds Trump days ahead of his presidency. *CNN*. Available from https://www.cnn.com.

Enten, Harry. 13 November 2015. Hillary Clinton is the most establishment-approved candidate on record. *FiveThirtyEight*. Available from https://fivethirtyeight.com.

Hilsenrath, Jon, and Bob Davis. 7 July 2016. Election 2016 is propelled by the American economy's failed promises. *Wall Street Journal*. Available from https://www.wsj.com.

Huq, Aziz Z., and Tom Ginsburg. 2017. *How to lose a constitutional democracy*. Rochester, NY: Social Science Research Network.

Inglehart, Ronald, and Pippa Norris. 2016. Trump, Brexit, and the rise of populism: Economic have-nots and cultural backlash. HKS Working Paper No. RWP16-026, Harvard University.

Ingraham, Christopher. 2016. Two new studies find racial anxiety is the biggest driver of support for Trump. *Washington Post*. Available from https://www.washingtonpost.com.

Iyengar, Shanto, and Sean J. Westwood. 2015. Fear and loathing across party lines: New evidence on group polarization. *American Journal of Political Science* 59 (3): 690–707.

Kilgore, Ed. 2017. Trump's dark, weird, inaugural campaign speech. *Daily Intelligencer*. Available from http://nymag.com.

Knuckey, Jonathan, and Myunghee Kim. 2015. Racial resentment, old-fashioned racism, and the vote choice of Southern and Nonsouthern whites in the 2012 U.S. presidential election. *Social Science Quarterly* 96 (4): 905–22.

Lauter, David. 2016. Donald Trump is now the least popular American Politician in Three Decades. *LA Times*. Available from http://www.latimes.com.

Levitsky, Steven, and Daniel Ziblatt. 2018. *How democracies die*. New York, NY: Crown.

McCoy, Jennifer, Tahmina Rahman, and Murat Somer. 2018. Polarization and the global crisis of democracy: Common patterns, dynamics, and pernicious consequences for democratic polities. *American Behavioral Scientist* 62 (1): 16–42.

Democracy Threat Index. 2018. Protect democracy. Available from https://protectdemocracy.org/
      threat-index.
Morgan, Stephen L., and Jiwon Lee. 2017. The white working class and voter turnout in U.S. presidential
      elections, 2004 to 2016. *Sociological Science* 4:656–85.
Mutz, Diana C. 2018. Status threat, not economic hardship, explains the 2016 presidential vote.
      Proceedings of the National Academy of Sciences. DOI: https://doi.org/10.1073/pnas.1718155115.
Newport, Frank, and Andrew Dugan. 2016. One in four Americans dislike both presidential candidates.
      Available from https://news.gallup.com.
Pew Research Center. 2016 election. Washington, DC: Pew Research Center. Available from http://www
      .pewresearch.org/topics/2016-election/.
Pew Research Center. 2016a. Partisanship and political animosity in 2016. Washington, DC: Pew
      Research Center for the People and the Press. Available from http://www.people- press.org/2016/06/22/
      partisanship-and-political-animosity-in-2016/.
Pew Research Center. 2016b. Clinton, Trump supporters have starkly different views of a changing nation.
      Washington, DC: Pew Research Center for the People and the Press. Available from http://www
      .people-press.org/2016/08/18/clinton-trump-supporters-have- starkly-different-views-of-a-changing-
      nation/.
Phillips, Amber. 2018. Even if Trump is blatantly ignoring the Russia sanctions law, there's not a lot
      Congress can do about it. *Washington Post*. Available from https://www.washingtonpost.com/.
Rasmus, Jack. 2016. Trump, trade and working class discontent. *Counterpunch*. Available from http://www
      .counterpunch.org.
Saad, Lydia. 2016a. Aversion to other candidate key factor in 2016 vote choice. Available from https://news
      .gallup.com.
Saad, Lydia. 2016b. Trump and Clinton finish with historically poor images. Available from https://news
      .gallup.com.
Schor, Elana. 2018. Senate fires bipartisan Russia warning at Trump. *Politico*. Available from https://politi
      .co/2A0g4Nk.
Silver, Nate. 2016. The mythology of Trump's 'Working Class' Support. *FiveThirtyEight*. Available from
      https://fivethirtyeight.com.
Skocpol, Theda, and Vanessa Williamson. 2016. *The Tea Party and the remaking of Republican conserva-
      tism*. Updated edition. New York, NY: Oxford University Press.
Stone, Walter J., Alan I. Abramowitz, and Ronald B. Rapoport. 23 June 2016. Why Trump was inevitable.
      The New York Review of Books. Available from https://www.nybooks.com.
Tesler, Michael. 2016a. Analysis: Views about race mattered more in electing Trump than in electing
      Obama. *Washington Post*. Available from https://www.washingtonpost.com.
Tesler, Michael. 2016b. Economic anxiety isn't driving racial resentment. Racial resentment is driving
      economic anxiety. *Washington Post*. Available from https://www.washingtonpost.com.
Tesler, Michael. 2016c. The education gap among whites this year wasn't about education. It was about
      race. *Washington Post*. Available from https://www.washingtonpost.com.
Yglesias, Matthew. 2016. Why I don't think it makes sense to attribute Trump's support to economic anxi-
      ety. *Vox*. Available from https://www.vox.com.
Yourish, Karen, Larry Buchanan, and Alicia Parlapiano. 2016. More than 160 Republican leaders don't
      support Donald Trump. Here's when they reached their breaking point. *The New York Times*. Available
      from https://www.nytimes.com.

Dynamics of Polarization in the Greek Case

By
IOANNIS ANDREADIS
and
YANNIS STAVRAKAKIS

This article focuses on the dynamics of polarization emerging within Greek political culture in the postauthoritarian setting. Following a brief historical framing, we trace Left–Right polarization between the two major parties of the period: Panhellenic Socialist Movement (PASOK) and New Democracy (ND). The party-based polarization of PASOK/ND was arguably the main axis of political antagonism in Greece from the 1970s until the end of the 2000s. By 2009, polarization had ebbed due to an ideological convergence of the two parties toward the center, but the onset of the 2009 economic crisis dislocated the established two-party system and facilitated the emergence of a new political landscape comprising many new political actors, most notably the Coalition of the Radical Left, SYRIZA. Using a predominantly quantitative methodology, we focus on a set of dimensions of polarization brought forward or re-activated within the context of economic crisis.

Keywords: crisis; Europe; Greece; polarization; populism

When can one conclude that a legitimate democratic agonism (meaning the respectful assertion of distinct political alternatives) has escalated into raw antagonism and that polarization has reached a risky threshold, mutating into a pernicious phenomenon? What role do political parties and other agents play in this process? How does Left/Right (L/R) polarization intersect with other culture-specific types of "formative rifts" (Somer and McCoy, this volume)? Is it possible to support qualitative accounts with quantitative data to make

Ioannis Andreadis is an associate professor of quantitative methods in the social sciences at the Aristotle University of Thessaloniki. He is a member of the steering committee of the Comparative Candidate Survey, and national collaborator for the Comparative Study of Electoral Systems.

Correspondence: john@polsci.auth.gr

DOI: 10.1177/0002716218817723

sense of polarization's trajectory in a particular setting? In this article, we address such questions by analyzing polarization in postauthoritarian Greece, from 1974 until 2015. We use historiographical, discourse, and quantitative analysis to explain polarization in the Greek case.

In Greece, party polarization along the L/R axis was exacerbated by its civil war (1945–49), which ended when pro-Western forces backed by Britain and the United States defeated the communist-led alliance. The anticommunist legacy of the ensuing Right-wing state, and of the military dictatorship (junta) that followed in 1967–74, laid the foundation for ideological antagonisms that followed the junta's collapse. That traditional cleavage has co-existed with other types of polarization organized around the ambivalent relationship between Greece and Europe, as well as Greece's relationship with populist and antipopulist strategies.

Greek political culture has been historically conceptualized in terms of a fundamental division that reflects the country's vacillating position within the European framework. The story goes back to the formation of the modern Greek state at the beginning of the nineteenth century. Since then, Europe has functioned for Greece as both a model and an observer. We know from historical research that Greek citizens, persistently feeling the ambivalence from other Europeans—who were both fascinated by ancient Greece and disappointed by modern Greece—increasingly resented the continuous need to prove to Europe the worth of modern Greek achievement. Greeks felt continuously judged on the progress of the new state following its war of independence (1821–1830) and on its acceptance into mainstream Europe, the European Economic Community (EEC), the European Union (EU) and, finally, the Euro-zone. Harvard anthropologist Michael Herzfeld has described this potent yet ambivalent relation as *crypto-colonialism* (Herzfeld 2002, 25).

In this context, the standard explanation for the polarized dynamics of Greek political culture posits a division between two distinct, antagonistic, cultural, and political orientations. The theory of *cultural dualism*, introduced by Nikiforos Dianandouros, understands the Greek political/cultural space as divided between two camps: pro-European modernizers and euro-skeptical traditionalists. In essence, this schema implies that the construction of a modern state in Greece led to "intense social, political, and cultural struggles in which potential beneficiaries and potential losers in the redefinition of power relations within Greece played the central role" (Diamandouros 1994, 8).

Most important, this division has often been associated with the debate around populism that has diachronically marked the Greek case—after all, Greece is often described as a populist democracy marked throughout by a deeply polarized political culture (Pappas 2014, 8). To the extent that Diamandouros's second camp of euro-skeptic traditionalists is predominantly populist (he himself calls it an "underdog culture"), polarization in Greek politics has been described as tending to "reduce the space for party competition to a single dimension, which

Yannis Stavrakakis has worked at the Universities of Essex and Nottingham and is currently a professor of political discourse analysis at the Aristotle University of Thessaloniki. Since 2014 he has been directing the POPULISMUS Observatory.

presumably exists between a majority (the masses, the people, the underprivileged, the poor) and some minority (the elites, the establishment, the privileged, the rich)" (Pappas 2014, 58). Although this picture does not adequately capture periods in which "modernization," the "middle ground," or the "center" has functioned as the holy grail of party competition and identification (1996–2009), it can illuminate important periods of recent history.

Over time, the relationship between the dimensions of polarization has fluctuated between a L/R cleavage, a pro-European/anti-European cleavage, and a populist/anti-populist one. Whether we call it crypto-colonialism or cultural dualism, none can deny that polarized dynamics have marked political culture in postauthoritarian Greece and require urgent attention, especially in times of crisis that threaten the cohesion of many polities internationally. In what follows, we develop many of these analytical angles, briefly covering some of the highlights of the early period in question but placing more emphasis on recent developments to capture how all these cleavages have interacted with each other, ushering in a period of instability and democratic careening.

Axes of Polarization in Postauthoritarian Greece

The polarization matrix in the early 1980s

The 1980s were dominated by Andreas Papandreou and his Panhellenic Socialist Movement (PASOK), a Left-wing populist party (Stavrakakis 2014, 2016) that highlighted the socioeconomic demands of sectors of the population that had been largely excluded in the long period between the civil war (1945–49) and the junta (1967–74). In the 1981 general election, PASOK won an outright majority in parliament with more than 48 percent of the vote. Politically, "PASOK opted for polarization rather than moderation. Indeed, the new government adopted an openly and consistently confrontational political strategy" (Kalyvas 1997, 84). This is not surprising given that PASOK represented social strata that had felt alienated from equal rights and legitimate access to decision-making for a long time (Katsambekis and Stavrakakis 2017, 6–7).

The polarization strategy was not limited to PASOK. Both PASOK and the Right-wing New Democracy (ND) party used a "discourse which presented the social and political space as divided into two opposed fields" (Lyrintzis 1987, 671). They claimed to represent incompatible political camps and made conscious and unrelenting efforts to undermine one another's legitimacy. Depictions of the enemy were thus instrumental in constructing the distinct identity of the two camps. On one hand, PASOK claimed that ND stood for authoritarianism, the oligarchy, and foreign interests (Kalyvas 1997, 86). Thus, "the Right was depicted as one and indivisible from the collaborationist Security Battalions of the Second World War through the Civil War, the subsequent repressive parliamentary regime and then the military dictatorship, up to its most recent reincarnation as New Democracy" (Pridham and Verney 1991, 46). On the other hand, "ND argued that PASOK's ultimate objective was to subvert the democratic regime,

FIGURE 1
Left/Right Polarization in Greece 1985–2015

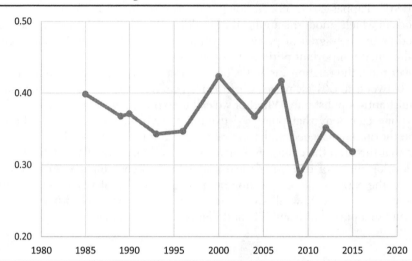

while the government was often referred to as the 'junta of PASOK'" (Kalyvas 1997, 88). Importantly, polarization was not just an elite phenomenon but affected the whole social fabric: it "was particularly felt at the mass level of politics as society became bitterly divided between the seemingly irreconcilable supporters of the two major parties." Even coffee shops were separated "throughout the country into 'green' and 'blue' according to the partisan identities of their patrons. The press and state-controlled electronic media also engaged in partisanship, thus further reinforcing social and political polarization" (Pappas 2014, 28).

How can we make sense of this polarization dynamic? What trajectory has it followed in the years since? Arguably, PASOK incarnated both a horizontal ideological (L/R), and a vertical populist (top/bottom, high/low) type of polarization. At the same time, its anti-EEC and anti-NATO discourses of the 1970s were soon replaced by a more pragmatic orientation, perhaps indicating that these were of overdetermined, secondary importance. Let us start by considering L/R polarization.

L/R polarization trends, 1985–2015

Figure 1 shows the development of L/R party polarization in Greece from 1985 to 2015.[1] Following the divisions of the early 1980s, polarization decreased, though it showed volatility. To better understand the mechanism producing variability in the L/R polarization index,[2] we can split the period into two parts. The first part, which can be described as the period of PASOK and ND dominance, covers the elections from 1985 until 2009. The second part covers the period of the financial crisis, the bailout agreement, and the enforcement of strict austerity measures that signaled the end of that dominance.

TABLE 1
Sum of Vote Shares of PASOK and ND

Year	1985	1989	1990	1993	1996	2000	2004	2007	2009
PASOK+ND	86.7%	86.9%	85.5%	86.2%	79.6%	86.5%	85.9%	79.9%	77.4%

FIGURE 2
Left/Right Self-Positioning of PASOK and ND Voters

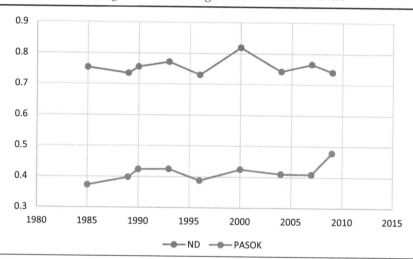

Table 1 shows the sum of vote shares received by PASOK and ND together from 1985 to 2009. In this period, this sum was very high (from 77.4 percent to 86.9 percent), indicating that Greece was under a two-party system. Thus, for this period it makes sense to focus on these two parties.

Party polarization in this two-party period took place mostly on the Left/Right (L/R) dimension. How did the L/R positioning of the two parties develop in this period? As Figure 2 shows, the period started with a large distance between PASOK and ND voters (0.38 in 1985), and it remained greater than 0.33 (i.e., more than one-third of the scale) in all election years until 2007. But the distance suddenly fell to 0.26 in 2009, as the voters of the two parties approached the center.

Comparing Figures 1 and 2 reveals that much of the polarization index variability between 1985 and 2004 can be attributed to movements of PASOK and ND voters. For instance, from 1985 to 1989 the voters of both parties moved toward the center and the distance between the parties became smaller. Figure 1 reveals a similar drop in the polarization index. Later, from 1996 to 2000, ND voters moved almost one-tenth of the scale to the Right (increasing their distance from PASOK), and in 2004 they fell back close to their 1996 position (decreasing their distance from PASOK). Figure 1 again shows a similar fluctuation of the polarization index during the same period. All in all, the trend is one of convergence: the two main parties and their voters moved toward the center, although the tendency was more pronounced on PASOK's part, possibly reflecting global trends among social-democratic parties.

Clearly, this trend involved a gradual softening of L/R polarization—which morphed into a center-Left/center-Right opposition—and the dominance of anti-populist actors and discourses in the party system and the public sphere. Arguably, democracy was initially consolidated in the context of a polarized political system in which Left-wing (populist/progressive) and Right-wing (anti-populist/conservative) forces, represented by PASOK and ND respectively, defended competing programs and thus built and disseminated antagonistic collective identities (see Voulgaris 2001; Stavrakakis and Katsambekis 2018). However, polarization soon gave way to a discourse of consensus, accompanied by constant denunciation of populism by both the PASOK of Costas Simitis and the ND of Kostas Karamanlis, who launched a new communication strategy of Bill Clinton-inspired "triangulation" in the late 1990s (Katsambekis 2016a).

Religious populism in the new century

Two anomalies interrupted the aforementioned trend of decreasing polarization, in 2000 and 2007. The second peak (in 2007) was not related to a significant movement of ND or PASOK voters: although the positions of the two major parties had not changed significantly (in comparison with 2004), polarization rose to one of its highest values in 2007. Two factors explain why polarization was no longer as strongly dependent on the ND and PASOK distance. First, the sum of the ND and PASOK vote share dropped below 80 percent. Second, the smaller parties that were represented in the Greek Parliament after the elections of 2007 embraced rather extreme L/R positions: The Communist Party of Greece (KKE, 0.13), the Coalition of the Radical Left (SYRIZA, 0.26), and the Popular Orthodox Rally (LAOS, 0.81).

At that time, SYRIZA was under the leadership of Alekos Alavanos, who took more radical positions than had his successor Alexis Tsipras. Under Tsipras, SYRIZA's L/R position moved closer to the center of the scale (contributing to the lower values of the L/R polarization index after 2009). In fact, the voters of all five parliamentary parties moved toward the center in 2009, resulting in the smallest value of the polarization index during the period in Greece.

The first peak of L/R polarization (2000) seems to coincide with one of the most striking developments in Greek politics around the turn of the century: the politicization of Church discourse. This politicization followed the decision by the center-Left (modernizing and antipopulist), Simitis-led PASOK government to exclude references to religion from Greek identity cards. This decision caused an extraordinary reaction on the part of the Greek Orthodox Church, a reaction that polarized Greek society and dominated political life and media coverage for most of 2000 and 2001.

The newly elected Archbishop Christodoulos led a campaign to oppose the decision, articulating a discourse that was marked by a clearly political profile. The campaign included mass rallies in Thessaloniki and Athens that were attended by hundreds of thousands of people, press conferences in the media, and an effort to gather as many signatures as possible calling for a referendum on the issue. This phase of populist mobilization ended in September 2001 after the Church's referendum demand was declared unconstitutional by both the constitutional court and the President of the Republic, a very popular conservative politician (Stavrakakis 2002, 2003).

What is significant here is that by the early 2000s the initial vehicle of populist polarization (PASOK) seems to have shifted toward an antipopulist, modernizing position (Lyrintzis 2005; Katsambekis 2016a). And with ND also following an antipopulist trajectory, the populist baton was passed on to a religious institution that articulated a populist strategy with nationalist and anti-European elements and a conservative ideology (hence the peak in L/R polarization). Yet this rather episodic occurrence had no salient, long-term effects on L/R polarization or on positions toward the EU (which was one of the main targets of the Archbishop's discourse, without, however, ceasing to be a target for funding programs initiated by the Church). At any rate, Archbishop Christodoulos's death in 2008 has denied the Church a more active role in recent years; his successor being somewhat more conciliatory.

The austerity effect, 2009–2015

In many international contexts, economic and social dislocations (such as the Venezuelan Caracazo in 1989, Argentina's default in the early 2000s, or the Greek debt crisis of the past few years) have triggered crises of representation that served as the springboard for polarization. Such crises are bound to create both populist mobilizations and antipopulist reactions, increasing polarization and potentially favoring a pernicious outcome. Especially in times of crisis, when ruling elites fail to deal with economic frustration and social dislocation, calls for political radicalization are often and summarily denounced as "populist," establishing a deep populist/antipopulist divide.

SYRIZA's meteoric rise in contemporary Greek politics, its elevation from a political outsider that attracted a mere 4.6 percent of the vote in the 2009 elections to a party of government that got 36.4 percent in the January 2015 elections (and almost replicating that result in September 2015) provides a suitable example. Between 2012 and 2015, the party's discourse chiefly involved (1) putting forward an antagonistic representation of the sociopolitical field along an us/them dichotomy, and (2) elevating "the people" to the position of the privileged signifier representing "us" in a manner allowing diverse groups hit by the crisis to identify themselves with this position (Stavrakakis and Katsambekis 2014; Katsambekis 2016b). Needless to say, this populist stance became the target of a variety of antipopulist discourses in politics and the media that singled out populism itself—a synecdoche of political evil projected onto SYRIZA—as the source of the crisis and of the failure to effectively deal with it (Stavrakakis 2014; Stavrakakis et al. 2018).

Radically diverging from the Eurocentric conventional wisdom that stereotypically casts populism as reactionary, nationalist, xenophobic, exclusionary, and anti-European, SYRIZA argued for a politically integrated and solidary Europe, defended immigrants and socially marginalized sectors, and pressed for social rights, claiming to fight for popular sovereignty, social justice, and democratization (Spourdalakis 2014; Stavrakakis and Katsambekis 2014; Stavrakakis et al. 2018). SYRIZA has attracted populist voters who support positions that are very different from the leftist positions of the party on both the economic and sociocultural L/R dimensions (Andreadis and Stavrakakis 2017). In fact, even conservative populist voters who have strong pro-EU attitudes seem to have chosen SYRIZA over the Right-wing populist party ANEL (Hawkins, Rovira Kaltwasser, and Andreadis 2018). In this sense, SYRIZA is very different from many other populist parties, including the populist PASOK of the 1980s, although many similarities exist at the level of political communication and discursive framing. SYRIZA's "paradox" was that it espoused a pro-European orientation that, at the same time, clashed with the dominant ordoliberal economic orientation of the euro-zone.

As we have seen, from 1974 onward a two-party system prevailed in which ND and PASOK, Right and Left, alternated in power. After the 1980s, the policies of the two parties gradually converged—with PASOK first adopting a social-democratic profile and then more liberalized economic policies—toward the antipopulist and EU-oriented center, and polarization subsided. What *dislocated* the system were the systemic failures associated with the 2008 global economic collapse and the way it was administered by dominant elites. GDP in Greece contracted by 20 percent between 2008 and 2012, and unemployment soared to 27 percent, with youth unemployment reaching 60 percent. The disastrous management of these systemic failures by the established political class resulted in wider intensification of social dislocations. This exacerbated indignation and discontent directed at the dominant regime of democratic representation (the two-party system) established after the transition to democracy, stimulating massive protest movements, including demonstrations, strikes, and square occupations (Stavrakakis et al. 2018). Once more, such a political choreography has not been peculiar to Greece alone; it bears striking resemblances to the historical trajectory of Latin American countries such as Venezuela and Argentina. But it has been one of the foremost examples of such a semiperipheral dynamic within the EU and the Euro-zone.[3]

In this context, the role of the Greek Indignants (*aganaktismenoi*) has been crucial (Pappas 2014, 83), signaling a second instance, after religious populism, in which civil society has taken the lead in reshaping the public sphere and over-determining political developments. And yet institutions remained largely insular to these demands. At this juncture, certain social actors started searching for new vehicles of political representation that would overcome the fragmentation and political impotence of the multitudes, organizing them and gaining access to power. Indeed, it was obviously impossible for the ensuing frustration, anger, and despair to leave party identification and the political process untouched during a series of consecutive early elections (twice in 2012 and then in early 2015). The parties affected included those entrusted to implement tough austerity policies by the European Commission (EC), the European Central Bank (ECB) and the

International Monetary Fund (IMF) (the so-called *troika*). Some of those parties, such as PASOK, have all but collapsed, with the main beneficiary being a former outsider, SYRIZA. As populism often does, SYRIZA thus emerged from the sidelines as a new response to the crisis of political representation, a crisis it partly created by attributing the blame for the socioeconomic dislocation since 2008 to the economic and political "establishment" (both national and European) to legitimize a populist re-democratization (Stavrakakis et al. 2018).

Polarization was a crucial strategy here, as it had been for Papandreou in the 1970s and 1980s (Pappas 2014, 29). Once more, then, the populist articulation of political antagonism has migrated to the Left, indeed the radical Left, following the short interval of religious populism in the early 2000s—and the radical Right populism of fringe parties such as LAOS that tried to capitalize on it. If, however, PASOK's surge in the early 1980s was conditioned by the demands of previously excluded sectors to enjoy equal rights and access to decision-making, SYRIZA's dynamic represented the demands of sectors hit by the crisis and alienated by the established party system and international/EU institutions.

In other words, if the PASOK of the 1970s and 1980s sought to express and represent social strata mainly Left of center, which had been excluded, marginalized, and mistreated for decades due to their ideological positioning (alleged or real), SYRIZA now claimed to represent those hit by austerity policies—those impoverished and marginalized because of the way the two traditional parties (PASOK and ND) had chosen to deal with the crisis. SYRIZA especially targeted people who were frustrated with PASOK's turn to neoliberal policies, which had devastating effects on the electoral base it had built from the mid-1970s onward.

And what about attitudes toward Europe and the EU? The selection of SYRIZA's coalition partner after the January 2015 elections, as well as the culmination of a bumpy negotiation with Greece's Euro-zone partners and lenders in an extremely polarized referendum (July 5, 2015), initially seemed to point toward a confrontation with the EU. Yet SYRIZA's eventual agreement to a new bailout memorandum may have signaled a turning point. As already noted, SYRIZA's attacks on the troika and the hegemonic policies of the Euro-zone did not involve an outright anti-European agenda, which would have clashed with the crypto-colonial identification regulating the attachment of many Greeks to the European project (Stavrakakis and Siomos 2016). As soon as the fantasy of "changing Europe" met its pragmatic limits, revealing the paradox plaguing SYRIZA's main demand ("Yes to the EU, No to austerity"), SYRIZA faced a dramatic dilemma. Like Papandreou's pragmatic U-turn in the early 1980s, the SYRIZA leadership opted to compromise, accepting the EU-imposed rules and opting for continuity in the country's geopolitical positioning. The compromise led to a split in the party, with the more Euro-skeptic faction establishing a new party, Popular Unity.

SYRIZA's compromise with the EU was largely endorsed by the electorate in the September 2015 elections, in which SYRIZA reproduced, more or less, the result of January 2015. At the same time, however, the anti-European attitude, formed in the context of the continuing brutal enforcement of austerity and the failure of SYRIZA's attempt to challenge it, only grew stronger. The party system

TABLE 2
Attitudes toward the EU and the Bailout Agreement per Party in 2012

	Blame foreigners		EU membership is bad	
	Mean	SD	Mean	SD
ND	0.57	0.213	0.20	0.289
SYRIZA-EKM	0.65	0.208	0.39	0.353
PASOK	0.61	0.276	0.26	0.291
ANEL	0.69	0.220	0.49	0.390
LS-XA	0.74	0.215	0.46	0.398
DIMAR	0.57	0.184	0.20	0.273
KKE	0.76	0.218	0.72	0.402
Total	**0.63**	**0.226**	**0.34**	**0.349**

in its form as of this writing—including SYRIZA—seems unable to represent this anti-EU sentiment in a consistent manner, but only the future can tell whether this will remain the case.

Polarization Beyond the Established Party System: New Challenges

The years 2012 and 2015 each saw two elections. Party polarization on the L/R dimension was low. Thus, we need to examine whether during this period the Greek electorate was polarized on other dimensions.

Our data from 2015 include numerous items that can be used to study polarization in additional dimensions, but the suitable variables in the 2012 study are limited. Table 2 shows the average scores on two dimensions based on questions asked in 2012. (The details of these questions are presented in the online appendix). The variables range from 0 to 1, with larger values indicating more negative attitudes toward the EU and the bailout agreements. For the first variable, the minimum value (0) corresponds to attributing no responsibility to external factors (the EU, Germany, the IMF, and credit rating agencies) and Greece's participation in Eurozone. The maximum value (1) appears when respondents think that all the aforementioned foreign actors are responsible for their economic situation.

The Greek electorate's average blame-foreigners score is 0.63. This average score indicates that Greek citizens think that foreign actors are largely to blame for their difficult economic situation. The polarization index for the blame-for-eigners dimension is rather low (0.10), indicating that most citizens are on the same side, that is, they agree on blaming foreign actors and institutions. The harsh austerity measures enforced under the bailout agreements are the main reason for the generally negative attitude toward the bailout and for blaming the

FIGURE 3
Negative Attitudes towards EU Membership (2004–2014) in Greece

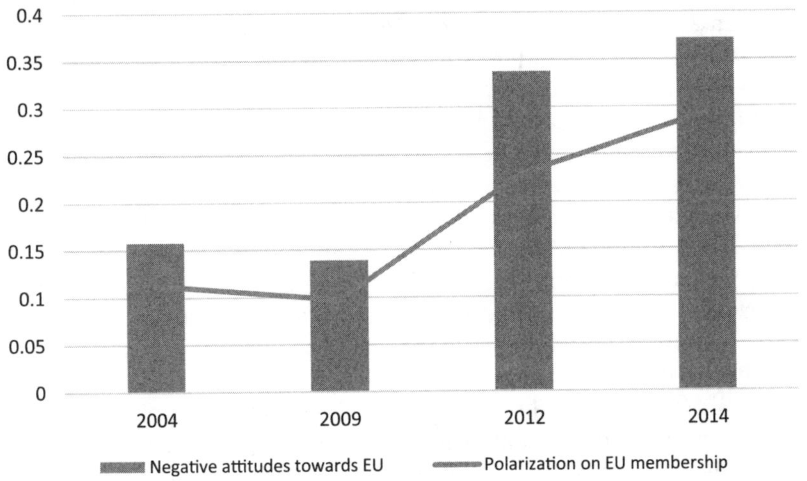

NOTE: Zero is the most positive; 1 is the most negative.
SOURCES: European Election Studies 2004, 2009, 2014 and Hellenic National Election Study 2012.

EU and other foreign actors, especially since, as Teperoglou et al (2014) have demonstrated, all Greek political parties that have elected members in the Greek parliament have encouraged this view (for more details about blame-shifting to the EU, see Teperoglou and Andreadis 2012).

Finally, the average score for the item that measures negative attitudes toward EU membership is much lower (0.34), indicating that, besides the aforementioned blame attribution, the majority of the 2012 Greek electorate wanted Greece to remain a member of the EU.[4] Of the two dimensions studied using ELNES 2012 data, this one has the higher polarization index (0.23), but, even in this case, the index is still not very high. This is because the only party with a clear negative attitude toward the EU is KKE, and its voters represent a small part of the Greek electorate.

To further illustrate the development of negative attitudes toward the EU, Figure 3 presents findings from the 2004, 2009, and 2014 European Election Studies datasets (Egmond et al. 2017; Schmitt et al. 2009; Schmitt, Hobolt, et al. 2016) and the Hellenic National Election Studies dataset (2012). The bars represent the mean value of attitudes toward the EU from 2004 to 2014 (0 is the most positive; 1 the most negative). In 2004 and 2009, before the crisis, the mean values are about 0.15, indicating that almost all Greeks evaluate EU membership as a good thing. After the crisis, the mean value increases significantly, to about 0.35 in 2012 and 2014, indicating that a significant part of the electorate no longer maintains its positive evaluation of EU membership. This development affects the trajectory of the polarization index along the EU membership dimension (depicted by the line on the diagram). In 2004 and 2009, the polarization index was very low (about 0.1), but as the portion of the electorate with negative attitudes toward EU membership grew, a rather different situation appeared after the crisis. In 2012, and even more so in 2014, polarization over EU membership is much higher, reflecting the role of European institutions in imposing austerity and the postdemocratic trend in decision-making.

For 2015, we have much richer data. ELNES 2015a includes a battery of questions about populist attitudes (see Stavrakakis, Andreadis, and Katsambekis 2017). It also includes statements from the Voting Advice Application (VAA) "HelpMeVote 2015" (Andreadis 2015). These capture the most important issues of political competition in Greece at the beginning of 2015 (the items used in this study are presented in Tables A1 and A2 in the online appendix). Three dimensions merit particular attention. The first comprises economic issues and attitudes toward the bailout agreements and the EU, the second comprises exclusively the items from a populism battery, while the third corresponds to sociocultural attitudes. On the sociocultural dimension, the polarization index is 0.17; on the populist dimension, it is 0.16. The highest polarization index, 0.29, occurs on the economy/anti-EU dimension. This finding shows that attitudes toward the EU were polarizing the Greek electorate, and that pro/anti-EU polarization was closely associated with the austerity measures enforced by the bailout agreements (similar conclusions can be drawn from following the Eurobarometer surveys).

Conclusion

Polarization has been present in Greek political culture throughout the postauthoritarian era, which began in 1974. As it reformulated cleavages emanating from the Greek Civil War, if not earlier, and purported to deal with a variety of challenges (e.g., democratic consolidation, socioeconomic incorporation of previously excluded strata, accession to the EEC, adoption of the Euro, and debt crisis), the political system has seen the dimensions and intensity of polarization fluctuate significantly. A brief review of some milestones in this trajectory, complemented by an analysis of discourse and opinion surveys, has helped us to somewhat clarify a complex choreography.

Polarization was established in the 1970s and early 1980s at both the leadership and popular level through the effective partisan performance of PASOK, which dominated the political field against a Right wing seen as incarnating, even in a much reduced form, the legacy of the exclusionary state that emerged after the Greek Civil War. Its institutionalization, however, also relied on the defeated ND's vitriolic reproaches of PASOK. During this period, the L/R axis, together with the populist/antipopulist frontier, seemed to attract most of the symbolic and affective dynamic of political polarization. Although positioning vis-à-vis Europeanization was also invoked at the discursive level, this failed to influence policy and slowly receded from the horizon, a fact that seems to corroborate the crypto-colonial hypothesis rather than the "cultural dualism" thesis. Arguably, during this period polarization operated more as a booster of than an obstacle to democratization, since it did not lead to pernicious effects.

From the mid-1980s onward, polarization seemed to moderate, and eventually the two main parties and their supporters seemed to converge on the middle ground, with the exception of the period around the identity cards crisis and the inclusion of religious belonging. This trajectory seemed to follow international trends of postpolitical consensus and was made possible by the upward social mobility marking this period, the achievement of reforms giving access to previously excluded groups, economic development through EU support, and the dominance of antipopulist modernization discourses.

In terms of quantitative data, during the first period (until 2009), polarization was measured on the L/R dimension only; it depends mostly on ideological movements of PASOK or ND. Yet a significant drop in L/R polarization can be observed toward the end of this period, in 2009. This trend coincides with the onset of the economic crisis and the increasing inability of the established party system to manage it in politically credible ways. In the second period, 2012–15, L/R polarization remained low, possibly signifying that the dynamic emergence of the radical Left SYRIZA was not premised on identification with its radical ideological profile on the part of broader social strata. It seems that SYRIZA managed to represent new demands that arose (or re-emerged) during the crisis for two reasons: all other established political forces from the Left and Right had been discredited, and SYRIZA assumed the representation of popular grievances developed on other axes.

Yet those grievances were paradoxical and contradictory. To the extent that the administration of the crisis partly emanated from abroad (and was experienced as such) and largely ignored popular grievances and protests, it caused an internal split in attitudes toward the EU and Europe. Faced with an overwhelming challenge, Greece's external environment was effectively represented in terms of a pervasive *split* between a "bad object" (the troika, EU institutions, etc.) and a "good object" (European orientation and belonging in general terms).[5] With its populist discourse, SYRIZA managed to express this inherently divided orientation against the established party system. And yet, exactly like PASOK in the 1980s, its orientation following the July 2015 referendum seems to reveal the reluctance of political elites (including the SYRIZA leadership), as well as a significant part of the electorate, to put in doubt the country's membership in the EU and its overall geopolitical positioning.

It may be that this development will leave an emerging Euro-skeptic orientation devoid of political representation. That will depend on whether the government as of this writing can partially satisfy—even at the symbolic level—demands pertaining to the elite vs. people dimension and alleviate economic grievances related to high unemployment, falling wages, and a collapsing welfare state; that is, to quote Melanie Klein, whether it can manage a more or less "smooth" passage from the "schizoid" to the "depressive" position (Klein 1975). In the 1980s, Andreas Papandreou managed to use polarization in a way that enhanced democratization on a variety of levels without destabilizing the country's European course. Dealing with a more intrusive Europe seeking to impose severe limits on economic and popular sovereignty, SYRIZA's task is much more formidable now. Much will depend on whether the currently orphaned anti-EU resentment will eventually find avenues of political representation establishing it, for the first time, as a salient axis of polarization. Could the Communist Party, KKE, or even Golden Dawn capitalize on this situation? Only the next general elections, scheduled for 2019, will adequately illuminate this question. At any rate, at a rhetorical level, and notwithstanding SYRIZA's change of course, the discourse toward SYRIZA of parties such as ND and PASOK remains very negative, indicating that the ongoing democratic careening has no predetermined outcome.[6]

Notes

1. The True European Voter (TEV) is the first source of data used in this study. The last available dataset in TEV is for the Greek Parliamentary elections of 2012. We have complemented these data with data from the Hellenic (Greek) Voter Study for the Parliamentary elections of January 2015 (ELNES 2015a). For further details, see Andreadis, Kartsounidou and Chatzimallis (2015) and http://elnes.gr.

2. For the calculation of the polarization index, we use the average ideological position of the respondents who voted for each political party, as an estimate for the position of the partisans of each party. Consequently, our polarization index is similar to the polarization index used by Dalton (2008). It has a value of 0 when the voters of all parties occupy the same position and 1 when voters are equally split between the two extremes of the scale. However, in real life, it is almost impossible to observe values close to the maximum value of the scale; in most cases, the values of this index are lower than the midpoint of the scale (see Table 1 in Dalton 2008, 907) For more details, see the online appendix.

3. Nicos Mouzelis had long ago elaborated the many similarities between semi-peripheral countries in Southern Europe and Latin America. See, in this respect, Mouzelis (1986).

4. We have rescaled this item on the [0, 1] range to make it comparable with the rest of the findings presented in this article. Lower values (near 0) indicate pro-EU and higher values (near 1) indicate anti-EU attitudes.

5. These concepts are drawn from psychoanalytic theory, in particular from the way Melanie Klein describes the so-called "schizoid" position (Klein 1975).

6. Many thanks are due to Jennifer McCoy, Murat Somer, and Giorgos Katsambekis for their invaluable comments on an earlier draft of this article.

References

Andreadis, Ioannis. 2015. The Greek voter according to HelpMeVote 2015 and ELNES 2015. Paper presented at the ECPR General Conference, Montreal.

Andreadis, Ioannis, Evangelia Kartsounidou, and Charalampos Chatzimallis. 2015. Innovation, an answer to lack of funding: The 2015 Hellenic National Election Voter Study. PSA Greek Politics Specialist Group Working Papers 22. Available from www.gpsg.org.uk/wp-content/uploads/2015/12/Working_Paper_22.pdf.

Andreadis, Ioannis, and Yannis Stavrakakis. 2017. European populist parties in government: How well are voters represented? Evidence from Greece. Swiss Political Science Review 23 (4): 485–508.

Dalton, Russell J. 2008. The quantity and the quality of party systems: Party system polarization, its measurement, and its consequences. Comparative Political Studies 41 (7): 899–920.

Diamandouros, Nikiforos. 1994. Cultural dualism and political change in postauthoritarian Greece. Madrid: Instituto Juan March.

Egmond, Marcel van, Wouter van der Brug, Sara Hobolt, Mark Franklin, and Eliyahu V. Sapir. 2017. European Parliament Election Study 2009: Voter Study. GESIS Data Archive, Cologne. ZA5055 Data file Version 1.1.1, doi:10.4232/1.12732.

Hawkins, Kirk, Cristobal Rovira Kaltwasser, and Ioannis Andreadis. 2018. The activation of populist attitudes. *Government and Opposition*. doi.org/10.1017/gov.2018.23.

Herzfeld, Michael. 2002. The absent presence: Discourses of crypto-colonialism. *The South Atlantic Quarterly* 101 (4): 899–926.

Kalyvas, Stathis. 1997. Polarization in Greek politics: PASOK's first four years, 1981–1985. *Journal of the Hellenic Diaspora* 23 (1): 83–104.

Katsambekis, Giorgos. 2016a. "The people" and political opposition in post-democracy: Reflections on the hollowing of democracy in Greece and Europe. In *The state we're in: Reflecting on democracy's troubles*, eds. Joanna Cook, Nicholas J. Long, and Henrietta L. Moore, 144–66. Oxford: Berghahn Books.

Katsambekis, Giorgos. 2016b. Radical left populism in contemporary Greece. *Constellations* 23 (3): 391–403.

Katsambekis, Giorgos, and Yannis Stavrakakis. 2017. Revisiting the nationalism/populism nexus: Lessons from the Greek case. *Javnost - The Public*. 24: 391–408.

Klein, Mélanie. 1975. *Envy and gratitude and other works 1946–1963*. London: Hogarth Press and the Institute of Psycho-Analysis.

Lyrintzis, Christos. 1987. The power of populism: The Greek case. *European Journal of Political Research* 15 (6): 667–86.

Lyrintzis, Christos. 2005. The changing party system: Stable democracy, contested "modernisation". *West European Politics* 28 (2): 242–59.

Mouzelis, Nicos. 1986. *Politics in the semi-periphery*. New York, NY: Saint Martin's Press.

Pappas, Takis. 2014. *Populism and crisis politics in Greece*. Abingdon: Palgrave Macmillan.

Pridham, Geoffrey, and Susannah Verney. 1991. The coalitions of 1989–90 in Greece: Inter-party relations and democratic consolidation. *West European Politics* 14 (4): 42–69.

Schmitt, Hermann, Stefano Bartolini, Wouter van der Brug, Cees van der Eijk, Mark Franklin, Dieter Fuchs, Gabor Toka, Michael Marsh, and Jacques Thomassen. 2009. European Election Study 2004 (2nd edition). GESIS Data Archive, Cologne. ZA4566 Data file Version 2.0.0, DOI:10.4232/1.10086.

Schmitt, Hermann, Sara B. Hobolt, Sebastian A. Popa, and Eftichia Teperoglou. 2016. European Parliament Election Study 2014, Voter Study, First Post-Election Survey. European Parliament, Directorate-General for Communication, Public Monitoring Unit. GESIS Data Archive, Cologne. ZA5160 Data file Version 4.0.0, DOI:10.4232/1.12628.

Somer, Murat, and Jennifer McCoy. 2019. Transformations through polarizations and global threats to democracy. *The ANNALS of the American Academy of Political and Social Science* (this volume).

Spourdalakis, Michalis. 2014. The miraculous rise of the "phenomenon SYRIZA." *International Critical Thought* 4 (3): 354–66.

Stavrakakis, Yannis. 2002. Religious populism and political culture: The Greek case. *South European Society and Politics* 7 (3): 29–52.

Stavrakakis, Yannis. 2003. Politics and religion: On the "politicization" of Greek church discourse. *Journal of Modern Greek Studies* 21:153–81.

Stavrakakis, Yannis. 2014. The return of "the people": Populism and anti-populism in the shadow of the European crisis. *Constellations* 21 (4): 505–17.

Stavrakakis, Yannis. 2016. Populism and hegemony. In *The Oxford handbook of populism*, eds. Paul Taggart, Cristobal Róvira Kaltwasser, Paulina Ochoa Espejo and Pierre Ostiguy, 535–53. Oxford: Oxford University Press.

Stavrakakis, Yannis, I. Andreadis, and Giorgos Katsambekis. 2017. A new populism index at work: Identifying populist candidates and parties in the contemporary Greek context. *European Politics and Society* 18 (4): 446–64.

Stavrakakis, Yannis, and Giorgos Katsambekis. 2014. Left-wing populism in the European periphery: The case of SYRIZA. *Journal of Political Ideologies* 19 (2): 127–29.

Stavrakakis, Yannis, and Thomas Siomos. 2016. SYRIZA's populism: Testing and extending an Essex school perspective. Paper presented at the ECPR General Conference, Charles University, 7–10 September 2016. Prague.

Stavrakakis, Yannis, and Giorgos Katsambekis. 2018. The populism/anti-populism frontier and its media-tion in crisis-ridden Greece: From discursive divide to emerging cleavage? *European Political Science*. DOI: 10.1057/s41304-017-0138-3.

Stavrakakis, Yannis, Giorgos Katsambekis, Alexandros Kioupkiolis, Nikos Nikisianis, and Thomas Siomos. 2018. Populism, anti-populism and crisis. *Contemporary Political Theory* 17 (1): 4–27.

Teperoglou, Eftichia, and I. Andreadis. 2012. Investigating consensus versus conflict between the Greek and Portuguese political elites during the economic crisis: A matter of ideology? Paper presented at the 2nd Plenary Conference of the CCS, 27–29 January 2012. University of Mannheim. Available from http://www.polres.gr/en/sites/default/files/CCS-2012.pdf.

Teperoglou, Eftichia, Andre Freire, Ioannis Andreadis, and Jose M. Leite Viegas. 2014. Elites' and voters' attitudes towards austerity policies and their consequences in Greece and Portugal. *South European Society and Politics* 19 (4): 457–76.

Voulgaris, Yannis. 2001. *The Greece of Metapolitefsi 1974–1990*. Athens: Themelio.

Party System Institutionalization and Pernicious Polarization in Bangladesh

By
TAHMINA RAHMAN

This article traces the development of political polarization in Bangladesh since its 1971 war of independence. I show how polarization is elite-driven, hinging mostly on competing views of the foundation myth of the nation. One major political bloc has emerged that ties national identity tightly to religion (Islam), where the other bloc prefers a national identity tied to ethnicity and use of the Bengali language. I show how an underdeveloped party system has contributed to the resulting political and societal polarization that stems from this ideological divide, which was created by elites as they attempted to consolidate party power. Further, I make a case that the activities of the International Crimes Tribunal (ICT)—established in 2010 to prosecute those who aided the Pakistani army in committing war crimes during the 1971 war—actually increased polarization and made it pernicious. Instead of healing the nation, the ICT exacerbated old political cleavages and instigated violence and social tension, making Bangladesh's young democracy more unstable and careening.

Keywords: polarization; Bangladesh; party system institutionalization; democratic careening

Bangladesh, a country where most people speak Bengali and practice Sunni Islam, presents a curious case of pernicious polarization. Political polarization there involves competing definitions of national identity, rather than divergent economic ideologies or class-based social cleavages. It takes the form of an Islamist/secular divide among the country's major political parties, where the Islamist parties focus on the religious element of national identity and the secular parties focus on language-based ethnic identity. This debate about national identity has spilled over into

Tahmina Rahman is a PhD candidate in political science at Georgia State University and an assistant professor of international relations at the University of Dhaka, Bangladesh.

Correspondence: trahman1@gsu.edu

DOI: 10.1177/0002716218817280

other areas of politics and society, creating long, protracted, and often violent disagreement over policy issues, producing poor policy decisions. It has also fostered social intolerance and often instigated violence. Since 2010, polarization has taken a particularly intense form over the issue of trial and punishment of people who committed crimes against humanity during the 1971 Liberation War.[1] This phase of polarization started over the legitimacy, transparency, and effectiveness of the International Crimes Tribunal (ICT), set up in 2010 to prosecute the war criminals, but it soon turned into a battle over a monopoly on the "true nationalist narrative."[2] The pro-Tribunal forces came to view and depict anyone opposing the Tribunal as Islamists who were trying to destroy the secular nature of the state. The anti-Tribunal forces saw an anti-Islamist and immoral social movement in the group that supported the Tribunal.

Bangladesh does not fit in the category of crisis-of-representation-induced polarization, as do Thailand or the Philippines (discussed elsewhere in this volume). As McCoy, Rahman, and Somer (2018) discuss, polarization is often a result of previously disenfranchised or under-represented groups' gaining political power and then alienating the opponent. This creates a backlash and divides society. But Bangladesh, one of the most stable democracies in South Asia, is a different story. The major parties here are quite broad-based and represent different groups/classes of people. The country has seen regular transfer of power between these parties through elections since 1991. Voter turnout is high, and people seem to be content with choosing their representatives from the existing parties. Most people still think democracy is the best method of governance (International Republican Institute 2017). Therefore, this is not a case of populist polarization caused by the political mobilization and empowerment of a previously unempowered or underrepresented group.

Neither has Bangladesh experienced any big exogenous shock such as an economic meltdown. In fact, the global financial crisis of 2008–09 did not greatly affect it, due to its relative insularity from the global economy. If anything, Bangladesh graduated from the category of "least developed" to the category of "developing countries" in 2017 (United Nations Department of Social and Economic Affairs 2018). A 2017 Asia Foundation survey found that, despite a large income gap, citizens are generally hopeful about where the country is heading (Rieger, Taylor, and Tweedie 2017).

Bangladesh has also consistently scored high on the global happiness index in 2009, 2012, and 2016.[3] So, there is little reason to conclude that economic discontent or lack of political enfranchisement is driving polarization in the country. In fact, major political parties in the country have a broad constituency base that cuts across social classes. Instead, polarization in Bangladesh is caused by competition over a monopoly on what LeBas and Munemo, in another contribution to this volume, call the "foundational myth" of a nation. The conflict is about what Bangladesh stands for, what its founding goals are, and what defines and distinguishes its people from other nationalities. It is about embracing either religion (Islam) or ethnicity (Bengali language) as the core component of national identity of its people—an unfinished project of nation-building that has been ongoing since Bangladeshi independence in 1971.

Although polarization in Bangladesh does not originate from either crisis-of-representation or class-based social cleavages, it is no less pernicious than other cases of severe polarization discussed in this volume of *The ANNALS*. Polarization at the political elite level has locked Bangladesh in what Somer and McCoy, in the introduction to this volume, refer to as *careening*, with an *increasingly authoritarian* turn. Although power regularly alternates between the two major parties through elections, policymaking is a contentious process, as policy issues are subsumed in the polarized divide over national identity. The polarized context impedes negotiation and consultation, and the governing party frequently makes unilateral decisions about nationally important issues. On the societal level, such polarization generates social distance between supporters of opposing political parties, where each group views the other as an existential threat to the identity and way of life of the Bangladeshi people.

This article demonstrates how an underdeveloped party system is a major contributor to the pernicious political and societal polarization in Bangladesh, arguing that polarization in Bangladesh is an elite-driven phenomenon. Although polarization over the Tribunal started at the civil-society level, the ingredients for such polarization are found in the major political parties. Their polarizing narratives since the authoritarian era (1976–1990)[4] prepared the ground for polarized civil society movements that feed on divisive nationalist narratives. Thus, polarization in Bangladesh has a cyclical nature, where unresolved debates over national identity are harnessed by the political parties to advance their agendas through their respective brands of civil society. These civil societies in turn exacerbate and sharpen the existing divide with the help of the political parties.

I trace the development of polarization in Bangladesh in three distinctive periods: elevation of social cleavages during the authoritarian period (1976–1990) as a way to solve the regime's legitimacy crisis; harnessing polarizing narratives during the first two decades of the post-authoritarian era to control electoral volatility (1991–2008); and crystallization of pernicious polarization over the Tribunal issue between 2010 and 2013.

Polarization as a Tool for Party System Institutionalization

Party system institutionalization refers to predictable patterns of intra-party competition. A highly institutionalized party system would exhibit a higher level of stability in terms of parties' maintaining strong bonds with the grassroots and retaining their core constituencies. A poorly institutionalized party system would be more chaotic in the sense that the parties might not have an adequate social bond with the grassroots level and, therefore, voters might switch parties more frequently, jeopardizing the electoral fortune of the parties.

Although scholars have identified many dimensions of party system institutionalization, the most relevant ones here are stability in party competition, lack of electoral volatility, and strong roots in society (Mainwaring and Trocal 2006, 206–27). In many emerging democracies, party system institutionalization, in terms of establishing a strong bond with the voters and stabilizing their electoral behavior, is a tricky business (Mainwaring and Zoco 2007). Because they did not arise out of socioeconomic changes like their western counterparts, the quickest way for these parties to create a dependable constituency is to organize people around some known social cleavage or cleavages (Manning 2005, 718). Manning explains that, in post-1990 Africa, parties "grew not out of socioeconomic cleavages or struggles over the nature of state authority, but out of elites' urgent need for electoral vehicles, which would allow them to compete in newly devised rules of the political game. Often the easiest basis for mobilizing support is via the politicization of ethnicity" (Manning 2005, 715).

While Manning offers a rather neutral assessment of cleavage-based party system institutionalization, others have been more critical. Randall and Svåsand caution us that "the very opportunity of party institutionalization provided by exclusive forms of cleavage, above all religion and ethnicity, could be at odds with the institutionalization of the party system through restricting the possibilities for cross party competition, and undermining the ethos of mutual acceptance amongst parties as well as the confidence of at least a section of the public in political parties" (Randall and Svåsand 2002, 9). Hence, polarization resulting from such cleavage-dependent politics could present the illusion of a party system that has achieved a high level of institutionalization, as evidenced by predictability in electoral turnout and the strength of the social relations between major parties and their constituencies.

In an emerging democracy like Bangladesh, party system institutionalization based on manufactured political cleavages that feed on founding myths of the nation can be counterproductive in terms of producing and sustaining a liberal democratic system. In a country that is nearly homogenous ethnically, linguistically, and religiously, political cleavages are not based on some objective measure of difference between groups, but artificially created to secure a constituency for different political parties. The Bengali/secular vs. Bangladeshi/Islamist divide goes back to the debate over what constitutes the core element of national identity, which started forming in the post-independence era under a military dictatorship. But its effect on the quality of democracy is similar to that of party system institutionalization based on ethnic/religious cleavages in other emerging democracies.

As data from Varieties of Democracy (Coppedge et al. 2018) show, since 1991 Bangladesh has consistently scored high in terms of party system institutionalization (0.7 on a 0 to 1 scale, where 0 is the worst and 1 is the best), a score that has not decreased over the years. But the same dataset shows that, since 2001, the country has consistently performed poorly in terms of respect for counterarguments and parties' willingness to compromise. This indicates that polarization might have regularized the institutional aspects of democracy, but at the same time it has made the uncooperative and confrontational nature of interaction between political parties a predictable pattern of behavior. Stability has not automatically translated into higher-quality democracy, at least not in terms of social and political tolerance and respect for pluralism.

After the return of democracy in 1991, major parties in Bangladesh needed to stabilize their respective constituencies. Both the liberal/center-Left Bangladesh Awami League (AL) and the conservative/center-Right Bangladesh Nationalist Party (BNP) appeared identical in their support for electoral democracy and market economy. Thus, they were mostly indistinguishable in terms of their programmatic appeals to the voters. They were also facing the challenge of electoral volatility from one general election to the other. In a winner-take-all arrangement such as Bangladesh's first-past-the-post parliamentary system, losing an election means losing all policymaking and rent-generating power. Therefore, to stabilize their constituencies and solidify voters into political camps, these parties fueled the country's identity debate. Although the political elite activated the latent identity cleavage, it has historical roots, largely as a result of the unfinished nation-building project in a country that became independent from two different rulers (Britain and Pakistan) in the same century, based on two different nationalist narratives.

Although a debate over national identity has always existed in Bangladesh, it sharpened in the years following the institution of the 2010 Tribunal. It took a particularly intense form in the first half of 2013. On February 5, 2013, people started gathering at Shahbag, a commuter hub in the capital, Dhaka, to condemn the Tribunal's verdict in a case involving an influential leader of the Islamist political party Bangladesh Jamaat-e-Islami (BJI). In Bangladeshi politics, BJI has not been very successful electorally, but over the years it has turned out to be a king maker via its political representation in the national assembly (Islam and Islam 2018, 12). Immediately after independence, BJI, along with other Islamist parties, was banned from Bangladeshi politics for their alleged collaboration with the Pakistani army in the 1971 liberation war. But Major Zia rehabilitated these stigmatized political elements during his military dictatorship. His successor, General Ershad, followed the same policy (Linter 2002, 3). By collaborating with the center-Right BNP, which has a moderate Islamist orientation, and by slowly cultivating a grassroots network throughout the country, BJI has been very successful in removing the stigma associated with the war. The rise of a generation of Bangladeshis who had not experienced the war first hand also helped to, as Linter says, "correct" the situation (Linter 2002, 3). Over the years, BJI achieved the status of the "largest and most active" Islamist party (Hossain and Siddiquee 2004, 384) in the country. This, along with the popularity of some of its top leadership as Islamist preachers, made the party politically influential. But not everyone has stopped questioning its role in the 1971 war. The segment of the population that associates itself more with the secular and language-based identity is particularly opposed to BJI's brand of politics.

Against this backdrop, the Tribunal sentenced BJI leader, Qader Molla, to life in prison, igniting a very polarized discourse. The Bangladesh Online Activist Forum (BOAN) called for gathering at Shahbag, where people demanded harsher punishment for Qader Molla, then the Assistant Secretary General of BJI, who was convicted of multiple crimes against humanity.

Soon Shahbag became center stage for what some analysts initially thought was the biggest nonpartisan apolitical movement in the post-authoritarian era.

But, as the movement grew stronger, it added more demands, such as banning religion-based politics and outlawing BJI for the involvement of its top leadership in war crimes. Around the same time, a counter-movement started to form, whose members did not consider the Tribunal to be legitimate. Rather, they viewed it as a puppet in the hands of the ruling government. They felt that by "targeting" the Islamist opposition forces for their involvement in the 1971 war, the ruling AL was making its path clear for the next general election, which was to take place in 2014. They were also concerned that abolishing religion from politics would downgrade the religious identity of the world's fourth-largest Muslim country. Hence, this counter-movement wanted the government to abolish the Tribunal and recommended serious punishment for Tribunal supporters for their anti-Islamist nature. As the anti-Tribunal movement started gaining support, it also added more demands for reorganizing the state and society to conform to a conservative version of Islam. Soon these two movements were embroiled in a polarized identity discourse. Pro-Tribunal forces worried that the activities of Islamist political forces (many of whom were charged with crimes against humanity) had been undermining the secular Bengali (language-based ethnicity) identity of Bangladesh. Conversely, the anti-Tribunal forces viewed the Tribunal as a political tool of the ruling AL government because the prosecution seemed to be targeting the top leaders of the opposition parties.

What evades the eyes of a casual observer, though, is what the AL and the BNP stood to gain from this polarization. Hence, an alternative explanation would take into account that what started as two separate civil society movements around the activities of the Tribunal might have become an identity crisis manufactured by the elites of these two political parties. These two movements represented the struggle between AL and BNP to create a stable niche for themselves. When these parties decided to support their preferred civil society movements, the fighting over the Tribunal expanded beyond its original focus, and polarization intensified. The following two sections discuss the structural roots of and the institutional incentives for the polarizing strategies that the major political parties employed in Bangladesh.

Structural Legacy: Unresolved Identity Crisis from Precolonial Bengal to Post-Independence Bangladesh

Confusion over what constitutes the core element of national identity in Bangladesh stems from two separate nationalist movements focusing on two different ingredients of nationhood—religion and language. Religion has played an influential role in the formation of national identity in South Asia, and Bangladesh is no exception. However, British colonialism changed the dynamics of religious politics in the region. Hindus and Muslims in the Indian subcontinent were pitted against each other in a divisive struggle to secure colonial patronage. Due to uneven socioeconomic development, the Hindu–Muslim divide did not lead to class conflict; instead it took the form of solidarity among the Muslims.

In this way, religious identity became a central instrument for political mobilization in colonial India. The Bengali Muslim political elite carefully constructed an identity for Bengali-speaking Muslims, who lagged behind the Hindus in terms of access to state institutions and resources. That is why the Bengalis had little trouble imagining themselves as part of a nation based on Islam when Pakistan was born in 1947 following the "two-nations theory."[5] However, the cultural differences between the two wings of Pakistan were too much to handle. The nonaccommodative and discriminatory posture of the Urdu-speaking elite in West Pakistan toward the East generated resentment among Bengalis (Misra 1972, 29).

West Pakistan's efforts to quell the eastern wing's cultural uniqueness further alienated Bengalis. Attempts at cultural homogenization and economic discrimination galvanized the Bengali Muslims in the East against the Muslims in the West. To assert their political and economic autonomy and cultural self-determination, Bengali Muslims started focusing on the other important element of their national identity—the Bengali language. Thus, a people who had supported the creation of an undivided Pakistan for Muslims started a liberation war to create their own nation-state around a language-based identity. The Pakistani army chose to play the religion card to justify genocide in East Pakistan, branding the Bengalis as kafirs or infidels. This galvanized East Pakistani public opinion against Islamist politics and gave the pro-liberation political elites an opportunity to focus on secularism as the cornerstone of Bengali nationalism (Huque and Akhter 1987, 202–03).

Islamist political entities in East Pakistan at that time sided with the Pakistani army because they were not persuaded that a separate nation-state for the Bengalis was a good idea. Elora Shehabuddin (2008, 589) explains: "During the 9-month war that followed, the Jamaat of the erstwhile East Pakistan gained notoriety in secularist and nationalist circles for speaking out against the country's independence, for collaborating with the West Pakistani army and for participating in mass rapes and killings." Some members of the political party now known as BJI participated in paramilitary forces, such as Razakar, Al-Badar, and Al-Shams, that committed war crimes. Thus, while secular elements in East Pakistan were cultivating an alternative nationalist narrative for Bengalis, the Islamists hung on to a religion-based narrative.

These two narratives provided fertile ground for competition over foundational myths in post-independent Bangladesh, where either language or religion has been opportunistically used as a basis of polarizing politics whenever a political crisis requiring mass mobilization has erupted. The divisive nationalist rhetoric and agenda of the political parties in present-day Bangladesh testifies to this trend. Partha Ghosh captures this dilemma nicely when he states: "If Bangladesh asserts its Islamic identity, it cannot justify its liberation struggle, as that was not only directed against Islamic Pakistan, but also was actively supported by 'Hindu' India. Alternatively, if it displays its Bengali credentials, it turns the risk of merging its identity beyond recognition into that of West Bengal" (Ghosh 1993, 698).[6]

The first constitution of independent Bangladesh was an effort to separate religion from politics. But AL (the party that led the country to independence) conflated secularism with the ethnic identity of the majority Bengali population. The "spirit of the liberation war" came to be defined as an ideology that respects people's private practice of religion but discourages religion's intrusion into state-craft (Majumder 2016). Therefore, the 1972 constitution enshrined secularism as one of four state principles. There was not much conflict over religious institu-tions' influence in the state affairs. The bitter history of religious nationalism in undivided Pakistan and the need to build a separate identity inspired the rise of secularism. Bangladeshi secularism in the early years was often called "poly-religious" by ultra-leftists because instead of banning religion from society and politics altogether, Bangladesh had a very lenient interpretation of secularism supporting freedom of religion (Khondker 2010, 190). All major religions received equal airtime on radio and television. People were free to practice reli-gion in the private sphere. Even the secular leaders themselves often used reli-gious symbolism and language in an effort to befriend the rich countries in the Arab world, which were a valuable source of foreign aid (Huque and Akhter 1987, 204).

However, the AL government did not have sufficient time to elaborate on this idea of secularism and to make it popular with the majority of Bangladeshis, who were suffering from famine and natural disasters immediately following inde-pendence. Concrete benefits of the liberation war—in the form of better living standards, equal opportunities, and more accountable government—were prior-itized over identity discourse. Growing anti-Indian sentiment did not contribute positively to the situation either. Rashiduzzaman explains: "The critiques of Awami League government and its leader, Sheikh Mujibur Rahman, the pro-fessed secularism … in the early 1970s was an Indian ploy to increase Hindu influence. The Bangladeshi Muslim's anxiety to stress their religious identity and growing anti-Indian feelings marked the beginning of opposition politics in the newly independent nation" (Rashiduzzaman 1994, 984). Although there were grievances at the mass level, no political entrepreneur was strong enough to capi-talize on them. But these grievances created a background against which the military dictatorship could institutionalize Islam in politics after the assassination of Sheikh Mujibur Rahman.

Following the assassination, Bangladesh experienced a 15-year military dicta-torship under Major Zia and General Ershad, successively. Zia tried to solve his legitimacy crisis by forming the Bangladesh Nationalist Party (BNP). The party appeared in 1978, and even though it carried the stench of dictatorship, it man-aged to become popular, for two reasons. The first is the "freedom fighter" status of its founding father. Zia was a decorated soldier who fought in the 1971 libera-tion war and commanded an entire sector. But the advantage of being on the right side of the liberation war was insufficient on its own for this party to flour-ish. Zia understood from the beginning that to carve out a niche, BNP needed a different ideology that challenged the AL's claim to represent true nationalism and distinguish BNP from AL (Mohsin 2004).

BNP's ideological void was soon filled with an alternative version of national-ism. In sharp contrast to the AL-championed Bengali nationalism—that is, a secular Bengali language–based national identity focused on the supposed ethnic homogeneity of the nation—BNP came up with a nationalism based on Islamist political identity, which is popularly known as Bangladeshi nationalism. Zia also took initiatives to give religion institutional standing in Bangladeshi politics by dropping secularism from the constitution and rehabilitating religion-based politics. Bangladesh Jamaat-e-Islami (BJI) restarted its political activity with the blessing of both Major Zia and General Ershad (Ganguly 2006). General Ershad, who rose to power after Major Zia's assassination, followed in his predecessor's footsteps by further institutionalizing Islam in Bangladeshi politics.

Since the reintroduction of democracy in 1991, the country has oscillated between calls for secular Bengali identity and an Islamist Bangladeshi identity as parties competing for power try to establish a secure constituency and shield themselves from electoral volatility. This brings us to a discussion of institutional incentives that encourage political parties in Bangladesh to use polarizing tactics.

Institutional Incentives for Polarization In a "Winner-Takes-All" System

Bangladesh has had a majoritarian first-past-the post system since 1991. In the 350-seat parliament (Jatiya Sangsad), members are elected from single-member constituencies through plurality votes (except for the 50 seats reserved for women). Although the country has dozens of big and small political parties, over the past 27 years it has been slowly moving toward a two-party system dominated by the ruling AL and the main opposition BNP. Defectors from both parties have often managed to establish new political parties, but they have not proven very successful at surviving on their own. Ultimately, they had to forge some kind of coalition with one or the other major parties to ensure their existence, partly because these smaller factions lack organizational strength and grassroots networks.

Nor does the country's ideological polarity allow for the growth of any alternative and new ideas. BJI, the far-Right party that lost its registration in August 2013, emerged in Bangladeshi politics during the dictatorial era. Its meager success in national elections has been compensated by its close association with BNP, which ensured cabinet positions for its members in the 2001–2006 administration. In addition to the BNP and the AL, a third major political party, JP, also emerged during the military dictatorship but has never formed a government on its own after restoration of democracy.

Immediately following independence, AL had a socialist platform, but over the years it has fully embraced a free market economy. The party is widely perceived as liberal/center-Left due to its commitment to secularism and language-based identity. Conversely, BNP, BJI, and JP are considered to be conservative parties because of their religion-based politics. Additional fringe socialist and Islamist parties have little to no parliamentary representation.

Political parties in Bangladesh are ill-equipped to perform their roles in a way that comports with a traditional Westminster model of government, for two reasons. The first is the "winner-takes-all" approach. Bangladesh is one of the most corrupt countries in the world, and institutional checks and balances are minimal or in some cases nonexistent. The party that wins political power through parliamentary election receives relatively unfettered access to state resources and institutions, which contributes to nepotism, politicization of the bureaucracy, and use of law enforcement agencies (and often the judiciary) to persecute political opponents and civil society members (Osman 2010). If the winning party achieves a supermajority in the parliament, it also gets to amend the constitution and change electoral laws in a way that might increase its chances of retaining power by restricting electoral competition or compromising its "free and fair nature" (M. Islam 2015). Riaz (2016) calls this the "dominant party approach," where both AL and BNP act in an authoritarian manner after coming to power through a democratic process. This is why, since 1991, Bangladesh has consistently received only a "partially free" rating from Freedom House.

When the opposition becomes a minority in parliament, it may not have much power to influence policymaking. Even when the opposition has a strong presence in the national assembly, it often prefers to take its demands to the street, organizing protests, sit-ins, and strikes, and using political violence instead of debating and discussing policies in the national assembly (S. Islam 2001). This is the second major problem that obstructs the political parties from performing their roles as responsible political actors, and it often contributes to drawn-out policy processes.

This culture of confrontation and noncompromise, coupled with the two major parties' authoritarian tendencies, is what sets the tone for electoral volatility in the country. The fact that the voters alternate in their choice of government every five years should not come as a surprise, but rather be treated as a reaction to the corrupt and near-authoritarian rule of the two major political parties in each cycle. Despite big promises and impressive election manifestos, when the parties finally start running the country, the lack of constitutional restrictions on rent seeking yields a return to corruption and squandering of state resources, which disenchants the population and tilts them toward the opposition,[7] Alamgir observes that, in the four elections that took place between 1991 and 2008, "nationwide balloting had dealt a loss to the incumbent coalition, with a margin of defeat perhaps reflecting the level of public unease with its conduct while in office. In 1996, AL won 50 seats that BNP had won five years earlier. In 2001, BNP won 89 seats that AL had won in 1996. And in 2008, AL won 145 seats that BNP had won in 2001" (Alamgir 2009, 42).

The political parties get creative in responding to this electoral volatility because being away from the treasury bench can mean more than losing the responsibility of running the country; it is linked to their power and privilege and often their very survival as political actors. Whenever one of the major parties is in opposition, it gives voice to public grievances against the ruling party by amalgamating those grievances in a neat package that classifies the problems on a national identity dimension. Since both parties act pretty much the same way while in power, their mobilizational tactics do not depend on articulating novel programs based on a certain class ideology. Rather, their tactics depend on their ability to bundle the existing problems of corruption and mismanagement with identity and cultural issues. Only against this backdrop of two dominant political parties and their divisive discourse can the rise of polarization over the Tribunal be understood.

International Crimes Tribunal (ICT) and the Crystallization of Politics of Polarization

As it had promised during the 2008 election campaign, AL established the International Crimes Tribunal in 2010. Although it was long overdue in terms of delivering justice for the victims of war crimes in 1971, the establishment of the Tribunal opened new wounds instead of healing old ones. As it started delivering verdicts, it encountered a legitimacy crisis from both pro-prosecution and anti-prosecution groups. Pro-prosecution groups like the Shahbag movement were unhappy because they thought the sentences did not correspond to the gravity of the crimes committed. The anti-prosecution faction saw the Tribunal as a puppet in the hands of the government, helping it to eliminate its political opponents in the name of justice. The status of the people charged with crimes against humanity (many of them were renowned politicians and Islamist figures in the country) and the swift planning and execution of the Tribunal overshadowed its legitimacy.

Commenting on achieving both procedural perfection and justice in the Bangladeshi context, Bergsmo and Novic write that "in the era of institutionalized complementarity, such a national attempt to investigate and prosecute war crimes should be welcomed by international community. Yet in the context of limited resources and a polarized political environment, effectively achieving reconciliation and deterrence will depend above all on professionalism and fairness" (Bergsmo and Novic 2011, 503). Against this background of a desire for both justice and fairness, identity politics began to unfold in February 2013 with the formation of the Shahbag movement.

Narratives and counter-narratives started emerging from both the pro- and anti-Tribunal movements, validating their respective positions and delegitimizing the claims of the opposing side. Even though they started as nonpartisan movements, they could not avoid the influence of polarizing political parties. For example, demands from the pro-Tribunal Shabag movement to ban BJI for the alleged collaboration of its leadership during the liberation war in 1971 and to prohibit religion-based politics started to bear an uncanny resemblance to the government narrative on the issue of war crimes (Gomez 2013).

As the government quickly co-opted the Shahbag movement, the anti-Tribunal forces started their own campaign to vilify it. They creatively appealed to the religious sentiments of the people as well as their frustration with law and order and corruption under the AL government. They bundled these issues together in a manner that incorporated the "illegitimacy" of the Tribunal and immorality of the people who were supporting it. Morality, legitimacy, and identity created a powerful political platform. BNP chairperson, Begum Khaleda Zia, widow of party founder Major Zia, publicly called the pro-Tribunal Shahbag movement a congregation of "immoral atheists." Some of the organizers of the Shahbag movement were in fact self-professed atheists. But it became a matter of serious concern when Begum Zia used her oratorical skills to create a link between the dormant "atheist/secularist" phobia in a large segment of the population and the reason to delegitimize the demands of the pro-Tribunal forces. Because secularism had never been defined properly in the Bangladeshi context by its promoters, the atheist identity of some organizers of the pro-Tribunal Shahbag movement became synonymous with secularism, and anti-Tribunal forces came to view them as the agents of the ruling party. Instead of removing this confusion from people's minds, both AL and BNP, along with their respective forms of civil society and partisan media, reinforced it by creating sharp lines between pro- and anti-Tribunal forces in terms of either their religious beliefs or their commitment to secularism.

Use of Rhetoric and Symbol and Polarization at the Mass Level

The rhetoric and symbols used by both sides intensified the debate by creating new moralistic categories of right and wrong, just and immoral. It is beyond the scope of this article to discuss in detail the politics of symbolism that transpired over the entire period of the Tribunal, but it is important to mention three defining moments between February and May 2013 that fueled polarization at the mass level.

The first was the murder of blogger Rajib, a self-proclaimed atheist blogger/ pro-Tribunal activist who was brutally murdered in front of his own house by anti-Tribunal activists. Pro-Tribunal and secular groups were quick to call Rajib the first victim of a renewed identity politics.[8] Anti-Shahbag FaceBook groups such as *Basher Kella*, on the other hand, condemned Rajib's atheist lifestyle and writings. Around the same time, some interesting vocabulary was introduced to identify pro- and anti-Tribunal forces. *Chaagu*, a very derogatory Bengali term meaning a person with the intellectual capacity of a sheep, became popular with the pro-Shahbag elements as a way to describe the anti-Tribunal elements. Anti-Tribunal people were even directly called *Razakars*,[9] or collaborators/traitors in the 1971 war. The anti-Tribunal group, on the other hand, started using the term *Awami League er Dalal* (boot lickers of Awami League) to identify the people who supported the Tribunal.

Before the Rajib episode had subsided, the Sayeede fiasco took place. Maulana Delwar Hossain Sayeede was a member of parliament and a very famous religious figure in the country when the Tribunal gave him a death sentence for his actions during the war. Anti-Tribunal forces started a rumor that Sayeede's face had appeared on the moon. In the Bangladeshi context, this propaganda had a strong polarizing effect. According to his supporters, the reason Sayeede's face was visible on the moon was because he was a saint-like person, incapable of committing the crimes he had been convicted of. Thus the Tribunal had been condemned by Heaven.

The immense power of such propaganda became apparent when violence erupted following law enforcement agencies' efforts to control the mob that took to the streets to overturn the verdict against Sayeede. The channels of communication used for this purpose were diverse. It started with announcements from local mosques over the microphone used for Azan (the call for prayer) in different parts of the country. Anti-Tribunal social media pages posted and reposted the rumor numerous times. Pro-Shahbag pages replied with caricature and mockery. Though it was not universally accepted by all Bangladeshis, the point remains that the polarizing actors told a story tapping into the religious feelings and grievances about the Tribunal among a section of society. They carefully chose the myth that appealed to the "inner Muslim" of even a nonpracticing Muslim in the country. Sayeede's death sentence and the subsequent propaganda campaign triggered a violent backlash involving burning public property, killing law enforcement officers, and brutal retaliation against civilians by the police.

The third major manifestation of mass polarization occurred when a little-known Islamist movement, *Hefazat-i-Islam* (HEI), started voicing its concerns over the "atheist" nature of the Shahbag movement and affiliated blogs. Initially HEI presented a 13-point set of demands to the government, one of which was a call to prosecute bloggers who, in their view, had committed blasphemy. To show their commitment, HEI organized a siege and grand rally in Dhaka on May 5, 2013. This protest brought thousands of people from all corners of the country to the capital. During this ill-coordinated, confusing protest against the government, violence erupted.[10]

During later investigations by journalists, some of the people who participated in the siege program revealed they knew little or nothing about blogging, social networks, or the Internet. They were made to believe that people demanding capital punishment for war criminals at Shahbag were all atheists and therefore had to be immediately stopped.

These events were neither isolated nor sporadic. They indicate a systematic manipulation of the population to further certain political interests. The Tribunal became a lightning rod around which major political parties, with their associated civil society movements, were creating and reiterating their narratives of right and wrong and their own standard of judging a good Muslim or a true Bengali. AL aligned itself with the Shabag movement by publicly supporting its cause, often calling it a movement worthy of upholding the spirit of the liberation war and the ideal of a secular Bangladesh. BNP chose to align with the anti-Tribunal movement. Thus, both parties contributed to a Manichean narrative that branded every pro-Tribunal citizen as an immoral/atheist/anti-Muslim/AL supporter and everyone opposing the Tribunal as a bigot/backward-looking/traitor/BNP/BJI supporter. The Tribunal successfully ended its job of prosecuting war criminals in 2015,[11] and all its sentences have been carried out (BBC News 2016). The Shahbag movement lost its momentum due to allegations of government co-optation in 2013, the same year it gained popularity. HEI did not stage any big showdowns after the May 5, 2013, event. Now that the dust has settled, the impact on democracy of this intense phase of polarization is more visible.

Outcome for Democracy

Political polarization in Bangladesh in the post-authoritarian era has been accentuated over time by increasing electoral volatility. The short but sharp form that it took during the Tribunal episode has created problems for a young democracy—in terms of dragging out legislative processes, encouraging demands for policy changes through extragovernmental forms of political participation (strikes, sit-ins etc.) instigating violence and social intolerance, eroding freedom of expression, and encouraging an authoritarian turn in the ruling government.

From an initial scan of the quality of democracy, not much has changed since the beginning of polarized politics after the restoration of democracy in 1991. Some of the features that we witness in present-day Bangladesh have always been a part of its political culture. The tradition of protests outside parliament by the opposition and the ruling party's tendency to use force to quell them is still present. This has impeded the normal functioning of parliament (Azad and Crothers 2012, 207). As Jahan (2002) explains this dismal situation: "Neither party is willing to accept electoral defeat and serve as a 'loyal opposition' in parliament. As a result, parliament has never functioned properly. Each election has been followed by prolonged boycott of parliament by the political opposition. The government in power has also indulged in acts of suppression and harassment of political opposition. Both parties have nurtured thugs and criminal elements to intimidate the opposition. Both have attempted to control government and nongovernment institutions by appointing partisan supporters to head key institutions" (p. 223).

The ruling AL government, which came to power with a landslide victory in 2008 and won the 2014 election almost uncontested, has been criticized for trying to control state institutions and harassing the opposition, neither of which is new in Bangladeshi politics. But what has changed since the last episode of polarization over the Tribunal is the increasing imbalance between the ruling party and the opposition. Two things are mostly responsible for this situation— the loss of the top and middle leadership of the opposition due to the Tribunal's verdicts and also the BNP's strategic blunder in boycotting the 2014 general election over the issue of a nonpartisan caretaker government.[12] AL won the election, and BNP lost its major opposition party status in parliament. The lack of a transfer of power between the two major parties in 2014, which had been a defining feature of Bangladeshi politics since 1991, strengthened the winner, AL, in a winner-takes-all system. In its 10 years of rule since 2008, the government has done many commendable things, such as prosecuting war criminals, and maintaining a steady GDP growth rate. But, at the same time, it has had the opportunity to continue for 10 long years the intimidating and oppressive tactics that are used by the victorious party in parliamentary elections. The prosecution of the top leadership of BNP and BJI at the Tribunal, canceling the registration of BJI as a political party, the recent long-term sentencing of BNP Chairperson Khaleda Zia on corruption charges have all rendered the opposition parties individually and collectively very weak. So, what had previously been a case of democratic careening now has some early indications of taking a turn toward authoritarianism.

Measures of the quality of democracy are useful in discerning this trend. Varieties of Democracy data for 2018 (Coppedge et al. 2018) indicate that Bangladesh is experiencing an alarming downturn in terms of freedom from political killing and torture by the government. If we compare today's government with previous governments after the reintroduction of multiparty democracy, we see that for the period of 1990 to 1999 Bangladesh scored at a medium level (0.48) on a zero to one scale of freedom from torture and killing, where a low score is less freedom and a high score is more. It moved up to 0.5 for the years 2000, 2001, 2002, and 2003 before falling to 0.4 for the next few years. In 2008, though, things started deteriorating as the country experienced more state-level physical violence. The score kept falling, and in 2016 reached its lowest level in the post-authoritarian era at .28.

The Economist Intelligence Unit's Democracy Index[13] also shows that overall, Bangladesh has fallen from the category of a flawed democracy in 2006, where elections were relatively free and fair and opposition harassment was at a minimal level, to the category of a hybrid regime in 2008, where widespread corruption, oppression of the opposition, a compromised judiciary, and curtailed freedom of expression are routine. In 2017, Bangladesh's democracy score dipped to its lowest point since the Index was started in 2006. Freedom House had consistently ranked Bangladesh as partially free since the restoration of democracy, but has expressed concern over the deteriorating civil and political rights situation in recent times and degraded the country's score beginning in 2014.

The most tenuous civil right in the country is probably the freedom of expression. Polarization over the Tribunal issue has had both direct and indirect effects on freedom of the press. The propaganda war on social media by both pro- and anti-Tribunal factions showed the immense power alternative media can wield in shaping public opinion. Considering that, it is little surprise that over the past five years the government has arrested what Human Rights Watch (2018) reports as "scores of people" under section 57 of the Information and Communication Technology Act for criticizing its activities on social media, blogs, and online newspapers. The indirect effect on freedom of expression comes from what Freedom House in 2018 called the "culture of impunity" created by the government's inability or unwillingness to prosecute perpetrators responsible for attacks on independent bloggers with an atheist orientation and human rights activists, while simultaneously arresting government critics (Freedom House 2018).

Freedom of expression and minority rights are also compromised by the religiously or linguistically exclusionary narratives on opposite sides that reinforce each other and disallow any conciliatory views. Minority rights are undermined as both poles exclude non-Bengalis and non-Muslims from their respective narratives. Even before controversy over national identity took this divisive form, the

AL government failed to recognize ethnic minority groups in the Chittagong Hill Tracts (people who do not speak Bengali) as indigenous groups. The 15th amendment to the country's constitution promulgated under AL established the hegemonic Bengali identity as the identity for all groups of people, overlooking ethnic and cultural diversity protected in the Chittagong Hill Tracts.[14] On the other hand, territorially based Bangladeshi nationalism put excessive emphasis on Islam as part of national identity. Such strict categorization leaves out the religious minorities in the country. Thanks to polarizing narratives privileging Islam, violence against religious minorities is on the rise in the country.[15]

A recent surge of attacks against religious minorities, atheist writers, and activists also indicates a problem with social cohesion and respect for diversity and pluralism. AL's victory over the Tribunal issue came with a price. Witnessing the popularity of the anti-Tribunal forces and the strength of their narrative, the government decided to appease the Islamists. So even though HEI could not stop the Tribunal, Islamists have managed to extract some concessions from the government from time to time on important social and cultural issues. The most controversial one is the decision to take all poems and stories written by non-Muslim writers out of primary- and secondary-level Bengali textbooks. Barry and Manik (2017) report: "First graders studying the alphabet were taught that 'o' stands for 'orna,' a scarf worn by devout Muslim girls starting at puberty, not for 'ol,' a type of yam; and a sixth-grade travelogue describing a visit to the Hindu-dominated north of India was replaced by one about the Nile in Egypt." This creeping Islamization of the education system might not seem that threatening, but in the broader perspective it represents a paradox—the very same party that upholds the secular spirit of the nation also institutionalizes Islam's privileged position in society. It encourages bigotry and instigates violence, as evidenced by the murder of several atheist bloggers in the past few years.

The identity-based divide has invaded all policy discussions and infused political discourse with partisan intractability. This has degraded the ability of the government and opposition to cooperate or reach consensus on unrelated policy issues such as education reform, quota system reform,[16] or the abolition of the caretaker government.

All in all, identity-based polarization delivered short-term benefits to political parties in Bangladesh. When it comes to consolidating democracy or solidifying the national identity of the people of Bangladesh after 47 years of independence, however, it has produced grim prospects on both counts.

Notes

1. Bangladesh became independent through a nine-month-long liberation war against Pakistan in 1971. The Tri-State Treaty, following the emergence of Bangladesh in 1972, among India, Bangladesh, and Pakistan obligated the Bangladeshi government to send the 92,000 Pakistani Prisoners of War and civilians back to Pakistan. Bangladeshi government enacted a special tribunal to prosecute those Bangladeshis who collaborated with the Pakistani military during the war under Bangladesh Collaborators' Ordinance 1972. As of October 31, 1973, some 2,848 people were prosecuted under this law and 752 of them were

sentenced. After the assassination of the first President of the Republic, Shiekh Mujibur Rahman, the process came to a standstill until Bangladesh Awami League (AL), the ruling party, established a tribunal to prosecute the collaborators in 2010 under the Bangladesh International Crimes (Tribunals Act) 1973. See also Judgments of International Crimes Tribunal-2, Bangladesh. Available from https://www.ict-bd .org/ict2/orders.php (accessed on May 13, 2018).

2. Bangladesh became a part of Pakistan in 1947 when the British colonial rulers left the subcontinent. It was known as East Pakistan then. Twenty-four years later it became independent from Pakistan and emerged as the sovereign nation-state now known as Bangladesh. Two different nationalist narratives galvanized the people during these two decisive moments in their national history. The focus of the anti-colonial movement was the Muslim identity of the people of Bengal in British India. But the focus of the liberation movement was the secular and language-based identity of the people that inhabited East Pakistan. No political party in post-independent Bangladesh ever presented a unifying nationalist narrative incorporating and balancing these two important and inalienable components (religion and language) of national identity of its people. Politics of polarization feeds on this unfinished nation building project.

3. Happy Planet Index, New Economics Foundation. Available from http://happyplanetindex.org/ (accessed June 30, 2018).

4. Right after independence in 1971, Bangladesh started as a democratic country. But after the assassination of the first president of the Republic in 1975, the country plunged into military dictatorship, which lasted until 1990. Multiparty democracy was restored in Bangladesh in 1991.

5. India was partitioned in 1947 based on a theory that identified Indian Hindus and Indian Muslims as two different nations. Muhammad Ali Jinnah has been credited for coming up with this theory and demanding a separate nation-state called Pakistan for Indian Muslims. Overlooking the linguistic and cultural diversities of the people practicing Islam and imposing an artificial national identity on them proved futile soon after the creation of Pakistan.

6. Bengali is also spoken by the people (mostly Hindu) in the West Bengal and Tripura States of India. The linguistic and cultural similarity between Bangladesh and some parts of India has often caused debate and controversy in Bangladesh as the need for a clearly distinguishable "Bangladeshi" identity became more and more pronounced. The need to create a separate identity for Bengali speaking and mostly Islam practicing people who are geographically located in independent Bangladesh fueled the *Bengali* versus *Bangladeshi* identity debate where *Bengali* indicates a secular ethnic identity and *Bangladeshi* indicates a religious and spatial identity.

7. Currently there is no evidence of an implicit or explicit agreement between the political elites of both parties regarding the conduct of rent-seeking behavior. The ruling party, whether AL or BNP, generally tends to prosecute the previous administration for their corrupt activity. This is done to gain an electoral advantage, not as a programmatic or idealistic undertaking, though it is often couched in these terms.

8. Different accounts credit different actors for using the label. Some identify BAL's Advisory Council Member Mr. Tofail Ahmed. Others credit BOAN's Rawshon Jhunu for coming up with this idea. It became a catch phrase among a section of pro-Shahbag people in the country.

9. Razakar was the anti-Bangladeshi paramilitary force organized by the West Pakistani army during the liberation war of 1971. It was involved in and contributed to crimes against humanity including murder, torture, rape, and arson. In post-independent Bangladesh it became a derogatory term used to label people who might come off as against the idea of an independent and secular Bangladesh.

10. The police brutality part and the correct number of Hefazat supporters being killed or injured that night has produced great controversy. The government denies any such allegation. But international non-governmental organizations such as Amnesty International and TV channels like Al-Jazzera report otherwise. Hefazat supporters' crime, on the other hand, is well documented. A dozen of TV and newspaper camera crews from leading national TV channels and newspapers were there to shoot the scene when Hefazat supporters were torching bookstores, public vehicles, and the office of Communist Party Bangladesh, and assaulted TV journalists.

11. Judgments of International Crimes Tribunal-2, Bangladesh. Available from https://www.ict-bd.org/ ict2/orders.php (accessed on May 13, 2018).

12. After the overthrow of the Ershad regime, it was necessary to assign the task of holding a free and fair election to a neutral body that would not tamper with election results. The nonpartisan caretaker government came into being as a result of consultation between the major political parties. All parliamentary elections in the post-dictatorial era (except for the one in January 2014) in Bangladesh have been

conducted under a caretaker government. The 2006 caretaker government overstepped its boundary and with the help of the military staged a soft coup. Instead of arranging the next general election within three months of the dissolution of the last parliament, it chose to run the country without people's mandate for more than a year until a spontaneous student movement led to its demise. Fearing that a future caretaker government might abuse its power again, the AL government abolished the system through the fifteenth amendment of the Constitution, a move that the main opposition party, BNP, did not welcome.

13. Economist Intelligence Unit's Democracy Index. Available from https://infographics.economist .com/2018/DemocracyIndex/ (accessed on July 30, 2018).

14. Approximately 5,089 square miles of southeastern Bangladesh is inhabited by over half a million people who do not share the majority population's ethnic identity. Tribal groups of various sizes live in this small territory. Military dictatorship's decision to outnumber these people with Bengali settlers started an insurgency that lasted for two decades. The 1997 Peace Accord that officially ended the insurgency gave the indigenous people some rights to govern themselves, but inadequate implementation of the Accord and the apathy of major political parties to the plights of these people gave rise to a renewed episode of violence where the government side has been accused of using disproportionate force. The latest constitutional amendment is considered another blow to the demands of the tribal people for recognition as distinct ethnic communities because now the Constitution labels every citizen of the country as a *Bengali*, irrespective of their ethnic identity.

15. According to the 2011 estimate Hindu, Buddhist, and Christian communities constitute 9.0 percent, 0.6 percent, and 0.3 percent of the population, respectively. Electoral violence specifically targeting the Hindu minorities has been on the rise. Since they are often viewed as supporters of AL, opposition parties try to intimidate the Hindu community by using physical violence. But violence also takes place in nonelection years against the minorities if the hostilities between the two major political parties become intense.

16. The quota system in Bangladesh is an affirmative action system that confers certain benefits to the family members of the freedom fighters of 1971 along with other disadvantaged groups in terms of education and employment opportunities. Government offices and public educational institutions reserve a certain number of positions for these communities as part of the affirmative action system practiced in the country. Recently there has been a debate about whether the system is dated and is obstructing the recruitment of meritorious people in government jobs and even giving undue advantage to quota-qualifying people in institutes of higher education. Pro-quota system people think that certain minority communities should still enjoy the benefits of the quota system. Those against the quota system want its reform to reflect the current situation of high unemployment in the country and relative improvement in the conditions of certain minority communities. Because one of the greatest beneficiaries of the quota system is the families of the freedom fighters of 1971, any opposition to the system is often portrayed as unpatriotic. At the time of the writing of this article in 2018, the quota-reform movement faced police brutalities, sparking another short-lived episode of intense polarization over national identity. Matia Chwodhury, the agricultural minister of the current AL government, allegedly equated participants of the quota-reform movement as "Razakars" (a term used to describe the Bengali collaborators who aided the Pakistani army in 1971). The main opposition party, BNP, meanwhile threw its weight behind the reform movement. A leaked telephone conversation between the exiled BNP acting chairperson Tarique Rahman and a Professor of Dhaka University revealed the party's plan to bank on the rising agitation over the quota system reform to mobilize people against the government right before the next parliamentary election. The AL government finally abolished quotas for first and second class jobs in civil bureaucracy, but the intense debate generated over it exposed the power of polarizing rhetoric used by both political parties.

References

Alamgir, Jalal. 2009. Bangladesh's Fresh Start. *Journal of Democracy* 20 (3): 41–55.

Barry, Ellen, and Julfikar Ali Manik. 22 January 2017. To secular Bangladeshis, textbook changes are a harbinger. *The New York Times*. Available from: https://www.nytimes.com/2017/01/22/world/asia/ bangladesh-textbooks-radical-islam.html.

BBC News. 4 September 2016. Bangladesh war crimes trial: Key accused. BBC News. Available from https://www.bbc.com/news/world-asia-20970123 (accessed July 29, 2018).

Bergsmo, Morten, and Elisa Novic. 2011. Justice after decades in Bangladesh: National trials for international crimes. *Journal of Genocidal Research* 13 (4): 503–10.

Coppedge, Michael, John Gerring, Carl Henrik Knutsen, Staffan I. Lindberg, Svend-Erik Skaaning, Jan Teorell, David Altman, Michael Bernhard, M. Steven Fish, and Agnes Cornell, et al. 2018. *V-Dem [Dataset v8]*. Varieties of Democracy (V-Dem) Project. Available from https://doi.org/10.23696/vdemcy18.

Abul Kalam Azad, and Charles Crothers. 2012. Bangladesh: An umpired democracy. *Journal of Social and Development Sciences* 3 (6): 203–13.

Freedom House. 2018. *Freedom in the World: Bangladesh Profile*. Washington, DC: Freedom House. Available from https://freedomhouse.org/report/freedom-world/2018/bangladesh (Accessed July 30, 2018).

Ganguly, Sumit. 2006. *The rise of Islamic militancy in Bangladesh*. Washington, DC: U.S. Institute of Peace. Available from www.usip.org. (accessed March 17, 2018).

Ghosh, Partha S. 1993. Bangladesh at the crossroads. *Asian Survey* 33 (7): 697–710.

Gomez, William. 2013. Shahbag: What revolution, whose revolution? Open Democracy. Available from www.opendemocracy.net. (accessed March 17, 2018).

Hossain, Ishtiaq, and Noore Alam Siddiquee. 2004. Islam in Bangladeshi politics: The role of Ghulam Azam of Jamaat-I-Islam. *Inter-Asia Cultural Studies* 5 (3): 384–99.

Human Rights Watch. 9 May 2018. Bangladesh Protect Freedom of Expression: Repeal Draconian Section 57 but New Law Should Not Replicate Abuses. New York, NY: Human Rights Watch. Available from https://www.hrw.org/news/2018/05/09/bangladesh-protect-freedom-expression (accessed May 13, 2018).

Huque, Ahmed Shafiqul, and Muhammad Yeahia Akhter. 1987. The ubiquity of Islam: Religion and society in Bangladesh. *Pacific Affairs* 60 (2): 200–25.

International Republican Institute. 2017. Bangladesh daily challenges: Public opinion on economics, politics, and security. Washington, DC: International Republican Institute. Available from file:///C:/Users/Tahmina/Documents/PI/conference%20papers/IRI_2018%20report.pdf (accessed July 17, 2018).

Islam, Md. Nazrul, and Md. Saidul Islam. 2018. Islam, politics, and secularism in Bangladesh: Contesting the dominant narratives. *Social Sciences* 7 (37): 1–18.

Islam, Mohammad M. 2015. Electoral violence in Bangladesh: Does a confrontational bipolar political system matter? *Commonwealth and Comparative Politics* 53 (4): 359–80.

Islam, Syed S. 2001. Elections and politics in post-Ershad era in Bangladesh. *Asian and African Studies* 10 (1): 160–73.

Jahan, Rounaq. 2002. Bangladesh in 2002: Imperiled Democracy. *Asian Survey* 43 (1): 222–29.

Khondker, Habibul Haque. 2010. The curious case of secularism in Bangladesh: What is the relevance for the Muslim majority democracies? *Totalitarian Movements and Political Religions* 11(2): 185–201.

Linter, Bertil. 2002. Religious extremism and nationalism in Bangladesh. Paper presented at Religion and Security in South Asia-An International Workshop. 19–22 August 2002. Asia-Pacific Center for Security Studies. Honolulu, Hawaii.

Mainwaring, Scott, and Mariano Trocal. 2006. Party system institutionalization and party system theory after the third wave of democratization. In *Handbook of party politics*, eds. Richard S. Katz and William J. Crotty, 206–27. Thousand Oaks, CA: Sage Publications.

Mainwaring, Scott, and Edurne Zoco. 2007. Political sequences and the stabilization of interparty competition: Electoral volatility in old and new democracies. *Party Politics* 13 (2): 155–78.

Majumder, Shantanu. 2016. Secularism and Anti-Secularism. In *Routledge handbook of contemporary Bangladesh*, eds. Ali Riaz and Mohammad S. Rahman, 40-51. New York, NY: Routledge Publishing.

Manning, Carrie. 2005. Assessing African party systems after the third wave. *Party Politics* 11 (6): 707–27.

McCoy Jennifer, Tahmina Rahman, and Murat Somer. 2018. Polarization and the global crisis of democracy: Common patterns, dynamics, and pernicious consequences of for democratic politics. *American Behavioral Scientist* 62 (1): 16–42.

Misra, K. P. 1972. Intrastate imperialism: The case of Pakistan. *Journal of Peace Research* 9 (1): 27–39.

Mohsin, Amena. 2004. Religion, politics and security: The case of Bangladesh. In *Religious radicalism and security in South Asia*, eds. Satu P. Limaye, Robert Wirsinga and Mahan Malik, 467–89. Honolulu, HA: Asia Pacific Center for Security Studies.

Osman, Ferdous A. 2010. Bangladesh politics: Confrontation, monopoly, and crisis in governance. *Asian Journal of Political Science* 18 (3): 310–33.

Randall, Vicky, and Lars Svåsand. 2002. Party institutionalization in new democracies. *Party Politics* 8 (1): 5–29.

Rashiduzzaman, M. 1994. The liberals and religious Right in Bangladesh. *Asian Survey* 34 (11): 974–90.

Riaz, Ali. 2016. Political parties, elections, and the party system. In *Routledge handbook of contemporary Bangladesh*, eds. Ali Riaz and Mohammad S. Rahman, 35–81. New York, NY: Routledge Publishing.

Rieger, John, Sara L. Taylor, and Pauline Tweedie, eds. 2017. *Bangladesh's democracy 2017: According to its people: A survey of the Bangladeshi people*. San Francisco, CA: The Asia Foundation. Available from https://asiafoundation.org/wp-content/uploads/2018/01/Bangladeshs-Democracy-2017-According-to-its-people.pdf (accessed July 7, 2018).

Shehabuddin, Elora. 2008. Jamaat-i-Islami in Bangladesh: Women, democracy and the transformation of Islamist politics. *Modern Asian Studies* 42 (2–3): 577–603.

United Nations Department of Economic and Social Affairs. 2018. Leaving the LDCs category: Booming Bangladesh prepares to graduate. New York, NY: United Nations Department of Economic and Social Affairs. Available from https://www.un.org (accessed June 30, 2018).

IV. The Illusory Promise of Democratic Reform: Success and Failure

Polarization in South Africa: Toward Democratic Deepening or Democratic Decay?

By
ROGER SOUTHALL

Under apartheid, white oppression of the black majority was extreme, and South Africa became one of the most highly polarized countries in the world. Confronted by a counter-movement headed by the African National Congress (ANC), the ruling National Party (NP) was eventually pressured into a negotiation process that resulted in the adoption of a democratic constitution. This article outlines how democratization defused polarization, but was to be hollowed out by the ANC's construction of a "party-state," politicizing democratic institutions and widening social inequalities. This is stoking political tensions, which, despite societal interdependence, are provoking fears of renewed polarization along class and racial lines.

Keywords: apartheid; democratization; polarization and proto-polarization; inequality; African National Congress; party-state

Before 1994, South Africa was one the most highly polarized countries in the world. White conquest and colonialism had buttressed the domination of a white minority and continuously reproduced poverty and powerlessness among a black majority for centuries. After the National Party's (NP) (whites only) election victory in 1948, apartheid was to deepen racial divisions and strip blacks of what rudimentary rights they had previously possessed. Yet apartheid was accompanied by capitalist development. Despite official policies to limit black urbanization, along with the ruthless suppression of black opposition, the minority regime was confronted in the 1970s by extensive popular revolt, whose principal locus was in the

Roger Southall is emeritus professor in sociology at University of the Witwatersrand. His publications include Imperialism or Solidarity? International Labour and South African Trade Unions *(University of Cape Town Press 1995)*, Liberation Movements in Power: Party and State in Southern Africa *(James Currey 2013), and* The New Black Middle Class in South Africa *(James Currey 2016).*

Correspondence: Roger.southall@wits.ac.za

DOI: 10.1177/0002716218806913

townships (segregated and undeveloped urban areas reserved for blacks). In addition, the regime was drawn into fighting (ultimately futile) wars against liberation movements in Zimbabwe, Angola, and Namibia. By the early 1990s, the apartheid state had been forced to the negotiating table; it had lost the anti-communist backing of western powers following the end of the Cold War; and its economy was in crisis. Even so, it remained the strongest military power on the African continent, and its opposition, headed by the African National Congress (ANC), recognized it was too strong to defeat. The outcome was a compromise between opposing elites, the essence of which was that the NP conceded to universal rights and a democratic regime, while the ANC accepted a capitalist economy (Ashman 2015; Marais 2011; Habib 2013).

The transition to democracy inaugurated an era of national reconciliation, as political polarization receded. Conflict was largely replaced by peace, underpinned by growth rates not seen since the 1960s. Developments of infrastructure, services, and welfare provided for substantial social progress and the raising of living standards for many in the black community (SAIRR 2018a). Nonetheless, given the endurance of historic inequalities along lines of race, space, class, and wealth, South Africa remains deeply divided. Whites (alongside international corporations) continue to dominate the private sector, while black communities endure astoundingly high levels of poverty and unemployment. Notwithstanding black upward mobility, class divisions remain stark, while the country's spaces remain highly segmented, with the large majority of the different racial groupings (Africans 80.5 percent; whites 8.5 percent; Coloreds 8.8 percent; and Indians 2.5 percent)[1] still living in areas that were racially demarcated and differentially serviced under apartheid. Politically, a highly praised constitution balanced majority against minority representation, guaranteed a host of individual freedoms, and dictated a separation of powers. However, simultaneously, apartheid's polarized history resulted in the post-1994 political dominance of the ANC as the representative of the overwhelming mass of the black, especially African, majority population.[2] In turn, this has facilitated the rise of a party-state elite bent on rapid accumulation, high levels of corruption, and a drift toward authoritarianism (Booysen 2011; Southall 2014a).

Fears are growing among observers that unless South Africa's cleavages are addressed by dramatic transformations accompanied by rapid economic growth, the country may yet again face the prospect of conflict and decline (Habib 2013; Johnson 2015). This poses urgent questions: Can South Africa's troubled democracy contain its past and present divisions? Or will it spiral back into a politics of polarization last seen during the latter years of apartheid—that is, a state where political actors on either side of a societal divide are unable to compromise, where conflict-management mechanisms fail, where violence replaces negotiation, and where society bifurcates into two hostile camps (McCoy, Rahman, and Somer 2018)?

Political Polarization in South Africa before 1994

The union of South Africa in 1910 had been designed to protect the interests of the mining industry while being permissive of political domination by the Boers (later Afrikaners), who constituted a majority of the white minority population. The interests of the mining industry (dominated by British and other foreign capital), commercial agriculture (dominated by local, notably Afrikaner, capital), and the white minority as a whole were secured by the denial of political rights to the black majority. This was backed by a massive appropriation of black land, the corralling of Africans in "native reserves," the imposition of repressive labor practices, entrenchment of a system of migrant labor from the reserves to the mines and white farms, and severe restrictions on the rights of blacks to reside in urban areas. However, by the 1940s, the deteriorating agricultural capacity of the reserves, alongside the expansion of manufacturing, had resulted in an inexorable drift of the black population into the towns. In turn, this stimulated black political consciousness (Lodge 1983).

The NP's victory in 1948 reversed hesitant attempts of the predecessor government to make pragmatic adjustments to the status quo, which would have recognized the permanence of black urbanization as an accompaniment of industrialization. Apartheid preached a rigid separation of the races. African political rights had already been further diminished during the 1930s. Further attacks upon the rights of all blacks followed during the 1950s and 1960s. These included new elements of divide and rule: Indians and Coloreds were to run their own affairs. Above all, the NP decreed that the African majority comprised discrete ethnic populations, each with their political *homelands* located in the reserves, where the regime sought to bolster despotic chieftain control. Meanwhile, the regime sought to reverse the continuing flow of blacks to urban areas by extending the migrant labor system to the secondary industry.

Prior to 1948, the ANC, formed by African middle-class elements in 1912, had restricted its role to lobbying for greater rights, only to suffer successive rebuffs. The NP's commitment to apartheid ensured that the ANC's hitherto conservative leadership was swept aside, and the NP's newly repressive measures were met by an upsurge of popular protest. Enforced division of the subordinated races only encouraged cross-racial unity. Yet when a Congress Alliance of Indian, Colored, and radical white and trade union organizations led by the ANC launched massive protest campaigns during the 1950s and early 1960s, the NP responded with brutal clampdowns, culminating in a series of infamous trials of the ANC and Congress leaderships, and the banning of their organizations following the imposition of a state of emergency after the Sharpeville massacre of 1961, when police gunned down protestors at a rally organized by the minority Pan-Africanist Congress.

The Sharpeville emergency was followed by a period of repressive stability, when black political quiescence was underpinned by foreign investment (attracted by the profits available from a docile and rightless black labor force) and rapid economic growth (Giliomee 1979; Terreblanche 2003). With the leadership of the ANC either in jail or in exile, the movement lost its momentum. However, apartheid proved unable to contain the industrializing logic of the political economy. Above all, the government was unable to stem the drift of rural Africans to burgeoning townships, which expanded rapidly on the fringes of white urban areas. Although the introduction of Bantu Education in 1953 had sought to school the African population for servitude, upward mobility of whites into higher skilled jobs opened opportunities for blacks and led to the growth of and increasing skills of the African workforce.

Such developments boosted black self-confidence. From the early 1970s, black workers confronted employers and police with militant strike activity and self-organization into trade unions. African youth became impatient with the political acquiescence of their parents' generation and rose in revolt in 1976, when schoolchildren's protests in Soweto[3] about unequal education ignited a massive extension of popular mobilization among anti-apartheid forces throughout the 1980s and early 1990s.

The regime responded with brutal violence and extensive security measures, yet simultaneously sought to defuse polarization by restructuring apartheid: first, by the incorporation of black trade unions into the industrial relations system in 1979; and second, by the introduction of a new constitution in 1983 whereby Indians and Coloreds were provided representation in parliament via the creation of separate chambers (alongside the established House for whites). Belated acceptance of black urbanization was signified by the creation of black *community councils* in urban areas and, in 1986, abolition of influx control, which restricted black movement. However, attempts to streamline apartheid were repudiated by the regime's opponents, prompting the formation of cross-racial unity within a United Democratic Front forged from a multiplicity of community-based civic organizations, religious groups, workers, and youth movements, which, in effect, became the surrogate of the exiled ANC.

By 1985, when diverse strands of black trade unions combined into a Congress of South African Trade Unions (COSATU), conditions were ripe for the effective re-creation of the Congress Alliance of the 1950s. The ANC's armed struggle was largely ineffective against the regime's military onslaught, but it nonetheless gained hugely in reputation among the black population, notably through what it termed *armed propaganda* in the mid-1980s. Its influence grew significantly during the 1980s. By the time the government had reached the conclusion that the confrontations with popular forces were becoming financially and economically unsupportable, in part because of divestment from South Africa of international companies and banks as a result of pressure from anti-apartheid campaigners globally, the ANC had largely reestablished its popular hegemony (despite the survival of significant minority political traditions).

The years of the political transition (1990–94) were turbulent. The major players, the ANC and NP, had very different conceptions of democracy, the former favoring direct, unitary, and popular forms of democracy; the latter preferring indirect, federal, and consociational forms protective of minority rights. Correspondingly, the ANC was backed by popular power, while the NP retained its grip on the state and security forces. Inevitably, there were violent battles on the streets and in rural areas. Militants clashed with the police and military, while the state and rogue elements stoked civil war between the ANC and the rival ethnic-Zulu Inkatha Freedom Party. Many thousands died violent deaths—yet ultimately these only reinforced the urgency of the negotiation process, and made the final carefully crafted agreement in 1993 more welcome.

The triumph of the postagreement 1994 election and the ANC-led coalition Government of National Unity (GNU) that followed it was that they combined majority rule with minority representation in government, symbolizing mutual accommodation by previously polarized forces. This, then, is a case of severe polarization leading to democratic reform, under the pressure of significant costs to the apartheid regime arising from international sanctions, domestic economic costs from strikes, and insurgent popular revolt. But would the democratic settlement remain viable given the massive socioeconomic inequalities and racial disparities that had been entrenched under apartheid?[4]

Democracy's Depolarizing Impacts and Limitations

The settlement forging democracy was a result of a sophisticated process of constitutional engineering conducted principally by ANC and NP elites that facilitated the adoption of a Bill of Rights; a hybridization between parliamentary and presidential systems of government; a quasi-federal devolution of powers to nine new provinces; and various checks and balances, including the establishment of *democracy-promoting* institutions such as a public protector (an ombudsperson with extensive investigatory powers). Above all, the executive and legislative bodies were subject to the constitution, with a new Constitutional Court becoming the final arbiter of whether policies and actions were constitutional (Corder, Federico, and Orru 2014).

The negotiation process (1990–94)—although forging an elite transition more than a meaningful liberation (Bond 1990)—was crucial in defusing distrust and allowing mutually exclusive political identities to give way to a broader sense of South Africanism. Although the daily realities of racial separation remained, newly inclusive political institutions saw the spanning of previously unbridgeable cleavages between the major political actors. The achievement was capped by the joyful holding of the first democratic election, and the pursuit of national reconciliation by Nelson Mandela, the democracy's first president. However, this elaboration of a transformative democracy was to be challenged by the political dominance of the ANC, allowing the new ruling party to erode the constraints formally imposed upon its authority by the newly adopted democratic constitution (Southall 2013).

The adoption of a party-list proportional representation (PR) system, for both national and provincial legislatures, pleased both the ANC, which was confident of winning the popular vote, as well as other parties that de facto represented political minorities. The outcome in 1994 was that the ANC's support fell just short of a two-thirds majority, with the NP and IFP securing sufficient votes to ensure their representation in the GNU, while a myriad of smaller parties formed the opposition.[5] Subsequently, after disagreements between the ANC and NP led to the latter leaving the GNU in 1996, the scene was set for the consolidation of the ANC's electoral dominance.

The ANC increased its share of the vote during the next two general elections (1999 and 2004), its predominance largely repeated in the different provinces (the major exception being the Western Cape, over which it lost control in 2004). Although the two subsequent elections saw a decline in the ANC's vote (down to 62 percent in 2014), the party was by now in firm control of the state machinery. Meanwhile, opposing parties remained fragmented, with their potential for unity constrained by divisions of race, ethnicity, style, ideology, regional affiliation, and their leaderships' personal ambitions. However, with the final collapse of the NP in 2005, the ground was firmed for the steady rise of the liberal Democratic Alliance (DA), which mopped up most of the conservative constituency left behind by the NP to become the major party of opposition (Southall 2014b).

The PR electoral system allowed for maximum political inclusivity. Notably, it avoided the fateful error committed by the Zimbabwean transitional electoral arrangements that provided for the separate representation of whites as whites (Southall 2013, 107–12). In contrast, the South African system ensured that any opposition party with ambition would need to garner support across race, ethnicity, and class (Horowitz 1991). This was to prove important in drawing racial minorities into postcolonial politics. Notably, it provided for the growth of the DA, whose support was to steadily expand beyond its predominantly white and Colored support base, and whose current major objective is to make inroads into the ANC's overwhelmingly black constituency. That it was to enjoy some success in this was indicated by the results of the 2016 local government elections when the ANC lost majorities in the three metros of Johannesburg, Tshwane (Pretoria) and Nelson Mandela Bay (Port Elizabeth), and was displaced by DA-led coalitions (underpinned by support from the Economic Freedom Fighters [EFF], a populist breakaway from the ANC). Even so, the DA and other opposition parties continue to face ANC political dominance.

From its beginning, the ANC sought to unite all Africans across class, tribe, and religion. The party embraced all those of whatever color who repudiated any form of discrimination by race. This culminated in its articulation of a creed of *nonracial democracy*. The apartheid-era subjection of so many activists to brutality and torture by apartheid security forces enhanced its commitment to human rights.

Nevertheless, there was another side to the ANC that disposed it to an exclusivity at odds with liberal democratic values. This flowed from two major sources. The first was the ANC's identity as an anticolonialism movement. At times, it was prone to conflate self-determination with democracy and to claim that the ANC embodied the spirit of the nation, and that it alone represented the will of the people. As the ANC has consolidated its power, so its leadership has on occasion claimed a quasi-divine right to rule. Hence, when he was president (2009–2018), Jacob Zuma proclaimed on a number of occasions that "The ANC will rule till Jesus comes" (Southall 2017).

The second source of authoritarianism in ANC thought lay in the party's historic alliance with the South African Communist Party (SACP). In practice, post-1994, the latter has always been subordinate to the former (to the extent that its members hold joint membership and campaign as the ANC electorally). Nonetheless, together, the SACP and ANC theorize the struggle against apartheid and capitalism as a struggle in two parts: first the realization of a national democratic revolution (NDR) and second, the defeat of capitalism and the advance to socialism.

The NDR expresses the ANC's ideological commitment to the total overthrow of an unjust socioeconomic system alongside its demand for democracy. This has proven sufficiently ambiguous to contain the aspirations of both nationalist and communist wings of the ANC's liberation alliance, as the NDR envisages the development of a black (or *patriotic*) bourgeoisie capable of challenging the domination of *monopoly capitalism* while simultaneously emphasizing the need for the liberation movement to ensure that the patriotic bourgeoisie remains loyal to the revolution. Yet what the NDR has also stressed has been the extension of liberation movement control over all organs of the state (the bureaucracy, the security forces, the parastatals and so on) if South Africa were to be *transformed* (ANC 1998).

Since 1994, the theory of the NDR has guided the ANC's deployment of loyal party cadres to key positions across all organs of state power (albeit with the judiciary largely left untouched). This has facilitated the rise of a party-state in which the executive dominates a supposedly independent civil service and all public institutions (although hitherto independent bodies like the universities have proved relatively successful in protecting their autonomy). Furthermore, while parliament has remained far more inclusive than it was under apartheid, the ANC has used its large majorities to undermine the will and capacity of the legislature to hold the executive accountable, with list-system PR making backbenchers overwhelmingly subject to the authority of party bosses.[6] Meanwhile, steam-rolled in parliament, opposition parties have often turned for redress to the courts, which on numerous occasions have ruled against the government. This in turn has prompted influential ANC figures to attack the judiciary as being counter-revolutionary and as thwarting the will of the people. Finally, given intra-party differences around economic policy (where calls for faster rates of transformation clash with a more cautious regard for the market), the theory of the NDR has served as an invaluable prop for attacks on opposition parties as representing unpatriotic minority interests. In sum, although the ANC formally upholds its liberal values, it is simultaneously inclined to rail against the constitution as an impediment to the true liberation of the people (Southall 2013).

Against this background, international reaction to ANC rule became increasingly negative, especially during the presidency of Jacob Zuma (April 2009–January 2018), when corruption billowed. As a result, the Democracy Index, compiled by the Economist Intelligence Unit, in 2016 downgraded South Africa to the status of a *flawed democracy*, that is one with free elections and respect for basic civil liberties, but also problems of governance, an underdeveloped political culture, and low levels of public participation. While South Africa is still a long way away from being classified as *authoritarian*, as was its neighbor Zimbabwe under President Robert Mugabe, there are fears that it could well move in the direction of Zimbabwe (EIU 2016). Indeed, the latter years of the Zuma presidency were characterized by high levels of popular protest, which contained within them seeds of polarization along both class and racial lines.

Protest and Proto-Polarization in Democratic South Africa

One of the major successes of South Africa's new democracy was its imposition of presidential term limits (not to exceed two terms of five years) and the ANC's acceptance of the hand-over of power from one president to another. The scene was set by Mandela's voluntary standing down from the presidency in 1999. He was succeeded by Thabo Mbeki, whose presidency confirmed the ANC's de facto acceptance of market-led economics while simultaneously stressing the need for black upward mobility and empowerment.

The capture of state power by the ANC inaugurated significant processes of redress. Policies of *equity employment* (or affirmative action) drove transformation. Blacks came to predominate in state employment even at the highest levels; and white dominance and ownership in the private sector was diluted by black economic empowerment. Such policies drove visible changes in the racial and class structure. Blacks experienced strong upward movement in the labor market and significant entry into the corporate and professional spheres; workplaces became mixed with remarkably few major dramas; praiseworthy strides were taken in the provision of housing and the extension of electricity, water, and other services to black communities; and the growth of a black middle class was accompanied by black African entry into former white, Colored, and Indian schools and suburbs (Southall 2016a). Further, the government has expanded its social protection, so that today there are more than 17 million people drawing old age pensions and social grants for war veterans, disability, child care, care dependency, and child support (SAIRR 2018, 742).

Although many of these advances were promoted by his leadership, Mbeki was to be ejected from office by the ANC in September 2008 before the expiration of his term. His ouster was a reaction to his run for a third term as party leader against the candidacy of Jacob Zuma, resulting in his defeat at the ANC's Polokwane national congress in December 2007. Despite Zuma having already been caught up in a morass of corruption allegations (which, inter alia, had led to his dismissal by Mbeki as Deputy President in 2005), Zuma had gained the backing of the left-wing of the ANC's liberation alliance (alienated by Mbeki's promarket policies) and many party elites (estranged by his authoritarian managerial style). Subsequently, Zuma became president after the ANC's election victory in 2009.[7]

The Zuma presidency brought to a head various pathologies of ANC rule that had begun to emerge in previous eras. Particularly, the party-state became a machine for material accumulation by the Zuma-aligned elements of the party elite. Merit qualifications were displaced by loyalty to the president in many public appointments, resulting in the erosion of numerous state entities' constitutionally decreed independence (Southall 2013). Suffice it to say that under Zuma, the party-state became riven by an extensive web of patronage and corruption, resulting in the increasing inefficiency and unaccountability of the state machinery.

The most scandalous signifier of these tendencies was the phenomenon of state capture, whereby the Guptas, a family that recently emigrated from India, allied themselves to President Zuma and his faction. Together, they used Zuma's control over the state machinery to staff key positions with cronies and drain the public service and parastatals of resources via the corrupt allocation of tenders to their opaque web of companies. Simultaneously, they systematically dismantled numerous agencies established to ensure the state's accountability (Pauw 2017; Public Protector 2017). Overall, as the party-state transmogrified into a vehicle for material accumulation and upward mobility by the party elite and those close to it, it undermined the integrity of government and its ability to deliver goods to ordinary citizens. Meanwhile, the investment climate deteriorated, economic growth declined, and public indebtedness increased. As a result, toward the end of the Zuma presidency, the ANC became increasingly divided and factionalized. As the availability of resources began to slow, and as corruption mounted and growth collapsed, the ANC's popularity rapidly diminished (Southall 2016b).

As the crisis intensified, there were manifold indications of discontent with ANC rule. Community protests targeting failures of service delivery and the unaccountability of overwhelmingly ANC-led local councils had spread like wildfire from the early 2000s (Alexander 2010; Von Holdt et al. 2011), many of these involving violent encounters between protestors and the authorities. Meanwhile, because the ANC's economic policies had failed to make a significant dent in apartheid era unemployment levels (which remained at between 25 and 40 percent of the labor force depending upon the definitions used; Mohamed 2010), and because workers were increasingly informally and precariously employed, they continued to live up to their reputation (earned from the 1970s) for militance (Bischoff 2015). When strikes broke out, such as during a major strike wave on the country's platinum belt in 2012–13, they often involved considerable violence—against management, *black legs*,[8] rival unions, security guards, or police (Chinguno 2015). The violence occurred despite the ANC having thoroughly overhauled the despotic industrial relations system it had inherited from apartheid. In turn, the police often responded by using violence of their own, the most notorious incident being their killing thirty-four protesting miners by gunfire at the Lonmin mine at Marikana on August 16, 2012, an incident that evoked memories of massacres committed by their apartheid predecessors (Marks and Bruce 2015).

Thereafter, a wave of student protests swept the system of higher education during the 2016 academic year. The protests were sparked by a student demonstration at the University of Cape Town demanding the removal of a statue of the colonial icon, Cecil Rhodes. Yet fundamentally the protests were about high fees, so they leapt rapidly from one university to another, igniting a widespread sense of grievance among black students who complained about continuing social exclusion within a still heavily white higher education system. It was therefore an easy transition from a social media driven demand that "#Rhodes must Fall!" to "#Fees must Fall!" to a more general campaign for the "decolonization" of the universities (Booysen 2016). This escalation rose to the level of arson, causing major damage on several campuses. While the use of fire earned the condemnation from across the party spectrum, its sympathizers responded—in terminology borrowed from black activists in United States—that it was expressive of an all-encompassing "black pain." The lesson drawn by observers was that the use of fire by the (relatively privileged) student movement was a metaphor for the broader problems of South Africa. It was the nation at large, not just the universities, that was already burning (Ismail 2016).

The student movement voiced anger among the younger black generation against continued white domination of the economy and much of the public sphere, despite the ANC's take-over of government. Their cry was echoed by numerous black commentators, who regularly decried what they labelled postcolonial domination by a white elite. In turn, confronted by mounting economic crisis, the Zuma faction within the ANC increasingly resorted to the related narrative that the NDR was being thwarted by "white monopoly capital" and that a campaign of "radical economic transformation" was urgently needed. Complaints that the 1994 democratic settlement had entrenched white privilege gained widespread currency, as momentum developed for reform of the constitution to facilitate more rapid land reform and "indigenization." In response, there is a strong undercurrent among whites of contempt for black rule disguised as criticism of Zuma's regime, with this surfacing in highly publicized examples of blatant racism.

Against this background of multiple discontents, polarizing racial discourse and political dysfunction, fears grew that South Africa was destined to experience a return to the political polarization experienced during apartheid. However, whereas under late apartheid a broad alliance of popular forces, cutting across class and race, confronted a despotic white minority regime, it was by no means fully clear whether the nascent popular movement was directing its anger principally against "white monopoly capital" or the ANC.

Proto-Polarization in South Africa: Toward Democratic Decay or Democratic Deepening?

If political polarization under apartheid provided the platform for a democratic settlement, that this settlement rested upon enduring socioeconomic inequalities has ensured that while polarization has diminished, it has only been partially defused, providing a constant potential for political mobilization. This would seem to point in two directions outlined by McCoy, Rahman, and Somer (2018). The first is that a failure to address the concerns of key constituencies may allow for mobilization of antisystem support by disaffected political elites, threatening the established democratic order; an alternative potential direction is that incumbent political elites respond constructively to the risks of polarization by addressing social inequalities, seeking support across opposing political blocs, and thereby reinforcing the legitimacy of democracy.

The underlying causes of South Africa's high levels of protest and violence are deeply etched in the political-economic order. The legacy of structural violence and racial division continues to run deep. Many blacks have experienced significant gains since 1994, with an emergent black middle class being a major beneficiary of democracy. Even so, it is Africans who remain at the bottom of the social heap while, relatively, the racial minorities have prospered. Second, the economy—characterized by dismally low savings and investment levels, low growth, massive unemployment, and extensive poverty—is failing too many citizens. Pursuit of neo-liberal market-led policies have led to the opening of the hitherto heavily protected apartheid economy, a major restructuring (and flight) of capital and a decline of manufacturing. Although job losses were more or less balanced by increased opportunities created by the growth of the financial and service sectors, there has been a marked shift toward informal and precarious employment. Furthermore, young people (15–34 years), many of them dismally educated, account for 65 percent of the unemployed.

It gets worse. South Africa remains one of the most unequal countries in the world, with its economy still overwhelmingly dominated (via control over value chains as much as ownership) by a small minority of whites (Oxfam 2017; World Bank 2018; Bosiu et al. 2017). Despite black advances, whites continue to enjoy strong relative advantage. In 2011, black Africans (80 percent of the population) owned gross private assets of 3.6 billion rands, while whites (just 9 percent) owned R10.4 billion (SAIRR 2012, 288). Overall, the gap between whites and blacks is increasing. Whereas whites' household incomes were 4.3 times larger than black Africans in 1996, they had become 5.8 times higher by 2014 (SAIRR 2016, 316). This reflects better life chances, as whites continue to gain preferential access to good schooling and have higher rates of graduation from universities, leading to higher standards of living.

Meanwhile, with fewer people formally employed than those receiving social grants,[9] the current economic trajectory is manifestly unsustainable, especially given a limited tax base (unless commodities, upon which the economy remains heavily dependent, enjoy an unexpected resurgence in prices). Simply put, the money to pay for the maintenance of South Africa's already modest welfare state is beginning to run out (Southall 2016b). Unsurprisingly, in the view of many citizens, the ANC has become self-destructively unresponsive to the needs of ordinary people, while its growing sense of insecurity is leading to the growing volatility of its political rhetoric.

Against this background of multiple discontents, economic uncertainty, and political dysfunction, the prospects are real that discontented political elites, within as well as outside the ANC, may claim that democracy (at least as it is established under the constitution) is not working for the mass of people, and mobilize around the need for faster and more far-reaching transformation. Such a shift in direction, which would doubtless be versed in terms of a populist black nationalism, would stoke fears of increased racial tensions, investment flight, and ultimately, a similar combination of economic meltdown and political authoritarianism that followed the regime's seizure of white farms in Zimbabwe from the early 2000s (Sachikonye 2012; Shumba 2018). In other words, South Africa seems at risk of returning to the level of political polarization experienced during the final years of apartheid—a scenario that would threaten democracy.

Against this, however, an equally strong argument can be made that South African democracy is sufficiently resilient to prevent a return to apartheid-era polarization. First, even though racial cleavages continue as a basis for political mobilization and many black activists use a racialized discourse, whites and blacks remain locked together in what Jacob Dlamini (2016) has termed a "fatal intimacy." Survey material suggests that South Africans of all races recognize that their identities and fate are closely bound together. One survey, conducted in 2015, reported that 54.1 percent of South Africans (59.8 percent of black Africans) felt that race relations had improved since 1994, 85.4 and 85.1 percent respectively felt that the different races need each other, and, interestingly, 62 percent and 58.3 percent felt that racial discourse was used by politicians to find excuse for their own failure (SAIRR 2016).

Meanwhile, although social cohesion is being severely tested by the increasing precariousness of employment among black workers, the latter continue to need their jobs and employers their workers. The level of inequality remains astounding, yet racial divisions are cross-cut by the growth of a black elite and middle class. Levels of intra-societal violence remain disturbingly high, yet they are as much contained within discrete communities by the still brutal spatial inheritances of apartheid as they are generalized across society. Additionally, South Africa remains a highly religious society, with religion continuing to play a significant role in diverting popular discontents away from political flashpoints.

Finally, it is particularly notable that the EFF, the populist breakaway from the ANC that has punted a radical nationalist platform around extensive nationalization of industries and expropriation of white-owned land, has gained only limited support. Simultaneously, it has opted to use institutional means of both parliament and the courts to expose and counter state-capture and other ANC corruption. Although the democratic fabric was severely eroded during the Zuma presidency, it was not destroyed. Indeed, it was because the ANC fears losing a majority at the next election (scheduled for 2019), and because, unlike in Zimbabwe, the competitive fairness of elections has been maintained, that the party opted for a change in political leadership offering the prospect of renewal.

Reform in the ANC, 2017–18

At its five-yearly National Congress in December 2017, Deputy President Cyril Ramaphosa, backed by anti-Zuma elements within the ANC, narrowly defeated Nkosazana Dlamini-Zuma, Zuma's ex-wife and strongly backed by his faction, for the party's leadership. To be sure, Ramaphosa's victory was severely circumscribed by the continuing strength of the Zuma faction within the party. Accordingly, he had to move very cautiously to consolidate his power. However, by early January 2018, he was strong enough to persuade a reluctant Jacob Zuma to stand down from the state presidency. Politically astute, managerially able, uncorrupt, and highly personable, Ramaphosa was widely viewed as the man to turn South Africa away from the excesses of the Zuma era and to restore it to economic growth and constitutional democracy.

Ramaphosa's rise to the presidency was due to a combination of factors. Significant elements within the ANC, many of them veterans of the struggle, had openly deplored the corruption that had billowed under Zuma and his related undermining of the constitution. Many party activists rebelled against the patterns of patronage within the ANC that had massively hollowed out intraparty democracy. Yet above all, party elites had taken note of the widespread demonstrations demanding that "#Zuma Must Fall," which had drawn support from across the racial and political spectrum during 2016–17. These had spread fear within party ranks that, as indicated by its major losses in the local elections, the ANC risked losing national power to opposition party coalitions in the forthcoming 2019 general election.

Ramaphosa's early months in power saw major changes. As of this writing in mid-2018, appointments to his first cabinet saw Zuma zealots cast aside or marginalized, competence prioritized, and treasury control over departmental spending firmly re-asserted. Major changes in personnel and direction took place in the country's major parastatals. A judicial inquiry into state capture has been facilitated, accompanied by backing given to the relevant state agencies to prosecute individuals suspected of corruption. Charges of corruption against Zuma, dropped after he became president, were re-instated, and he faces the very real prospect of being sent to jail. The Guptas' empire was being dismantled, looted resources were being reclaimed, and the Guptas themselves became likely to face trial. Meanwhile, Ramaphosa was spearheading major efforts to attract major flows of investment back to South Africa (Everatt 2018).

Hence, it is that the ANC is busy re-forging its bonds with its mass constituency. With Ramaphosa at its head, it is probable that it will again secure a majority (albeit reduced) in the 2019 election, not least because the DA—its major competitor—is presently struggling with internal divisions. Meanwhile, there are some encouraging signs that the ANC is turning away from the disastrous Zuma trajectory. Precipitated by the extent of civil society protest, this shift is taken by many to demonstrate the resilience of the country's democracy.

Nonetheless, long-term prospects remain uncertain. Disappointment among the black population at the limits of the democratic settlement is mounting; community protests against perceived ANC arrogance have continued into the new era; and Ramaphosa's renewal of the ANC has yet to see the removal of Zuma strongmen within key provinces, prompting questions of whether the party can really reform.

Much depends on whether Ramaphosa's reformist agenda succeeds or falters. If it succeeds by achieving higher economic growth, reducing corruption, and improving service delivery by government, then political polarization may be diffused and the legitimacy of democracy enhanced. But if it fails, the prospects of deepening political polarization, resulting in Zimbabwe-style authoritarianism and political decay, will be worryingly increased.

Notes

1. Coloreds, descended from a wide variety of ethnic ancestries (African, Asian, and European), were officially defined as one of South Africa's four official population groups under apartheid.

2. South Africa still grapples with racial terminology. *Black* here is used to refer to Africans, Indians, and Coloreds inclusively.

3. Soweto, with a population of some 1.3 million, was Johannesburg's largest black township. For the Soweto Revolt, see Hirson (1979).

4. Comprehensive overviews of South African history include Terreblanche (2002) and Welsh (2009).

5. The transitional interim constitution provided the right of parties gaining 10 percent of the vote to claim proportionate representation in the GNU. This provision was dropped following the finalization of the constitution by parliament in 1996.

6. The ANC party hierarchy has the political clout to "redeploy" the party's representatives out of the legislature, to another posting, or, as the ultimate sanction, to expel an MP from the party, which under the constitution would mean they would lose their seat in parliament.

7. Veteran ANC activist Kgalema Motlanthe replaced Mbeki as president until Zuma took over in 2009.

8. Employees continuing to work during a strike.

9. Total employed (nonagricultural) was 16.1 million versus 17.2 million social grant recipients in 2017 (SAIRR 2018, 246, 744).

References

African National Congress (ANC). 1998. The state, property relations and social transformation, *Umrabulo* 5: 3.

Alexander, Peter. 2010. Rebellion of the poor: South Africa's service delivery protests—a preliminary analysis. *Review of African Political Economy* 37 (123): 25–40.

Ashman, Samantha. 2015. The South African economy: The minerals-energy-finance complex redubbed? In *New South African Review 5: Beyond Marikana*, eds. Gilbert Khadiagala, Prishani Naidoo, Devan Pillay and Roger Southall, 67–85. Johannesburg: Wits University Press.

Bischoff, Christine. 2015. Cosatu's organisational decline and the erosion of the industrial order. In *Cosatu in crisis: The fragmentation of an African Trade Union Federation*, eds. Vishwas Satgar and Roger Southall, 217–45. Johannesburg: KMM Press.

Bond, Patrick. 1990. *Elite transition: From apartheid to neo-liberalism in South Africa*. Sterling, VA: Pluto Press.

Booysen, Susan. 2011. *The African National Congress and the regeneration of political power*. Johannesburg: Wits University Press.

Booysen, Susan., ed. 2016. *Fees must fall: Student revolt, decolonization and governance in South Africa*. Cape Town: Witwatersrand University Press.

Bosiu, Teboho, Nicholas Nhundu, Anthea Paelo, Mmamoletji Thosago, et al. 2017. Growth and strategies of large and leading firms—Top 50 firms on the Johannesburg Stock Exchange. *CCRED* Working Papers 17. Available from https://papers.ssrn.com/sol3/papers.cfm?abstract_id=3013670.

Chinguno, Crispen. 2015. Strike violence after South Africa's democratic transition. In *Cosatu in crisis: The fragmentation of an African trade union*, eds. Vishawas Satgar and Roger Southall, 246–67. Johannesburg: KMM Review Publishing Company.

Corder, Hugh, Veronica Federico, and Romanu Orru. 2014. *The quest for constitutionalism: South Africa since 1994*. Dorchester, UK: Ashgate.

Dlamini, Jacob. 2016. *Askari: A story of collaboration and betrayal in the anti-apartheid struggle*. Auckland Park: Jacana.

Economist Intelligence Unit (EIU). 2016. Revenge of the deplorables. Available from http://felipesaha-gun.es/wp-content/uploads/2017/01/Democracy-Index-2016.pdf.

Everatt, David. 2018. Dare South Africans dream again as they celebrate their 23rd Freedom Day? Available from http://theconversation.com/dare-south-africans-dream-again-as-they-celebrate-their-23rd-freedom-day-95660.

Giliomee, Hermann. 1979. The Afrikaner economic advance. In *The rise and crisis of Afrikaner power*, eds. Heribert Adam and Hermann Giliomee, 145–76. Cape Town: David Philip.

Habib, Adam 2013. *South Africa's suspended revolution: Hopes and prospects*. Johannesburg: Wits University Press.

Hirson, Baruch. 1979. *Year of fire, year of ash: The Soweto revolt—roots of a revolution?* London: Zed Press.

Horowitz, Donald. 1991. *A democratic South Africa? Constitutional engineering in a divided society.* Berkeley, CA. University of California Press.

Ismail, Zenobia. 2016. Fire, freedom and disrepair. Available from http://www.universityworldnews.com/article.php?story=20160621132415750.

Johnson, R.W. 2015 *How long will South Africa survive the looming crisis?* Cape Town: Jonathan Ball Publishers.

Lodge, Tom. 1983. *Black Politics in South Africa since 1945.* Johannesburg: Ravan Press.

Marais, Hein. 2011. *South Africa pushed to the limit: The political economy of chance.* Cape Town: University of Cape Town Press.

Marks, Monique and David Bruce. 2015. Marikana and the politics of public order policing. In *New South African review 5: Beyond Marikana.* eds. Gilbert Khadiagala, Prishani Naidoo, Devan Pillay, and Roger Southall, 207–28. Johannesburg: Wits University Press.

McCoy, Jennifer, Tahmina Rahman, and Murat Somer. 2018. Polarization and the global crisis of democracy: Common patterns, dynamics and pernicious consequences for democratic politics. *American Behavioral Scientist* 62 (1): 16–42.

Mohamed, Seeraj. 2010. The state of the South African economy. In *New South African Review 1: Development or decline?* 39–64. Johannesburg: Wits University Press.

Oxfam. 2017. *Even it up: Time to end extreme inequality.* Available from https://www.oxfamamerica.org/static/media/files/even-it-up-inequality-oxfam.pdf.

Pauw, J. 2017. *The president's keepers: Those keeping Zuma in power and out of prison.* Cape Town: Tafelberg.

Public Protector. 2017. *State of capture.* Report No. 6 of 2016/17. Available from www.ppprotect.org.

Sachikonye, Lloyd. 2012. *Zimbabwe's lost decade: Politics, development and society.* Harare: Weaver Press.

Shumba, Jabusile. 2018. *Zimbabwe's predatory state: Party, military and business.* Pietermaritzburg: University of Kwazulu-Natal Press.

South African Institute of Race Relations (SAIRR). 2012. *South Africa Survey 2012.* Johannesburg. South African Institute of Race Relations.

South Africa Institute of Race Relations (SAIRR) 2018. *Life in South Africa: Reasons for Hope.* Available from https://irr.org.za/reports/occasional-reports/files/life-in-south-africa-reasons-for-hope.pdf.

South African Institute of Race Relations (SAIRR). 2016. *The state of South Africa's race relations.* Johannesburg: Institute of Race Relations.

South African Institute of Race Relations (SAIRR) 2018. *South Africa Survey 2018.* Johannesburg: South African Institute of Race Relations.

Southall, Roger. 2013. *Liberation movements in power: Party and state in Southern Africa.* Scottsville. University of Kwazulu-Natal Press.

Southall, Roger. 2014a. Democracy at risk? Politics and Governance under the ANC, *The ANNALS of the American Academy of Political and Social Science* 652:48–69.

Southall, Roger. 2014b. The contradictions of party dominance in South Africa. In *The quest for constitutionalism: South Africa since 1994*, eds. Hugh Corder, Veronica Federico, and Romano Orru, 155–68. London: Ashgate.

Southall, Roger. 2016a. *The new black middle class in South Africa.* Woodbridge, UK: James Currey.

Southall, Roger. 2016b. The coming crisis of Zuma's ANC: The party state confronts fiscal crisis. *Review of African Political Economy* 43 (147):73–88.

Southall, Roger. 2017. The political theology of Jacob Zuma, *The Conversation.* Available from https://theconversation.com/the-political-theology-of-jacob-zuma-71176.

Terreblanche, Sampie. 2002. *A history of inequality in South Africa 1652-2002.* Scottsville, SA: University of Kwazulu-Natal Press.

Von Holdt, Karl, Malose Langa, Sepetla Molapo, Nomfundi Mogapi, et al. 2011. *The smoke that calls: Insurgent citizenship, collective violence and the struggle for a place in the new South Africa.* Johannesburg: Centre for the Study of Violence and Reconciliation; Society, Work and Development Institute, University of the Witwatersrand.

Welsh, David. 2009. *The rise and fall of apartheid.* Cape Town: Jonathan Ball.

World Bank. 2018. *Overcoming poverty and inequality in South Africa: An assessment of drivers, constraints and opportunities.* Washington, DC: World Bank.

Elite Conflict, Compromise, and Enduring Authoritarianism: Polarization in Zimbabwe, 1980–2008

By
ADRIENNE LeBAS
and
NGONIDZASHE MUNEMO

How do elites play a role in crafting polarization? And what effects do elite-led conflicts have on democracy and mass politics? To examine these questions, we compare two separate episodes of party-based polarization in Zimbabwe, from 1980 to 1987 and from 2000 to 2008. Each of these moments of polarization ended in an elite power-sharing settlement, but a comparison of the two moments yields insights about both the causes of polarization and its effects. We find that the episodes of polarization were rooted in elite instrumentalization of conflict. They differed, however, in the extent to which they activated foundational myths and built larger master cleavages. We suggest that the latter episode conforms more closely to McCoy, Rahman, and Somer's pernicious polarization, which we argue is marked by deeper societal penetration and segregation than other forms of political polarization and is also less amenable to resolution.

Keywords: polarization; Zimbabwe; institutions; elections; conflict

D o elites play a role in crafting polarization, and under what conditions do polarizing strategies produce durable changes in mass politics? When do citizens remain captive in polarized camps, and when do they become free to reconstitute themselves into new democratic majorities? These questions are central to the fate of democracy in divided societies, since the reconstitution of interests and formation of new majorities is vital for democratic health. Where membership in a minority comes to be perceived as fixed, as often occurs during polarization, this calls into question the idea of

Adrienne LeBas is an associate professor of government in the School of Public Affairs at American University. She is the author of the award-winning From Protest to Parties: Party-Building and Democratization in Africa *(Oxford University Press 2011), as well as several articles on political parties, violence, and public opinion.*

Correspondence: lebas@american.edu

DOI: 10.1177/0002716218813897

a shared civic realm in which ideas and interests can be debated. For Appadurai, *predatory majorities* are especially likely to emerge in democratic contexts where individual citizens cannot easily move from a minority to a majority group, and group-based violence becomes more likely (Appadurai 2006). In terms of when these kinds of fixed group identities emerge, the literature has tended to focus on ethnicity, religion, and other ascriptive identities as particularly dangerous in terms of violence and democratic survival (e.g., Montalvo and Reynal-Querol 2005; Østby 2008; Cederman et al. 2011). Ethnicity and religion are presumed to be the natural raw materials with which elites will "gamble for resurrection" when faced with electoral defeat or popular protest (De Figueredo and Weingast 1999; Kaufman 2001). Especially where there is a history of group violence, democratization is seen to go hand-in-hand with exclusionary ethnic mobilization (e.g., Horowitz 1985; Snyder 2000).

We argue that political science tends to wrongly elevate the importance of ascriptive or semi-ascriptive differences, such as ethnicity and religion, in the analysis of political polarization. In a number of cases, this focus on ethnicity or other ascriptive difference has obscured the roles played by other forms of difference in shaping political debate. This article calls for greater and more nuanced attention to the roles that ideology and conceptions of the state can play in fostering polarization. We find that episodes of polarization are rooted in elite instrumentalization of conflict, as one would expect, but they differ in the extent to which they activate foundational myths and build enduring cleavages at the popular level. We argue that polarization is likely to penetrate to the societal level—and be sustained over time—when it capitalizes upon foundational myths about the nation and the state's purpose. These differences *may be* associated with an ascriptive identity, insofar as political narratives built around pluralism or regional autonomy might be attractive to ethnic or religious minorities. But these kinds of foundational debates can be cross-cutting and can generate polarization even if they have little association with pre-existing identity-based cleavages.

In democracies, polarizations built around foundational arguments are more likely to be sustained over time, leaving strong marks on partisan loyalties and a country's overall political trajectory. In his analysis of regime instability and democratic *careening*, Slater (2013) identifies one foundational argument around which polarization is often structured: should democracy enhance vertical or horizontal accountability? Or, in other words, should democratic institutions be structured to check concentrations of power or to amplify the power of the electorate? In more recent work, Slater and Arugay argue that tensions over vertical versus horizontal accountability can play out—and polarize societies—via debates over executive abuses of power (Slater and Arugay 2018).

Arguments over institutional constraint do not exhaust our options. In Zimbabwe, the polity has been divided over the centrality of the liberation war

Ngonidzashe Munemo is an associate professor of political science and associate dean for institutional diversity and equity at Williams College. He is author of Domestic Politics and Drought Relief in Africa: Explaining Choices (*Lynne Rienner Press 2012*), *and several articles on Zimbabwean politics, state response, and social protection.*

and the role it should play in civic and political life. In other countries, arguments over ethnic federalism or rotational power have similar polarizing and system-threatening force, as the cases of Ethiopia and Nigeria suggest. In still other countries, polarization may be built around challenges to group status or narratives of differential citizenship (King and Smith 2005; Straus 2015; LeBas 2018). All these types of polarizing debates may contain elements of claims for either greater horizontal (popular inclusion) or vertical (checks on centralization) accountability, but they cannot be reduced to this disagreement. Just as the character of polarizing debates may vary, so do their consequences. In the two episodes discussed here, polarizing debates led to very different kinds of political settlements. Furthermore, as LeBas argues elsewhere, polarization may result in short-run declines in political freedom yet still have longer-term positive effects on institution-building and democracy (LeBas 2018).

To show the effect of ideological disagreement on polarization, we compare two separate episodes of party-based polarization in Zimbabwe. Zimbabwe is a particularly good case in which to assess how episodes of polarization might differently impact mass politics. The country has been a procedural democracy with multiparty elections since independence in 1980, but elections have rarely been free and fair. Violence and intimidation have been consistent features of election campaigns, and violence has often been accompanied by rhetoric that paints opposing forces as subversive, traitors to national interests, or otherwise illegitimate political actors (Kriger 2005). The Zimbabwe African National Union-Patriotic Front (ZANU-PF) has won every election from 1980 to the present, but its party dominance can only be seen as secure for the period 1987–2000. That period of party dominance was bookended by two periods of severe political polarization.

The first period of polarization was from 1980 to 1987, when conflict between the country's two nationalist parties turned violent and ultimately left up to 20,000 dead. The second was from 2000 to 2009, when a new opposition party, the Movement for Democratic Change (MDC), challenged the ruling party that emerged from the first moment of crisis. According to the MDC and civil society groups, several hundred were killed, more than 6,000 individuals were abducted, and thousands more violently attacked during this second period of polarization.[1] Both of these episodes seem to accord with standard relational definitions of polarization that stress the emergence of a single social boundary around which social and political space are reordered (McAdam et al. 2001; LeBas 2006; McCoy et al. 2018). During both periods in Zimbabwe, elites deployed rhetoric that accused others of treason; state-sponsored violence targeted individuals who were suspected of loyalty to the other side; and politics was reshaped around a single us/them boundary. In both cases, polarization emerged during a moment of political opening but ended in a more closed political regime, one that could be best described as competitive authoritarian. Finally, each period of polarization ended with elite power-sharing settlements and explicit guarantees of an end to violent conflict, though these power-sharing arrangements should not be seen as a sign of genuine political opening or liberalization. Power-sharing was associated with further political closure during the first period and left the degree of freedom largely unchanged during the second period.[2]

Despite some similarities, there were significant differences between these episodes. These differences may help to explain when polarization penetrates to the mass level and is durable over time. In Zimbabwe, the first episode of elite conflict would seem to have been the more dangerous and polity-threatening episode, since elite conflict was structured around ethnicity. Yet violence and rhetorical escalation ended abruptly with an elite pact. There is no evidence that the new elite coalition had difficulty reining in party hardliners or the armed wings of either party, and there were no substantial attempts to reinforce or politicize the ethnic divide. In contrast, we suggest that the latter episode of polarization conforms more closely to "pernicious polarization" (McCoy et al. 2018), which we argue is marked by deeper societal penetration and segregation than other forms of political polarization and is also less amenable to resolution than other types.

Seven years after the power-sharing settlement that ended the most intense period of polarization and violence, MDC and ZANU-PF supporters still live in separate worlds in terms of public opinion and civic space. Friendships, social worlds, and sometimes even churches are structured on partisan lines. NGOs and public figures are assumed to be biased toward one of the two parties, even if they claim to be nonpartisan or nonpolitical. And new information is processed on partisan lines, such that MDC and ZANU-PF supporters disagree strongly about responsibility for events, such as the postelection military shootings of civilians, and may even dismiss events that conflict with their prior views as "fake news." Put simply, civil society remains segregated, violence continues, and both elites and opposition still use polarizing language to mobilize their base constituencies. The following pages focus on the differences between this episode of polarization and the earlier 1980–1987 period, which we argue was less systemically transformative.

Political Conflict with Limited Polarization, 1980–1987

The political conflict that developed immediately after independence in Zimbabwe was between the two major nationalist parties: the Zimbabwe African National Union (ZANU), the victor in the independence elections of 1980, and its main rival, the Zimbabwe African Peoples Union (ZAPU). The acrimony between ZANU and ZAPU had its roots in ideological and strategic divisions among nationalists that were reproduced over the course of the struggle for independence (Sithole 1999; Alexander et al. 2000; Mlambo 2014). In the immediate aftermath of independence, the pre-existing enmity between the rival nationalist parties was fanned and stoked by elites during a period of intense violence.

There were several conditions that, on the face of it, would seem to predispose the conflict between ZANU and ZAPU to pernicious polarization. These include a history of violent competition, regional/ethnic patterns of recruitment and support, the presence of armed party militia or armies on both sides, and strong and explicit indications from ZANU that it wished to establish sole control over the newly independent polity. Yet elites were not able to turn the ZANU-ZAPU division into an impermeable boundary around which social and political life was reordered. Quite different from what we see later with the MDC, the outcome of the ZANU-ZAPU conflict was the unification of the two nationalist parties, an enduring elite pact, and relatively little evidence of lingering polarization at the mass level.

Prelude to polarization

Zimbabwe became independent on April 18, 1980, but it was bound by the terms agreed to by the nationalist parties and the Zimbabwe Rhodesia transitional government at the 1979 Lancaster House Conference. The agreement required that ZAPU and ZANU gather their armies at designated assembly points prior to the February elections, and it established a parliamentary system of government with twenty reserved seats for Zimbabwe's white population, which composed at the time only about 8 percent of the population, and eighty "common roll" seats to be filled through proportional representation.[3] Though ZANU (led by Robert Mugabe) and ZAPU (led by Joshua Nkomo) had negotiated as a united Patriotic Front (PF) at Lancaster House, they contested the elections as separate parties. Both parties' fighters gathered at assembly points, and ordinary voters were unsure that the ceasefire would hold. This affected the climate in which the 1980 elections took place. Election observer reports indicate widespread voter intimidation, as well as threats by ZANU cadres of a resumption of war should the party lose the elections (Kriger 2005, 4–6; Laakso 2002, 329–30).

The results reflected the different regional bases of the two parties and, for the most part, reflected the ethnic geography of Zimbabwe. Thus, ZANU dominated the provinces where their army had been operative, winning more than 80 percent of votes in Mashonaland East and Central, in Masvingo, and in Manicaland (Cliffe et al. 1980, 46). ZAPU, on the other hand, won 86 percent of votes cast in Matabeleland South and 79 percent of votes in Matabeleland North. Put differently, ZANU did well in areas with Shona-speaking voters, and ZAPU performed strongly in Ndebele-speaking areas. Though observers often present the 1980 elections as an ethnic census, especially given what was to follow, this is not exactly the case. Despite its ethnic core constituency, ZAPU won more than 27 percent of the vote in the ethnically mixed Midlands province, and it won a parliamentary seat and 13 percent of the vote in the overwhelmingly Shona-speaking Mashonaland West.

These ZAPU victories seemed, at least initially, to be accepted by ZANU. The party invited ZAPU to join it in a coalition government, and four ZAPU Members of Parliament joined the government as ministers, including ZAPU leader Joshua Nkomo. By July, only a few months after the unity government was announced, Finance Minister Enos Nkala declared at a rally that ZANU's goal and desire "from now on [was] to crush Joshua Nkomo and forget about him."[4] In November 1980, ZANU elites continued their attacks on ZAPU by declaring to their supporters at a rally that "from today the PF[ZAPU] has declared itself the enemy of ZANU."[5] At this rally, Nkala went on to urge ZANU supporters in Bulawayo to form vigilante groups so that they could "challenge [ZAPU] on its home ground" (Alexander et al. 2000, 186).

Conditions were equally tense at the assembly points, where the ZANU-linked Zimbabwe African National Liberation Army (ZANLA) forces were taking control over the new Zimbabwe National Army. Some members of ZAPU's army, the Zimbabwe People's Revolutionary Army (ZIPRA), refused to come to the assembly points, and others left after arrival.[6] In late 1980, the first large-scale clashes between ZANLA and ZIPRA fighters broke out, and conflict spilled from the assembly point camps into urban townships. ZANU rhetoric likely played a role in inflaming tensions. ZANU-PF politicians insinuated that ZAPU politicians were involved in the violence, and, in February 1982, ZANU-PF Prime Minister Robert Mugabe announced that arms caches had been discovered on lands belonging to high-ranking ZAPU politicians.

The discovery of the arms caches brought the emerging conflict between ZANU-PF and ZAPU elites and fighters to a head. Accusing ZAPU of plotting to overthrow the government, Mugabe fired most ZAPU ministers from his coalition government and detained several senior ZIPRA commanders.[7] In dismissing his coalition-partners, Mugabe declared that: "ZAPU and its leader, Dr. Joshua Nkomo, are like a cobra in a house. The only way to deal effectively with a snake is to strike and destroy its head."[8] Both the language and the strategies employed by elites were consistent with pernicious polarization. The dismissal of Nkomo and other senior ministers from the coalition government prompted another wave of ZIPRA defections from the new national army and from the assembly points. Nkomo fled Zimbabwe and remained in exile until 1985.

Civilians and the ZANU–ZAPU conflict

Did this elite confrontation penetrate to the societal level, and in what ways? Though marginal groups of violent ZIPRA dissidents posed little threat to the regime (see Alexander et al. 2000), the ZANU government mobilized significant military force to the affected regions, with disastrous impact on civilians.[9] The operation was termed *Gukurahundi*, which roughly translates from Shona as "the storm that washes away the chaff," and its political or partisan nature was clear. The thousands-strong Fifth Brigade was drawn exclusively from former ZANLA combatants and was under the direct control of the Office of Prime Minister Robert Mugabe. In a report published in 1997, the Catholic Commission for Justice and Peace (CCJP) estimated that the Fifth Brigade was responsible for the following casualty toll in the single district of Tsholotsho alone: the killing of 1,500 civilians; the disappearance of another 350; the detention of close to 3,000 civilians, of whom roughly 380 were tortured; the sexual assault of 250 women by troops; and 1,500 injuries of other kinds (LRF 1997).

Consistent with other episodes of polarization, violence was accompanied by attempts to shape loyalties and enforce ideological compliance. Those caught in the brigade's dragnet were often marched to schools or other public places at gunpoint and forced to sing Shona songs in praise of ZANU in what was imagined as a re-education campaign of sorts. Sources are in agreement that the intent of the operation was less tracking down dissidents than creating a climate of intense fear among presumed ZAPU loyalists in the run-up to the 1985 elections. Also consistent with other episodes of polarization, the conflict allowed for no intermediate ground between "us" and "them." In practice, ZANU-PF politicians and military personnel conflated partisan and ethnic identity. In their rich account of the civilian experiences of the conflict in the 1980s, Alexander, McGregor, and Ranger reveal a clear pattern of targeting Ndebele civilians on the presumption that all Ndebele were ZAPU supporters and were therefore dissidents: "the child of a snake is also a snake" (Alexander et al. 2000, 222). Fifth Brigade commanders were also reported to have explained their actions as meting revenge on the Ndebele for the nineteenth-century raids of their ancestors on the Shona: "you have been killing our forefathers, you Mandebele." It is therefore unsurprising that Alexander at al. conclude that one of the brigade's most notable impacts in the conflict was "in hardening ethnic prejudice, and in bolstering a strong identification between ethnicity and political affiliation" (2000, 224). This was not entirely one-sided. To the present, some Zimbabweans mention roadblocks, forced evictions, and even killings of Shona-speaking residents of western Zimbabwe, though these attacks by ZIPRA or other armed actors were rare in comparison to the government's attacks on Ndebele-speaking victims.

Estimates of the total number of civilians killed vary significantly, from the 2,000 deaths directly documented by the CCJP to the more than 20,000 total deaths estimated by the CCJP and Amnesty International.[10] To some extent, the violence can be viewed as imposing an ethnic cleavage from above, with the clear intent of shaping election results.

The military occupation of western Zimbabwe continued through the 1985 elections, and both atrocities against civilians and direct repression of ZAPU made campaigning impossible. Kriger reports that more than eighty ZAPU officials were abducted or disappeared during the 1985 election campaign, and, by the time of polling, "outside Bulawayo, virtually every urban and rural ZAPU office had been closed or burned down" (Kriger 2005, 8). During the campaign, as Kriger documents, ZANU-PF politicians consistently used inflammatory rhetoric that may have encouraged violence (Kriger 2005, 8–13). The results, remarkably, indicate some degree of robust support for ZAPU: ZAPU retained 88 percent of the votes that had been cast for the party in 1980, and it lost only 5 of its 20 parliamentary seats.

"Power-sharing," party fusion, and the end of polarization

Shortly after the 1985 polls, perhaps convinced of its inability to eliminate its political rival via force, ZANU opened negotiations with ZAPU. Though violence and atrocities continued in western Zimbabwe, Nkomo returned from exile. In December 1987, ZANU and ZAPU signed the Unity Accord, which formally merged the two parties into ZANU-PF. Senior ZAPU members were given prominent cabinet posts, and, after constitutional changes adopted in 1990, Joshua Nkomo became one of two national vice presidents. The division of cabinet and other political positions was written into the new ZANU-PF constitution, as was the commitment to pursue the establishment of a one-party state. Although ZANU-PF did not succeed in creating a *de jure* one-party state, unification with ZAPU eliminated any potential for viable multi-party competition and laid the groundwork for the consolidation of a competitive authoritarian regime. In August 1987, ZANU-PF abolished the twenty seats reserved for white Zimbabweans and replaced them with candidates nominated and elected by parliament. ZANU-PF was left in control of 99 of 100 seats in parliament. In October 1987, the constitution was again amended to create an executive president with extensive powers. Robert Mugabe was the only presidential candidate nominated by parliament and was swiftly elected by the assembly. Zimbabwe transitioned from a parliamentary to a presidential system, but the centralization of powers that accompanied the party merger was much more important in shaping the post-1987 regime's character and conduct.[11]

Surprisingly, ethnic polarization at the elite level faded quickly. The Unity Accord substantially increased Ndebele representation in the cabinet, resulting in more ZAPU ministers than in the first 1980 postindependent cabinet (Laakso 2003, 132). Since the signing of the unity accord, former ZAPU members have always held at least one of the vice presidential positions. Even after Mugabe's overthrow in the "soft coup" of November 2017, this tradition continues. The accord also required the two parties to merge their entire organizational structures to the branch and cell levels. Given the geographic division of the two parties' support bases, this may have required less merging than relabeling, and the task may have been helped by the decimated nature of many ZAPU district, branch, and cell structures by 1987. But, more fundamentally, the ideals and basic political attitudes of ZANU and ZAPU activists and politicians were not terribly different. Both parties espoused varieties of socialism, viewed the ruling party as the vanguard of the people, and were sympathetic to strands of traditional cultural revival.[12] More importantly, the two parties' elites believed that the liberation war should be central to party ideology and central to all party attempts to mobilize mass constituencies.

Nor were there indications that ethnic polarization reshaped political loyalties. Despite the toll that the Fifth Brigade exacted in western Zimbabwe, there were few signs that Ndebele citizens were necessarily hostile to ZANU-PF or opposed to the Unity Accord. In a snap poll conducted at a joint party rally in western Zimbabwe in January 1988, *The Herald*, Zimbabwe's state newspaper, reported that few attendees knew about the alliance but cheered when informed that ZAPU members had been appointed ministers in the ZANU-PF government (quoted in Laakso 2003, 132). Voting patterns in western Zimbabwe do not suggest simmering resentments or an unwillingness to vote for ZANU-PF or even for former ZAPU cadres who had "sold out" the party and joined government. In the 1990 elections, voter turnout was marginally lower in Matabeleland than it was in the rest of the country (47 percent compared with 56 percent elsewhere), but there were few signs of a voter revolt. ZANU-PF won all twenty-four parliamentary seats in Matabeleland North and South in 1990 and 1995, and the party consistently won well over 80 percent of votes cast in rural constituencies nationwide.

Nor did party campaigns suggest that ethnicity was an issue. In 1990, the newly unified ZANU-PF did face a robust challenger. The Zimbabwe Unity Movement was formed by Edgar Tekere, a member of ZANU's high command during the war and a popular former secretary-general of the party. Tekere and his party won 17 percent of the presidential vote and roughly 20 percent of the national parliamentary vote, mostly in urban areas. The Shona-speaking Tekere made no special attempts to politicize the prior violence against ZAPU supporters known as *Gukurahundi*, and his party's program focused on economic conditions, corruption, and centralization of executive power—with no mention of human rights abuses or the atrocities in Matabeleland (Sylvester 1990, 389-392).[13] Ethnicity—or, indeed, any aspect of politics in Matabeleland—did not seem important enough to merit more than passing mention in academic articles on the election (Sachikonye 1990; Sylvester 1990).

This is not to suggest that *Gukurahundi* did not or does not matter to Ndebele Zimbabweans. Ethnic resentment over the lack of justice for the victims certainly lingers, and there are occasional suggestions that there exists a subtle, embedded political tribalism in Zimbabwean electoral politics (e.g., Muzondidya and Ndlovu-Gatsheni 2007). But our general point is that—in comparison with the polarization discussed below—the 1980s elite-level polarization was limited. Despite the rhetorical hardening and violence associated with this confrontation, there are few signs that polarization penetrated to the mass level. It did, however, result in a speedy closure of democratic possibility in Zimbabwe. From the mid-1980s to 2000, there was no space for viable political challenge in Zimbabwe. A new period of polarization was required to force such an opening.

Opposition Emergence and Pernicious Polarization, 2000–2013

The second period of polarization emerged from confrontation over a political opening. At first, this involved the formation of a constitutional reform pressure group, and then the launch of a new party. The beginnings of Zimbabwe's second period of polarization can be traced to mass protests in the 1990s and, especially, societal debate over the reform of the 1979 Lancaster House Constitution (LeBas 2011). Similar to other cases of polarization discussed in this volume, the rise of a new political challenger was a vital ingredient in Zimbabwe's descent into polarization. In 1997, a civil society coalition led by the labor movement formed the National Constitutional Assembly (NCA), which started a constitutional outreach and advocacy program that was intended to parallel the government's own constitutional reform program. Many of the principal organizations involved in the NCA formally launched the MDC in late 1999. After the government's own draft constitution was defeated in a popular referendum in February 2000, ZANU-PF began to see the MDC's civic coalition as a significant threat. Land invasions, violent targeting of opposition activists and supporters, and mass evictions followed. Despite this, the MDC attracted a substantial base of voters in 2000 and was able to maintain it for multiple electoral rounds, even in the wake of continued state-sponsored violence and repression.

As with the first period of polarization, this period resulted in substantial political closure and authoritarian retrenchment. But this period of political polarization also differed in two important ways from earlier polarization between ZANU-PF and ZAPU. First, the MDC challenged ZANU-PF's version of the history of the Zimbabwean state, which elevated anti-imperialist struggles to the level of a foundational state credo. ZANU-PF and ZAPU had been in agreement about two things, both of which were challenged by the MDC. The nationalist movements saw liberation war credentials as a near-prerequisite for holding political office. The MDC nominated several candidates who were too young to have served in the liberation armies. More troubling from the standpoint of ZANU-PF, the MDC leadership included several individuals who had been adults during the liberation war but had not joined the armed struggle.

Further, the MDC was an avowedly pluralist political movement, which argued for a diversity of opinion within government. This was a sharp change from the political culture of ZANU-PF, which prioritized solidarity and viewed the party-state as leading—rather than following—popular constituencies. Unlike the two nationalist parties, ZANU-PF and the MDC were not united by their liberation war credentials, nor did the two parties share a similar orientation toward the state and the role of a ruling party, as ZANU-PF and ZAPU had.

For these reasons, we argue that polarization split the country down very different lines and generated enduring political disagreement between individuals on either side of the polarized boundary. Put differently, though polarization was crafted and reinforced by elite confrontation and state-sponsored violence, it also penetrated to the societal level and reshaped political allegiances in a more durable way than did the first period of polarization.

Emergence of polarization

ZANU-PF's response to electoral challenge and regime threat in 2000 was three-fold. First, it launched a series of mass land invasions of white-owned farms, in an attempt to shore up its popular support base among rural Zimbabweans. Second, it launched a campaign of state-sponsored violence that targeted MDC candidates, party organizers, and those suspected to be supporters of the party, such as teachers residing in rural areas. Up to 12,000 MDC supporters and activists fled the rural areas for the relative safety of the cities, and thousands more were displaced by the farm invasions. Finally, the ruling party deployed a violent rhetoric aimed both at discounting political opposition as treasonous and at reinforcing the liberation war as the central lynchpin of the country's politics (Ranger 2004).

The direct costs of polarization were not borne by MDC supporters and activists alone. In an eloquent demonstration of polarization's flattening of all politics into a single us/them distinction, formal and informal restrictions were placed on civil society organizations, and journalists and lawyers also became targets of violent attacks, arbitrary arrest, and abduction. Actions taken by government to target perceived opposition supporters also harmed economic activity and remade urban spaces. Businesses in the formal sector that did not express explicit support for the government found themselves subjected to electricity load-shedding during business hours, and others found their workplaces invaded and their unionized workers harassed by a newly formed, ZANU-PF-sponsored splinter union. In late May 2005, the Zimbabwean government implemented *Operation Murambatsvina*, an "urban beautification" campaign that forcibly displaced up to 700,000 Zimbabweans. As Potts underlines, this was not merely the removal of "squatters" or the clearance of illegal settlements; instead, the bulk of homes destroyed were backyard shacks constructed in formal, legal high-density areas (Potts 2006). The Zimbabwean government's own statistics suggest that 570,000 Zimbabweans were displaced during the operation (Tibaijuka 2005, 32). Victims of Murambatsvina were disproportionately opposition supporters.

But the process at work should not be seen as simply state repression or the imposition of a disloyal or treasonous identity on any who voted against ZANU-PF. Instead, as LeBas has argued elsewhere, it is best to see this entire period as a reciprocal process of polarization that reinforced the solidarity and commitment of constituencies on either side of the political divide (LeBas 2006; LeBas 2011). In 2000 and in subsequent years, violence was disproportionately associated with state security forces, ZANU-PF party militia, and war veterans who were loyal to the ruling party (Kriger 2005). But the MDC and its civil society allies deployed their own polarizing rhetoric, reinforced us/them boundaries, and, especially within the grassroots structures, rejected any movement toward moderation or compromise. As time passed, the MDC created its own parallel structures that did not shy away from using violence and coercion to enforce party aims (LeBas 2006), and a culture of aggressive "hardcore activism" took root in some of the MDC's affiliated structures (Hodgkinson 2013).

Polarization stabilized support for the two parties. This is perhaps the strongest evidence that polarization was reciprocal, as one-sided repression would have yielded a collapse of opposition support. Instead, we see continued loyalty and even the hardening of support among MDC activists and supporters, despite a consistent campaign of repression by ZANU-PF against both. In 2000, the MDC ran candidates in all 120 parliamentary constituencies and won 57 of those seats. Its support was concentrated in Zimbabwe's cities and in ZAPU's former strongholds in western Zimbabwe, but it performed well, and won parliamentary seats, in rural Shona-dominated constituencies as well. Though the party did not perform as strongly in the 2002 presidential and the 2005 parliamentary elections, it still won roughly 40 percent of the overall vote in both contests, despite rigging, intimidation, and violence. In the 2008 presidential and parliamentary elections, the MDC had split into two rival factions, but they collectively won more than 50 percent of the national vote and 110 of Zimbabwe's 210 parliamentary seats. The

MDC's Tsvangirai won the presidential election outright, but ZANU-PF insisted that he fell short of the 50 percent needed to avoid a run-off. The period before the presidential run-off was associated with the worst spell of violence since *Gukurahundi*: 200 died at the hands of state security forces, and 36,000 were displaced.

Polarization and civilians

The penetration of political polarization to the mass level is also evident in public opinion data collected during this period. In the Afrobarometer's second round of public opinion polling in 2004, roughly 48 percent of ZANU-PF supporters said they were "very" or "fairly satisfied" with democracy in Zimbabwe, while only about 10 percent of MDC supporters said the same.[14] Thirty-five percent of MDC supporters said they trusted the president "not at all" versus only 2 percent of ZANU-PF supporters; trust in other institutions, ranging from the police to courts to parliament, followed the same pattern. In the multiple rounds of Afrobarometer polling since then, these stark differences between MDC supporters and ZANU-PF partisans have remained remarkably constant. To a large extent, the partisan boundary in Zimbabwe shapes citizens' attitudes toward democracy, toward their country's institutions, and even toward the acceptability of political violence. In the most recent Afrobarometer polling, conducted in the run-up to July 2018 elections, voting intentions were almost entirely monopolized by the two poles with less than 2 percent of voters expressing a preference for parties other than MDC Alliance and ZANU-PF (Bratton and Masunungure 2018).

How can we know whether this polarization is partisan, as we argue here, or ethnic? In a study of Zimbabweans' attitudes toward transitional justice and punishment of offenders for past human rights abuses, Bratton (2011) finds evidence consistent with our argument about both periods of polarization. As we would expect, MDC supporters are 36 percent more likely to demand justice than are supporters of the ruling party, but Ndebele-speakers—the victims of the first episode of polarization—are no more likely to demand justice than any other Zimbabweans (Bratton 2011, 372–74). Political polarization, yes; ethnic polarization, no.

We argue that elite confrontation and polarization in the 1980s did not have the effects on mass attitudes suggested by this public opinion data. Why might that be the case? First, to a greater extent than in 1980 to 1987, political conflict from 2000 to 2009 had an impact on ordinary Zimbabweans regardless of where they lived. Because rural teachers were often viewed as "closet" MDC supporters, political polarization took a particularly heavy toll on education in Zimbabwe. Attacks on teachers continued after the 2000 elections were over, and the first wave of forced rural school closings started in 2001 (Zimbabwe Human Rights NGO Forum 2002). In the run-up to the second round of the 2008 elections, the Progressive Teachers Union of Zimbabwe (PTUZ) reported violent attacks on teachers in schools, the use of schools for political meetings and militia bases, and forced student attendance at political meetings. What is notable is the geographic reach of these incidents: the schools affected in the first two weeks of May 2008 spanned twenty-three districts across the entire country. PTUZ reported that 65,000 to 75,000 teachers had been displaced from rural areas by 2010, and UNESCO reported in 2008 that 94 percent of rural schools had shut down due to political persecution.[15]

These events took a toll on basic services and economic conditions nationwide. Schools operated with fewer teachers, clinics suffered staff shortfalls (especially later, with the collapse of professional salaries in 2002–2003), and other government programs lost skilled staff. As some rural areas became "no-go" areas for opposition, many Zimbabwean nongovernmental and community-based organizations ceased operations, and access to international food assistance was politicized as well (Human Rights Watch 2003). The collapse of the agricultural sector, price controls, and the resulting hyperinflation devastated the Zimbabwean economy, giving rise to *kukiya-kiya* (make-do) economy in which ordinary people turned to hoarding, trade in contraband, fraud, and even crime to make ends meet (Jones 2010).

Power-sharing and the continuation of mass polarization

As in 1987, the path out of polarization was power-sharing. In late 2008, under extreme pressure from South Africa and other regional actors, ZANU-PF signed a power-sharing agreement that named MDC leader Morgan Tsvangirai as prime minister, distributed ministerial positions evenly between the two MDC factions and ZANU-PF, and created a new decision-making body that was intended to give opposition a voice in the executive. The Global Political Agreement resembled past political settlements in Zimbabwe, including the 1987 Unity Pact. Like them, it did little to depoliticize the state security forces or carry out the institutional reforms needed to push Zimbabwe toward democracy (Bratton 2014). The GPA was also immediately undercut by public statements by ZANU-PF's leading politicians and by the military heads who suggested continuity with past polarizing rhetoric. On the eve of signing the power-sharing agreement, Mugabe said that the MDC and ZANU-PF were "as different as fire and water" (quoted in Cheeseman and Tendi 2010, 220). Zimbabwe's military chiefs refused to salute Tsvangirai at his inauguration, citing his lack of liberation war credentials, and high-ranking military officials referred to him as a security threat or as "taking orders from foreigners" throughout the power-sharing period.[16] The contrast with the period following the 1980 Unity Accord, during which there seemed to be near-seamless military and political integration of the two nationalist parties, is notable. Most troubling, violence continued throughout the power-sharing agreement. This included waves of new farm invasions, armed clashes between MDC and ZANU-PF youth, continued state targeting and detention of MDC officers and elected officials, and violence and intimidation during by-elections.

Though power-sharing seemed a continuation of the politics of polarization for ZANU-PF, it had striking effects on the MDC and, especially, on its electoral support (LeBas 2014). The party abandoned the confrontational rhetoric that had shored up its identity as distinct from ZANU-PF. MDC party leaders—now flush with the benefits of ministerial positions—allowed grassroots structures to erode, failed to maintain close relationships with civil society, and seemed to abandon their commitment to internal democracy. By 2012, grassroots MDC activists were disillusioned by allegations of corruption, the remote nature of party leadership, and what seemed an abandonment of the party's commitment to internal democracy. In 2013, MDC voters seemed to come out for the party once more but to little effect. Though roughly the same number of votes were cast for the MDC in 2013 as in 2008, these translated into only 34 percent of the overall vote and just over 25 percent of parliamentary seats. This was partly due to the redrawing of electoral constituencies, which diluted MDC votes and made winning in a single-member-district more difficult. But it was also due to an incredible expansion in the size of the electorate and the overall number of votes cast for ZANU-PF, which the MDC and some civil society observers saw as a further indication of a fraudulent voters' roll. The extent of rigging is unknown.

ZANU-PF viewed this defeat as an end to polarization, and both overt repression and polarizing rhetoric diminished. Both ZANU-PF and the MDC became more consumed with internal squabbles and purges than with elite-level confrontation. Does this mean polarization has diminished? As noted above, partisan loyalties and vote intentions in the months before the recent elections remained sharply polarized between ZANU-PF and a newly reconstituted MDC Alliance, which together monopolize voting intentions. In the 2015 Afrobarometer poll, patterns of distrust and disapproval also seemed largely unchanged from earlier rounds: 21 percent reported that they were either "not at all satisfied" with democracy in Zimbabwe or volunteered that Zimbabwe is not a democracy, and a further 18 percent refused to answer the question. Twenty-five percent of Zimbabweans reported that they fear violence and intimidation at the polls "a lot," and this number rises to 40 percent of MDC supporters versus 19 percent of ZANU-PF supporters. Finally, a majority of Zimbabweans (63 percent) think the country is going the wrong way, but the gap in belief between MDC supporters and ZANU-PF supporters was 40 percent in 2015.[17]

In 2018, we see similar polarization on party lines around beliefs about media access and freedom (Bratton and Masunungure 2018, 16). To a large extent, even though elite polarization has diminished, ordinary Zimbabweans' attitudes remain polarized.

Conclusion

Zimbabwe's party dominance has twice been challenged. In both cases, the response from the ruling ZANU-PF has been the vilification of opposition and the hardening of authoritarianism. Prior to 1987, the ruling party faced a significant challenge from ZAPU. From 2000 until 2009, the ruling party won close victories over a new opposition party, the MDC. During both of these periods, individuals of the "wrong" ethnicity or presumed partisan affiliation were targeted for dispossession, forced displacement, and violence (Alexander et al. 2000; LeBas 2006). Yet, as we have shown, the primary cleavage that structured the ZANU-ZAPU confrontation—ethnicity—has proven a less enduring division in Zimbabwean politics. Thus, while the period produced intense conflict coming from elite instrumentalization, its impact on Zimbabwe was less durable and less threatening to the system than was the ZANU-MDC confrontation of the 2000s. Not only did the extreme polarization of 2000–2009 penetrate deeply to the level of mass attitudes, but it seems to still shape contestation and confrontation in Zimbabwe.

We argue that the durability of this later period of polarization in Zimbabwe is because it was built around both rival views of the liberation war and different conceptions of the state. For ZANU-PF, the liberation war remains the key event in Zimbabwean history, and its view of the link between state and citizen is plebiscitary rather than participatory. Opposition politics since 2000 have challenged these foundational myths, attempting to open political space and even to directly discredit ZANU-PF's claims about the liberation war's legacy.

Recent dramatic events in Zimbabwe seem consistent with our intuition here. In late November 2017, forces within the ruling party used an illegal military intervention to force long-serving President Robert Mugabe from office. New Zimbabwean President Emmerson Mnangagwa, who was directly involved in oversight of the Fifth Brigade in Matabeleland and long-term vice president to Mugabe, attempted to strike a conciliatory tone and promised that the July 2018 elections would be free and fair. After nearly two decades of isolation under Mugabe, Mnangagwa invited the United States and the European Union to send election observers, and he indicated that his primary goal would be to repair relations with donors and the international financial institutions. The July 2018 elections were not perfect, but the opposition MDC campaigned freely throughout the country for the first time. Both the media and ordinary Zimbabweans seemed free to criticize the incumbent party.

This brief moment of political opening, however, proved illusory. Shortly after results confirming Mnangagwa's victory were announced, the military opened fire on MDC protesters, killing six, and the police raided MDC offices and violently disrupted a press conference held by MDC leader, Nelson Chamisa. The MDC alleged that the results were rigged and filed a lawsuit with the courts. As this article goes to press, the ruling party's repression of opposition and civil society continues, economic crisis in Zimbabwe deepens, and both sides have returned to the language of warfare and confrontation. Despite the Mnangagwa administration's attempt to break with the past, polarization between ZANU-PF and the MDC has proven easy to rekindle. This reinforces our intuition that political polarization is more durable—and less amenable to resolution—when it is structured around foundational disagreements about the state and the nation, as it is in Zimbabwe.

Notes

1. Monthly data for some of this period are available from the Zimbabwe Peace Project (www .zimpeaceproject.com), and earlier NGO monitoring reports are available at the clearinghouse website, www.kubatana.net. Violence and abductions continued after 2009. The highest number of killings and abductions occurred during the election periods of 2000 and 2008.

2. Freedom House scores from 1980 to 2017 do not capture all these changes, but they are suggestive of political closure. Following independence, Zimbabwe's score peaked at a 3,4,PF in 1981 and then declined to 4,6,PF in 1986. Following the Unity Accord, it worsened further to a 6,5,PF in 1988. After the launch of the MDC, the score worsened further, and it remained a 7,6,NF or a 6,6,NF through the 2008–2013 power-sharing period. Neither LeBas nor Munemo feel that the Freedom House rankings are accurate for Zimbabwe, particularly for the post-2000 period.

3. There were few powers attached to the largely ceremonial presidency at this point, and ZANU's leader Robert Mugabe became prime minister upon independence.

4. Senator Enos Nkala quoted in "I Aim to Crush Nkomo, Nkala Tells Rally," *The Herald* (7 July 1980).

5. Enos Nkala quoted in "Nkala Warns PF at Rally," *The Herald* (10 November 1980).

6. As Alexander points out, fighters on both sides refused to come to the assembly points, and many may have opposed the ceasefire to begin with. After the elections, however, ZANU politicians began to present the non-compliance as an exclusively ZIPRA phenomenon and suggested that it was due to dissatisfaction over ZAPU's electoral loss (Alexander 1998, 153).

7. The two remaining ZAPU members in the government were John Nkomo and Cephas Msipa. Msipa's insistence on raising the issue of military atrocities in Matabeleland during cabinet meetings subsequently led to his dismissal.

8. Robert Mugabe quoted in Nkomo (2001, 2).

9. The most detailed account of the operation and its impact on civilians is found in the first-person testimonies of Matabeleland and Midlands residents collected by the Catholic Commission for Justice and Peace (LRF 1997). Our account relies heavily on the CCJP and on subsequent interviews and fieldwork conducted by Alexander, McGregor, and Ranger in the 1990s (Alexander et al. 2000).

10. "Victims relive Gukurahundi massacres that taint Mnangagwa," *The Zimbabwean* (30 January 2018).

11. Political decisions were taken by ZANU-PF as an organ rather than by the president. President Mugabe's attempts to break with this regime norm resulted in his ouster in a military intervention in November 2017.

12. The overlap between ZANU-PF and ZAPU preoccupations and world views is evinced by the similar themes and language deployed in the theater performed in the two movements' military camps during the war (Kaarsholm 1990). See also the discussion of the new party's manifesto and 1990 electoral campaign in Sylvester (1990).

13. The full scale of atrocities would not be known until later, but civilian massacres were discussed in both ZANU Central Committee meetings and in Parliament, so Tekere would have had some knowledge of conditions in western Zimbabwe.

14. All Afrobarometer data available for download at www.afrobarometer.org.

15. "Fear grips teachers ahead of elections," *The Zimbabwean* (18 December 2012).

16. See, for instance, "Zimbabwe army: PM Tsvangirai is security threat," *British Broadcasting Service* (23 June 2011).

17. The first report on the 2018 Afrobarometer results does not break down responses on these key indicators by party.

References

Alexander, Jocelyn. 1998. Dissident perspectives on Zimbabwe's post-independence war. *Africa: Journal of the International African Institute* 68:151–82.

Alexander, Jocelyn, JoAnn McGregor, and Terence Osborn Ranger. 2000. *Violence and memory: One hundred years in the 'dark forests' of Matabeleland*. Zimbabwe: Heinemann and James Currey.

Appadurai, Arjun. 2006. *Fear of small numbers: An essay on the geography of anger*. Durham, NC: Duke University Press.

Bratton, Michael. 2014. *Power politics in Zimbabwe*. Boulder, CO: Lynne Rienner Publishers.

Bratton, Michael. 2011. Violence, partisanship and transitional justice in Zimbabwe. *The Journal of Modern African Studies* 49:353–80.

Bratton, Michael, and Eldred Masunungure. 2018. Public attitudes toward Zimbabwe's 2018 elections: Downbeat yet hopeful? Afrobarometer Policy Paper No. 47.

Catholic Commission for Justice & Peace and the Legal Resources Foundation. 1997. *Breaking the silence, building true peace: A report on the disturbances in Matabeleland and the Midlands, 1980-1988*. Harare: Catholic Commission for Justice & Peace and the Legal Resources Foundation.

Cederman, Lars-Erik., Nils B. Weidmann, and Kristian Skrede Gleditsch. 2011. Horizontal inequalities and ethnonationalist civil war: A global comparison. *American Political Science Review* 105:478–95.

Cheeseman, Nic, and Blessing-Miles Tendi. 2010. Power-sharing in comparative perspective: The dynamics of "unity government" in Kenya and Zimbabwe. *The Journal of Modern African Studies* 48:203–29.

Cliffe, Lionel, Joshua Mpofu, and Barry Munslow. 1980. Nationalist politics in Zimbabwe: The 1980 elections and beyond. *Review of African Political Economy* 7 (18): 44–67.

De Figueredo, Rui, and Barry R. Weingast. 1999. The rationality of fear: Political opportunism and ethnic conflict. In *Civil wars, insecurity, & intervention*, eds. Jack Snyder and Barbara Walter. New York, NY: Columbia University Press.

Hammar, Amanda. 2003. The making and unma(s)king of local government in Zimbabwe. In *Zimbabwe's unfinished business: Rethinking land, state and nation in the context of crisis*, eds. Amanda Hammar, Brian Raftopoulos and Stig Jensen, 119–54. Harare: Weaver Press.

Hodgkinson, Dan. 2013. The "hardcore" student activist: The Zimbabwe National Students Union (Zinasu), state violence, and frustrated masculinity, 2000–2008. *Journal of Southern African Studies* 39:863–83.

Horowitz, Donald L. 1985. *Ethnic groups in conflict*. Berkeley, CA: University of California Press.

Human Rights Watch. 2003. *Not eligible: The politicization of food in Zimbabwe*. New York, NY: Human Rights Watch.

Jones, Jeremy L. 2010. Nothing is straight in Zimbabwe: The rise of the Kukiya-Kiya economy 2000–2008. *Journal of Southern African Studies* 36:285–99.

Kaarsholm, Preben. 1990. Mental colonisation or catharsis? Theatre, democracy and cultural struggle from Rhodesia to Zimbabwe. *Journal of Southern African Studies* 16:246–75.

Kaufman, Stuart J. 2001. *Modern hatreds: The symbolic politics of ethnic war*. Ithaca, NY: Cornell University Press.

King, Desmond S., and Rogers M. Smith. 2005. Racial orders in American political development. *American Political Science Review* 99:75–92.

Kriger, Norma. 2005. Zanu(PF) strategies in general elections, 1980–2000: Discourse and coercion. *African Affairs* 104:1–34.

Laakso, Liisa. 2003. Regional voting and cabinet formation. In *Twenty years of independence in Zimbabwe*, eds. Staffan Darnolf and Liisa Laakso, 122–39. New York, NY: Palgrave Macmillan.

Laakso, Liisa. 2002. When elections are just a formality: Rural-urban dynamics in the dominant-party system of Zimbabwe. In *Multi-party elections in Africa*, eds. Michael Cowen and Liisa Laakso. New York, NY: Palgrave.

LeBas, Adrienne. 2014. Another twilight in Zimbabwe? The perils of power sharing. *Journal of Democracy* 25:52–66.

LeBas, Adrienne. 2018. Can polarization be positive? Conflict and institutional development in Africa. *American Behavioral Scientist* 62:59–74.

LeBas, Adrienne. 2011. *From protest to parties: Party-building and democratization in Africa*. Oxford: Oxford University Press.

LeBas, Adrienne. 2006. Polarization as craft: Explaining party formation and state violence in Zimbabwe. *Comparative Politics* 38 (4): 419–38.

McAdam, Doug, Sidney Tarrow, and Charles Tilly. 2001. *Dynamics of contention*. New York, NY: Cambridge University Press.

McCoy, Jennifer, Tahmina Rahman, and Murat Somer. 2018. Polarization and the global crisis of democracy: Common patterns, dynamics, and pernicious consequences for democratic polities. *American Behavioral Scientist* 62:16–42.

McGregor, JoAnn. 2002. The politics of disruption: War veterans and the local state in Zimbabwe. *African Affairs* 101:9–37.

Mlambo, Alois S. 2014. *A history of Zimbabwe*. New York, NY: Cambridge University Press.

Montalvo, José G., and Marta Reynal-Querol. 2005. Ethnic polarization, potential conflict, and civil wars. *American Economic Review* 95:796-816.

Muzondidya, James, and Sabelo Ndlovu-Gatsheni. 2007. "Echoing silences": Ethnicity in post-colonial Zimbabwe, 1980–2007. *African Journal on Conflict Resolution* 7:275–97.

Nkomo, Joshua. 2001. *Nkomo: The Story of My Life*. Harare: Sapes Books.

Østby, Gudrun. 2008. Polarization, horizontal inequalities and violent civil conflict. *Journal of Peace Research* 45:143–62.

Potts, Deborah. 2006. "Restoring order"? Operation Murambatsvina and the urban crisis in Zimbabwe. *Journal of Southern African Studies* 32:273–91.

Ranger, Terence. 2004. Nationalist historiography, patriotic history and the history of the nation: The struggle over the past in Zimbabwe. *Journal of Southern African Studies* 30:215–34.

Sachikonye, Lloyd. 1990. The 1990 Zimbabwe elections: A post-mortem. *Review of African Political Economy* 17 (48): 92–99.

Sithole, Masipula. 1999. *Zimbabwe: Struggles within the struggle, 1957–1980*. Harare: Rujeko Publishers.

Slater, Dan. 2013. Democratic careening. *World Politics* 65 (4): 729–63.

Slater, Dan, and Aries A. Arugay. 2018. Polarizing figures: Executive power and institutional conflict in Asian democracies. *American Behavioral Scientist* 62:92–106.

Snyder, Jack. 2000. *From voting to violence: Democratization and nationalist conflict*. New York, NY: W.W. Norton.

Straus, Scott. 2015. *Making and unmaking nations: War, leadership, and genocide in modern Africa*. Ithaca, NY: Cornell University Press.

Sylvester, Christine. 1990. Unities and disunities in Zimbabwe's 1990 election. *The Journal of Modern African Studies* 28:375–400.

Tibaijuka, Anna Kajumulo. 2005. *Report of the fact-finding mission to Zimbabwe to assess the scope and impact of Operation Murambatsvina*. New York, NY: United Nations.

Zimbabwe Human Rights NGO Forum. 2002. *Teaching them a lesson: A report on the attack on Zimbabwean Teachers*. Harare: Zimbabwe Human Rights NGO Forum.

Conclusions

Reflections: Can American Democracy Still Be Saved?

By
NANCY BERMEO

This article reflects on whether the erosion of democracy in the contemporary United States can be halted. Using the cases and conclusions from McCoy and Somer's eleven country collective project, it argues that democracy's decline is not inevitable. A case for cautious optimism emerges from analyzing the coalitions around democracy's disassemblers and democracy's defenders. The actors disassembling democracy have activated cleavages and adopted a style of rule that exacerbates fault-lines on the Right. The actors defending democracy have thus far done what's needed to eventually build the sort of winning coalition that has proven successful elsewhere. Creating broad, cross-class networks, mobilizing peaceful protest, and drawing on mass values that are still supportive of democracy bolster the likelihood of successful defense.

Keywords: democracy; polarization; opposition; Trump; Republican Party; business lobbying; Democratic Party

As every morning's news sets our heads spinning, it is natural to steady ourselves with historical parallels and to speculate about the future with an eye to the past. McCoy and Somer's collective project enables us to do precisely this. By analyzing the association between polarization and democracy in eleven countries across four continents, it provides a broad platform for viewing the turbulence of the Trump administration in comparative perspective.

What can the effects of pernicious polarization on democracies elsewhere teach us about

Nancy Bermeo is currently a PIIRS senior scholar at Princeton University and a Nuffield senior research fellow at Oxford University. Her books include Parties, Movements and Democracy (with Deborah Yashar; Cambridge University Press 2016), Mass Politics in Hard Times (with Larry Bartels; Oxford University Press 2014) and Ordinary People in Extraordinary Times (Princeton University Press 2003), an award winning study of the breakdown of democracy.

Correspondence: nancy.bermeo@politics.ox.ac.uk

DOI: 10.1177/0002716218818083

democracy in the United States? More precisely, do the analyses presented here foreshadow democracy's continued erosion, democracy's collapse, or the potential for democracy's defense? Though each case study contributes to an answer, the editors' conclusion provides two general theoretical leads that are especially helpful.

The first is that the effects of polarization on democracy are shaped not simply by the coalition of "polarizing figures" in charge but by the "reaction of opponents" as well. By drawing our attention to two specific sets of actors, the collection highlights the sometimes forgotten fact that democracies never die of natural causes. Democracies become dictatorships when one set of actors attempts to disassemble democratic institutions and another set of actors fails to marshal an appropriate defense.

The collection's second especially helpful lead concerns the factors that help to determine whether the defense of democracy will succeed. The editors conclude that "the possibility of handling" polarization "democratically" is decisively shaped by the nature of the cleavages activated by polarizing elites, and the relative capacity for electoral mobilization exhibited by each camp. A close look at cleavages and capacity among incumbent and opposition actors in Trump's America suggests that an effective defense of U.S. democracy is sorely needed but still possible.

Incumbent Elites

The right-wing coalition associated with Donald Trump has fault-lines that may hamper its capacity to disassemble American democracy in the future. One of the most significant involves the divide between political elites in the White House and a subset of economic elites in globalized sectors of the economy. Despite changes in tax and regulatory policy, which have clearly worked to their benefit, a subset of prominent business elites is offering public resistance to both the content and the nature of Trump's rule.

We must not forget that capitalists in the United States have been very well served by neo-liberal democracy. They have no need for an authoritarian executive, or for dramatic institutional change because their control of policymaking has heretofore been firm (Hacker and Pierson 2010; Gilens 2012; Page, Bartels, and Seawright 2013). Unlike their counterparts in Thailand before the 2006 coup (and unlike many other democracies that collapsed), U.S. capitalists are not being threatened by either an economic crisis or a redistributive Left.

Rather than playing the role of silent coalition partners, some of the most dynamic and powerful sectors of our capitalist elite have emerged to oppose Trump's policymaking. They have come out vehemently against trade tariffs.[1] They have strongly opposed xenophobic immigration policies.[2] And when Trump expressed sympathy for the racist and anti-Semitic right-wing marchers in Charlottesville, so many members of his hand-picked Business Council resigned that he was forced to abolish it.[3] Most recently, the Koch Brothers' Americans for Prosperity group not only pledged to campaign against Republicans who backed

Trump's agenda but openly criticized "Trump's Washington" for "divisiveness" and for "the deterioration of the core institutions of society."[4] In line with what happened in the Philippines under Estrada (Arugay and Slater, this volume), key capitalist elites are uneasy with any further concentration of executive power and are demanding more "horizontal accountability" instead.

Capitalist resistance to the concentration of executive power may be partially driven by libertarian values, but its main impetus is material. Governing an economy by tweets and executive orders may send signals of decisiveness to Trump's base and may provide direct benefit to Trump's personal cronies but it harms the interests of most capitalists who need predictability and who have long benefitted from the multiple access points and lobbying opportunities afforded by the separation of powers. In any case, the cronyism and patronage that buy loyalty in smaller and weaker economies is of less marginal value to our spectacularly large and globalized economic elite. Most U.S. capitalists do not depend on government contracts or protection. They have thrived in open markets and been advantaged by skilled and unskilled labor crossing relatively open borders.

The divide between the incumbent administration and economic globalists is closely linked to Trump's nationalist activation of cultural cleavages. These cleavages may constitute a second coalitional fault-line. Xenophobia and racial resentment were decisive in Trump's 2016 victory and are foundational to his support base (Abramowitz and McCoy, this volume). Yet there are reasons to question whether these cleavages can be the basis of a lasting majoritarian coalition. Xenophobia and racism run deep in American society, but demographic and generational changes are weakening their resonance. Only 3 percent of the American public sees racism as unproblematic and the share deeming it a "big problem" has doubled since 2011 to nearly 60 percent. A full 37 percent of Republicans and Republican leaners take this view (Neal 2017) and nearly a third believe that "we need to continue making changes to give blacks equal rights with whites" (Pew Research Center 2018b). Anti-immigrant sentiment has been declining since 1995 (ANES), and despite the president's fear-mongering, a full 68 percent of registered voters and 44 percent of Republicans still believe that "America's openness is essential to who we are as a nation." An impressive 80 percent of adults under 30 hold this view (Pew Research Center 2018b). Racist and xenophobic messages may have magnetic appeal for Trump's base, but they may also be a liability for retaining Republican moderates and Independents. The party's lethal loss of suburban House seats in the 2018 midterm elections illustrates precisely this (Scherer and Dawsey 2018).

If the Republican Party were strong, these opinions (and voters) might be ignored without cost, but Trump is weakening his party. This is a third problem for the coalition. In 2017, the percentage of registered women voters identifying as Republican plummeted to only 25 percent (Pew Research Center 2018a). Nearly a quarter of young Republicans shifted Democratic between January 2016 and March 2017 alone (Pew Research Center 2017b). Overall, the rate of defection is now steeper than it has been since 2005 (Kamarck, Pokul, and Zeppos 2018). Successful democracy disassemblers such as Chávez, Thaksin, Erdoğan, and Orbán built and expanded political parties. Trump has done the opposite. Even on the eve of decisive midterm elections he was channeling the fruits of fundraising overwhelmingly toward his own 2020 campaign rather than toward vulnerable fellow-partisans (Vogel 2018).

The weaknesses outlined above may harm incumbent capacity to build a winning electoral coalition in the future. It pays to remember that even as Trump won the presidency in 2016, he lost the election by some 3 million votes and that only 25 percent of eligible voters actually cast a ballot backing him. (The comparable figures for Chávez, Orbán, Estrada, and Duterte average over 33 percent). Trump has a rock-solid base, but it lacks the width and dynamism to make victory a sure thing. He took office with approval ratings that were far lower than his two predecessors and they have been stagnant ever since, despite a buoyant economy (Dunn 2018). The midterm loss of forty House seats and more than seven governorships shows the coalition's vulnerability.

Opposition

At the time of writing, in early December 2018, the defenders of democracy are behaving as if they had already internalized the tactical themes of this collection. Unlike their counterparts in failed democracies, opponents of the incumbent administration have built cross-class alliances, avoided unconstitutional actions, and eschewed violence. While depriving disassemblers of an excuse to silence critics in the name of security, they have had extraordinary success at mobilizing *peaceful* resistance. Peaceful protest—involving between 14 and 21 million Americans—is at an historic high and a sharp spike in voter registration and turnout is likely to give Democrats the advantage.

But the diversity of the opposition may matter most. As I have shown elsewhere, democracy endures when key actors distance themselves from would-be authoritarians, *prosecuting* and *condemning* all those who engage in lawlessness and antidemocratic behavior even when they present themselves as allies (Bermeo 2003). We have seen pathetically little distancing from the Republican Congress and this is deeply problematic, but we *are* seeing prosecution and condemnation from a broad range of other important actors.

The judiciary is still managing to prosecute elite lawlessness. It has convicted or indicted at least eight of the president's closest associates so far and challenged a host of xenophobic and other executive orders. Even stalwart Republican judges such as South Carolina's Dave Norton have joined in.[5] Of course, Trump is filling the bench with his own appointments, but we sometimes see distancing from them too: Dabney Friedrich is now the fourth judge to rule against legal challenges to the Mueller investigation.

Condemnation from the Left abounds but the defense of democracy is being advanced by figures associated with the Right as well. Condemnation from George Will and former Republican operatives such as Steve Schmidt are surely consequential, but condemnation from actors associated with the FBI, the intelligence community, the military, and leading donors is likely to resonate with a broader audience. Hope for an effective defense of American democracy lies in the fact that more than 200 former intelligence and security officials signed a cascade of open letters rebuking the president as a menace to free speech; that the admiral who headed the Bin Laden Raid stated publicly that Trump's attacks on the media are "the worst threat to democracy" in his lifetime (Vogel 2018); and that Seth Kalman, formerly the biggest GOP donor in New England, recently pledged $20 million to help Democrats retake Congress and become "a check on Donald Trump and his runaway presidency" (Kranish and Lee 2018).

Support for basic democratic values remains strong among ordinary Americans and this means that wise and principled leaders can still shape a winning coalition for democracy's defense. A recent LAPOP poll found that political tolerance for those who "hold diverging views" was nearly identical to Canada's, that support for coups was even lower than Canada's, and that only 14 percent of Americans had orientations that put "democracy at risk" (Cohen, Lupu, and Zechmeister 2017). Despite pernicious polarization, an impressive 84 percent of the public agrees that it is "very important that the rights and freedoms of all people are respected." A full 83 percent believe that a democracy requires "a system of checks and balances" and a striking 89 percent agree that democracy depends on "elections that are open and fair" (Pew Research Center 2017a). The historically high turnout in the 2016 midterms illustrates that abstract opinions about elections can affect the behavior of ordinary voters.

Democratic victories in the House, in state legislatures, and in gubernatorial races in key states such as Arizona, Michigan, Wisconsin, and Kansas suggest that the incumbent coalition is already suffering from the frailties I detailed above. But no one can predict whether the potential for democracy's defense will be realized. And no one can know whether and when the damage already done to norms and institutions can be corrected. Backsliding and defense are iterative games. Moreover, every unhappy democracy is unhappy in its own way and, thus, the routes to breakdown are myriad. Voter suppression, court-packing, gerrymandering, media manipulation, and infighting might stymie democracy's defenders. But the differences between the U.S. case and the cases of democratic breakdown analyzed in this collection suggest that the worst case scenarios may still be avoided. Time will tell.

Notes

1. Fierce opposition to Trump's earliest tariff the "Buy American" Border Adjustment Tax, came from The Business Roundtable (with its $7 trillion in revenue), the Global Automakers Association, the National Automobile Dealers Association, the Retail Industry Leaders Association, the National Retail Foundation, and major individual retailers such as Target and AutoZone.

2. More than ninety major corporations, including Apple, Facebook, Microsoft, Twitter, Netflix, and Yelp, immediately opposed the February 2017 immigration ban. More than 300 companies immediately opposed the president's policies toward DACA and H-1B visas. These included IBM, Google, Amazon, Apple, Microsoft, Facebook, Best Buy, and Wells Fargo.

3. The resigning executives included Kenneth Frazier of Merck Pharmaceuticals, Brian Krzanich of Intel, Kevin Plank of Under Armour, Scott Paul of the Alliance for American Manufacturing, and Inge Thulin of 3M.

4. These are the words of Americans for Prosperity leader Brian Hicks, *Washington Post*, July 29, 2018.

5. In response to an executive order suspending implementation of the Clean Water Rule, Norton wrote, "the pivot from one administration's priorities to the next [requires] at least some fidelity to law and legal process. … The court cannot countenance such a state of affairs" (Wittenberg and Reilley 2018).

References

Bermeo, Nancy. 2003. *Ordinary people in extraordinary times: The citizenry and the breakdown of democracy*. Princeton, NJ: Princeton University Press

Cohen, Mollie, Noam Lupu, and Elizabeth Zechmeister, eds. 2017. *The political culture of democracy in the Americas 2016/17: A comparative study of democracy and governance*. Available from https://www.vanderbilt.edu/lapop/ab2016/AB2016-17_Comparative_Report_English_V2_FINAL_090117_W.pdf.

Dunn, Amina. 1 August 2018. *Trump's approval ratings so far are unusually stable – and deeply partisan*. FactTank. Washington, DC: Pew Research Center.

Gilens, Martin. 2012. *Affluence and influence: Economic inequality and political power in all America*. Princeton, NJ: Princeton University Press.

Hacker, Jacob S., and Paul Pierson. 2010. *Winner take all politics: How Washington made the rich richer and turned its back on the middle class*. New York, NY: Simon & Schuster.

Kamarck, Elaine, Alexander Pokul, and Nicholas Zeppos. 14 June 2018. Trump owns a shrinking Republican Party. FIXGOV, Brookings Institution. Available from https://www.brookings.edu/blog/fixgov.

Kranish, Michael, and Michelle Ye Hee Lee. 29 October 2018. Pittsburgh Synagogue Shootings Deepen Divide Jewish Community over Trump. *Washington Post*.

Langer, Gary, and Benjamin Siu. 2018. Election 2018 exit poll analysis: Voter turnout soars, Democrats take House. ABC News. Available from https://abcnews.go.com/Politics/election-2018-exit-poll-analysis-56-percent-country/story?id=59006586.

Neal, Samantha. 29 August 2017. *Views of racism as a major problem increase sharply, especially among Democrats*. FactTank. Washington, DC: Pew Research Center.

Page, Benjamin, Larry Bartels, and Jason Seawright. 2013. Democracy and the policy preferences of wealthy Americans. *Perspectives on Politics* 11 (1): 51–73.

Pew Research Center. 2 March 2017 (2017a). Large majorities see checks and balances, right to protest as essential for democracy. Washington, DC: Pew Research Center.

Pew Research Center. 17 May 2017 (2017b). Partisan identification is "sticky" but about 10% switched parties over the past year. Washington, DC: Pew Research Center. Available from http://www.people-press.org/2017/05/17/partisan-identification-is-sticky-but-about-10-switched-parties-over-the-past-year/21-3/.

Pew Research Center. 20 March 2018 (2018a). Wide gender gap, growing educational divide in voters' party identification. Washington, DC: Pew Research Center. Available from http://www.people-press.org/2018/03/20/1-trends-in-party-affiliation-among-demographic-groups/.

Pew Research Center. 4 October 2018 (2018b). 2018 midterm voters: Issue and political values. Washington, DC: Pew Research Center. Available from http://www.people-press.org/2018/10/04/2018-midterm-voters-issues-and-political-values/.

Scherer, Michael, and Josh Dawsey. 7 November 2018. How the democrats won the House. *Washington Post*.

Vogel, Kenneth. 18 October 2018. Money is rolling in, but for the president, not vulnerable Republicans. *New York Times*.

Wittenberg, Ariel, and Amanda Reilly. 16 August 2018. Clean water rule judge shifts legal brawl. E&E News PM.

Toward a Theory of Pernicious Polarization and How It Harms Democracies: Comparative Evidence and Possible Remedies

JENNIFER McCOY
and
MURAT SOMER

This article compares the dynamics of polarization in the eleven case studies analyzed in this special issue to draw conclusions about antecedents of severe political and societal polarization, the characteristics and mechanisms of such polarization, and consequences of severe polarization for democracy. We find that the emergence of pernicious polarization (when a society is split into mutually distrustful "Us vs. Them" camps) is not attributable to any specific underlying social or political cleavage nor any particular institutional makeup. Instead, pernicious polarization arises when political entrepreneurs pursue their political objectives by using polarizing strategies, such as mobilizing voters with divisive, demonizing discourse and exploiting existing grievances, and opposing political elites then reciprocate with similarly polarizing tactics or fail to develop effective nonpolarizing responses. We explain how the political construction of polarization around "formative rifts" (social or political rifts that arise during the fundamental formation/reformation of a nation-state), the relative capacity of opposing political blocs to mobilize voters versus relying on mechanisms such as courts or the military to constrain the executive, and the strategic and ideological aims of the polarizing actors contribute to the emergence of its pernicious form. We analyze the consequences for democracy and conclude with reflections on how to combat pernicious polarization.

Keywords: polarization; democracy; democratic erosion; populism; opposition strategies

Polarized polities around the world are suffering democratic erosion. The articles in this volume analyze eleven case studies, showing how pernicious polarization—polarization

Jennifer McCoy is a distinguished university professor of political science at Georgia State University. She is a specialist in comparative politics and democratization and Latin American politics; she coordinates the international research group on political polarization and democratic consequences. She is the author or editor of six books, the most recent being International Mediation in Venezuela *(with Francisco Diez; United States Institute of Peace 2011).*

Correspondence: jmccoy@gsu.edu

DOI: 10.1177/0002716218818782

234

ANNALS, *AAPSS*, 681, January 2019

that divides societies into "Us vs. Them" camps based on a single dimension of difference that overshadows all others—can occur in very diverse settings and produce harmful effects for democracy.

We recognize that political polarization is associated with both democratic strengthening and democratic erosion (Somer and McCoy 2018). Polarization can help to strengthen political parties and institutionalize party systems because it enables them to mobilize voters around identifiable differences. Offering voters clear choices and serving as heuristic cues can be helpful to democracy. Polarization is also potentially transformative in its capacity to address an imbalance in the popular vs. oligarchic versions of democracy (Slater 2013 and Stavrakakis 2018), or to open up a strong state as discussed by Somer in this volume. Democratic reform to enhance inclusion can be the goal when polarizing challengers organize to represent previously underrepresented groups. Polarization can thus serve democratization when used by political actors equipped with an inclusive agenda to contain polarization before it turns pernicious.

Even then, however, polarizing politics always carries the risk of taking on a life of its own, eviscerating cross-cutting ties and nonpartisan channels for compromise, and becoming pernicious. Polarizing challengers often provoke an elite backlash and counter-mobilization to stymie their transformative attempts, rather than a recognition of their reformist and inclusionary potential in building a constructively agonistic and pluralist democracy (Stavrakakis 2018). This elite backlash, in turn, can motivate the polarizing challengers to double down and strive to protect themselves by changing the rules and creating hegemonic power. Thus, whether polarization serves a constructive or destructive purpose for democracy depends on the behavior of both incumbents and oppositions, new political actors and traditionally dominant groups.

This collaborative project is focused on severe political and societal polarization, and moves beyond the conventional conceptualization of polarization as ideological distance between political parties and candidates. Instead, we are interested in situations in which people's identities and interests line up along a single divide, one in which people form into political groups that are seen in a competitive, "either-or" relationship with each other, overshadowing people's other, normally cross-cutting, identities. This pernicious state results from polarization's tendency—if not contained—to make the "normal multiplicity of differences in a society increasingly align along a single dimension (where) cross-cutting differences become instead reinforcing, and people increasingly perceive and describe politics and society in terms of "Us" vs. "Them" (McCoy, Rahman and Somer 2018).

Murat Somer is a professor of political science and international relations at Koç University, Istanbul. He specializes in comparative politics and democratization, and his research on polarization, religious and secular politics, ethnic conflict, and authoritarianism has appeared in books, book volumes, and journals, such as Comparative Political Studies, American Behavioral Scientist *and* Democratization.

NOTE: The authors appreciate the research assistance provided by Sara Ali, Tahmina Rahman, and İlker Kocael.

In this relational conceptualization, polarization has the tendency to extend from the partisan world to the realm of everyday social relations. In extreme cases, political identity can become all-encompassing as people view those in the "other" camp with distrust, suspicion, or fear, and cease to interact with them—even segregating themselves in their neighborhoods, social relationships, and news-feeds with like-minded people.

The dividing line between the camps may be simply support of, or opposition to, a personalistic political leader, such as pro- and anti-Trump in the United States, *chavistas* and anti-*chavistas* (for and against former president Hugo Chávez) in Venezuela, or pro- and anti-Erdoğan people in Turkey. But that dividing line may also reflect competing value systems (such as religious vs. secular), different visions of democracy (such as representative vs. participatory), or different definitions of citizenship and what rights should be afforded to immigrants. Group identity, which may act as a proxy or marker for the other aggregated divisions, is the key, linking citizens to a particular leader or partisan identity.

In this article, we compare our case studies in light of four basic questions. First, we examine how pernicious polarization emerges. Are there common antecedents of polarizing episodes in each country's history, such as social cleavages, economic crises, or democratic experiences? Second, we explore the characteristics and dynamics of pernicious polarization in action.

Third, we ask how pernicious polarization impacts democratic institutions and norms. Here polarization shifts from the outcome we are trying to explain, and becomes the explanatory factor itself—the independent variable. In McCoy, Rahman, and Somer (2018), we envisioned four possible outcomes for democracy, three of them negative and one positive: i) government gridlock and governmental control that careen between the parties representing the two camps; ii) democratic erosion or backsliding under the new elites who have to come to power, as they gradually concentrate power and exclude prior dominant groups or dissenters; iii) democratic erosion or even collapse as old power groups reassert control; and iv) a more positive outcome of democratizing reform in response to democratic crises of careening or backsliding.

Finally, we compare our cases to see if any patterns emerge in the structural or institutional factors or even the specific nature of the polarization that might help us to predict which of these democratic outcomes could result in a given country.

Emergence of Pernicious Polarization

How do democracies move from normal competitive politics among adversaries with plural identities to pernicious polarization? Social scientists do not agree on the structural, institutional, agentic, and elite vs. mass-based causes of severe polarization (Bermeo 2003; Abramowitz 2010; Druckman, Peterson, and Slothuus 2013; Campbell 2018). Armed with our relational and political conceptualization of polarization and response, we first focus on the interaction of underlying social cleavages and grievances (that is, structural factors), and the strategies and discourse of political elites who politicize them (that is agentic factors). We then turn to institutional antecedents.

Structure vs. agency: Underlying cleavages and grievances and elite discourse

Enterprising political actors who understand the power of polarizing tactics often build on existing cleavages in a society to simplify and emphasize differences and help to build politically winning coalitions. But our cases show that polarization is not explained by the simple existence of underlying social cleavages. That is, underlying social cleavages are often present, but are not always the basis of polarization. Neither is their existence sufficient to predict when polarization occurs. Take ethnic and religious cleavages as an example. Zimbabwe with its identifiable ethnic cleavage did not consistently express political interests around those cleavages, and did not consistently experience political polarization. Poland, Hungary, and the Philippines, on the other hand, with more homogenous populations in terms of language, religion, and ethnicity, nevertheless experienced episodes of deep polarization. Therefore, we need to understand when and how social-political cleavages turn into pernicious polarization.

To examine the role of social and political cleavages in polarization, we distinguish between the salient *discursive* dimension of polarizations, and the *underlying social and political cleavages*. As we discussed in the introductory article to this volume, we refer to long-standing and deep-cutting divisions that either emerged or could not be resolved during the formation of nation-states, or, sometimes during fundamental re-formations of states such as during transitions from communism to capitalism, or authoritarian to democratic regimes, as "formative rifts." Whenever polarization arises on the basis of a formative rift, we hypothesize that it is more likely to produce pernicious consequences for democracy.

Table 1 shows these dividing lines for each of our case studies. Some of the categories are actually empty signifiers, meaning that the speaker and the listener can assign whatever content they wish to the term. The populist rhetoric distinguishing the virtuous "people" from the conspiring "elite" is an excellent example of empty signifier (Hawkins et al 2018; Mudde and Kaltwasser 2018). For a populist, the "people" may refer to the "real Americans" or heartland supporters of Donald Trump, or the native-born Hungarians for supporters of Victor Orbán. The "elites" might be the establishment political parties, the more educated, the "deep-state" intelligence agencies and bureaucracy, Wall Street bankers, or foreign governments aligning with local opponents.

In addition to the traditional social cleavages of class, religion, ethnicity, and geography, political cleavages can emerge based on issues or values. In polarized contexts, such cleavages are sometimes simplified to a "Left-Right" discourse, whose actual content varies from the traditional economic ideological scale (referring to the degree of intervention or regulation of the state in the economy) to the more cultural dimensions described in this volume by Vegetti for Hungary (cosmopolitan/nationalist; traditional/modern) or Rahman for Bangladesh (religious, linguistic, and ethnic definition of the nation). In some of our cases, a political ideology cleavage around the concept of democracy emerged:

TABLE 1
Discursive Dimensions of Polarization and Underlying Cleavages

Categories	Description	Salient Discursive Dimension of Polarization in:	Underlying Cleavage or Formative Rift in:
Populist	Elite/people (always discursive; empty signifiers)	Venezuela Thailand Greece Hungary Turkey Poland Philippines U.S.	NA
Religious/Secular, or Church/State	Religious vs. secular values, beliefs, behavior and belonging; Role of religion in public life and national identity	Turkey Bangladesh	U.S. Turkey Poland Bangladesh
Cosmopolitan/ Nationalist	Pro- or anti-EU, pro- or anti-globalist	Hungary U.S. Greece	NA
Cultural values	Traditional/Modern; Conservative/Liberal; Communitarian/ Universalist	United States Turkey Poland	Greece Turkey U.S. Hungary Poland
Values and Interests of Place and Status	Urban/Rural or Center/ Periphery and the associated values, institutions and markers; Regionalism; Territorial distribution of power and economic resources	Turkey	U.S. Thailand Turkey
Economic ideology or Class	Market/Socialist; Liberalism/Solidarism; Austerity/Anti-austerity; Government role in economy	United States Poland Thailand	Venezuela Greece Thailand Poland
Political Ideology: concept of democracy and source of legitimacy	(Participatory/represen-tative; Majoritarian democracy vs liberal freedoms; National liberation/revolutionary vs liberal)	Venezuela Thailand Philippines Turkey Zimbabwe 1 Zimbabwe 2	Venezuela Thailand South Africa (post apartheid) Zimbabwe
Citizenship rights and national identity as formative rifts	Foreign- or native-born; Racial and ethnic minori-ties; Ethnicity/language	U.S. Hungary	U.S. South Africa Zimbabwe Turkey Bangladesh

participatory (radical) vs. representative (liberal) democracy in Venezuela, or royal-elitist "Thai democracy" vs. majoritarian democracy in Thailand.

Polarization around formative rifts—those we predict to be most enduring and with pernicious outcomes—occurs in several of our cases. In three of the countries in this volume, the competing foundational myths about the nation and the state's purpose, as described by LeBas and Munemo, centered on the legacy of the liberation wars and the actors claiming its legacy: ZANU and ZAPU in Zimbabwe, the ANC in South Africa, and Awami League in Bangladesh. In all three cases, the leaders of the anticolonialist liberation wars claimed a monopoly on the mantle of "liberation" and thus to serve as the true representatives of the people as nation, leading to democratic crises when challengers threatened that monopoly. Unresolved disputes over the basis of national identity further inflamed polarization in Bangladesh in the debate over whether religious identity or language/ethnicity should serve as the primary basis of national identity. Another kind of formative rift—"protean formative rift"—is evident in Turkey, described by Somer's study in this volume. Here, the so-called center-periphery (Shils 1961; Mardin 1973) rift since the late Ottoman times on one hand produced "republican-centrist" narratives reflecting the values, identities, and institutional premises of the "center" (Somer 2014). These, for example, described who the heroes and villains were during the foundational periods of modernization and nation-state formation, and what should be the indispensable principles of the republic. On the other hand "conservative-revisionist" narratives emerged, which challenged many claims, if not the core, of the republican-centrist narrative. These two narratives more or less corresponded to the prosecular and proreligious political identities, respectively, which were not entirely mutually exclusive. Since the transition to multiparty politics in 1950, these competing narratives had not produced pernicious polarization until the parties adopted polarizing tactics around them in the 2000s and overcame the rough balance of power between the electoral majorities of center-right parties and the institutional dominance of a secular-republican ideology, particularly in the military and judiciary.

Finally, in the United States, the basic question of citizenship and who enjoys the rights espoused by the founding fathers—Thomas Jefferson's "these truths" of political equality, natural rights, and sovereignty of the people (Lepore 2018)—has been debated since the founding of the republic and its differentiated citizenship for African slaves, Native Americans, and women. Subsequent divisions focused on birthright citizenship and naturalized citizenship. As Jill Lepore (2018) argues, at the heart of these conflicts is the dispute over the origin of truth, whether from God or the laws of nature. The deep polarization over these competing narratives of citizenship rights and roles of faith and reason led to a civil war, severe legal and informal discrimination for a century following the Civil War until the 1964 Civil Rights Act, and repolarization in the late-twentieth-century, which turned particularly rancorous during the Obama and Trump administrations.

Abramowitz and McCoy in this volume examine how racial resentment in the United States—responding to perceived unfair benefits or redress for historical legacies of discrimination—helps to explain voter realignment after the 1964

Civil Rights Act and to predict the vote for Trump in the 2016 U.S. elections. They further describe how Donald Trump's candidacy "reinforced some of the deepest social and cultural divisions within the American electorate—those based on race and religion." This feature of the current U.S. polarization that feeds off a formative rift creates a potential for pernicious polarization, which should worry democratic social and political actors from both sides of the aisles.

As is clear from the table, the discourse of polarization does not always match underlying social or political cleavages or formative rifts. Instead, polarizing actors more often seek to exploit grievances centered on political, economic, or cultural complaints; to activate latent resentments based on underlying cleavages and formative rifts; or bundle formative rifts together with other cross-cutting divisions. Mass grievances at the societal level are usually detectable and often exploited and exacerbated by elite political rhetoric. Polarizing speech articulates or even suggests a grievance, stoking fears, anxieties, and resentments that then become expressed as hostility, bias, and eventually enmity. By choosing the cleavage or grievance to highlight, political elites drive the polarization in important ways (Enyedi 2005; Lebas 2006).

We identify three primary types of grievances:

Political grievance or crisis of representation. Important segments of the population may perceive a lack of representation for a variety of reasons. They may have been actively excluded, such as blacks in apartheid South Africa or the American South prior to the civil rights era. Voters may also feel unrepresented if they perceive a lack of difference among colluding political parties viewed as either corrupt (i.e., too *little* polarization) or as unresponsive technocrats divorced from the people. For example, scholars have identified unresponsive technocratic or expert governments as the explanation for rise of populists in the United States and Europe (Luce 2018; Berman 2017).

Among our cases, a crisis of representation was ably exploited by Chávez's outsider candidacy in Venezuela, as voters rejected the traditional political parties that they blamed for economic crisis, mismanagement, and corruption in the 1990s; i.e., too *little* polarization. Similar mobilization of marginalized or alienated sectors occurred with Thaksin in Thailand in his support from the relatively poor rural and northern parts of the country; the AKP in Turkey, as they mobilized Islamists together with other social, cultural, and geographical groups that felt hindered or disempowered by bureaucratic and economic elites; the civil society movement organized around constitutional reform and more pluralist representation in government and becoming the MDC opposition party in Zimbabwe; Estrada's appeal to the marginalized poor in the Philippines; and of course the challenge to apartheid South Africa.

Economic grievance. Short-term economic crisis makes an easy target for political challengers. The populist Syriza party rose to dominance after three decades of alternation between two traditional political parties in Greece led to their implosion in the wake of the 2009 economic crisis, as did Chávez's movement in

Venezuela after the hyperinflation of the 1990s. Similarly, economic crisis and missteps by his opponent helped to propel Orbán's Fidesz into office in Hungary in 2010 and motivated businessman Thaksin to run for office in Thailand following the 1997 Asian financial crisis. Turkey's 2001 financial crisis helped the AKP initially to come to power with the electorate disillusioned with the existing parties.

Longer-term income inequality and relative deprivation can also serve as a mobilizing tool by targeting the economic anxiety of the "left-behinds." The PiS party in Poland mobilized Catholics with their ideology of "solidarism" vs. liberalism, highlighting the relative deprivation felt by Poles who perceived a decline in their economic well-being and social esteem relative to the liberal elites benefitting from the post-Communist transformation. In Turkey, developmental policies based on import-substitution until the 1980s favored urban industrial interests at the expense of rural interests, forming a grievance held by the countryside that was represented successfully first by center-right parties and then by the AKP who bundled it together with other cleavages. Donald Trump argued that immigrants and foreign trade were "stealing jobs" from U.S. workers feeling left behind after decades of growing income inequality, using a polarizing globalist vs. nationalist message that pitted America against the world.

Cultural grievance. Cultural grievances around the rights of specific religions, or Church vs. State arguments, *kulturkampfs* between secularized and conservative lifestyles among members of the same religion, as well as moral debates around gender and sexual rights or issues of sex and death can become the most polarizing because moral issues are the most difficult on which to compromise (Skitka and Morgan 2014). The "cultural backlash" theory has also been argued to better predict populist votes in the United States and Great Britain than the economic anxiety theory (Inglehart and Norris 2016), while racial resentment was at least as important as economic anxiety in the Trump vote (Abramowitz and McCoy, this volume).

Cultural grievances also emerge from a perceived loss or threat of loss of social or economic status by a dominant group in society, as explained by dominant status group theory (King and Wheelock 2007; Outten et al 2012; Sidanius and Pratto 2001). In these cases, changing demographics and political realignments can produce anxiety among such groups and, commonly, a receptivity to polarizing populist messages. The reaction of white, male, Christian, Trump supporters to the presidency of a biracial man in the United States, and to the growing diversity of the United States (in terms of race, religion, sexual orientation, and gender relations in the workplace) exemplifies a perceived loss of social and economic status (Mutz 2018). Similarly, Fidesz party leader, Viktor Orbán, successfully articulated a desire to keep Hungary for ethnic Hungarians, capitalizing on the threat posed by the refugee crisis of Syrians and northern Africans entering Europe as a campaign theme. In Thailand, the backlash against Thaksin's coalition of rural and Northern voters from the urban middle class and Southern voters was based, at least in part, on a perceived loss of social status as the urbanites lost electoral dominance to the rural majorities. Similarly, *kulturkampf*(s) between the less and more educated, between the more religious-conservative and rural and the more secular and urban, and even between proreligious and prosecular women activists underlie the polarization between the supporters and opponents of the AKP and Erdoğan.

Institutional antecedents and democratic historical experience

As our cases show, pernicious polarization can emerge in newer as well as established democracies. All of our cases had either a medium-term (20–40 years) experience with democracy, or a long-term history (more than 40 years). Thus, we argue that the length and quality of democratic history are more likely to impact the consequences of polarization for democracy, than to explain its emergence.

Likewise, we maintain that severe polarization can occur in democracies with various institutional setups, but the design and strength of institutions may impact the severity of polarization and its consequences for democracy. Hence, our cases include parliamentary as well as presidential democracies and those with proportional as well as majoritarian electoral systems. Our cases imply that institutional strength should be understood to entail, in addition to features such as credibility and adaptability (North 1990; Mahoney and Thelen 2010), the agentic dimension of how judiciously and consistently people manage the state institutions and implement formal and informal institutional rules at critical junctures. We return to these points in subsequent sections.

Institutional design can be expected to provide incentives and opportunities for polarizing political leaders and parties to pursue different strategies and seek to build different coalitions. Since proportional representation (PR) systems provide more opportunities for multiple, smaller parties to enter legislatures even when they represent similar cleavages and compete for overlapping constituencies, polarizing entrepreneurs may at least initially focus on the inward-looking strategy of consolidating their own bloc. In turn, since majoritarian electoral systems discourage smaller parties and the internal fragmentation of major electoral blocs, polarizing actors may concentrate on the outward-looking strategy of attacking and chipping away at the electoral support of the rival blocs.

As we discuss further in the section ahead on the dynamics and consequences of polarization, in general, single-member districts or mixed electoral systems (with some single-member and some proportional representation districts) are more likely to give disproportionate representation to the largest vote-getting party than are purely PR systems. We expect majoritarian electoral systems to deepen the democracy-eroding effects of polarization, and majoritarian and proportional systems to generate different incentives and opportunities for polarizing political agents.

In some of our cases, the polarizing period began with one party winning an absolute legislative majority, giving it the opportunity to then remake the rules to further its own advantage. This was the case in Bangladesh, Hungary, Poland, the Philippines, South Africa, Turkey, and the United States. Of these, the AL in Bangladesh, Fidesz in Hungary, the ANC in South Africa, and the AKP in Turkey all went on to reform the constitution, further enhancing the electoral advantage for the majority party and augmenting executive power. Erdoğan's constitutional reform even changed the parliamentary system to an (executive) presidential one; he then went on to win the 2018 elections with significant new powers.

In other cases, the governing party at the beginning of the polarization period ruled in coalition, but subsequently gained absolute majorities and attempted constitutional reforms and major legislative changes. Thaksin first won power in Thailand in 2001 benefitting from a 1997 constitutional reform that aimed to strengthen political parties and the prime minister. His attempt to further change the constitution failed in 2001, but his party won subsequent elections with absolute majorities, only to be repeatedly deposed by a royalist-elitist-military coalition until the military took power indefinitely in 2014. Hugo Chávez won the presidency in Venezuela in 1998 without a legislative majority, but engineered a constitutional reform the following year, strengthening presidential powers and changing electoral rules, and another in 2009 abolishing term limits; his party won electoral majorities in every election until 2015.

Polarizing leaders also attempted, but failed, to change the constitution early in their mandates in Poland (PiS party in 2015) and the Philippines (Estrada in 1999). The PiS went on to implement the changes anyway with their legislative majority after changing the composition of the Constitutional Tribunal to a more compliant one. Zimbabwe's polarizing periods each started out with ZANU-PF in power, but ended with power-sharing agreements as the challengers gained electoral strength and ZANU-PF was reluctant to give up power. The second polarization period (2000–2008) in fact started as a consequence of constitutional reform efforts, when the civil society movement defeating the government's reform proposals formed a new political party in 2000 and won a legislative majority. They lost some ground in subsequent elections in the wake of severe repression but split the legislature in 2008 elections and formed a power-sharing government to end the electoral stand-off, a result that defused the polarization but left the ZANU-PF as the dominant power.

Only the United States and Greece did not see a constitutional reform effort. In the United States, scholars debate the role of institutional design in producing polarization (Sides and Hopkins 2015). Nevertheless, the partisan-led model of redistricting in most states creates a system of gerrymandering that gives the advantage to the party in power—in this case, to the Republican Party as they won power in a majority of states in the 2000s. And the democratization of party primary systems (adopted by both parties in the 1970s) contributed to the incentives for more extreme candidates to be selected by the activist partisans who tend to vote in primaries. Thus, polarization contributed to even greater polarization. New, stricter voter identification laws championed by the Republican Party, changes to campaign finance rules, and allegations of voter suppression also appeared to indicate efforts to enhance partisan electoral advantages. Given the difficulty of changing the constitution, the increasingly partisan battles over Supreme Court nominations revolve, in large part, around constitutional interpretation. In addition, important institutional rule changes result from and continue to shape the polarizing dynamic, such as removing the filibuster from judicial nominations.

Polarizing Dynamics: Common Patterns and Variations

One of the most notable characteristics of pernicious polarization is the Manichean, moralizing character of political discourse. Leaders and supporters alike describe their own and opposing political groups in black and white terms as good and evil. They ascribe nefarious, often immoral, intentions and demonstrate prejudice and bias against those in the opposing camp. In this sense, polarization politically activates the latent tendencies in the population toward ethnocentrism—generally favorable views toward the in-group, and unfavorable stereotyping of the out-group (Kinder and Kam 2009).

As we noted in the introductory article, many of our cases involve populist leaders, who often bundle populism with other polarizing themes and messages. Further, populist leaders generally employ polarizing language and often generate antipopulist counter-mobilizations. Therefore, we are examining populism as one of the discursive dimensions of polarization. Scholars of populism identify Manichean discourse as one of three elements of populism, the other two being pro-people and anti-elite (Hawkins et al. 2018; Mudde and Kaltwasser 2017). In the majority of our cases, polarizing politicians regularly divide the populace into the "good" people and the "evil" elites. Populist leaders rail against the establishment or the elites, blaming them for the plight of the people, while upholding the virtues of the undefined "people" whom they claim to represent.

When opponents reciprocate with derogatory antipopulist language, the polarizing dynamic spirals. For example, in Venezuela, supporters of Hugo Chávez were called *chusmas* (gangs) by their opponents, while Chávez's supporters referred to the middle- and upper-class opposition as *sifrinos* (a slang term from a song about a rich, brainless woman caring only about luxury consumption) (McCoy and Diez 2011). Kongkirati in this volume describes the Manichean language on both sides in Thailand: "It is an uncompromising warfare between the 'good' and the 'bad'; 'moral, clean, enlightened' and 'immoral, corrupt, stupid' people; 'patriots' and 'traitors'; and 'aristocrat' and 'commoners.'" In the United States, Donald Trump gives derogatory nicknames to political opponents and critics, while categorizing entire sectors with pejoratives, such as "fake media." Trump opponents often imply his supporters are racist or ignorant.

But we see the same Manichean discourse denigrating opponents while lauding supporters even in cases that are not as saliently populist in their politics, implying that it reflects a general feature of polarizing politics, whereby the "elites vs. people" frame salient in populism constitutes a subtype of it. For example, Rahman describes the language used by both parties in Bangladesh in the polarizing episode of the International Crimes Tribunal: "*Chaagu*, a very derogatory *Bengali* term meaning a person with the intellectual level of a sheep, became popular with the pro-Shahbag elements to describe the anti-Tribunal elements." Meanwhile the opposition BNP leader "publicly identified the pro-Tribunal Shahbag movement as the congregation of 'immoral atheists.'" In Zimbabwe, LeBas and Munemo report that in the earlier conflict between ZANU and ZAPU, ZANU showed a "clear pattern of targeting Ndebele civilians on the presumption that all Ndebele were ZAPU supporters and were also dissidents: 'the child of a snake is also a snake.'" In the second polarizing period between ZANU-PF and the MDC, the symbolic delegitimation of the coopted opposition leader continued even after the power-sharing agreement appointing the MDC leader prime minister was signed: "Zimbabwe's military chiefs refused to salute Tsvangirai at his inauguration, citing his lack of liberation war credentials, and high-ranking military officials referred to him as a security threat or as 'taking orders from foreigners' throughout the power-sharing period."

Social psychologists have found that social identity leads group members to hold positive sentiments toward in-group members and negative sentiments toward out-group members. The more salient the identity, the stronger the loyalty toward in-group members and the prejudice and antipathy toward out-group members tend to be (Tajfel and Turner 1979; Gaertner et al 1993). The dynamics of intergroup conflict in particular lead members of a group to exhibit sympathy and loyalty to members of their group, while they exhibit antipathy and prejudice toward members of the out-group.

We argued in McCoy, Rahman, and Somer (2018) that "severely polarized democracies exhibit the tribal nature of intergroup dynamics, in which members become fiercely loyal to their 'team,' wanting it to win at all costs, and strongly biased or prejudiced against the other group. The psychology of polarization becomes fundamental as mechanisms of dehumanization, depersonalization, and stereotyping all contribute to the emotional loathing, fear, and distrust of the out-partisans" (p. 23). Politicians use symbols and language to create an "us" and "them" identity and thus contribute to these psychological mechanisms, whether intentionally or unintentionally.

In polarized politics, negative campaigning reinforces the antipathy toward the out-party's candidates and supporters. As a consequence, we often see a rise in negative partisanship, as Abramowitz and McCoy show in their case study of the United States in this volume—when vote choices are informed by a voter's *dislike* of an opposing candidate more than their liking of their own candidate. The use of insults to characterize opponents contributes to the psychological categorization of individuals, and the very usage of pronouns, where entire categories of persons are referred to not by name, but as the impersonal "them," depersonalizes and makes it easy to dehumanize them. Language of blame is commonly used, where blame is placed on "them," the out-group, who are victimizing "us," the in-group.

In polarizing settings, people who hold moderate opinions and maintain interests and identities that cut across the dividing line are increasingly ostracized, diminishing any chance of dialogue between opposing groups. As the Venezuelan case shows, it becomes nearly impossible to claim a neutral or middle position in a polarized polity as the most vocal proponents of each camp (usually the most radical positions) attempt to label or categorize not only individuals, but also media, and educational and civic organizations as belonging to one side or the other. Those who attempt to have a dialogue or compromise with the other side are then labeled as traitors or sell-outs (McCoy and Diez 2011; Garcia-Gaudilla and Mallen, this volume). Likewise, Somer in this volume argues how trimodal polarization in Turkey turned incrementally bi-modal as potential "bridge-makers" in the middle were wiped out and it became increasingly difficult for people to remain nonpartisan and maintain a critical position toward both blocs at the same time.

In fact, in pernicious polarization, intra-bloc tensions often escalate as high as do the inter-bloc tensions, whereby the hardliners and softliners within each bloc may fiercely blame each other. In the Turkish case, an example of this is the ongoing dispute between those opposition actors who had opposed a critical set of constitutional reforms, which the AKP government passed in a crucial 2010 referendum, by arguing these changes would crack the door open for AKP hegemony and authoritarianism; and those who had defended the reforms by arguing that they were not enough, but they were worth supporting, using the campaign slogan "insufficient but yes," as Somer discusses in his contribution. In Venezuela, it includes the divide within the opposition to President Maduro about whether to spur a presidential resignation or ouster through street protests, or focus resources on the tedious work of grass-roots organization-building to compete electorally. More recently, intra-opposition divides included the debate over whether to participate at all in unfair elections. Such divides can fragment an opposition and help to consolidate the rule of the dominant party.

Structural changes also tend to happen in the economy, bureaucracy, and key sectors, such as the media, that enable or reinforce the weakening of the middle ground in public and political discourse. Accordingly, ownership and/or management of institutions shift to opportunistic or ideological loyalists of one bloc or the other. This results in a situation where, for example, independent journalists find it increasingly more difficult to shape the news, or, worse, maintain their jobs.

Thus, a summary of the most striking features of pernicious polarization in our cases that distinguish it from a healthy pluralism in democratic society:

a) Division of the electorate into two hostile camps, where multiple cleavages have collapsed into one dominant cleavage or boundary line between the two camps.

b) The political identity of the two camps becomes a social identity in which members feel they belong to a "team" and demonstrate strong loyalty to it.

c) Political demands and interests become formed around those identities.

d) The two camps are characterized in moral terms of "good" and "evil."

e) The identities and interests of the two camps are viewed as mutually exclusive and antagonistic, thus negating the possibility of common interests between different groups.

f) A greater cohesion grows within groups, and greater conflict and hostility between groups.

g) Stereotyping and prejudice builds toward the out-group due to lack of direct communication and/or social interaction.

h) The center drops out and the polarized camps attempt to label all individuals and groups in society as one or the other.

i) Institutions, including media, become dominated by one bloc or the other through discursive changes as well as changes of ownership, management, and staff, weakening the middle ground in public and political discourses.
j) The antagonistic relationship manifests in spatial and psychological separation of the polarized groups.

Life of its own

Once the forces of polarization are set in motion, they often take on a life of their own. Social and political incentives make it increasingly more convenient for individuals to go along with polarization, and, if and when a critical mass is reached, powerful cascade (bandwagon) effects can be activated (Kuran 1995; Somer 2001). Though the polarizing dynamics may be initiated and sustained by political entrepreneurs for their own political benefits, it can become self-propagating and entrap those very political actors. Somer describes in this volume the process in Turkey: when Erdoğan's AKP used polarizing tactics to mobilize voters and win, it "triggered changes that transformed the AKP itself and the mainstream political field at large. … [T]his logic of polarization locked both the party and its rivals in a web of intended, unintended, and mutually reinforcing policies and discourses, which were antidemocratic or had democracy-destroying consequences."

As polarization extends into other areas of social interaction and sharpens Us vs. Them identity politics, interactions along all other planes diminish considerably, channels of communication between groups break down, and intragroup solidarity increases at the expense of intergroup cohesion. Palonen (2009) describes the "totalizing" nature of polarization as it extends from the political to societal realms—a process perhaps most advanced in our set of cases of Venezuela and Hungary, but increasingly in the United States and Turkey as well.

The dominant political frontier creates a point of identification and confrontation in the political system, where consensus is found only within the political camps themselves. Polarization is reproduced in all political and social contests with an intensity that distinguishes it from mere two-party politics. It is a totalizing system, as it aims to dominate the existing system of differences and identities. (Palonen 2009, 321)

Variations

We have already discussed variations in the types of underlying cleavages and grievances. There are also variations in the political motivations or strategic aims underlying the use of polarizing strategies, and the actual strategies used by polarizing incumbents and oppositions, to which we now turn.

Strategic and ideological aims of polarizing elites

The strategic and ideological aims underlying elites' use of polarization as a political strategy also vary. We identify three basic patterns giving rise to the political use of polarization: the more stationary and pro-status-quo pattern of intra-elite power struggles and party competition, and the inclusionary and exclusionary versions of transformative politics in which mass-based popular demands for fundamental change are channeled and exploited by a political entrepreneur able to capitalize on this demand.

In the first pattern, intra-elite conflicts drive rival elites to compete for political power by mobilizing voters to boost their electoral chances. They may do so on the basis of appeals to populism or other claims to represent a sector of the population or the people. These are not so much democratizing efforts to include new sectors into the polity and economy, as they are elite instrumentalism to further their own interests. These efforts may turn into a polarized struggle between elites able to capitalize on the vertical accountability of popular sovereignty and elections in competition with other elites who dominate the horizontal accountability of institutional checks and balances to constrain the executive (Slater and Arugay 2018).

Intra-elite competitions characterized polarization in Bangladesh and Zimbabwe following national liberation wars from colonialism, in which rival elites claimed the mantle of representing revolutionary legitimacy (Rahman; LeBas and Munemo, this volume) and "manufactured" differences to be able to compete electorally, and in Thailand and the Philippines as disaffected elites created their own political movements to further their own agendas (Kongkirati; Arugay and Slater, this volume).

In the second and third patterns, polarization becomes a transformative political strategy, in which the dominant political motive and discursive focus seem to be either progressive-inclusionary, seeking to include previously marginalized sectors, or reactionary-exclusionary, seeking to exclude threatening outsiders. In these patterns, polarizing politicians challenge the status quo, often with populist undertones. While demand from the electorate is not absent in the first pattern of intra-elite power struggles, in the cases of transformative polarization, the masses play a more proactive role in demanding and mobilizing for change, which is then channeled by a political entrepreneur, often a political outsider who seizes the political opportunity.

In the progressive-inclusionary version, polarizing confrontation is required to achieve democratizing reforms, argue the challengers. Turkey under Erdoğan, which Somer in this volume analyzes as a case of "polarizing-cum-transformative politics," and Venezuela under Chávez, arguably the cases with the most revolutionary political aims, are the exemplars of pernicious polarization becoming self-propagating and producing authoritarian outcomes under the new elites. In both cases, polarizing actors successfully mobilized and then acted upon the new status- and redistribution-seeking, upwardly mobile and progressive impulses of previously marginalized groups.

In the reactionary-exclusionary version of transformative polarization, the restoration of declining dominant group status requires excluding interlopers, assert the challengers. Hence, polarizing actors act upon the reactionary and exclusive impulses of masses who feel they have suffered loss of status and resources. Hungary's Viktor Orbán, Poland's Jaroslaw Kaczyński, and Donald Trump in the

United States all use system-delegitimizing rhetoric and populist appeals to capitalize on existing fears and anxieties and create new ones, particularly focusing on anti-immigrant and racial appeals. Their parties practice asymmetric polarization at the elite level, as Tworzecki describes, with the victorious challengers breaking with the prevailing liberal-democratic consensus and moving their parties toward ever more extremes.

Incumbent strategies

Once in power, polarizing elites choose a strategy to govern and to conduct relations with the opposition, conditioned on their own capacity. Most polarizing incumbents work to entrench their electoral advantages. In fact, a prevalent trend during polarization in our cases, described above, is the temptation to amass sufficient power to change the rules, once in power, to further advantage the majority party and strengthen executive power. Electoral rules that produce disproportionate representation provide incentives for new and old elites to mobilize voters in either the Machiavellian intra-elite power struggles illustrated by the Philippines, or the counter-establishment struggles illustrated by Venezuela.

Similarly, incumbent polarizing parties typically attempt to govern on their own and eschew norms for bipartisan or multi-partisan decision-making. As Figure 1 shows, all of our cases experienced a decline in willingness to compromise during the polarization periods (indicated by willingness to consult with other actors, or respect for counter-arguments), except for Greece and the Philippines. Bangladesh started at a low rate of compromise within the bipolar party system after independence, and continued at a low rate as polarization intensified after 2010.

Incumbents must decide how to achieve and then maintain a winning majority to be able to govern, including whether to continue polarizing or to depolarize. Here we analyze the common options for a polarizing strategy identified in our cases of severe polarization, and in the last section we return to theoretical options to depolarize. The strategies to maintain power that are most pernicious for democracy, then, are to govern unilaterally without consulting the opposition, to ally with smaller parties to form a majority, to coopt the opposition, or to repress dissent, discussed here:

    a. *Govern with own majority and without consultation with the opposition*, contingent on electoral rules and popular mobilization capacity. Hungary (Fidesz), Turkey (AKP), the Philippines (Estrada), and the United States (Trump). In South Africa, the ANC has been the dominant majority party since 1994, but re-polarization is only incipient.

    b. *Ally with smaller, extreme parties*, when unable to gain a majority on their own. This was the case at least initially for polarizing parties in Thailand, Bangladesh, Poland, and Venezuela. In Greece, Syriza allied with an extreme populist party on the opposite side of the ideological extreme.

    c. *Defang the opposition by cooptation, co-habitation, or power-sharing settlement.* Zimbabwe's two episodes illustrate ZANU-PF's strategy of defanging

(text continues on p. 253)

FIGURE 1
Country Scores on Freedom, Press Freedom, Parties Willingness to Consult,
and Respect for Counterarguments, 2000–2016

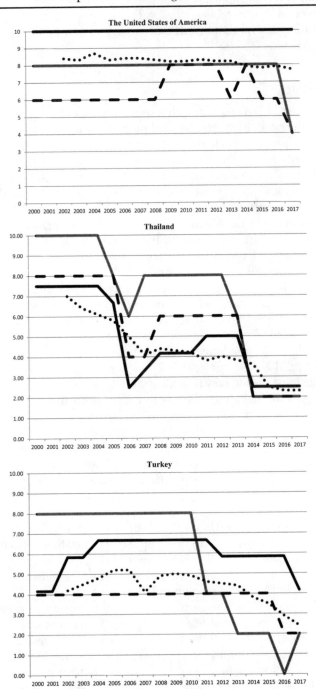

(continued)

FIGURE 1 (CONTINUED)

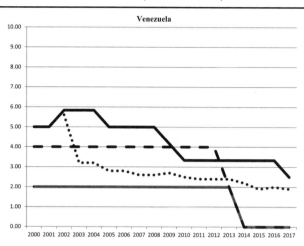

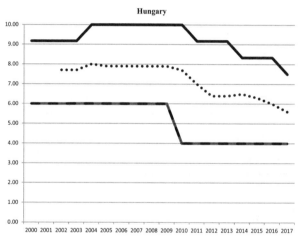

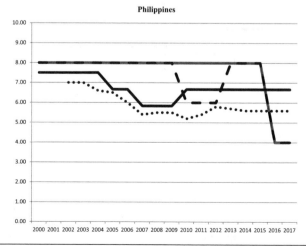

(continued)

FIGURE 1 (CONTINUED)

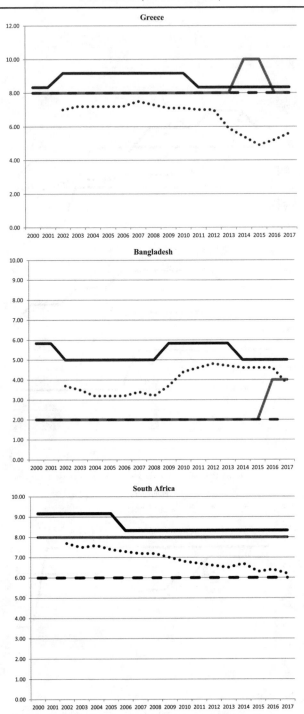

(continued)

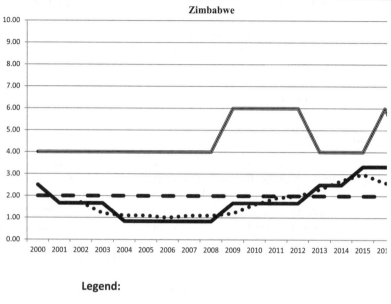

FIGURE 1 (CONTINUED)

Data Sources: Freedom House, freedomhouse.org: *Mean Freedom Rating* was originally on 1–7 scale and converted to 0–10. And then reversed in a way for the highest value to show highest freedom. *Press Freedom Reversed* was originally on 0–100 scale and converted to 0–10. And then reversed in a way for the highest value to show highest press freedom. V-Dem Series 7: *Parties Range of Consultation* was originally on 0–5 scale and converted to 0–10. *Parties Respect for Counterarguments* was originally on 0–5 scale and converted to 0–10. Coppedge et al. (2017).

the opposition with power-sharing agreements in which specific positions are guaranteed for the opposition, but ZANU-PF retains the dominant role. As LeBas and Munemo show, such power-sharing settlements do not guarantee de-polarization, particularly once the polarization extends into society, and do not necessarily represent a democratizing move.

To remain in power, incumbent parties may adjust to new circumstances and develop cocktail strategies. Turkey's AKP and Erdoğan, for example, have been combining their main majoritarian strategy with cooptation by regularly recruiting popular and critical politicians from smaller opposition parties into their own ranks, and, since 2016, by building alliances with several erstwhile critical extreme-nationalist parties, some of which are becoming satellite parties.

d. *Govern through repression.* Common practices include legal maneuvers to exclude rival candidacies and tilt the electoral playing field, stack the courts, or outright repression of dissent and speech—jailing dissidents, curtailing civic freedoms, and cracking down on popular protests. Both Turkey and Venezuela, in particular, exemplify this strategy in recent years.

Opposition strategies

As we have argued, polarization is both political and relational (Somer and McCoy, this volume; McCoy, Rahman, Somer 2018). Thus the reaction of opposition parties and social groups is critical to the dynamics of polarization. Our case studies demonstrate that the relational component can change over time within a polarizing episode and within a single country. A rough balance of power between two poles may entail similar capacities to mobilize people at the polls or in the streets, resulting in alternating elections or clashing street protests. But a balance of power may also entail an advantage in numbers in the polls or the streets, on one side, and an advantage in institutional control on the other. A good example is Thailand, where the populist Thai Rak Thai party (and its successors) had a consistent advantage in numbers in the polls, and an ability to mobilize street protests, while the opposing royalist-elite factions had an institutional advantage, particularly in the military and the courts, while also mobilizing street protests. Eventually, with the opposing coalition unable to overcome the populist electoral advantage, the military staged its culminating coup in 2014.

Venezuela's two decades of Bolivarian Revolution demonstrates how the balance of power can shift under polarization. Chávez moved to balance his initial institutional weakness and legislative minority by proposing a constituent assembly and new constitution, both with electoral rules favorable to his party and enhanced presidential powers. The resulting power balance gave him a legislative majority and partial control of major public institutions, while his opposition mounted massive street protests and a military coup temporarily removed him from office. After Chávez survived a recall referendum in 2004, a demoralized opposition ceded legislative control in an ill-conceived electoral boycott, while Chávez's party moved to gain control over the Supreme Court, Electoral Council, media, and civil society organizations. For a decade, Chávez's party dominated political decision-making in a unipolar asymmetry, while the society continued to be polarized, until the political opposition regrouped to win a super-majority in the 2015 legislative elections. Growing opposition threatening electoral chances of Chávez's successor, Nicolás Maduro, led the Maduro government to rely increasingly on repression of popular protests and dissent, electoral manipulation, and growing authoritarianism to remain in power.

Opposition political strategies thus include the basic decisions whether to reciprocate polarizing tactics or try to depolarize politics based on inclusive and unifying platforms, whether to compromise and share power with the incumbent or unite against the incumbent, and whether to use electoral and institutional accountability mechanisms (judicial rulings or impeachment proceedings) or extra-constitutional or nondemocratic efforts to constrain or remove the incumbent, as described below:

a. *Counter-mobilize and reciprocally polarize.* Political oppositions may unite to counter the polarizing incumbents' power either electorally, i.e. by mobilizing voters through new strategies, programs and discourses, in the streets through protests, or in the institutions. If they adopt reciprocal strategies using polarizing and Manichean discourse they often reinforce the pernicious logic of polarization in a downward spiral that may threaten the democratic system even further. Turkey's Gezi protests in 2013, for example, exemplified massive grassroots mobilization vilifying the government's polarizing and authoritarian policies and bringing together diverse societal groups demanding democratization; but they ended up antagonizing progovernment groups and accelerating polarization, government oppression, and democratic breakdown. Stavrakakis (2018) highlights, for example, the dehumanizing antipopulist rhetoric not only within Greek politics and media, but also at the European Union level, where political leaders and journalists referred to the populist challenge to austerity as abnormal, using medical terms (Greece as a "corrupt, ailing body"), subhuman terms ("Neanderthal, cave man"), or monster terms ("monster of populism, executioner of democracy, beast of populism") (pp. 53–54). Stavarakakis fears that elite refusal to recognize the democratizing aspect of populist challengers will further the spiral of pernicious polarization.

An example of reciprocal norm violation is the tit-for-tat behavior of the Republican and Democratic parties in the United States that led to a steady erosion of bipartisanship in judicial appointments during the Obama and early Trump administrations. The Republican Senate majority finally pulled the plug on bipartisan confirmations of Supreme Court justices, with the so-called nuclear option when they abandoned the filibuster rule and thus any pretense at bipartisan appointments (Abramowitz and McCoy, this volume).

Counter-mobilization strategies by opposition coalitions created a rough balance between two poles (with electoral and/or institutional power) at least at times under the polarizing episodes in Bangladesh, Greece, the Philippines, Thailand, the United States, Venezuela, Turkey, and Zimbabwe.

b. *Overcome opposition fragmentation.* Opposition groups may fail to unite to effectively confront a polarizing incumbent party, either because of inter-party rivalries or because traditional parties have been rejected by voters in favor of new challengers. Yet opposition failures to overcome fragmentation that we observe in our cases may also reflect a built-in dynamic of polarization: opposition groups may find it a challenging task to unite without employing the strategy of "counter-mobilize and polarize" and face the resulting pitfalls we discussed above.

With fragmented or disorganized opposition, the incumbent party can more easily change the rules and dominate institutions, making it even harder for opponents to organize to challenge the now hegemonic party. The experiences of Venezuela, Hungary, Turkey, Poland, and Thailand at some point during their polarization episode exemplify this pattern, fostering polarization with the new elites gaining dominance. In the Philippines, after the forced removal of Estrada in 2001, both sides in the bipolar struggle fragmented and realigned, with Estrada forces and Aquino forces aligned against Arroyo. This intra-elite struggle re-equilibrated with the return of oligarchic democracy under Benigno Aquino in 2010, only to be threatened again with the ascent of the illiberal populist Rodrigo Duterte.

c. *Compromise and share power.* A variation on the pattern of opposition fragmentation is Zimbabwe's cohabitation, or power-sharing settlements, in which the opposition party lost its mobilization capacity once joining in the power structure as a junior partner. Such loss of mobilizational capacity may not occur whenever the party in question has an ethnic or regional basis. This was the case with Turkey's pro-Kurdish party that partially cooperated with the AKP government for the sake of a peace settlement in 2014–15. In this situation, however, the ethnic-regional cleavage may reinforce opposition fragmentation and weakness, as indeed happened in Turkey.

d. *Unconstitutional or nondemocratic means to constrain or remove a polarizing incumbent.* In the extreme, oppositions use nondemocratic means to try to remove a polarizing incumbent. Examples include the attempted coups in Venezuela and Turkey, manipulated impeachment processes in the Philippines, and threatened military interventions in Turkey in the AKP's early periods and repeated judicial and military interventions in Thailand. The risk here is that such maneuvers threaten to generate a backlash among supporters of the beleaguered incumbent and those who oppose antidemocratic actions, increasing and even broadening his/her support.

e. *Legal institutional means to constrain executive abuse of power.* Our cases also illustrate many instances of judicial interventions against polarizing and authoritarian incumbents where one would be unjustified or hard pressed to argue that these interventions were formally unconstitutional. Examples are the ongoing legal investigations and threatened impeachment cases against U.S. President Trump (Abramowitz and McCoy, this volume), the Constitutional Court case to shut down the AKP in Turkey in 2008 (Somer, this volume), and the National Assembly's votes to investigate and censure Venezuelan President Maduro (García-Guadilla and Mallen, this volume).

f. *Oppose polarization and work for de-polarization.* Since we analyze in this project only democracies that have been suffering varying degrees of severe polarization, our sample is biased against cases where de-polarization strategies were successful. However, our case analyses provide important insights regarding the difficulties of this strategy, and examples of attempted and partially or locally successful de-polarization to which we return in the last section.

Consequences for Democracy

We mentioned in our introduction to this article that polarization can sometimes serve useful democratic ends and should not be regarded as a necessarily bad feature of governance. In this volume, Greece in the 1980s and 1990s, Bangladesh in the early post-independence years, and even Zimbabwe in the 2000s reflect a constructive role of polarization in contributing to early institutionalization of party systems. Two kinds of danger may arise, however, while this is happening. The first emerges when the consolidation of the polarized blocs occurs asymmetrically, that is one side becomes politically strong, while the other may remain fragmented. The reasons may be agentic, organizational, or structural, for example, related to the country's ethnic and ideological makeup. Whatever the underlying reasons, such asymmetry increases the possibility of democratic erosion under the hegemony of new elites, as happened in Turkey, or under the return of old elites who feel existentially threatened, as occurred in Thailand.

The second danger for democracy is when the polarizing parties engage in aggressive discourse and behavior that delegitimize their opponents and the political system. They then unleash the dynamics described above and across our cases, often leading voters to perceive greater polarization than the policy differences among parties warrant, to discount substantive information, and to develop more confidence in "less substantively grounded opinions" (Druckman, Peterson, and Slothuus 2013). These two perils for democracy can sometimes reinforce each other. Asymmetry, for example, can induce actors to up the ante vis-a-vis their polarizing and antagonizing rhetoric, either because of insecurity or hegemonic ambitions.

Often, a very slippery slope connects the simplification of politics as a struggle between two major rival blocs, which is a constitutive feature of most polarizing politics, to the vilification of these rivals and the effective emasculation of any ties cutting across the dividing line, features of pernicious polarization. Many dynamics that turn polarization pernicious are built-in and hard to control for the very political actors that initiate it. For example, as soon as a political party begins to over-simplify political disagreements and vilify its rivals, this also begins to transform the party itself by advantaging less principled actors, at the expense of more principled actors within the party (Somer, this volume). Likewise, it is not always clear how opposition actors can respond to polarizing incumbents "constructively." When they abstain from counter-polarization, for instance by not vilifying an incumbent, they may be seen as accepting and thus legitimizing the incumbent's unscrupulous tactics and violation of accepted democratic norms. When they counter-mobilize with their own polarizing tactics and malign their opponents, on the other hand, they may contribute to pernicious polarization and end up accelerating democratic erosion (Somer, this volume).

What is more, the practice of demonizing opponents feeds the unfavorable views of opposing parties and their supporters, and the emotional reactions of affective polarization that distances party supporters from each other. This social distancing based on partisanship is evidenced heartbreakingly in the polling in Turkey and United States, which shows unwillingness to live near, marry into, or have their children play with families supporting opposing parties (Somer, this volume; Abramowitz and McCoy, this volume; McCoy, Rahman, and Somer 2018). *The Economist's* Democracy Index even downgraded U.S. democracy in 2016 for its growing social polarization and its negative impact on the functioning of democracy (*Economist* 2017).

Rhetoric is crucial because political elites give cues to their voters that influence political attitudes (Zaller 1992, 1994). System-delegitimizing rhetoric, such as the Polish PiS party's refrain that the country is "in ruins" due to elite profligate spending (Tworzecki, this volume), or Donald Trump's dark inaugural speech blaming past administrations for the "American carnage," contribute to perceptions of a democracy deficit. Large sectors of the electorate may then demand systemic change, despite evidence of positive economic growth and, in the case of Poland, even strong happiness scores (Tworzecki, this volume; Abramowitz and McCoy, this volume). Distrust in representative institutions—especially legislatures and political parties—further undermines the legitimacy of the political system.

Several of our cases demonstrate how attacks on the media by incumbents contribute to declining faith in the media and information as well as growing tolerance of restrictions on free speech for critics and journalists by the incumbents' supporters. Even with formal censorship absent, individual journalists and media institutions, like the rest of the citizenry, may feel the pressure of the "either-or" logic of polarizing politics. They may feel compelled to pick one side or the other so that they can preserve their jobs or readership, nonpartisan journalism thus becomes increasingly difficult. As Figure 1 shows, all our cases experienced a deterioration in Freedom House's measure of press freedom during the periods of intense polarization. Political polarization was associated with a polarized media in all our cases except South Africa, and in the cases moving toward authoritarianism, an intentional aim to gain government control over private media, either through outright closures or purchases, or through tax or judicial harassment (Hungary, Turkey, Venezuela, and Zimbabwe).

Finally, growing affective polarization and negative partisanship contributes to a growing perception among citizens that the opposing party and their policies pose a threat to the nation or an individual's way of life. Most dangerously for democracy, these perceptions of threat open the door to undemocratic behavior by an incumbent and his/her supporters to stay in power, or by opponents to remove the incumbent from power (McCoy, Rahman, and Somer 2018; Svolik 2018).

The cumulative effect of severe polarization as we have defined it here is a deterioration in the quality of democracy, leading to backsliding, illiberalism, and in some cases reversion to autocracy. Figure 1 shows the declines in freedom as measured by Freedom House, while Figure 2 shows the declines in liberal democracy measured in the Varieties of Democracy database during and in some cases after the periods of polarization identified in our cases.

Predicting the outcomes for democracies

One of our key motivating questions is to understand how and when the expected benign polarization of normal politics becomes transformed into pernicious polarization with harmful consequences for democracy. And further, to

FIGURE 2
Liberal Democracy Country Scores and Polarization Episodes

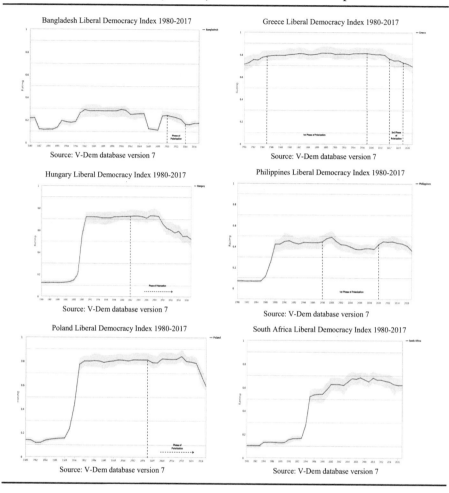

(continued)

identify the factors that might predict different outcomes for democracy. The answers may spell the difference between democratic reform and deepening democratic instability, and democratic collapse.

We have already discussed the important role of elite behavior and discourse, and demonstrated the ubiquitous occurrence of demonizing and denigrating discourse about opponents and critics in polarized contexts. We return to strategic behavior below, but first we consider institutional conditions at the meso and macro levels of political party systems, electoral systems, and systems of government. We then present a preliminary theory of polarization with pernicious consequences, focusing on the nature of the dividing line and how the balance of

FIGURE 2 (CONTINUED)

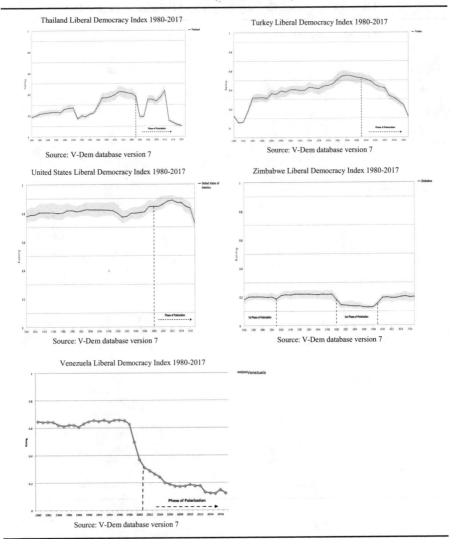

SOURCE: Coppedge et al. (2017).

power dynamics in the relationship between the political poles inform their strategies and constrain the outcome for democracy.

Institutional factors: Constraints on executive power and destabilizing aspects of polarization, or incentives for polarization and de-democratization?

Institutions alone neither explain when pernicious polarization occurs, nor can they definitively resolve it. But some institutional factors emerge from our analysis as important facilitating conditions; namely, the nature of the electoral system, powers delegated to the head of government, and strength and use of accountability mechanisms.

Electoral system. We find that the most extreme cases of polarization among our countries emerge in contexts of majoritarian electoral systems that produce a disproportionate representation for the majority or plurality party, and that, once in power, the polarizing parties and incumbents attempt, and often succeed, in engineering additional constitutional and legal changes to enhance their electoral advantage. In one case that disproportionate system backfired when the Venezuelan opposition finally won a two-thirds majority in government with a popular vote of only 56 percent after 15 years of the Bolivarian Revolution.

Proportional representation electoral systems do not guarantee escape from pernicious polarization, though, if they employ majoritarian-enhancing mechanisms. For example, Turkey has a proportional representation system but also a high threshold for parties to win seats (10 percent of the votes), along with a disproportionate distribution of seats favoring rural areas. The Greek electoral system, after 2012, awards a "bonus" of fifty seats to the largest party, which helped Syriza to gain a majority.

As McCoy, Rahman, and Somer (2018), and Vegetti (this volume) point out, the winner-take-all logic produced by institutional rules in disproportionate majoritarian electoral systems, combined with the psychological elements of the "us-versus-them" discourse employed in severely polarized party systems, provide perverse incentives for de-democratization. The zero-sum perceptions of such systems led governing parties to further work to cement their electoral advantages with revised electoral formulas, gerrymandered electoral redistricting, restrictive voter registration, and other such constitutional and legal reforms in Bangladesh, Hungary, Turkey, the United States, and Venezuela. The resulting electoral immobilism entrenched with institutional disproportionate rules contributes to the extension of political polarization to the societal level, and makes polarization even more difficult to overcome (Vegetti, this volume).

System of government. Whether a country is a parliamentary or presidential democracy alone does not seem to determine incentives for polarization. Instead, the determining factor appears to be direct election of the head of government, the powers attributed to the executive by constitutional authority, and a majoritarian electoral system giving disproportionate representation to the largest party. As indicated in Table 2, among our cases, five are presidential systems with direct elections, while six are parliamentary with relatively strong prime ministers (in Turkey and Thailand, the powers of chief executive were enhanced prior to polarization). Nevertheless, nine of the eleven have disproportionate representation: seven with majoritarian electoral systems (single member districts or mixed electoral systems) and two with proportional representation electoral systems with bonus to the largest party.

TABLE 2
Institutional Factors

| | | System of Government | |
		Directly elected president	Parliamentary
Electoral System	Majoritarian (or PR with bonus)	Philippines Turkey (since 2014)° United States Venezuela Zimbabwe	Bangladesh Hungary Greece Turkey (until 2017)° Thailand
	Proportional	Poland (limited powers)	Poland South Africa

°Turkey's parliamentary system with a strong president changed to direct election of president in 2014 and then to an executive presidential system in 2017.

Party system institutionalization. The level of party system institutionalization does not appear to predict the rise of polarizing leaders (whether populist or national liberation), nor the outcome for democracy. Our cases include highly institutionalized party systems (United States, Bangladesh, Hungary, Turkey, Poland), moderately institutionalized systems (Zimbabwe, Venezuela), and weak systems (Philippines, Thailand) according to Varieties of Democracy (Coppedge 2018). The cases with the least pernicious polarization—South Africa, Greece—have strong systems.

Accountability institutions. Institutional constraints on executive abuse of power via mechanisms of accountability and checks and balances can be a double-edged sword under polarization. Among our cases, we see both democratic and undemocratic uses of accountability institutions by oppositions to constrain executive abuse of power, as well as the undemocratic use of such institutions by an autocratizing party/incumbent to maintain power and weaken its challengers. Thus the strength of these institutions, as well as the motivations of the coalitions that dominate them, are crucial to determine whether they play a democratizing or autocratizing role.

Slater and Arugay (2018) contrast the Machiavellian strategies of street protest and constitutional hardball used by political actors unable to compete electorally in intra-elite power struggles in Thailand and the Philippines with Madisonian strategies of relying on constitutional mechanisms to constrain executive overreach in Taiwan and Indonesia. In Turkey and Venezuela, antipopulist forces had sufficient presence in the military, courts, and bureaucracies to restrain populists in the early years. But they soon resorted to extraconstitutional measures to strive to contain the populists' electoral advantages, rather than conducting the coalition-building, democratizing internal reform and voter mobilization necessary to compete at the ballot box (Somer; Garcia-Guillen and Mallen, this volume). In turn, Erdoğan and Chávez transformed those very institutions over time and populated them with loyalists. They then used the accountability institutions in an undemocratic way against opponents and internal dissenters in an increasingly repressive manner.

Toward a Theory of Pernicious Polarization's Harm to Democracy

We have argued that agency plays a fundamental role in pernicious polarization in democracies, and that both supply and demand factors are important. On the demand side, popular grievances or elite disaffection leading to intra-elite power struggles underlie all our cases. Yet on the supply side (the political leaders), the most pernicious polarizations involve divisions that are brought to the forefront of the national agenda or even manufactured by elites. Grievances and latent cleavages exist, but they are most often activated, exploited, or distorted—in the sense that the normal complexity of politics is wiped out and cross-cutting and otherwise de-polarizing identities are rendered politically irrelevant—by political elites who choose the issue or grievance to highlight and create the divisive us-and-them perceptions.

We find that the *relation* between political actors and the *political* use of polarization as a strategy predict its effects. That is, just as crucial as the supply of polarizing figures is the reaction of opponents. If they adopt similar polarizing strategies rather than internal reforms and unequivocally prodemocracy electoral mobilization and civic engagement, they are likely to provoke outcomes of either "careening" or a hegemonic party with autocratizing tendencies.

Figure 3 presents two conditioning factors that we consider to be critical in predicting the severity of polarization and its potential consequences for democracy: polarization formed around formative rifts, and the relative balance of power in electoral mobilizing capacity of the two camps. These factors shape the political uses of polarization and the reactions of political actors to it, as well as the possibilities for a polity to handle its polarizing episode democratically.

We hypothesize that polarizations shaped around formative rifts are more enduring and pernicious. As discussed above, unresolved historical debates over what constitutes the core component of national identity or the basis of citizenship rights seem to underlie contemporary polarizations in Bangladesh, Zimbabwe, Turkey, South Africa, and the United States. We hypothesize that the cleavages formed around these unresolved national debates are particularly difficult for politics precisely because they involve state identity and belonging. As LeBas (2018, 61) suggests, "Pre-existing binary narratives of group belonging and citizenship make polarization more devastating when it occurs" by rendering intergroup disputes more difficult to resolve through bargaining.

While LeBas posits this type of polarization is more likely to generate violence and democratic breakdown, we argue that it is more likely to have the negative consequences for democracy described in this article because it questions who has the right to live in a polity as a full citizen—membership vs. non-member-ship—and whether one group can claim exclusive legitimacy to represent the citizens in government. Polarization thus becomes threatening and causes mutual polarizing reactions in a relational way, leading to democratic erosion. It becomes an *enduring* feature of democratic politics because the competing political iden-tities extend into the society such that even if one camp is able to dominate over the other and temporarily defuse the polarization episode, the latent polarization residing in the society will facilitate its resurgence unless the political actors take constructive steps toward resolving the national debates.

We further hypothesize that the relative balance of power between the poles, and, in particular, the existence of cross-class parties capable of mobilizing popu-lar electoral support, shapes the strategies of political actors and the dynamics of polarization. Where the party system has developed competing mass-based par-ties, political actors are more likely to engage in electoral competitions even when formative rifts around competing foundational myths about the heroes and villains of national independence and national identity lead to severe polarization, such as in Bangladesh. However, if some exogenous or self-imposed condition or crisis, or a long-lasting problem such as corruption, weakens attachment to tradi-tional parties and opens the door to political outsiders, the relative balance of power shifts, as does the political calculation of political actors. When capacity for electoral mobilization is or becomes very unbalanced, access to institutional sources of power become important in shaping the dynamics of polarization. As Slater and Arugay (2018) argue, contemporary polarizations in South East Asia result from changes ushering in disequilibria between the two fundamental accountability mechanisms of democracy: vertical accountability of voting, and horizontal accountability of restraints on executive power.

In cases where the opposition either never had or lost the capacity to match the electoral mobilization capacity of the new populists, opponents are likely to turn to institutional sources of power in the courts, military, and bureaucracy. Where attempts to use institutional mechanisms to constrain or defeat a polar-izing leader fail, the incumbents can consolidate their institutional power through constitutional changes and majoritarian politics. Indeed, in many of our cases such as the Philippines, Thailand, Turkey, and Venezuela, the opponents at some point became impatient and resorted to extraconstitutional measures to try to remove the incumbent, rather than democratize internally and rebuild their elec-toral mobilization capacity. In other cases, like Hungary and Zimbabwe after the second polarizing period in the 2000–08, the oppositions weakened and divided, unable to constrain the hegemonic party.

Thus, as indicated in the top, right of Figure 3, a rough balance of electoral mobilization capacity and politics polarizing around formative rifts is expected to lead to sustained polarizing politics and likely alternation of power with diminishing quality of democracy, until one side gains the upper hand through court appoint-ments and electoral law changes to enhance their electoral advantage, as happened in Turkey and Bangladesh. Even if polarization is temporarily defused with one party consolidating its power, it is likely to reemerge as the society remains polar-ized with the failure to address the underlying issues of the formative rifts.

FIGURE 3
Predicted Outcomes of Pernicious Polarization

		POLARIZATION AROUND FORMATIVE RIFT	
		YES	NO
INSTITUTIONALIZED MASS-INCLUDING PARTY SYSTEM (both poles have cross-class parties with mobilization capacity)	YES	Predicted Outcome: ENDURING SYMMETRICAL POLARIZATION WITH DEMOCRATIC EROSION United States Zimbabwe Bangladesh Turkey South Africa	Predicted Outcome: INDETERMINATE Hungary (populist transforms traditional Party) Poland (populist transforms traditional Party) Venezuela (trad. party system weakens/realigns) Greece (trad party system weakens/realigns)
	NO	Predicted Outcome: SHORT-LIVED POLARIZATION CRISES WITH RETURN OF OLD ELITES AND DEMOCRATIC COLLAPSE [Egypt]	Predicted Outcome: CAREENING or OLD ELITES RETURN EXTRA-CONSTITUTIONALLY Thailand Philippines

The exception to this outcome arises in one of two conditions: i) when opposing elites refrain from delegitimizing polarization tactics, and focus instead on mutual tolerance and restraint, as in early post-apartheid South Africa under Nelson Mandela; or ii) a hegemonic party chooses to reform internally, holding its own leaders accountable and democratizing its own organizational structures. While the removal of corrupt leaders in Zimbabwe and South Africa in 2017 by their own parties theoretically holds out the latter possibility, early signs indicated that the hegemonic stance of ZANU-PF under Emmerson Mnangagwa and the ANC under Cyril Ramaphosa may continue. Likewise, as of mid-2018, the Republican Party in the United States continued to resist holding President Trump accountable for his divisive rhetoric and policy stances upending U.S. foreign policy, while it allowed the special counsel to continue its investigation into Russian meddling in the 2016 elections and any collusion with the Trump campaign.

In the top, right of Figure 3, where a rough balance of electoral capacity is paired with polarization around more contemporary issues and grievances, the outcome is indeterminant. It theoretically should allow for a compromise around the polarizing issue and thus defuse the polarizing crisis. However, the outcome depends in part on the reaction of oppositions. As Slater and Arugay (2018) argue, in Indonesia and Taiwan opponents treated polarizing figures who abused executive power with patience and constraint, engaging in Madisonian tactics to check the executive through constitutional mechanisms, and thus avoid destabilizing polarizing politics.

In contrast, oppositions that weaken and divide internally, and/or engage in extra-constitutional, undemocratic attempts to remove a polarizing leader, are likely to see a counter-productive outcome as sympathy builds for the attacked leader and opposing parties fail to carry out the organizational rebuilding and voter outreach necessary to challenge the incumbent in the electoral arena. For example, over the course of the 18-year Bolivarian movement led by Chávez and Maduro, the opposition veered among extra-constitutional maneuvers, attempts at mobilizing a popular challenge in the streets and ballot box, and internal rivalries and divisions. The 2002 coup attempt against Chávez allowed him to paint his opponents and the U.S. government, who backed them as undemocratic, and they failed to defeat him electorally until his death. After uniting, the opposition finally won decisively the 2015 legislative elections. In response, Maduro resorted to increasingly undemocratic and repressive measures, backed by the military, even as the society depolarized and the vast majority turned against him. In Figure 3 Turkey is another example, where an apparent 2016 coup attempt against Erdoğan paralyzed, divided and garnered condemnation even from the opposition, and gave him an excuse to further crackdown on his opponents and purge the civil service, teachers and university professors, and courts of any suspected dissidents.

In Hungary, the opposition also engaged in polarizing tactics, with each bloc refusing to accept the other as legitimate political interlocutors. Fidesz's early supermajority electoral win, however, in 2010 allowed it to further change the electoral laws to its advantage and cement its dominant status. The inability of opposition parties to form a single coalition impeded their ability to challenge Fidesz's electoral dominance.

International influence can also play an important role. Greece's EU membership and debt made it particularly vulnerable to regional pressure. Andreadis and Stavrakakis in this volume describe the Greek ambivalence toward the EU—a majority joined in blaming EU financial elites for the unpopular austerity measures, but they are divided on the question of EU membership. This helps to explain Syriza's skirting of the issue by accepting a compromise over its debt rather than risk ouster from the EU, while continuing to blame outsiders for the difficult economic situation.

The bottom, left of Figure 3 is a null set for our study, but we might think of the short-lived democratic transition after Mubarak's removal in Egypt as an example of a majoritarian party government under the leadership of Morsi's Muslim Brotherhood government that polarized around formative rifts related to religion and state identity. The opposition's inability to unite and pose an electoral challenge to the Muslim Brotherhood, along with Morsi's polarizing behavior, led the opposing political elite to support a military coup to remove Morsi from power.

The bottom, right of Figure 3 represents cases with an imbalance in electoral mobilization capacity and polarizing politics around more temporal issues such as contemporary grievances or the polarizing behavior of a populist and aggrandizing figure. The cases of Thailand and the Philippines examined in this volume fit this category, with an outcome of careening between oligarchic democracy and mass populist democracy. We expect this outcome as intra-elite power struggles play out using the different resources of democratic power—institutional horizontal accountability mechanisms and vertical electoral mobilization.

Future Research and Possible Antidotes to Pernicious Polarization

What factors might prevent self-propagating pernicious polarization? And once it is set in motion, is it possible to turn around? We have argued that pernicious polarization emerges from the interaction of grievances around representation deficits, economic inequities, or cultural clashes, and the politicization of those grievances by elites using polarizing strategies for their own purposes. As societies change by growing more racially or religiously diverse, more wealthy or unequal, or suffer crises of the economy or corruption, then perceptions of inequity or changing social status can fuel demands for change and spur the supply of polarizing leaders and parties, often by bundling populist rhetoric together with other polarizing strategies. The reaction of once-dominant groups and elites to the rise of challengers is crucial in determining the path toward polarization. As Slater notes, "Democratic stability rests upon the readiness of oligarchies to expand substantive access to the political system, not simply upon the willingness of rising opposition to 'work within the system'" (2013, 60).

Every society and democracy has inequalities and hierarchies. If those on the bottom are allowed a political representation and respected as a challenger, rather than outright enemy, a society can have an agonistic, pluralist democracy rather than an antagonistic and polarized one (Stavrakakis 2018; Mouffe 2014). But if the newly mobilized actors take an antidemocratic and delegitimizing stance, such as European fascists did, or contemporary authoritarian populists do, or if their ascent to political power generates an antipopulist backlash, discrediting and delegitimizing the new actors, it will likely generate an irreversible logic of polarization locking in the actors. The most likely result is increased conflict and democratic erosion. Hence, the discourse, actions, and political strategies of the rising new actors as well as those shaping the backlash against them are crucial.

While our cases do not offer any definite answers as to how pernicious polarization can be prevented or reversed, they offer indirect insights we aim to explore in future research. None of our cases suggests that reactionary popular mobilization in the streets against polarizing actors with illiberal or authoritarian tendencies proved successful in achieving de-polarizing and democratizing results, at least by themselves. Judicial attempts—within constitutional boundaries—to constrain polarizing figures prone to the abuse of power are more promising for *preventing* severe polarization (Slater and Arugay 2018). However, our

THE ANNALS OF THE AMERICAN ACADEMY

cases do not offer evidence that they can be effective in reversing polarization and democratic erosion *after* the onset of severe polarization, precisely because the polarized views of the constraining agents and the polarizing figure alike reduce the legitimacy of the constraint mechanisms.

Simultaneously, our analysis shows that the most severe examples of polarization followed from some elites' reframing of their societies' formative rifts in divisive and provocative fashions to achieve power, and from opposing elite reactions. Further, the two countries with the steepest democratic erosion resulting in authoritarian outcomes under new elites (see Figure 2) were the two with the most ideologically revolutionary aims—the inclusionary transformative cases of Erdoğan in Turkey and Chávez in Venezuela. All this suggests that the choices and strategies of incumbent and opposition elites in political and civil societies— who can act as both gatekeepers and proactive problem-solvers—can play critical roles in preventing and reversing pernicious polarization and its negative consequences for democracy. Rather than unconstitutional interventions, reactionary mass mobilization, and even legal sanctions, the most propitious strategy for prodemocratic elites appears to be developing successful electoral strategies, making programmatic and organizational internal reforms, and supporting democratizing institutional reform proposals.

South Africa, Turkey, and Greece provide useful lessons of within case variation. Despite Turkey's long-existing formative rifts, a moderate polarization actually constituted its most promising period with respect to democracy under the AKP in 2002–2007. At that time, the AKP government subsumed its polarization around the formative rifts under a broader consensus message of EU accession (Somer, this volume). In this period, the AKP government and the opposition cooperated for EU-inspired democratic and economic reforms and the government was checked by strong—albeit semi-authoritarian—horizontal accountability mechanisms, until a constitutional crisis over the new president's election escalated polarization. Hence, presumably, Turkey could have produced an outcome of democratic reforms if its political elites had made different choices. This could have happened, for example, if they had agreed on a president trusted by both sides and worked on democratizing the semi-authoritarian horizontal accountability mechanisms, and if the opposition had focused its energies on removing the AKP by programmatically and organizationally reforming themselves rather than, as they tried, through popular mobilization and quasi-constitutional judicial interventions.

Apartheid South Africa was democratized with institutional and electoral arrangements that carried their own seeds of both vulnerability and resistance to repolarization. Although the first post-apartheid presidency under Nelson Mandela avoided the polarizing temptation, successive leaders in the African National Congress used their dominant-party status to grow increasingly hegemonic and self-serving. As Southall points out in this volume, the ANC's origin as a national liberation movement allowed it to conflate self-determination with democracy and to claim that it alone represented the will of the people, similar to the Bangladesh and Zimbabwe cases. The party's comparative advantage in mobilizing voters led its political opponents to turn to horizontal accountability mechanisms—namely the courts—for redress, while ANC figures attacked the judiciary as "counter-revolutionary." At the same time, the electoral hegemony of the ANC meant there was little political polarization and little choice in representation, making the hegemonic party-state subject to corruption and authoritarian tendencies. Consequently, Zuma's ouster in 2017 and Ramaphosa's early reforms held out the possibility of another potentially positive democratizing outcome—that of a hegemonic party reforming itself from within, and possibly dissolving the basis of polarization by addressing representation deficits.

Greece's early postauthoritarian democratic politics were heavily polarized at the political and societal levels as partisans of the two major parties took on party identity as social identity. Yet Andreadis and Stavrakakis argue in this volume that this was benign polarization in that it strengthened two programmatic parties that began to converge rather than diverge. Depolarization was disrupted with the 2009 economic crisis, much like a decade earlier in Venezuela, when the two-party system in each case was blamed by voters for mismanagement and even collusion (thus too little polarization), and outsiders emerged. Syriza's establishment-vilifying rhetoric actually masked a more complex polarization in Greece along three dimensions (austerity/anti-austerity; pro- and anti-European sentiment; and a broader consensus blaming EU actors for the painful austerity requirements). The outcome was a unique coalition of Left and Right extremes and a period of political instability. Greece's current vulnerability is a deficit in representation of the anti-EU membership position, leaving open space for a new political actor to emerge with potentially pernicious consequences.

These cases indicate at least three potential depolarization mechanisms: democratizing internal reforms of the hegemonic party; democratizing reforms and electoral mobilization by the opposition; and pluralist political representation options for various cleavages to participate within the party system. But we need more theoretically informed and fine-tuned research on depolarization strategies in different cases. By definition, any nonpolarized democracy could offer an example where strategies of depolarization or preventing severe polarization were effectively implemented by actors representing the opposition, the government, or both. However, our cases, too, entail many opposition actors who partially or predominantly attempted to depolarize their polities with different degrees of success, such as South Africa's Democratic Alliance (DA) or U.S. legislators who have been working across the aisle under the Obama and Trump administrations. Future research should place more emphasis on analyzing the dynamics and dilemmas of the depolarization strategies and what makes these strategies more or less successful.

References

Abramowitz, Alan I. 2010. *The disappearing center: Engaged citizens, polarization, and American democracy.* New Haven, CT: Yale University Press.

Berman, Sheri. 2017. The pipe dream of undemocratic liberalism. *Journal of Democracy* 28 (3): 29–38.

Bermeo, Nancy. 2016. On Democratic Backsliding. *Journal of Democracy* 27 (1): 5–19.

Bermeo, Nancy Gina. 2003. *Ordinary people in extraordinary times: The citizenry and the breakdown of democracy.* Princeton, NJ: Princeton University Press.

Campbell, James E. 2016. *Polarized: Making sense of a divided America*. Princeton, NJ: Princeton University Press.

Coppedge, Michael, John Gerring, C. H. Knutsen, S. I. Lindberg, S. E. Skaaning, J. Teorell, and J. Krusell. 2017. V-Dem Methodology v7. Varieties of Democracy (V-Dem) Project.

Coppedge, Michael, John Gerring, C. H. Knutsen, S. I. Lindberg, S. E. Skaaning, J. Teorell, and J. Krusell. 2018. V-Dem Methodology v8. Varieties of Democracy (V-Dem) Project.

Druckman, James N., Erik Peterson, and Rune Slothuus. 2013. How elite partisan polarization affects public opinion formation. *American Political Science Review* 107 (1): 57–79.

Economist. 2017. Democracy Index 2017. Available from https://www.eiu.com/topic/democracy-index.

Fitch, Andy. 2018. Partisan conflict separate from the policy: Talking to Frances Lee. *LARB (blog)*. Available from https://blog.lareviewofbooks.org/interviews/partisan-conflict-separate-policy-talking-frances-lee/.

Gaertner, S. L., J. F. Dovidio, P. A. Anastasio, B. A. Bachman, and M. C. Rust. 1993. The common ingroup identity model: Recategorization and the reduction of intergroup bias. *European Review of Social Psychology* 4 (1): 1–26.

Handlin, Samuel. 2018. The logic of polarizing populism: State crises and polarization in South America. *American Behavioral Scientist* 62 (1): 75–91.

Hawkins, Kirk A., Ryan E. Carlin, Levente Littvay, and Cristóbal Rovira Kaltwasser, eds. 2018. *The ideational approach to populism: Concept, theory, and analysis*. 1st ed. New York, NY: Routledge.

Inglehart, Ronald, and Pippa Norris. 2016. Trump, Brexit, and the rise of populism: Economic have-nots and cultural backlash. Harvard Kennedy School Working Paper, RWP16-026, Cambridge, MA.

Kinder, Donald, and Cindy Kam. 2010. *Us against them: Ethnocentric foundations of American opinion*. Chicago, IL: University of Chicago Press.

Kinder, Donald R., and Nathan P. Kalmoe. 2017. *Neither liberal nor conservative: Ideological innocence in the American public*. 1st ed. Chicago, IL: University of Chicago Press.

King, Ryan D., and Darren Wheelock. 2007. Group threat and social control: Race, perceptions of minorities and the desire to punish. *Social Forces* 3:1255–80.

Kongkirati, Prajak. 2016a. Thailand's polarization: Intra-elite struggle and mass based conflict. Atlanta, GA: Georgia State University.

Kongkirati, Prajak. 2016b. Thailand's failed 2014 election: The anti-election movement, violence and democratic breakdown. *Journal of Contemporary Asia* 46 (3): 467–85.

Kongkirati, Prajak. 2016c. Evolving power of provincial political families in Thailand: Dynastic power, party machine and ideological politics. *South East Asia Research* 24 (3): 386–406.

Kuran, Timur. 1995. *Private truths, public lies: The social consequences of preference falsification*. Cambridge, MA: Harvard University Press.

LeBas, Adrienne. 2006. Polarization as craft: Party formation and state violence in Zimbabwe. *Comparative Politics* 38 (4): 419–38.

LeBas, Adrienne. 2018. Can polarization be positive? Conflict and institutional development in Africa. *American Behavioral Scientist* 62 (1): 59–74.

Lee, Frances E. 2016. *Insecure majorities: Congress and the perpetual campaign*. 1st ed. Chicago, IL: University of Chicago Press.

Lepore, Jill. 2018. *These truths: A history of the United States*. 1st ed. New York, NY: W.W. Norton & Company.

Levin, Shana. 2004. Perceived group status differences and the effects of gender, ethnicity, and religion on social dominance orientation. *Political Psychology* 25 (1): 31–48.

Luce, Edward. 2018. *The retreat of Western liberalism*. Reprint edition. New York, NY: Grove Press.

Mahoney, James, and Kathleen Thelen, eds. 2010. *Explaining institutional change: Ambiguity, agency, and power*. New York, NY: Cambridge University Press.

Mardin, Şerif. 1973. Center-periphery relations: A key to Turkish politics. *Daedalus* 102 (1): 169–90.

McCoy, Jennifer, and Francisco Diez. 2011. *International mediation in Venezuela*. Washington, DC: United States Institute of Peace.

McCoy, Jennifer, Tahmina Rahman, and Murat Somer. 2018. Polarization and the global crisis of democracy: Common patterns, dynamics, and pernicious consequences for democratic polities. *American Behavioral Scientist* 62 (1): 16–42.

Mounk, Yascha. 2018. The undemocratic dilemma. *Journal of Democracy*. Available from https://www.journalofdemocracy.org/article/undemocratic-dilemma.

Mudde, Cas, and Cristobal Rovira Kaltwasser. 2017. *Populism: A very short introduction*. 2nd ed. New York, NY: Oxford University Press.

Mutz, Diana C. 2018. Status threat, not economic hardship, explains the 2016 presidential vote. *Proceedings of the National Academy of Sciences* 115 (19): E4330–39.

North, Douglass C. 1990. *Institutions, institutional change and economic performance*. New York, NY: Cambridge University Press.

Outten, H. Robert, Michael T. Schmitt, Daniel A. Miller, and Amber L. Garcia. 2012. Feeling threatened about the future: Whites' emotional reactions to anticipated ethnic demographic changes. *Personality & Social Psychology Bulletin* 38 (1): 14–25.

Palonen, Emilia. 2009. Political polarisation and populism in contemporary Hungary. *Parliamentary Affairs* 62 (2): 318–34.

Sidanius, Jim, and Felicia Pratto. 2001. *Social dominance: An intergroup theory of social hierarchy and oppression*. 1st ed. Cambridge: Cambridge University Press.

Shils, Edward. 1961. Centre and periphery. In *The logic of personal knowledge: Essays presented to Michael Polanyi*, ed. Michael Polanyi, 117–30. London: Routledge & Kegan Paul.

Skitka, Linda J., and G. Scott Morgan. 2014. The social and political implications of moral conviction. *Political Psychology* 35 (February): 95–110.

Slater, Dan. 2013. Democratic careening. *World Politics* 65 (4): 729–63.

Slater, Dan, and Aries A. Arugay. 2018. Polarizing figures: Executive power and institutional conflict in Asian democracies. *American Behavioral Scientist* 62 (1): 92–106.

Somer, Murat. 2001. Cascades of ethnic polarization: Lessons from Yugoslavia. *The ANNALS of the American Academy of Political and Social Science* 573:127–51.

Somer, Murat. 2007. Moderate Islam and secularist opposition in Turkey: Implications for the world, Muslims and secular democracy. *Third World Quarterly* 28 (7): 1271–89.

Somer, Murat. 2014. Moderation of religious and secular politics, a country's 'centre' and democratization. *Democratization* 21 (2): 244–67.

Somer, Murat. 2017. Conquering versus democratizing the state: Political Islamists and fourth wave democratization in Turkey and Tunisia. *Democratization* 24 (6): 1025–43.

Somer, Murat, and Jennifer McCoy. 2018. Déjà vu? Polarization and endangered democracies in the 21st century. *American Behavioral Scientist* 62 (1): 3–15.

Stavrakakis, Yannis. 2018. Paradoxes of polarization: Democracy's inherent division and the (anti-) populist challenge. *American Behavioral Scientist* 62 (1): 43–58.

Svolik, Milan W. 2018. When polarization Trumps civic virtue: Partisan conflict and the subversion of democracy by incumbents. Available from https://cpb-us-w2.wpmucdn.com/campuspress.yale.edu/dist/6/1038/files/2018/09/polarization_manuscript-2ex9y63.pdf.

Tajfel, Henri, and J. C. Turner. 1979. An integrative theory of intergroup conflict. In *The social psychology of intergroup relations*, eds. W. G. Austin and S. Worchel, 33–37. Boston, MA: Brooks/Cole.

Zaller, John R. 1992. *The nature and origins of mass opinion*. 1st ed. New York, NY: Cambridge University Press.

Zaller, John R. 1994. Strategic politicians, public opinion, and the Gulf crisis. In *Taken by storm: The media, public opinion, and U.S. foreign policy in the Gulf War*, 1st ed., eds. W. Lance Bennett and David L. Paletz, 250–74. Chicago, IL: University of Chicago Press.

Zsolt, Enyedi. 2005. The role of agency in cleavage formation. *European Journal of Political Research* 44 (5): 697–720.

Corrigendum

Bolsen, Toby, James N. Druckman, and Fay Lomax Cook. 2015. Citizens', Scientists', and Policy Advisors' Beliefs about Global Warming. *The Annals of the American Academy of Political and Social Science* 658 (1): 271–95. doi: 10.1177/0002716214558393

There is an error in the bottom half of Figure 2 in Bolsen, Druckman, and Cook (2015), which displays the predicted belief "Global Warming Is Anthropogenic" for conservatives and liberals at the minimum and maximum levels of knowledge. In the original Figure 2, the values for minimum knowledge and maximum knowledge conservatives and liberals were mistakenly transposed; therefore the slopes of the lines are the opposite of what was correctly communicated in the corresponding text. Also in the original Figure 2, *lower values* correspond to a greater belief that climate change is human-caused; this is unduly confusing, owing to the fact that we reverse-coded data from estimations presented in Table 2.

A revised Figure 2 (below) presents new simulated predicted values using *Clarify* for minimum knowledge and maximum knowledge liberals and conservatives in the public sample, with higher values indicating greater belief

FIGURE 2
Bottom half: higher scores associated with a greater belief that global warming is a result of anthropogenic causes

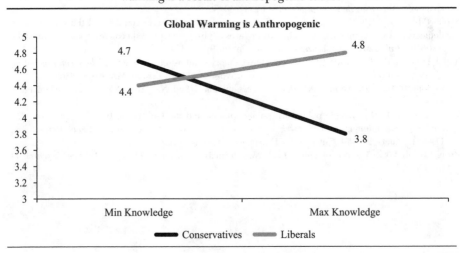

DOI: 10.1177/0002716218811652

that climate change is human-induced and less belief that it is the result of Earth's natural changes. The figure shows, as reported in Table 2 of the original manuscript and discussed in the article, that there are no significant differences in the beliefs of liberals and conservatives at low levels of knowledge; however, significant differences between these groups manifest at higher levels of knowledge.

THE IMPACT OF THE SOCIAL SCIENCES: How Academics and their Research Make a Difference

Simon Bastow, Patrick Dunleavy, and Jane Tinkler, *all from London School of Economics*

Foreword by Kenneth Prewitt, *Columbia University*

In the modern globalized world, some estimates suggest that around 40 million people now work in jobs that 'translate' or mediate advances in social science research for use in business, government and public agencies, health care systems, and civil society organizations. Many large corporations and organizations across these sectors in the United States are increasingly prioritizing access to social science knowledge. Yet, the impact of university social science continues to be fiercely disputed. This key study demonstrates the essential role of university social science in the 'human-dominated' and 'human-influenced' systems now central to our civilization. It focuses empirically on Britain, the second most influential country for social science research after the US. Using in-depth research, the authors show how the growth of a services economy, and the success of previous scientific interventions, mean that key areas of advance for corporations, public policy-makers, and citizens alike now depend on our ability to understand our complex societies and economies. This is a landmark study in the evidence-based analysis of social science impact.

PAPERBACK ISBN: 978-1-4462-8262-5 • FEBRUARY 2014 • 326 PAGES

LEARN MORE AT SAGEPUB.COM!